Praise for *The Myth of the ADHD Child*, Revised Edition

"At a time when ADHD and the medications used to treat it are growing by leaps and bounds, Thomas Armstrong asks parents to think critically about the ADHD diagnosis, to value the uniqueness of their children's different rhythms of learning, attending, and behaving, and to appreciate and use the wide range of non-drug strategies that are out there to help their kids prosper in school and flourish in life."

Michele Borba, EdD, bestselling author of *The Big Book of Parenting Solutions*, *Building Moral Intelligence*, and *UnSelfie: Why Empathetic Kids Succeed in Our All-About-Me World*

"Parents everywhere should read this book, not just those with kids diagnosed with ADHD! Thomas Armstrong presents a wealth of strategies, ideas, tips, and resources that will help parents nurture kids who feel good about themselves, who have skills for coping with life's challenges, and who practice learning strategies that will help them succeed in the classroom and beyond. I wholeheartedly recommend *The Myth of the ADHD Child*!"

Jack Canfield, coauthor of the bestselling Chicken Soup for the Soul series and *The Success Principles*

". . . absolutely essential reading for parents, teachers, and others concerned with children who struggle. Armstrong provides a lucid and comprehensive response to the tragic overuse of medication for America's children. Bursting the myths of an established brain deficit, a single cause, and long-term effectiveness of drugs, Armstrong discusses parental options with compassion."

L. Alan Sroufe, PhD, professor emeritus of child psychology, Institute of Child Development, University of Minnesota

"This is a fabulous book. Not only does Armstrong explain with balance and clarity the evidence-based problems associated with the concept of ADHD; he also provides a wealth of practical ideas, resources, and approaches to help the parents of any kid who is presenting with challenging behavior, especially those who have or might attract a diagnosis of ADHD. Professionals and parents alike will benefit enormously from reading this."

Sami Timimi, MD, consultant in child and adolescent psychiatry, Lincolnshire Partnership NHS Foundation Trust; visiting professor of child psychiatry and mental health improvement, University of Lincoln

T0176325

The Myth

of the

ADHD Child

101 WAYS TO IMPROVE
YOUR CHILD'S BEHAVIOR AND ATTENTION SPAN
WITHOUT DRUGS, LABELS, OR COERCION

REVISED EDITION

Thomas Armstrong, PhD

A TarcherPerigee Book

tarcherperigee

An imprint of Penguin Random House LLC
375 Hudson Street
New York, New York 10014

First published under the title *The Myth of the A.D.D. Child* by Dutton,
a member of Penguin Putnam Inc. 1995
This revised edition published by TarcherPerigee 2017

Library of Congress Cataloging-in-Publication Data
Names: Armstrong, Thomas, author.
Title: The myth of the ADHD child : 101 ways to improve your child's behavior and attention span
without drugs, labels, or coercion / Thomas Armstrong, PhD.
Other titles: Myth of the A.D.D. child | Myth of the attention-deficit hyperactivity disorder child
Description: Revised edition. | New York, New York : A TarcherPerigee Book,
[2017] | Revision of: Myth of the A.D.D. child. 1995. | Includes bibliographical references and index.
Identifiers: LCCN 2016056894 (print) | LCCN 2017001964 (ebook)
| ISBN 9780143111504 (paperback) | ISBN 9781101992807 (ebook)
Subjects: LCSH: Attention-deficit hyperactivity disorder—Diagnosis—Moral and ethical aspects.
| Behavior disorders in children—Treatment. | Child rearing. | Attention-deficit hyperactivity disorder—
Treatment—Moral and ethical aspects. | Problem children—Behavior modification.
| BISAC: FAMILY & RELATIONSHIPS / Children with Special Needs.
| FAMILY & RELATIONSHIPS / Learning Disabilities.
Classification: LCC RJ506.H9 A76 2017 (print) | LCC RJ506.H9 (ebook)
| DDC 618.92/8589—dc23
LC record available at https://lccn.loc.gov/2016056894

Printed in the United States of America

Book design by Elke Sigal

This book is dedicated to my father,
William B. Armstrong, MD

CONTENTS

Contents

Contents

Contents

PREFACE

Just as a person remembers exactly where he was when a great public figure was assassinated, so too I remember exactly where I was when I first learned about ADD, or attention deficit disorder, as it was then called. It was in the mid-1980s, and I was standing in the book stacks of the ed-psych library in Tolman Hall at the University of California, Berkeley, where I was doing research for what eventually became my third book: *In Their Own Way: Discovering and Encouraging Your Child's Personal Learning Style.*[1] I was perusing a copy of *Academic Therapy Quarterly*, a special education journal published in Novato, California, and I saw an article about a new disorder related to attention. My first thought was, "This doesn't sound good at all." Making a disorder out of attention? Saying there are deficits for this highly personal and idiosyncratic process of directing the mind? It seemed to me that attention was a function that could be affected by many objective and subjective factors: the weather, a big meal, a loud bang on a TV show, a dog barking, anxiety, joy. But above all, it seemed clear to me that children generally pay attention mostly *to what interests them.*

I began to wonder if this new attention deficit disorder wasn't just a sneaky way to define a specific set of conditions authorities deem worthy of attention. My intuition whispered to me that what this really was about was an underlying concern among the originators of this new disorder that there were things any normal person *should* be interested in and pay attention to, and that apparently these kids with ADD weren't doing that. Thus, they must have a medical disorder. After all, how could one not to want to turn one's full attention to a teacher's unutterably boring lectures? What would possess a child that he could or would not focus his complete attention on a workbook or textbook instruction to fill in a blank or circle the right answer? What gall! What effrontery!

It's my concern with this hidden agenda of underlying values regarding what one should and shouldn't pay attention to that made me suspicious of ADD/ADHD from the very start. There were hints in this new disorder of 1950s Soviet psychiatry, where to have the wrong beliefs or values could lead to a diagnosis of mental illness. Moreover, we weren't doing this to our dissident scientists, philosophers, or writers, we were doing it to our children! Children whose instincts are so natural, whose minds are so fragile and beautiful, whose natures lack guile or cynicism. And to top it off, medical doctors were giving these kids medications meant to direct their attention away from what really interested them and toward what the ADHD powers-that-be determined they *ought* to be paying attention to. There were haunting echoes of George Orwell's *1984* in all of this.

My misgivings and concerns festered for a few years while I pursued other interests. But twenty years ago, I wrote the first edition of this book, which was titled: *The Myth of the A.D.D. Child: 50 Ways to Improve Your Child's Behavior and Attention Span without Drugs, Labels, or Coercion.* Right after publication, I began hearing from irate readers who thought I was saying that their kids weren't inattentive, hyperactive, and/or impulsive. Most of these people had not actually read the book. If they *had*, they would have discovered that I say no such thing. But most of the responses I received were supportive, the majority coming from mothers who told me how they'd been to hell and back trying to get answers as to why their kids were having difficulties, how they'd been given lots of conflicting advice, how they had concerns about giving their kids powerful medications, and how they appreciated having fifty practical nondrug strategies to use to help their kids. Interestingly enough, the ADHD community itself (made up of key proponents, researchers, and advocates) was silent with regard to the book (a smart strategy, I guess, for dealing with people whose views you do not wish to see advertised or promoted in a public forum).

Now, twenty years have passed and what you hold in your hands (or are reading on a screen, or listening to through a speaker) is essentially a completely new book. So much has happened since the original hardcover publication of this book in 1996 (the paperback edition was released in 1997) that it seemed to me nothing short of a complete rewrite would do. The biggest change since the original publication of the book (other than the transformation of this term from ADD into ADHD) is the overwhelming expansion of ADHD diagnoses both nationwide and worldwide and the skyrocketing rates of medication prescriptions to treat it. This new expanded edition of the book incorporates the latest research on ADHD, including the growing critical literature and research supporting new nondrug strategies to help inattentive, hyperactive, and/or impulsive kids. The only part of the original book that remains is the section of fifty strategies, which have been shortened to fit our increasingly short-attention-span culture, and then edited and updated with new research and resources. Most important, *I've added fifty-one new practical strategies* for parents, teachers, and other child workers to use in helping kids with their behavior and attention issues.

The book is divided into three main sections. In the first section, I look at the basic shortcomings of what I call the *ADHD myth*. I compare ADHD to the science fiction creature "the Blob" in its continual expansion and incorporation of new markets both here in the United States and around the world. Then I examine why the ADHD myth or paradigm is not a very good story, pointing to its many inconsistencies, faulty logic, unsupported conclusions, and other imperfections. Finally, I look at why powerful psychoactive medications should not be used as a first-line treatment for inattentive, distractible, and/or impulsive children. I detail some of the minor, moderate, serious, and potentially life-threatening side effects of drugs such as Adderall, Concerta, and Strattera.

In Section II, I examine seven reasons why there's been such a dramatic rise in ADHD diagnoses in America and the world. I suggest in this section that we have an epidemic of ADHD diagnoses largely because:

1. We don't let kids be kids anymore.
2. We don't let boys be boys anymore.
3. We disempower our kids at school.
4. We pass our stresses on to our kids.

5. We let our kids consume too much junk media.
6. We focus too much on our kids' disabilities and not enough on their abilities.
7. Too many people have a vested economic interest in seeing the epidemic continue.

I also examine the defensive strategies that ADHD proponents typically use in response to criticisms of ADHD and explain why those arguments seem to be pretty lame and simplistic. Finally, I propose a paradigm that puts the child in the center of a multiperspectival model, allowing us to consider a far broader range of practical strategies to help kids diagnosed with ADHD than is possible with the current narrowly-focused, neurobiologically centered worldview.

The third section of the book (making up the last two thirds of the text) is devoted to 101 practical nondrug strategies that can be used to help improve the attention and behavior of kids diagnosed with ADHD. I cover a broad range of approaches including:

- *Behavioral strategies.* To improve your child's outward behavior (positive time out, positive contracts, positive behavior modification programs, logical consequences)
- *Biological strategies.* To improve your child's biochemistry through nutrition (limiting junk food, providing a balanced breakfast, removing allergens and additives from the diet, adding omega-3 fatty acids)
- *Cognitive strategies.* To improve the way your child thinks (self-monitoring skills, organizational strategies, emotional self-regulation, goal setting)
- *Creative strategies.* To expand your child's ability to express herself in a positive way (expressive arts, music, entrepreneurship, novel learning experiences)
- *Educational strategies.* To improve your child's performance at home and school (hands-on learning, home–school communication, study strategies, online learning)
- *Ecological strategies.* To enhance your child's ability to succeed at home and school by modifying the environment (time in nature, an animal to care for, limiting junk food, eliminating distractions)

- *Emotional strategies.* To improve your child's ability to manage his feelings (emotional self-regulation, stress management, self-awareness tools, individual and family therapy)
- *Familial strategies.* To create a positive family climate within which your child can thrive (family meetings, family exercise and recreation, humor and laughter opportunities, success celebrations)
- *Physical strategies.* To make use of your child's bodily-kinesthetic vitality to improve his behavior and attention span at home and school (martial arts, daily exercise, rough-and-tumble play, yoga)
- *Social strategies.* To improve the way your child relates to others (social skills training, communication strategies, peer learning, child–teacher rapport)

I also provide a questionnaire (on pages 82–87) that will help direct you toward precisely those strategies that will meet the needs of your unique child, and I make frequent references to strategies throughout the text to help you determine which approaches might have the greatest benefit for your child. For many of the strategies, I've provided resources for further help and information. I've also included more than 400 references (see pages 297–338) that support the claims and assertions I make in the book and that provide research evidence of the effectiveness of the 101 strategies covered.

Please note that throughout the book I avoid using the terms *ADHD child* and *child with ADHD* because I feel this implies a merging of the child's identity (in whole or in part) with a concept that I do not believe is either valid or helpful to these kids. Instead, I use expressions such as *the child who was diagnosed with ADHD* and *the ADHD-identified child* because the diagnosis itself was a social event (that is, the act by the physician of diagnosing a specific disorder) that occurred in the life of the child in real time and thus functions as a true statement. Given the potential negative impact that the ADHD label can have on a child or teen, I recommend that parents, teachers, and other child helpers avoid the labeling approach ("the ADHD child") and adopt the socially-conscious way ("the ADHD-diagnosed child") of describing a child's or teen's relationship to an ADHD diagnosis.

I'd like to thank the many people who have helped me over the years to make possible the original book and now this new revised and expanded edition. They include the many children and adolescents I taught in my special education classes in the United States and Canada who in today's world would have been diagnosed with ADHD; Diane Divoky, who co-authored a book in the 1970s, *The Myth of the Hyperactive Child*, that was the inspiration for this book and book's title; the thousands of teachers I've given workshops to over the past thirty years on the topic of ADHD and the whole child; the countless parents who have phoned, e-mailed, and written me with concerns about their ADHD-diagnosed kids; my educational publisher, ASCD, which supported the 1999 publication of my teacher's book on ADHD, titled *ADD/ADHD Alternatives in the Classroom*; Sharna Olfman and Gwynedd Lloyd, who invited me to write chapters on ADHD, play, and the media for their books *All Work and No Play* (2003) and *Critical New Perspectives on ADHD* (2006); Deb Brody, my original editor at Dutton for *The Myth of the ADD Child*; Sara Carder, my current editor at TarcherPerigee of this revised and expanded edition; my ex-wife Barbara Turner; and last but certainly not least, my literary agent, Joelle Delbourgo, who is the agent I'd always dreamed of having as a younger writer. I hope that you find this book thought-provoking and also a positive guide in helping your ADHD-diagnosed children and adolescents realize their full potential as vital, creative, and accomplished human beings.

SECTION I

The ADHD Myth and Its Shortcomings

CHAPTER ONE

The ADHD Blob Rolls
Over America and the World

Recently, I happened to catch an old cult classic movie from the 1950s called *The Blob*.[1] It's the story of a tiny gelatinous substance brought to earth via a meteorite that begins to wreak havoc on a small town in America, devouring everything in its path. As it rolls over people, the blob incorporates them into its mass and as it does so, it grows larger and larger. I won't spoil the story by telling you how the movie ends (*Hint:* It has something to do with climate change), but I will say that while I was watching the film I thought of America's ADHD epidemic. The notion of there being an attention deficit disorder in the human mind began as a tiny blob of an idea when it was first presented in a speech to the Canadian Psychological Association in 1972 by its president, McGill University psychologist Virginia Douglas. She suggested that what at the time was being called *hyperkinesis* had more to do with attention problems than with the behavior of hyperactivity.[2] From there, the ADHD blob grew in size at cognitive science laboratories throughout the 1970s (cognitive psychology having displaced behaviorism in the late 1960s as the psychology field most likely to receive research funding from universities, foundations, and governmental agencies). In 1980, attention deficit disorder was given official recognition as a psychiatric disorder in the United States by the American Psychiatric Association in their *Diagnostic and Statistical Manual of Mental Disorders III* (DSM-3).[3]

Then, in the 1980s the ADHD blob gobbled up an entire village with the founding of Children and Adults with Attention-Deficit/Hyperactivity Disorder (CHADD), a parent advocacy group that began lobbying the U.S. Congress to recognize what was then called ADD as a legally handicapping condition under federal disability laws. In the late 1980s and early 1990s the media began spreading the word about this new phenomenon on talk shows, in feature articles, and through popular culture (in the 1992 movie *Wayne's World*, for example, Wayne frequently reminded his somewhat scattered buddy Garth to take his Ritalin).

Big drug companies, sensing an opportunity to make a huge profit from this new attention disorder, started to financially support CHADD and fund individual doctors, ADHD researchers, and professional organizations. In 1997, the federal Food and Drug Administration (FDA) relaxed its restrictions on selling drugs to consumers and began permitting ads for ADHD drugs in women's magazines, on television commercials, and through other publicity outlets, creating even broader exposure of ADHD to the public consciousness and creating an even greater demand for drugs to treat it.[4]

In the 2000s, the ADHD blob rolled over a huge new community as it extended its reach to include ADHD in adults, through Web sites, blogs, social networking sites, chat rooms, and forums that discussed the impact of ADHD on work, marriage, relationships, and general coping skills. Now, in the 2010s, the ADHD blob has overtaken and digested another large region, the world of early childhood, with kids as young as two years old being identified as having ADHD and medicated for their attention deficits.[5] As I sit back and contemplate all that has gone on since 1972, I ask myself: Is there anywhere the ADHD blob, now a gargantuan amorphous entity, has not yet visited? The answer: the rest of the world, where ADHD is spreading rapidly, with rates rising as much as tenfold over the past few years in some countries.[6]

Why I Call ADHD a Myth

Before I get any further into this chapter, there's one thing that I want to set straight. When I say that ADHD is a myth, *I am definitely* not *saying that there are no restless, inattentive, hyperactive, impulsive, and/or disorganized children (and adults) in America and the rest of the world.* I worked for several years as a special education teacher, and during my tenure, I taught so many kids who displayed these traits that I began to think that *all* children acted in this way. I have no illusions about the millions of restless, inattentive, and/or impulsive children out there in homes and classrooms across the country and the world who are exasperating parents, testing the patience of teachers, and creating havoc in families and schools at epidemic levels. The reason I need to stress this fact is that when I wrote the first edition of this book twenty years ago, many people (especially those who had been diagnosed with ADHD or whose children had been diagnosed with ADHD) became apoplectic, thinking that I was saying that they or their kids had no problems. I have received a fair number of angry letters and e-mails from people over the years who felt that I was insensitive to their issues, blind to their symptoms, and completely out to lunch with my proclamation that ADHD is a myth. Not wishing to repeat this unpleasant experience, I need to state here plainly what I mean when I say ADHD is a myth. I'm using the word *myth* in this book in terms of its original meaning from the Greek word *mythos*, which means "story." Over the course of the past forty-five years, *a story* has emerged to explain why some children are restless, inattentive, disorganized, hyperactive, and/or forgetful (among other behaviors). This story has been collectively told by many different agents of society, including psychologists, psychiatrists, university researchers, educators, parents, the pharmaceutical industry, the media, and those who have themselves received a diagnosis. Like any myth, it's a story that has different versions, but overall there's a general consistency to the basic narrative.

THE ADHD MYTH

ADHD is a neurologically based disorder, most probably of genetic origin (although prenatal smoking and lead poisoning are also known to be contributing factors), which afflicts around 11 percent of America's children aged five to seventeen.[7] Significantly more boys appear to have this disorder than girls (boys, 14 percent, girls, 6 percent), although girls who have evaded detection for years are increasingly being identified as having the version of ADHD that is referred to as "ADHD Inattentive Type." ADHD is characterized by three main features: hyperactivity (fidgeting, trouble playing quietly, always moving, leaving classroom seat, talking excessively), impulsivity (blurting out answers in class, interrupting others, having problems waiting turns), and/or inattention (forgetfulness, disorganization, losing things, making careless mistakes, being easily distracted, daydreaming). Current thinking has identified three major groups of ADHD children, one group that appears more hyperactive and impulsive, another that seems more inattentive, and a third that has all three features. The symptoms must have lasted at least six months, have originated by the age of twelve, and have been observed in multiple settings (for example, home and school).[8]

There are no lab tests, biomarkers, or other objective methods available to diagnose this disorder. Assessment tools include parent, child, and teacher interviews; a thorough medical examination; and the use of specially designed behavior rating scales and performance tests. There is no known cure for ADHD, but it can be successfully treated in most instances using a psychostimulant medication such as Ritalin, Adderall, or Concerta. Other drugs have also been used as well, including antidepressants such as Wellbutrin, blood pressure medications such as clonidine, and norepinephrine reuptake inhibitors such as Strattera. Nondrug interventions include behavior modification, parent training, a structured classroom setting, and information given to parents and teachers on the proper way of handling ADHD behaviors at home and in school.

There is no known cause of ADHD, but current thinking has it as involving structural abnormalities in the brain and biochemical imbalances in areas of the brain that are responsible for attention, planning, and motor activity, including the striatum, the cerebellum, the limbic system, and the prefrontal cortex. Neurotransmitters that appear to be dysregulated in ADHD include dopamine and norepinephrine.

Children who have been diagnosed with ADHD can experience significant school problems, suffer from low self-esteem, have difficulty relating to peers, and encounter problems in complying with rules at home leading to conflict with parents and siblings. Some kids with ADHD also have learning disabilities, conduct disorders (destructive and/or antisocial behaviors), Tourette's syndrome (a disorder characterized by uncontrollable motor or verbal tics), and/or mood disorders including depression and anxiety. While ADHD

*seems to disappear for some children around puberty, it can represent
a lifelong disorder for up to 80 percent of those initially diagnosed.*[9]

Although this description of ADHD omits many fine points and details
and although there are disagreements within the ADHD community in regard to some of these issues, I believe there is very little in my description
that most ADHD experts would seriously dispute. I want to emphasize again,
however, that this is a *story*. It may be supported by thousands of medical
studies, as claimed by a 2002 International Consensus Statement on ADHD
signed by more than eighty of the leading authorities in the field, but it is still
a story gleaned from those research findings.[10] We should remember that in
ancient times, myths were stories that people told to account for unexplained
phenomena in their lives (for example, wars, storms, illness, and death). Here
too we have an unexplained phenomenon: Millions of children in our culture
are restless, inattentive, impulsive, and disorganized despite our best efforts
to parent and educate them, and as in ancient times, we want to have a way of
making sense of this situation. Naturally the storytelling elements used in
the modern age (research, clinical data, epidemiological studies, and so on) are
far more sophisticated than those used in ancient times (such as supernatural
entities, magic, and divine revelation). Nonetheless, the intent is still the
same: to provide a coherent narrative, easily understood by the average person, for why millions of children are not acting in the way that we suppose
they should act.

As we'll see in the next chapter, my biggest problem with the ADHD myth
is that it's just not a very good story. Yes, it looks good on the outside with the
fine veneer of medical authority, scientific rigor, and governmental support.
However, when one digs deeper into the story, inconsistencies start to appear,
other interpretations of the same data begin to emerge, and alternative stories
to account for the same restless, inattentive, and impulsive behaviors start to
appear, especially when we include other fields of inquiry beyond neuroscience,
psychiatry, and clinical psychology, such as sociology, anthropology, evolutionary biology, economics, gender studies, media studies, developmental psychology, and family systems theory. In the next chapter, I discuss some very specific
problems with the ADHD myth, and in subsequent chapters, I share a number
of alternative interpretations or stories that can also account for the millions of
restless, inattentive, and impulsive children in our homes and schools.

CHAPTER TWO

Why the ADHD Myth
Is Not a Very Good Story

A good story has certain essential elements in it. It should have a compelling beginning, a strong middle, and a convincing and conclusive ending. The ADHD story, on the other hand, has a feeble beginning, a confusing middle, and an ending that appears wildly out of control. ADHD historians often like to situate the beginnings of the disorder in an 1845 German storybook of morality tales for children called *Struwwelpeter* (Shock-Headed Peter).[1] The book contains a poem titled "Fidgety Phillip" about a child who wiggles, giggles, tips his chair, and can't sit still. This description would fit many young children alive on the planet today. Finally, he pulls off the tablecloth (with the food still on the table) and hides or is trapped underneath it. Again, we're talking about an incident that could happen (and probably has happened) to many families at one point or another in their lives. The book of poems from which this story was taken also includes vignettes of a child with poor grooming habits, a boy who won't eat his soup, and a boy who goes outside during a storm with an umbrella and is sent flying through the air. What are the current disabilities for which these particular poems provide historical beginnings?

The History of ADHD: A Bad Novel in the Making?

The second foundational event occurring at the beginning of the ADHD story concerns a British doctor named George Still. In a series of three lectures to the Royal College of Physicians in 1902 London, Still spoke about children who possessed a "morbid defect of moral control" not accountable to "feeble-mindedness" or medical illness.[2] To use this as one of the key plot points for the beginning of a story about a disorder now said to afflict more than six million children in the United States alone is, and I say this as someone who has written fiction myself, a weak literary move. Still was talking about only a very few children (he cites around twenty in his lectures), not 10 percent of all children worldwide. The children in his case studies behaved in ways not even remotely similar to the American Psychiatric Association's DSM-5 criteria for ADHD. Still's patients defecated in bed, stole, and lied; one even went up to two kids in the playground and "banged" their heads together, in Three Stooges fashion, causing them great pain. Finally, Still attributes the behaviors of these children to a "moral defect," constructing a cause that is absent from today's neurobiological thinking about the origins of ADHD (although he does claim to be able to identify moral defects by the size of the children's heads!). To use a single fictional child in a poem, and twenty children from medical case files to serve as the beginning of a story affecting the lives of millions of children and adults worldwide is, in my opinion, to build a narrative structure on quicksand.

From its humble and irrelevant beginning, we advance to the middle of the story, when things start to get a bit confusing and a little crazy. After World War I, children who had survived the worldwide encephalitis epidemic and apparently displayed symptoms looking like ADHD were said to be suffering from "post-encephalitic behavior disorder." In the 1930s, two German physicians, Franz Kramer and Hans Pollnow, referred to children with ADHD-like symptoms as having "hyperkinetic disease of infancy." Based on cases of children who had shown these symptoms after suffering from actual brain damage, doctors in the 1940s began to use the term *minimal brain damaged* to describe children who acted this way. In the 1960s, many scientists became dissatisfied with this term because of the absence of any detectable brain damage, so they coined a new term to describe these kids' situation: *minimal brain dysfunction*, or MBD. In 1968, with the publication of the second edition of the psychiatric bible, *The Diagnostic and Statistical Manual of Mental Disorders*, the term *hyperkinetic reaction of childhood* became the correct nomenclature to use in describing and diagnosing this disorder. Even with all these name changes, the number of children considered to be suffering from whatever term happened to be used at the time was very small.

Then we come to 1972 and Virginia Douglas's seminal speech on attention deficits, which led to the third edition of the DSM in 1980, and the establishment of "attention deficit disorder" (ADD) "with and without hyperactivity" as a psychiatric disorder. Finally, we have a protagonist in the story and a name that will survive in one form or another up to the present day, although the naming process will look a little like a scammer's shell game. In the revision to the third edition of DSM in 1987, this disorder was renamed "attention deficit hyperactivity disorder." In 1994, the DSM-4 divided this disorder into three components: ADHD predominantly inattentive type, ADHD predominantly hyperactive-impulsive type, and ADHD combined type.[3] The current edition of the manual, the DSM-5, kept this distinction but extended it to adults and changed the maximum age of onset of the disorder from seven to twelve.

Clearly we're dealing with a story whose author keeps changing the plot as he goes along. What's next? Actually, there's a new subplot ADHD researchers are toying around with concerning a disorder called "sluggish cognitive tempo."[4] They'd like to apply this new label to many of the kids identified as having ADHD. Perhaps the comic strip character Sluggo could be considered as a poster boy. To add confusion to this unstable plot, much of the rest of the world uses an entirely different classification method than the DSM-5 called the International Classification of Diseases (ICD). *This* classificatory system uses a *different* term altogether from ADHD: hyperkinetic disorder, or HKD. The system defines the condition more narrowly than the DSM-5, viewing the prevalence of HKD as including 1 to 3 percent of all children instead of 5 percent, which is the figure cited by the American Psychiatric Association, which in turn is far less than the figure currently cited by the Centers for Disease Control and Prevention (CDC) of 11 percent.[5]

The discrepancy between these figures represents another reason why the ADHD myth isn't a very good story: The prevalence rates of the disorder vary all over the place. As noted in a recent report from the CDC, "the percentage of children estimated to have ADHD has changed over time." According to their research, in 2003, 7.8 percent of children had an ADHD diagnosis, in 2007 it rose to 9.5 percent, and in 2011 it rose again to 11 percent. Every year since 1997, the number of kids diagnosed with ADHD has risen 3 percent. And prevalence rates for this disorder vary widely from state to state, with a low of 5.6 percent in Nevada to a high of 18.7 percent in Kentucky.[6] Russell

Barkley, one of the key figures promoting the ADHD story, says that the rate "hinges on how one chooses to define ADHD, the population studied, the geographic locale of the survey, and even the degree of agreement required among parents, teachers and professionals. . . . Estimates vary between 1–20 percent."[7] So then, it's all about how you tell the story, and after all, one can be creative with statistics. Unfortunately, the narrative line suffers.

The Emperor's New Diagnosis

Another big reason why the story of ADHD is so squishy and unreliable is that the tools used to diagnose it are almost entirely subjective. As behavioral neurologist and ADHD critic Richard Saul points out:

> You may notice that there is something striking about the way we define this "illness"—that is, by its symptoms, rather than its cause. If we were to define a heart attack by chest pain, then the appropriate cure would be painkillers, rather than the revival and repair of the heart. Other examples are easy to find: Nasal congestion can be a symptom of a cold, allergy, or many other conditions, but a runny nose is not a diagnosis.[8]

The DSM-5, which is the ultimate arbiter of ADHD diagnoses in America, reads a bit like a restaurant menu, for which the diagnostician is asked, in relation to "inattention" for example, to identify at least six out of nine symptoms, including "is often easily distracted" and "often avoids or dislikes, or is reluctant to do tasks that require mental effort over a long period of time (such as schoolwork or homework)."[9] There is nothing in either of these descriptions to suggest any kind of a social context that might give the responder a better chance of providing a more informed decision. One person might be living in an environment where there are constant distractions from television, people arguing, phones ringing, door bells sounding, computers with their bells and whistles, music playing, and the like, while another might live in a house where silence reigns supreme. But there are no allowances for weighing the noisy setting against the quiet one. Similarly, a child may avoid, dislike, or be reluctant to do his homework because it is boring, or too difficult, or because there's too much of it (some educators even suggest that homework should not be assigned in the first place because of studies suggesting that it has no intrinsic educational value).[10] These types of social contexts, life complications, and research findings are not factored into the DSM criteria, and people are pretty much left to their own devices about making an educated guess based solely on subjective judgment as to whether one of these ADHD indicators actually applies to the child in question.

Besides the physician, the two key sources that decide whether a child is or isn't ADHD are the child's own parents and his schoolteachers. Think about it: How would you like your *own* mental health status to be decided by your relatives and former teachers? Doctors provide parents and teachers with rating scales, checklists, or questionnaires and ask them to rate the child, often on a four- or five-point scale, on a number of behaviors. These checklists and rating scales are used in almost 90 percent of the cases where children receive a diagnosis of ADHD.[11] A recent study suggests that the Conners Abbreviated Symptom Questionnaire (Conners ASQ) "may be the most effective diagnostic tool in assessing ADHD because of its brevity and high diagnostic accuracy."[12] I looked up the Conners Abbreviated Teacher Rating Scale on the Internet and discovered that it consists of *only twelve items*![13] Imagine this: A high school teacher with thirty kids competing for her attention every forty-two minutes being handed this rating scale and asked to determine whether the student fidgets: "not at all," "just a little," "pretty much," or "very much."[14] And on the basis of such quick judgments (keep in mind that she may be completing this questionnaire between class periods as students are coming into the room), the student may find himself labeled with ADHD and medicated. The insanity of this sort of seat-of-the-pants rating circus, which then masquerades as a quantitative "score" in a psychologist's report, brings to mind the sheer circularity of the ADHD myth, as evidenced in this brief but potent dialogue suggested by retired psychologist Philip Hickey:

> *Parent:* "Why is my child so restless and inattentive?"
> *Psychiatrist:* "Because he has an illness called ADHD."
> *Parent:* "How do you know he has this illness?"
> *Psychiatrist:* "Because he is so restless and inattentive."[15]

Meanwhile the search goes on for some objective way to determine who is ADHD and who is not. Recent contenders for potential biomarkers include atypical responses to a finger-tapping activity, olfactory sensitivity (children diagnosed with ADHD are believed to be more sensitive to odors than typically developing kids), and iron levels in the brain.[16] Despite this search for objective evidence of the existence of ADHD, an international consensus statement on biomarkers for ADHD declared: "No reliable ADHD biomarker has been described to date. . . . Most likely, no single ADHD biomarker can be identified."[17]

Label without a Cause

The difficulty in determining objectively who actually has ADHD may be due in large part to the fact that scientists still don't know what causes it. This may seem strange for a disorder that has had literally thousands of studies seeming to support it, but if we read between the lines we discover that while these studies often do differentiate between groups of children identified as ADHD and typically developing kids, it's not completely clear that this is because something called ADHD is responsible for the difference. For example, there are a number of studies that show significant differences between children diagnosed with ADHD and non-ADHD control groups on measures of executive function (such as working memory, inhibition, and planning).[18] However, other research has revealed that the brains of children identified as ADHD, while developing normally, lag behind typically developing children by about three years.[19] Executive functions are associated primarily with the prefrontal cortex, an area of the brain that typically doesn't fully develop until the early twenties even in typically developing individuals.[20] Consequently, it may be that the differences being measured are not a result of some entity called ADHD but because of differences in the rates of maturation of the brain between kids with the ADHD label and typically developing control subjects. We'll explore this topic of cortical maturation in greater detail in chapter 4.

Most versions of the ADHD story make reference to structural and functional abnormalities in the brains of children with the diagnosis, and they use brain scan research as proof that the disorder is inborn and not caused by environmental influences. However, University of Minnesota psychologist and professor emeritus L. Alan Sroufe notes that:

> While the technological sophistication of these studies may impress parents and nonprofessionals, they can be misleading. Of course the brains of children with behavior problems will show anomalies on

brain scans. It could not be otherwise. Behavior and the brain are intertwined. . . . However brain functioning is measured, these studies tell us nothing about whether the observed anomalies were present at birth or whether they resulted from trauma, chronic stress or other early-childhood experiences. One of the most profound findings in behavioral neuroscience in recent years has been the clear evidence that the developing brain is shaped by experience.[21]

Studies suggest, for example, that traumatic stress can have a big impact on both the structure and function of the hippocampus, the amygdala, the prefrontal cortex, and other critical areas of the brain during childhood and adolescence.[22] We'll explore the role that adversity can have in giving rise to an ADHD diagnosis in chapter 7.

Similarly, a great deal of research has been conducted by scientists in an attempt to prove that there is a genetic basis for ADHD, with heritability levels estimated to be as high as 80 percent, about the same as the heritability for height.[23] However, in the gold standard of heritability tests, comparing identical and fraternal twins, one study revealed that there was "no significant influence of genetic factors for activity, attention, and impulsivity," while another concluded that "the genetic risks implicated in ADHD generally tend to have small effect sizes or be rare. . . . Thus, they cannot be used for prediction, genetic testing or diagnostic purposes beyond what is predicted by a family history."[24] Moreover, the cutting edge in genetics these days focuses on gene–environment interactions: Specific genes can result in a child's being either vulnerable or resilient in response to specific adverse events, and environmental influences can trigger or turn off the expression of specific genes responsible for regulating brain development. Several studies, for example, have demonstrated how specific genes interact with environmental influences such as maternal criticism or trauma in early childhood to produce not only the symptoms associated with ADHD but also some of the structural brain abnormalities associated with it.[25]

Don't Go Co-Morbid on Me

Finally, there is the troubling matter of "co-morbidities" in the ADHD story. This cheery term refers to a situation in which a child can have ADHD, for example, *and also* have a learning disability and/or bipolar disorder and/or an anxiety disorder and/or a number of other mental disorders or behavioral conditions, including autism spectrum disorder, eating disorders, and conduct disorders. In one large-scale study of almost fifteen thousand children and adolescents diagnosed with ADHD in Denmark, 52 percent had at least one other psychiatric condition.[26] This raises a number of troubling questions. Where does one disorder leave off and the other one begin? Could it be that what diagnosticians regard as ADHD is in fact the manifestation of another disorder? If we could peel away the contents of these co-morbid disorders, how much ADHD would be left? The fact that physicians are increasingly prescribing antidepressants for ADHD makes me wonder to what degree these kids could be suffering from depression of one kind or another (unipolar depression, bipolar depression, dysthymia, etc.), which fuels their inability to concentrate, their restlessness, and their impulsivity. One study, for example, identified a co-occurring lifetime rate of 18 percent between bipolar disorder and ADHD, and other studies have suggested that a co-morbidity of ADHD and bipolar disorder might represent a distinct clinical subtype.[27] Given the popularity of the ADHD diagnosis in America, there's a danger that children could be quickly identified as having ADHD when, in fact, there might be the deeper and more troubling issue of depression lurking within and left untreated. In the next chapter, I'll take a look at one more reason ADHD isn't a very good story: because the ADHD diagnosis exposes children to potentially harmful medications that may not be necessary in the first place.

CHAPTER THREE

Why Medicating Kids to Make Them Behave Is Not a Very Good Idea

Several years ago, when Ritalin was the drug of choice for ADHD, I walked into a small classroom in a northern California community center and sat down in one of the twenty-five or so chairs set up for the CHADD (Children and Adults with Attention-Deficit/Hyperactivity Disorders) support group meeting. The talk for the evening was on medication for ADHD kids and was to be delivered by a local pediatrician. In the front of the room was a large piece of newsprint taped to the chalkboard with the words "A.D.D. Kids and Drugs" at the top. Underneath this inscription, there was a hand-drawn picture of a sad face (a circle with dots for the eyes and nose and a drooping line for the mouth), and next to it, a happy face. Below the title and faces was a list of several names of drugs, including central nervous system stimulants (Ritalin, Dexedrine, Cylert), antidepressants (desipramine, imipramine), antipsychotics (Haldol, Orap), anticonvulsants (Tegretol), anti-anxiety agents (BuSpar), and blood-pressure medications (Inderal, clonidine). A line with an arrow connected the sad face to the happy face. The implication seemed to be that these drugs would turn a sad kid into a glad kid.

The physician soon appeared and spent the next hour and a half talking with a group of twenty parents and me about the pros and cons of using each of the listed drugs to control hyperactivity, impulsivity, and inattentiveness. The talk was peppered with frequent questions from the audience. One parent asked: "I've heard Ritalin improves organizational problems, but I haven't seen it in my kid. Is there another drug that can?" Another mentioned that her son had been on Ritalin a month and now cries easily. One mother of twins shared her own story: "I have twins that have been on Ritalin for six years. I've heard Ritalin is the first choice, but it's short-acting. Brad's one way, then another, and I find it hard to deal with his roller-coaster behavior."

After the physician had discussed research about how certain drugs can actually stimulate children to seek the approval of adults, a parent spoke up: "I'm always telling my kid to follow his own decisions. He's very popular. I can't imagine stressing that he do all these things just to get approval. What about individual choice?" The physician's response was curious. He replied: "How much free choice do we really have in life?" How much free choice, indeed. Psychoactive drugs have now made it possible for parents and professionals to encourage compliance in children through purely biological means. All the messiness involved in growing up—the battle of the child's will against the adult's will, the endless restless curiosity, the sudden bursts of anger, excitement, or jealousy—all this unpleasantness can now be avoided. One simply needs to classify the unruly child within a soundly scientific framework, give him a diagnostic label—attention deficit hyperactivity disorder—and control him through a psychopharmaceutical cornucopia of state-of-the-art medications. No longer do parents have to ask so many of the difficult questions: "Why is my son so angry at life?" "How can I learn to communicate with my daughter?" "Why is my child not excited by school?" Instead, they can consult with the doctor: "This drug isn't working so well. Do you have one that won't make her migraines worse?" "The stimulant you prescribed is helping him focus, but he's still aggressive—what have you got to control that?" "My child's medication wears off during math class. What should I do?"

A History of Chemical Compliance

The use of medicines to control children's behavior is certainly not new. The second-century Greek physician Galen prescribed opium for restless, colicky infants. During the heyday of the Industrial Revolution, working moms and dads used to soak their crying infants' teething rags with liquor to create a soporific effect. In the late 1800s, overwhelmed parents flocked to Winslow's Soothing Syrup, a morphine-based elixir that was then available without a prescription. But it wasn't until the 1930s that the use of behavior-controlling drugs took on an air of sophistication by being administered under the supervision of a licensed physician. It was in 1937 that Providence, Rhode Island, physician Charles Bradley observed how regular doses of Benzedrine, an amphetamine, calmed down a group of children with behavior problems and helped them focus more effectively on schoolwork.[1] His discovery went unheeded by the medical community during the 1940s and 1950s, when tranquilizers seemed to be the primary means of subduing difficult children. However, in the early 1960s, researchers at Johns Hopkins University discredited the use of tranquilizers in pacifying unruly kids and saw promise in a new group of psychostimulants, including dextroamphetamine sulfate (known by its brand name, Dexedrine) and methylphenidate hydrochloride (Ritalin, developed by the pharmaceutical firm Ciba-Geigy), an amphetamine-like drug originally approved by the Food and Drug Administration (FDA) in 1955 to control mild depression and senility in adults.[2]

Ritalin soon became the drug of choice for controlling hyperactivity. According to a survey conducted by Daniel Safer and John Krager for the Baltimore County Health Department, 40 percent of all prescriptions for behavior problems in 1971 were for Ritalin and 36 percent for Dexedrine. By 1987, the situation had dramatically altered, with Dexedrine accounting for only 3 percent of all prescriptions and Ritalin taking the lion's share—93 percent—of the behavior-control drug market.[3] Over the course of the 1990s, psychostimulant drug use increased a whopping 700 percent in the United States, accounting for nearly 90 percent of the entire world's supply.[4] During the 1990s and 2000s, other drugs began to supplant Ritalin as a first-line treatment for ADHD. In 1996, Richwood Pharmaceuticals (which later merged with Shire) brought onto the market Adderall, a mixture of amphetamine and dextroamphetamine salts. In 2000, Johnson & Johnson began to market Concerta, a long-acting version of methylphenidate hydrochloride. In 2006, Eli Lilly introduced Strattera, a norepinephrine reuptake inhibitor and the first nonstimulant drug to be approved for ADHD. In 2016, the drug company Neos Therapeutics received FDA approval for Adzenys XR-ODT, a slow-dissolving candy-flavored psychostimulant.[5] Since 2010, ADHD medication prescriptions, fueled partly by new diagnoses among adults, have increased 8 percent a year and by the year 2020 are expected to account for $17.5 billion in drug sales.[6] Lawrence Diller, a developmental pediatrician and author of *Running on Ritalin: A Physician Reflects on Children, Society, and Performance in a Pill*, observes: "These production quotas continue to grow and grow. One hundred ninety-four tons of legal stimulants were produced in this country in 2013. That's enough to mold into 27 round, blue 20-mg Adderall pills for every man, woman and child in America."[7]

While these drugs do increase compliance with parent and teacher demands, and while they do result in short-term improvements in attention, behavior, and executive functioning, these advantages come at a price for many children. In this chapter, I outline a number of these disadvantages. Please note: I'm not a Scientologist or a Christian Scientist. I don't believe that psychiatrists are in league with drug companies to control the minds of our children (although, as you'll see, there's more going on between doctors and pharmaceutical companies than meets the eye). I don't believe that Concerta, Adderall, Strattera, and other drugs for ADHD should never be used with children. *Instead, I believe that medications, if prudently prescribed and resolutely monitored in conjunction with the implementation of some of the nondrug strategies described in this book, can represent an important tool for physicians that in some instances can lift children out of a cycle of social, behavioral, and/or academic failure. But I believe that, for the most part, nondrug alternatives ought to be considered first and tried before embarking on a regime of behavior-altering medication.*

Prescribing Speed in a Speedy Culture

The problem is that medications are prescribed too easily and too quickly by physicians without much thought as to nondrug alternatives, and they're not sufficiently monitored by doctors. "How are most people in the United States diagnosed with ADHD?" asks Stephen Hinshaw, professor of psychology at the University of California, Berkeley, and co-author of *The ADHD Explosion: Myths, Medication, Money, and Today's Push for Performance*: "A 10-to-15-minute visit with a pediatrician or a general practitioner. That's it; there is no reimbursement [from insurance companies] for a long, careful, thorough assessment."[8] Reports indicate that families from higher socioeconomic backgrounds have prodded doctors to prescribe ADHD drugs for their children to cope with increasing academic pressures.[9] Conversely, some physicians have used ADHD medications for children from lower socioeconomic backgrounds even if they don't qualify for a diagnosis of ADHD as a means of giving them a leg up in school.[10] More recently, doctors have been provided with guidelines by the American Academy of Pediatrics stating clearly that behavior therapy is the most effective strategy for treating very young children diagnosed with ADHD and should be used before prescribing medication. Yet many physicians have ignored these recommendations and continue to prescribe medication as a first-line treatment.[11] Doctors have also prescribed ADHD medications for children under the age of four, despite AAP guidelines that don't even address the use of medication for children ages three and under.[12]

Perhaps the most up-front difficulty with many ADHD drugs is that they are powerful and potentially addictive. The U.S. government's Drug Enforcement Administration (DEA) lists most ADHD medications as schedule II drugs (out of five schedules), which they define as: "drugs with a high potential for abuse, with use potentially leading to severe psychological or physical dependence. These drugs are also considered dangerous."[13] Included in the list, along with Adderall, Ritalin, and other psychostimulants, are cocaine, OxyContin, and Vicodin. While ADHD experts have long suggested that taking ADHD drugs will make it less likely that a person will descend into drug addiction later on, research now suggests that this simply isn't the case and that a person is neither more nor less likely to become addicted to illegal substances in later life as a result of their taking ADHD medications.[14] This research is based on averages over thousands of individuals, and for specific individuals the issue may not be so clear cut. The diagnosis of ADHD is associated with a greater likelihood of substance abuse in adolescence, so perhaps turning to a drug (even a legal one) for help in solving life problems may not be the best way of modeling how to cope with today's complex world. The fact that ADHD drugs are themselves abused should add to concern that they not be used as a first-line treatment for symptoms associated with a diagnosis of ADHD, but instead be relegated to secondary or tertiary status if nondrug approaches don't prove to be effective.[15]

Then there's the finding that these drugs don't actually work as intended in the long run. Most ADHD drugs are short acting, even those that are called long acting (which refers to the fact that their effects last over the course of many hours, rather than just a few hours). As soon as the child stops taking the drug, the beneficial effects disappear. In that sense, ADHD medications are like behavioral Band-Aids, suitable for controlling symptoms in the short run, but poor mechanisms for making a lasting contribution to the child's welfare over the long haul. One of the best-known and most-respected studies examining the effectiveness of ADHD treatments was the National Institute of Mental Health's collaborative multisite Multimodal Treatment Study of Attention-Deficit Hyperactivity Disorder (MTA) in children, a longitudinal study initiated in 1992 which determined in 2001 that medication was the best treatment for ADHD.[16] Eight years later, however, researchers concluded that medication use in the study did not predict functioning six to eight years later (there were four treatment groups: drugs only, behavior therapy alone, drugs with behavioral therapy, and routine community care). The researchers wrote in their follow-up report in 2009: "In nearly every analysis, the originally randomized treatment groups did not differ significantly on repeated measures or newly-analyzed variables (for example, grades earned in school, arrests, psychiatric hospitalizations, or other clinically relevant outcomes)."[17] James Swanson, a psychologist at the University of California, Irvine, and one of the original study's authors, commented in an article published in the science journal *Nature*: "I don't know of any evidence that's consistent that shows that there's any long-term benefit of taking the medication."[18]

The Dark Side of Psychoactive Drugs

Then there are the side effects. Some common side effects of psychostimulants are decreased appetite, insomnia and other sleep difficulties, abdominal pain, nausea and vomiting, headaches, and anxiety.[19] These symptoms by themselves, while unpleasant, are often short-lived and can be lessened or eliminated by a physician who carefully monitors the child while he's taking the medication and changes dosages or drugs as needed (although as mentioned earlier, this careful monitoring may not always take place, in which case, as a parent, you should immediately seek a doctor who does a better job of following up). It also should be noted, however, that for the children who have to take the drugs, even short-term discomfort represents a distinct downside (a question to the reader: Would you continue to take a painkiller like Tylenol if it gave you any of the above symptoms?).

What is more troubling are the potential long-term adverse effects. Some studies have reported the occurrence of abnormal cardiovascular events from psychostimulants and atomoxetine (Strattera), including increases in blood pressure and heart rate, and rarely, myocardial infarction, stroke, and even sudden cardiac arrest.[20] The American Heart Association has recommended that before patients are treated with ADHD medications, there should be a thorough evaluation, including patient and family history, paying special attention to the presence of any cardiac conditions.[21] There are also potential risks of psychosis stemming from psychostimulant use, especially if there's a family history of mental illness. In a recent study, researchers compared two groups of children aged six to twenty-one, all of whom had one or both parents with major depressive disorder, bipolar disorder, or schizophrenia. Psychotic symptoms (most often, hallucinations) were present in 62.5 percent of youth who had taken stimulants compared with 27.4 percent of participants who had never taken stimulants.[22]

There are also concerns that taking ADHD drugs may harm bone health. Jessica Rivera, an orthopedic surgeon with the U.S. Army Institute of Surgical Research, Fort Sam Houston, San Antonio, Texas, and colleagues identified 5,313 children eight to seventeen years old in the CDC's National Health and Nutrition Examination Survey. They discovered that children on ADHD medication had lower bone mineral density (BMD) in the femur, femoral neck, and lumbar spine, compared to the children who were not taking ADHD drugs.[23] Perhaps most ominously, a survey of mortality data for children aged seven through nineteen years revealed a higher incidence of psychostimulant use preceding unexplained sudden death compared to individuals who had never taken psychostimulants and died in auto accidents.[24]

Less serious than the risks just mentioned, but nevertheless significant to the children taking the drugs, are the psychosocial and emotional costs of taking ADHD medications. One study suggested that adolescents with the ADHD diagnosis who were taking medications were more likely to be victimized by bullies than teens identified as ADHD who were not taking the drugs.[25] A number of reports indicate that ADHD drugs are widely used for nonmedical recreational use; adolescents and young adults are giving or selling their prescribed pills to their friends and colleagues who use them as study aids or who snort them like cocaine for the stimulant high they give.[26] Such illicit use of these drugs can lead to dire consequences. Data from the Johns Hopkins Bloomberg School of Public Health reveals that emergency room visits related to the misuse of Adderall increased dramatically for young adults between 2006 and 2011.[27] Finally, and perhaps most significant for the children and adolescents who have to take these medications, some kids simply don't like taking the drug. While studies reveal that children generally view ADHD drugs favorably, reports from individuals, especially adolescents, tell a different story.[28] In one study of young adolescents, comments included statements such as these: "If I weren't taking the meds, I'd go to school happy and I think I'd have a much better day" (male, age thirteen) and "I just like notice when I don't take the medication I'm happier, I'm more perky. I can get along with people" (female, age twelve).[29] In another study, one adolescent reported: "It felt like I'm not myself when I take my tablets," and another said: "[It's] like the tablets are taking over me and I can't control myself, the tablets are in control of me."[30] Perhaps the best indication of teenagers' feelings about ADHD drugs is that over the course of adolescence, most choose to stop taking them. One longitudinal analysis of a cohort of teens reported usage rates of prescribed ADHD medications dropped 95 percent from age fifteen to age twenty-one.[31]

What then are we to make out of all these data? Should parents have their kids medicated or not? I'm not a medical doctor, so I am not in a position to either recommend or discourage the use of ADHD drugs in any given situation. *But I do know that you should never discontinue a medication that your child is currently taking or change the dosages except under the direction and supervision of a licensed medical doctor* (family doctor, pediatrician, general practitioner, psychiatrist, etc.). What I *would* suggest is that you take this book along with you to the doctor's office and share with your physician the 101 nondrug strategies that are given in the remainder of the book. Discuss with your doctor whether he or she feels that some of the strategies listed might be worth trying *before* initiating a regime of drug therapy or whether the strategies might be used as a *supplement* to drug therapy to keep the dosage as low as possible.

One study has suggested that when a lower dose of stimulant medication is paired with a placebo pill (that the child knows is a placebo), it is more effective than a higher dose of stimulant medication.[32] If this is the case, then certainly pairing some of the nondrug strategies in this book with a lower dosage of stimulant medication should also prove to have beneficial effects for many children and adolescents. If you don't currently have a doctor for your child, I would recommend you start by seeing a developmental-behavioral pediatrician. This subspecialty of physicians trains clinicians who are more likely to view your child's situation within a broader psychosocial context and not rely on ADHD drugs as the *sole* treatment for your child. Many are in private practice, others are affiliated with a clinic, hospital, medical center, or university. You can search for a developmental-behavioral pediatrician in your area by going to WebMD at: doctor.webmd.com/find-a-doctor/specialty/developmental -behavioral-pediatrics.

In any case, I hope that the information in this chapter is helpful to you in making decisions about medications for your child. To make a better and more informed choice about whether to medicate, I would also recommend that you read books that have a more favorable attitude toward ADHD drugs, including Russell A. Barkley's *Taking Charge of ADHD: The Complete Authoritative Guide for Parents*, and Edward M. Hallowell and John J. Ratey's *Delivered from Distraction: Getting the Most Out of Life with Attention Deficit Disorder*.[33] Armed with information taken from a variety of viewpoints, you'll be more likely to make the very best decisions (in conjunction with your doctor) to help your child succeed in school and life.

SECTION II

Why There's a Nationwide and Worldwide ADHD Epidemic

CHAPTER FOUR

Reason #1 for America's ADHD Epidemic: We Don't Let Kids Be Kids Anymore

All babies manifest the three classic warning signs of ADHD: hyperactivity, distractibility, and impulsivity. Unless fast asleep, they're in constant motion, hyperactively exploring their surroundings at every opportunity. They're easily distracted by any unexpected noise or stimulus in their field of vision; a person entering the room, a new toy, a light being turned on or off. And finally, they're impulsive, suddenly exploding into ecstatic squeals of delight or conversely writhing with plaintive tears of disappointment. Over time, however, something happens that we call *maturation*. The growing child's brain goes through a complex series of neurodevelopmental processes that include the creation of new brain cells (neurogenesis), the elimination of excess connections linking brain cells (pruning), and the insulation of nerve pathways (myelination). These activities make the brain more efficient in processing signals from the outside world and manifest themselves outwardly in observable changes in the child's behaviors.

The growing child gradually assumes more control over his impulses (less impulsivity), is better able to focus attention on things (less distractibility), and can stay in one place for greater lengths of time (less hyperactivity). By the time a person reaches early adulthood, the flailing gross motor gyrations of the baby have become the adult's nervous tapping finger on the desk. The scatteredness of the baby becomes, at most, the restless (and often creative) mind of the adult. The impulsiveness of the baby turns into the inner voice of

27

the adult saying to himself after a rude encounter, "Boy, I'd like to punch that guy in the mouth!" but not acting on the impulse.

The ADHD Brain: Marching to the Beat of a Different Timekeeper

A key point to keep in mind about human development is that the pathway for getting from the immature behaviors of the baby to the mature actions of the adult is different for everybody. The brains of children develop at different rates. Neuroscientists now tell us that the brains of children who have been diagnosed with ADHD mature two to three years later than typically developing children, particularly in those areas of the brain that are involved in planning, inhibition of behavior, focus, and other executive functions.[1] An important addendum to this observation is the finding that the so-called ADHD brain, though delayed in development, develops normally. *That is, the brain of the child identified as ADHD is not a flawed brain, a broken brain, or a disordered brain; it is a developmentally delayed brain. And this in turn means that we should not be regarding children diagnosed with ADHD as suffering from a neurological disorder but, rather, as manifesting a developmental difference.*

This makes a great deal of sense when we examine the prevalence statistics of ADHD over time from childhood into adulthood. One study concluded that the rate of ADHD in a given age group declined by 50 percent every five years, such that an ADHD prevalence figure of 4 percent of all children (this study was done in 1996 when rates were much lower) decreases to 0.8 percent of all twenty-year-olds, and 0.05 percent of all forty-year-olds.[2] A more recent study suggested that by age twenty-five, only 15 percent of all individuals identified as having ADHD in childhood met the full criteria for the disorder (making it a rate of 0.6 percent of all young adults using the calculations of the first study).[3] The overarching question is, Where did the ADHD go? The answer: Most of those with the ADHD diagnosis *grew out of it.* They matured. Because they represented a group of people whose brains matured two or three years later than typically developing people, they took a little more time to grow up.

The idea that ADHD represents a question of brain maturation is also supported by research suggesting that, other things being equal, a child who is the youngest in his class is more likely to be identified as having ADHD and given ADHD medication. One study revealed that Icelandic children between the ages of seven and fourteen who were in the youngest third of their class were 50 percent more likely than those in the oldest third of the class to be prescribed psychostimulants.[4] Another study of almost one million children aged six to twelve years in British Columbia indicated that boys born in December were 30 percent more likely to receive a diagnosis of ADHD than boys born in January (the December students being the youngest in their class and the January children being the oldest).[5] A Taiwanese study, which came to the same conclusions, observed: "Relative age, as an indicator of neurocognitive maturity, is crucial in the risk of being diagnosed with ADHD and receiving ADHD medication among children and adolescents."[6] If you're a parent of a child who is one of the youngest students in her class, you need to be very cautious about any diagnosis of ADHD or recommendation that your child be medicated.

The Disappearance of Childhood in Our Culture

Paying attention to developmental factors in understanding the ADHD epidemic raises a larger issue. We are no longer letting kids be kids in our culture. We expect children to do things they are not developmentally ready for. I thought my psychotherapist wife was joking one day when she told me that one of her child clients, a preschooler, had an hour of homework to do every day. I am consistently alarmed at news accounts announcing an increase in academic learning and a decrease in free play and hands-on exploration in our kindergartens and preschools. In a recent study, researchers at the University of Virginia compared the views and experiences of kindergarten teachers in 1998 with those of their counterparts in 2010. Here's what they discovered: in 1998, 31 percent of teachers believed children in kindergarten should learn to read; by 2010, this figure had skyrocketed to 80 percent. In 1998, 87 percent of kindergarten teachers said they had a dramatic play area in their classroom; by 2010, this figure had fallen to only 50 percent. In 1998, 20 percent of kindergarten teachers said they used math worksheets daily; by 2010, this had increased to 35 percent.[7] Recent news reports point to an increase in suspensions in preschool, the rise of parents tutoring their preschool children to get them ready for kindergarten, and an increasing number of preschools focusing on academic learning.[8]

We now expect typically developing children to do things that their brains are not ready for, let alone ADHD-diagnosed kids whose brains lag behind their peers by two to three years. Is it any wonder that we have an epidemic of children manifesting symptoms of inattention, impulsivity, and hyperactivity? A major step toward fighting our nation's ADHD epidemic would be to restore our nation's kindergartens and preschools to centers where kids can be kids, where they can play, dramatize, paint, sing, bounce on the teeter-totter, build with blocks, and express their childlike nature in other creative ways. Remember that the word *kindergarten* means "children's *garden*."

Decades ago, children spent far more time playing out in nature in free unstructured ways than they do today. I remember playing for hours outside my home with neighborhood kids, engaging in games of tag that extended over several city blocks, playing King of the Mountain while standing on mounds of dirt that had been dug up by construction crews, building simple forts with scrap wood, putting on pretend music concerts (I lip-synched Elvis's "You Ain't Nothin' But a Hound Dog" at the age of five to a group of neighborhood kids), and even arranging play marriages (the neighborhood gang took my "wife" and me in a little red wagon to the Dairy Queen for our "honeymoon"). According to Jaak Panksepp, distinguished research professor of psychobiology at Bowling Green State University: "Play is now increasingly rule-bound and organized by adults and seems increasingly lost in our evermore regulated and litigious society where too many kids have little freedom to negotiate the social terrain on their own terms."[9]

Panksepp believes that one of the reasons for skyrocketing rates of ADHD in our society has to do with the decline in rough-and-tumble activities such as chasing, climbing, wrestling, and playing physical games. In experiments with rats that had had their frontal lobes intentionally damaged, he and his researchers observed symptoms similar to those of ADHD. However, when the rats were given opportunity to play, those symptoms diminished. Panksepp also noted that when psychostimulants were administered, the rats were less likely to play.[10] He believes that free play is crucial to the development of the frontal lobe executive functions involved in social learning; precisely the areas that ADHD experts claim are impaired in children identified as having attention deficit hyperactivity disorder. Add to this, recent studies indicating that ADHD symptoms actually decrease when children are out in nature (see Strategy #5: Make Time for Nature), and you begin to see how behavior and brain function appear to be directly tied to sociological changes in how our children spend their free time in today's complex high-tech world compared with the way it was fifty or sixty years ago, before the ADHD blob was even a tiny globule.[11]

Not Broken Brains, but Better Brains

What adds even more dramatic tension to this already untenable developmentally-based situation is that the so-called immaturity of ADHD-diagnosed children actually turns out to be a positive thing. *It may, in fact, be better to have a delayed brain than to have a typically developing brain.* The best evidence for this comes from the field of evolutionary biology where a concept called *neoteny* (a Latin word meaning "holding youth") puts a primacy on youthful behavior. Neoteny refers to the retention of juvenile traits into maturity.[12] The great Harvard evolutionary biologist Stephen Jay Gould hailed neoteny as perhaps the key factor in human evolution.[13] He noted, for example, how a juvenile chimpanzee looks much more like a human than it does an adult ape because those childlike traits were not "held" into the adulthood of his species. In humans, on the other hand, the small face, the vaulted cranium, and the large brain related to body size of the child are traits that *are* retained into human maturity. He writes: "If humans evolved, as I believe, by neoteny . . . then we are, in a more than metaphorical sense, permanent children."[14]

Neoteny also has its psychological dimensions. In his book *Growing Young*, Princeton anthropologist Ashley Montagu suggested a number of neotenous childlike traits that we should try to retain in our adulthood, including: creativity, imagination, playfulness, curiosity, vitality, humor, wonder, and joy.[15] These are traits that many children diagnosed with ADHD display. Unfortunately, parents and teachers often tend to regard these features as negative traits: daydreaming, rough-housing, silliness, and impulsivity. Many of the strategies described in this book take the qualities that so-called immature ADHD-labeled children manifest and turn them into positive neotenous traits that can serve to support their well-being and the realization of their full potential.

ADHD and Adolescent Behavior: What's the Difference?

Developmental considerations should also impact the way we look at *adolescents* who have been diagnosed with ADHD. The statistics are frightening. Over 16 percent of boys between the ages of twelve and sixteen have been diagnosed with ADHD in the United States at some point in their lives, according to a CDC tabulation.[16] Keep in mind that a key component of the ADHD myth is that the executive functions of individuals with ADHD (the ability to plan, reflect, inhibit impulses, focus, and so on) are impaired compared with typically developing control groups and that the executive functions are closely associated with the prefrontal lobes of the cerebral cortex. What we've learned over the past fifteen years from the brain scans of typically developing adolescents engaged in cognitive tasks is that the frontal lobe executive functions are going through a critical stage of reorganization and maturation.[17]

While adolescents can make "cool cognition" judgments about things by the age of fifteen or sixteen (when they're in a controlled laboratory environment), they have great difficulty with decision making when their peers are present or if they're in the midst of an emotional situation (a condition termed *hot cognition*).[18] The point is that the brains of adolescents are going through an important period of maturation, and this is a *normal* developmental process. Claims by the ADHD community that the ADHD-diagnosed adolescent brain's prefrontal lobes are impaired and the adolescent mind's executive functions are compromised fail to consider that virtually all adolescents are going through this process. Adolescence is a time fraught with passions, poor decision making, lack of inhibition, failure to comply with authority, and many other challenges, and it's likely that ADHD-type behaviors have a greater association with being an adolescent than with having a disorder called attention deficit hyperactivity disorder. And because adolescents often don't want to take their ADHD medications and discontinue their use, it's especially important that we develop nondrug, age-appropriate strategies to help them through this challenging time in their lives.[19]

Finally, there's the response from ADHD believers who bridle at this sort of developmental analysis and angrily chide those who would say, "It's just growing pains; he'll grow out of it." They cite studies predicting that children who manifest ADHD symptoms at three years of age will have those same symptoms at age six, and so we should intervene as early as possible to keep ADHD in check.[20] This defense implies a choice between active medical intervention on the one hand and doing nothing on the other. But this is a false dichotomy. No one is saying, "Oh, he'll grow out of it," and then putting the child into an empty room for several years. Children grow up in cultural settings that either support their growth or suppress it. A key feature of the child and adolescent brain is its *neuroplasticity*.[21] This means that the sorts of experiences a child or teen is exposed to as he grows up have a crucial role in determining what type of brain he'll end up with. We'll come back to this concept in Strategy #33: Teach Your Child How His Brain Works, but for now, we need to recognize that to say something like "He'll grow out of it" can be a cop out if there's no further thought as to how to support the child's or adolescent's development. Yes, it's likely that he *will* grow out of his ADHD, but you still need to make sure that the child or teen is given the very best social, emotional, cognitive, physical, and creative enrichment possible. Whether you believe in ADHD or not, *every child* needs to be provided with an optimal environment that supports his or her growing. That's what the 101 strategies described in Section III are all about.

CHAPTER FIVE

Reason #2 for America's ADHD Epidemic: We Don't Let Boys Be Boys Anymore

One of the most consistent findings in the field of ADHD is the preponderance of boys who are diagnosed with ADHD. Using the latest statistics available covering ADHD diagnoses in the United States from 2011 to 2013, 13.3 percent of all boys were identified as having ADHD compared with 5.6 percent of girls. For ages twelve to seventeen, the figure was 16.3 percent of all boys and 7.1 percent of all girls.[1] Why so many boys? Some have suggested that girls may be underidentified because they tend to have the subtype of ADHD designated Inattentive Type. Because the symptoms of this subtype are largely internal (forgetting things, being mentally disorganized, daydreaming, etc.), they are not as likely to be observed by parents, teachers, or doctors compared with boys whose "externalizing" behaviors cause them to be identified with the Hyperactive/Impulsive or Combined subtypes of ADHD.[2] Others have suggested that there may be a gender bias toward the study of boys in the research literature of ADHD.[3] The question is, Why are boys favored among diagnosticians when it comes to a disorder involving hyperactivity, impulsivity, and/or inattentiveness? The answer may be found in our culture's changing conceptions of how boys are supposed to act in our society.

The Decline of All-Boy Behavior

Pulitzer Prize–winning *New York Times* science journalist Natalie Angier suggests that the surge in ADHD may be due to the fact that we no longer accept traditionally boyish behavior as normal. She writes:

> *Until quite recently, the plain-spun tautology "boys will be boys" summed up everything parents needed to know about their Y-chromosome bundles. Boys will be very noisy and obnoxious. Boys will tear around the house and break heirlooms. They will transform any object longer than it is wide into a laser weapon with eight settings from stun to vaporize. They will swagger and brag and fib and not do their homework and leave their dirty underwear on the bathroom floor. But they will also be . . . boys. They will be adventurous and brave. When they fall down, they'll get up, give a cavalier spit to the side, and try again. . . . A boy being a shade too boyish risks finding himself under the scrutiny of parents, teachers, guidance counselors, child therapists—all of them on watch for the early glimmerings of a medical syndrome, a bona fide behavioral disorder. . . . Is he fidgety, impulsive, disruptive, easily bored? Perhaps he is suffering from attention-deficit hyperactivity disorder, or ADHD, the disease of the hour and the most frequently diagnosed behavioral disorder of childhood.*[4]

In the early 1990s, when I was writing a monthly column for *Parenting* magazine, developmental psychologist David Elkind told me in an interview something very similar to what Angier was saying: that what used to be called "all-boy behavior" was now being pathologized as attention deficit disorder. And that was long before 13.3 percent of boys had been labeled ADHD.

Vive La Brain Difference!

At the risk of sounding like a simpleton, let me say this: Boys are different from girls. Girls' brains mature earlier than boys'; in some respects, as much as ten years earlier.[5] Does this sound familiar? Yes, just as we discussed in the previous chapter, the brains of typically developing children mature years earlier than kids diagnosed with ADHD. Someone who believes that a boy's brain should mature at roughly the same age as a girl's is likely to be disappointed in that expectation and will begin to regard that boy's brain as disordered, particularly in those regions of the brain that mature last (not until early adulthood): the executive function areas of the prefrontal cortex.[6] There are also qualitative differences in specific areas of the brain based on sex, especially in those areas where there are a lot of sex steroid hormone receptor densities, including sex differences in the right hippocampus (important for learning and memory), the bilateral amygdala (involved in social status and the experience of strong emotions like joy and anger), and cortical gray matter (the major component of the central nervous system).[7] These basic neurological differences in the rate of brain maturation and brain structure lead directly to big differences in the behaviors and psychological characteristics that differentiate boys from girls.

Preschool boys engage in more vigorous physical activity in school than girls.[8] In language tasks, boys need to employ multiple areas of the brain (visual or auditory), depending on how the words are presented, while girls use a unifying language neural network to process words.[9] Boys aren't as adept as girls are in self-regulating emotions (such as using effective coping strategies for dealing with stress).[10] Boys are less able to inhibit behaviors than girls, who display more effortful control over their actions.[11] And perhaps most significant, in a study involving eleven hundred girls and eleven hundred boys, boys performed worse than girls on tasks involving attention and planning.[12] And remember, we're talking about *typically developing* boys and girls.

Gender Bias in the Classroom

It should immediately be evident that all the things that girls are better at than boys are precisely the types of behaviors and abilities that are needed in a typical preschool, kindergarten, elementary school, and secondary school classroom. Add to this the fact that the earlier stages of schooling (early childhood and elementary school education) are dominated by women teachers, and it becomes apparent that the playing field is tilted strongly in favor of girls performing better than boys in school, and manifesting fewer of the symptoms of ADHD. Using statistics from 2015, 96.8 percent of all preschool and kindergarten teachers and 80.7 percent of all elementary and middle school teachers are women.[13] In one study of preschool teachers' attitudes toward play, female teachers were more likely to value calm play and emphasize the importance of social development, whereas male teachers tended to stress the importance of physical development in play.[14] In another study, clinicians were observed to be more likely to diagnose a boy with ADHD than a girl, even if the boy did not meet all the criteria for a diagnosis.[15] In the home environment, research on ADHD is dominated almost entirely by mothers' reports and involvement, and if fathers play a role at all, it is usually in downplaying the significance of the medical aspects of the ADHD diagnosis and opposing the use of medications in treating their child.[16] All of these studies add up to the fact that *being a boy is a risk factor for receiving a diagnosis of ADHD and a prescription for psychoactive medication.* If we once again let boys be boys in our culture, it's likely that the rates of ADHD would decline sharply at all age levels.

CHAPTER SIX

Reason #3 for America's ADHD Epidemic: We Disempower Our Kids at School

In talking with parents of children who have been diagnosed with ADHD over the years, I've often heard mothers say: "We take him off his medication in summer and on weekends." I've also heard something similar from doctors who refer to giving an ADHD-diagnosed child a "drug holiday." When I first heard about these holidays I asked myself, What do summers and weekends have in common? Almost immediately came the answer: *There's no school.* The implications seemed to me almost too disturbing to contemplate: doctors were prescribing medications for kids to make them conform to the requirements demanded of them by modern schooling. Taken in this sense, ADHD medications seem to function like the performance drugs that athletes take (often illegally) to boost their capacities within a given sport. But I knew it couldn't be that simple. ADHD symptoms are supposed to be observed both at school and at home. But if this is true, then why were so many parents taking their kids off psychostimulants when they weren't in school? Why didn't they keep them on drugs around the house when school wasn't in session? As someone who'd been a special education teacher for several years working with kids who had attention, behavior, and learning problems, I already knew the answer. Kids needed the drugs to sit for long periods of time at their desks listening to teachers' lectures. They needed medications to focus on the rote worksheets and committee-written textbooks that teachers assigned. They needed drugs to pay close attention to the questions on a high-stakes standardized test. Conversely, they *didn't need them* when they were out playing basketball in a community center, or hiking in the woods with their family, or planting flowers in a garden, or play wrestling with a neighbor, or engaged in an art project with a sibling, or playing a board game with friends.

So I began to realize that a big part of the diagnosis for ADHD and the use of medications appeared to have a lot to do not with school itself but with the particular manner in which school was conducted. The kids in my special education classrooms were much more engaged and had fewer symptoms of ADHD when we were involved in creating puppet shows, or singing songs, or drawing pictures, or building villages with clay, or, in one case, fishing in a pond near my home after school. In this latter case, I particularly recall one child who was an absolute terror in my classroom whenever he was required to do seatwork (such as answer questions in worksheets, workbooks, and textbooks) becoming the most highly mannered and pleasant boy during our fishing escapade.

Boring Classrooms May Be Causing ADHD Symptoms

So perhaps, then, ADHD medications aren't simply "school adaptation drugs" but more properly are "bad schooling practices adaptation drugs." I say this as an educator of more than forty years who understands that the best type of learning is active learning, when children and adolescents are engaged in hands-on, experiential, collaborative, real-life, creative learning activities that require them to construct new ideas and make new connections to practical problems that are out there in the real world. My heroes in education who have pointed the way toward how our schools need to be run include Maria Montessori, John Dewey, Jean Piaget, Jerome Bruner, John Holt, Jonathan Kozol, Howard Gardner, Deborah Meier, Susan Ohanian, and Alfie Kohn.[1] I contrast this type of active approach to learning with what I would term "worst practices" learning, by which students sit for most of the day at their school desks listening to colorless lectures, filling out brain-dead worksheets, taking paper-and-pencil tests, and engaging in rote (that is, memorized) learning. If there were a single moment in a classroom that summed up this type of educational approach, it would be actor Ben Stein lecturing on the Hawley-Smoot Tariff Act to high school students in the 1986 movie *Ferris Bueller's Day Off*:

> In 1930, the Republican-controlled House of Representatives, in an effort to alleviate the effects of the . . . Anyone? Anyone? . . . the

Great Depression, passed the . . . Anyone? Anyone? The tariff bill? The Hawley-Smoot Tariff Act? Which, anyone? Raised or lowered? . . . Raised tariffs . . .[2]

It turns out that kids who have been diagnosed with ADHD have real problems with worst practices learning, but respond very favorably to active "best practices" learning. One of the first (and still to my mind just about the only) researchers within the ADHD community to have recognized this is Sydney S. Zentall, a professor of special education at Purdue University. Over the past forty years, she has amassed a body of literature that supports the idea that children diagnosed with ADHD require *a higher level of environmental stimulation* than typically developing children. She refers to this as "the theory of optimal stimulation."[3] Just as psychostimulants calm ADHD-diagnosed kids down, so too can stimulation in a classroom help them focus and become better engaged in academic material. Her research reveals, for example, that kids identified as ADHD do better academically and behaviorally when they can engage in spontaneous verbalizations and when color is used to highlight information.[4] Another study she was involved with indicated that simply giving ADHD-diagnosed students a brief choice on a computerized math task, providing a spoken voice giving the math problem, and then displaying visual feedback of their answers was enough to "normalize" their performance.[5]

Other researchers have discovered the same thing. In one study, children in grades one through four were matched and divided into two groups, with one group diagnosed with ADHD and the other a control group. They were then observed during regular classroom sessions. The researchers focused on how the two groups performed under two learning conditions: (1) when involved in passive learning (listening to a lecture, silently reading a book, looking at a worksheet) and (2) when engaged in active learning (writing, reading aloud, talking with a teacher or student about the topic at hand). Results indicated that students in the group identified with ADHD exhibited lower rates of academic engagement and higher rates of off-task behavior than the control group in the passive learning situation. No surprises there. But what was interesting was that there were no differences between the two groups when they were *all* engaged in the active learning condition (the observers were "blind" to who was or wasn't ADHD-identified). In other words, ADHD-labeled kids were indistinguishable from so-called normal kids when they were actively engaged in learning. The study's authors concluded by saying: "Although all students should benefit from increased opportunities to actively respond to academic material, this may be especially true of students with ADHD."[6]

What amazes me is *how small the changes needed to be to normalize the behaviors of the children diagnosed with ADHD.* Educators should be doing *far more* than this though. They should be engaging ADHD-identified kids in building hands-on projects, developing inventions, taking field trips, creating art, interviewing community members, carrying out ecological investigations, having debates, organizing a model United Nations, and much more. But one has to ask the big question: To what extent are these types of stimulating learning activities going on for *all* kids these days in school? And the answer is not very often. In fact, worst educational practices are even more prevalent than they were decades ago when Zentall first began her work. Therein lies a big reason for the massive increase in the diagnosis of kids with ADHD. Let me explain why this is so by telling you a sad story about what has occurred in American education over the past fifty years.

A SAD TALE: AMERICAN EDUCATION GOES DOWNHILL—1966–2016

In the 1960s and 1970s, propelled by the work of thinkers like John Holt, Jerome Bruner, Jonathan Kozol, and other progressive educators, American education was alive with positive and active learning initiatives that included open education, expressive arts learning, affective education, schools without walls, and other forms of student-centered learning. In 1983, however, Secretary of Education Terrell Bell released a national report from the National Commission on Excellence in Education titled "A Nation at Risk," which criticized the mediocre standards of American education. The report observed: "If an unfriendly foreign power had attempted to impose on America the mediocre educational performance that exists today, we might well have viewed it as an act of war." The report called for a far more rigorous curriculum, tougher academic requirements, and higher standards.[7] At this point, the tide began to shift from student-centered learning to teacher-directed education, from learning to testing, from exuberance in learning to accountability of what had been learned. During the 1990s, a series of conferences was convened and attended by state governors, CEOs of large corporations, and federal officials who began to hammer out a set of initiatives intended to create a national mandate for a more accountable, teacher-directed school system. This effort came to a head finally with the passage of the federal law No Child Left Behind, which was signed into law by President George W. Bush, in January 2002. It required schools in the United States to make "adequate yearly progress" on standardized tests or face increasingly severe penalties. In 2009, an effort at further school reform was initiated by state governors and state superintendents of education with the establishment of the Common Core State Standards Initiative. It was a measure designed to establish a uniform set of academic standards from kindergarten through grade twelve to be adopted by each state in the country. Upon taking office in 2009, President Barack Obama created a new federal program called Race to the Top, which awarded federal funds to states that engaged in educational reforms such as:

- *Establishing data systems to track student achievement*
- *Creating a value-added component to teacher evaluations to assess teacher performance in part on the basis of the test results of their students*
- *Establishing academic programs solidly grounded in the Common Core State Standards*

Finally, in 2015, Congress passed the Every Student Succeeds Act (ESSA), which replaced the No Child Left Behind act and gave more flexibility to the states to determine school quality, but still within these test-driven teacher-directed accountability standards.

What makes this story so sad is its emphasis on standardized testing, its focus on a uniform academic curriculum, its transformation of students into sources of data, and its method of evaluating teachers based on student test results. If you tried to, you couldn't have created a more dismal learning environment, one that serves to stifle the expression of creative energies, narrow the scope of human fulfillment, dull the natural curiosity of children, suppress the love of learning every child is born with, and ignore the wide diversity of methods that are available for introducing students to the incredible world around us.

ADHD-Diagnosed Kids: Our Canaries in the Coal Mine?

This sort of "accountability curriculum" is bad for *all* kids. As former assistant U.S. Secretary of Education Diane Ravitch noted: "What we're teaching today is obedience, conformity, following orders. . . . We're certainly not teaching kids to think outside the box."[8] But the students who particularly suffer are the ones who have the greatest neurobiological antipathy to a test-driven workbook-centered approach to learning. I'm talking about the kids whom we label ADHD and medicate, often because the schools have failed to optimally stimulate them. There's a growing body of research to support this view. A recent article in *Pediatrics*, a journal of the American Medical Association, for example, postulates a connection between the push for academic achievement that has occurred over the past two or three decades in the United States and the increase in the number of kids diagnosed with ADHD. The authors write: "It is not surprising that increased academic demands would lead to the diagnosis of ADHD. Although it is a neurobiological condition with genetic causes, ADHD is defined by behaviors that are age dependent, related to the demands of the environment, and occur on a spectrum of typical behavior of children. Diagnosis is based primarily on teacher and care giver reports, which should be influenced by expectations for behavior. As young children face increased academic demands, some will be seen as outliers and will be diagnosed as having ADHD."[9] Another study revealed that what is true for young children is also true for kids between the ages of six and thirteen. Using National Survey of Children's Health reports from 2003, 2007, and 2011, the researchers discovered that children who were at or near the poverty line in states that had passed educational accountability laws after No Child Left Behind were more likely to be diagnosed with ADHD compared with kids at the same socioeconomic level from states that had passed such laws years earlier.[10] A further study put it more bluntly: "Children in states with more stringent accountability laws are more likely to be diagnosed with Attention Deficit/Hyperactivity Disorder (ADHD) and consequently prescribed psychostimulant drugs for controlling the symptoms."[11]

So, what do kids labeled ADHD have to say about their experience of learning in today's accountability classroom? According to one survey, children diagnosed with ADHD report feeling less support for their autonomy, less related to their teachers, and less competent in the classroom compared to their non-ADHD-diagnosed peers. They also perceived their classrooms as more controlling.[12] For those who might say "these are the classrooms we've got and ADHD-diagnosed kids need to get with the program and take their ADHD medications, if that's what is required of them," it might be pointed out that children are not programmed by nature to learn in this fashion. In ancestral hunter-gatherer communities, children learned the skills of the culture through direct engagement with the natural world. Much of that learning happened through play. Children had to learn how to navigate their world, identify plants, make tools, cook, and learn many other practical hands-on skills. Now, all of a sudden they have to sit for long periods of time staring at a black-and-white board with small markings on it and scratch those markings onto pieces of white paper with thin wooden sticks. Is it any wonder that we have a growing number of children who find their attention wandering to things that are far more interesting to them? In coal-mining communities, it was customary for miners to take a caged canary with them into the mine. If the oxygen in the mine began to decrease due to a blockage of some sort or noxious gases, the canaries, having less respiratory capacity than humans, would fall off their perch. This would alert the miners that there wasn't enough air for them to breathe, and they would leave the mine. The children whom we diagnose with ADHD are our canaries in the coal mine, warning us that there isn't enough air to breathe in our classrooms and that we'd better get to work fast and construct more humane, playful, and engaging classrooms before the walls of our culture cave in completely.

CHAPTER SEVEN

Reason #4 for America's ADHD Epidemic: We Pass Our Stress on to Our Kids

A key component of the ADHD myth is that it's a neurobiological disorder. This "fact" is convenient because it isolates the disorder from any taint of association with family problems, suboptimal parenting, child abuse, poverty, and other social ills. As ADHD defenders continue to say over and over again in response to critics, ADHD is not caused by poor parenting. If there are suggestions of a stressful family life in the home of an ADHD-diagnosed child, it's generally concluded by these defenders that it is the *child* who most likely caused the family stress due to his out-of-control, noncompliant, restless, and/ or disorganized behaviors.[1] When I typed the terms *child stress* and *ADHD* in the search engine Google Scholar, I discovered that *the overwhelming majority of the journal articles had to do with the child causing parental stress*, not the parent causing the child's stress. But psychologists Soly Erlandsson and Elisabeth Punzi have referenced the belief of Françoise Dolto, a French child psychiatrist and psychoanalyst, that "the parent who is deeply bothered by his/her child's behavior is the one who needs treatment." Erlandsson and Punzi continue:

> Today, shifting the focus from the child to the parents is, however, al-most perceived as a threat not only to the parents but—ironically—also to the experts on ADHD. It is not the parents' fault that their child is acting divergently. Such behavior problems in the child can,

however, be linked to an unbalanced situation in the family and to the family history. Instead of examining the family dynamics and masked dysfunctions in parents, it is of course less complicated to put the blame on the child.[2]

It's certainly not my intention to blame parents for their children's diagnosis of ADHD. But I also feel that it's not acceptable to blame the victim (the child) for the impact of her ADHD behaviors on family members. As an academic psychologist, I've been steeped for decades in a literature that regards the early events of a child's growing-up years—especially those involving the parents—as pivotal. Parents have an enormous formative influence on their kids, affecting behavior, personality, and future outcomes for the rest of their children's lives. My mentors for this perspective have included, among others, Sigmund Freud, Carl Jung, Alfred Adler, Erik Erikson, John Bowlby, Carl Rogers, and Albert Bandura.[3] There is virtually no mention of these foundational thinkers in the ADHD literature. Instead, if the topic of parents is brought up in books and journal articles on ADHD (and it very frequently is), the discussion has to do with how to help the parents cope with the ADHD-identified child's disorder, how to help explain ADHD to the child, how to use behavior modification strategies to control the child's symptoms, how to handle compliance with medication, how to communicate and cooperate with the child's school regarding the ADHD behavior, and of course, how to deal with the ADHD-identified child's role in creating family stress.[4] In the past five years, however, there's been an emerging literature focused on the idea that a child's surroundings, and in particular, the presence of poverty, stress, parental criticism, and/or trauma and abuse can be significant contributory factors to an ADHD diagnosis. In this chapter, I look at some of this literature and examine what it can tell us about the ADHD epidemic in America and the rest of the world.

Adversity as an ADHD Trigger

If a child grows up in an environment where parents fight about finances, where drug use is common, and where violence is a daily occurrence—as is often the case in areas of poverty—then the ability to self-regulate emotions, concentrate on academics, set goals, and engage in other important executive functions can be greatly diminished. A recent systematic review of studies on psychosocial factors in ADHD revealed that out of forty-two studies on this topic, thirty-five found a clear association between socioeconomic disadvantage and ADHD. The data suggested that children in families with low socioeconomic status (SES), were 1.85 to 2.21 times more likely to have been diagnosed with ADHD than their peers in high SES families.[5] Other studies have demonstrated that it is the SES level that contributes to the ADHD diagnosis and not the child's ADHD symptoms that drove the family into poverty.[6]

Key factors within low SES families that contribute to an ADHD diagnosis include prenatal smoking, family conflict, and poor maternal emotional attachment to the child. Other factors include partner cruelty, substance abuse, parental criminal behavior, and lack of parental involvement with the child.[7] A survey of more than one million children in Sweden observed an association between younger single-parent mothers with less education (factors associated with a low SES) and a diagnosis of ADHD in one or more children.[8] Studies have also shown that children in foster care are three times more likely than non-foster-care kids to have a diagnosis of ADHD.[9]

Parents or caregivers provide the primary developmental template for a child's social, emotional, and cognitive development. If this relationship is impaired by dysfunctional interactions, then ADHD symptoms may be one possible outcome. Some research, for example, suggests that if a child is exposed to high levels of parental criticism, he is less likely to undergo the remission in ADHD symptoms that often occurs as a child moves through adolescence into young adulthood (a development that we explored in chapter 3).[10] Other surveys point to the role of early emotional trauma as a factor contributing to a diagnosis of ADHD. One study taken from the National Longitudinal Study of Adolescent Health, for example, revealed associations between ADHD Inattentive Type and self-reported parental or guardian neglect, physical abuse, and even sexual abuse.[11] Another study of 13,054 adults from the 2005 Canadian Community Health Survey indicated that there was a seven times higher likelihood of being diagnosed ADD/ADHD if the subject had been abused in childhood, after controlling for age, race, gender, parental divorce, parental addictions, and long-term parental unemployment.[12]

The stress of violence may be an important contributor to the structural and functional brain abnormalities seen in children diagnosed with ADHD. As British child health expert Elspeth Webb puts it: "Children exposed to early violence display altered responses to confrontation and conflict; in essence they are 'hard-wired' to be anxious, distractible, highly aroused, and impulsively aggressive in situations of conflict. . . . These children present with hyperactivity, distractibility and impulsive aggression, and thus, it is easy to see how they might fulfill criteria for a diagnosis of ADHD."[13] One study revealed that high stress exposure resulted in greater levels of norepinephrine release (the neurotransmitter regulated by Strattera, among other drugs) and that this in turn was associated with poorer attention performance in individuals diagnosed with ADHD.[14] During stressful encounters, the hypothalamus-pituitary-adrenal (HPA) axis that is central to regulating our responses to stressful life experiences becomes impaired, and areas of the limbic system, including the hippocampus (important for memory and learning), begin to display abnormalities. Similarly, trauma has a negative impact on the dopaminergic system in the brain, which is the main neurotransmitter targeted by ADHD drugs.[15] Finally, there is evidence that the executive functions associated with the prefrontal cortex are impaired by early traumatic experiences.[16]

The Great ADHD Smokescreen

One of the consequences of the ADHD community's chronic denial of the role of family strife and social adversity in contributing to ADHD symptoms is that these conditions then tend to get swept under the rug, while the presenting problems—the child's symptoms—are controlled with medications that provide only temporary relief, and the deeper problems are left unaddressed. As L. Alan Sroufe, lead researcher in a forty-year study of two hundred children born into poverty, puts it:

> "What we found was that the environment of the child predicted development of A.D.D. problems. . . . Plenty of affluent children are also diagnosed with A.D.D. Behavior problems in children have many possible sources. Among them are family stresses like domestic violence, lack of social support from friends or relatives, chaotic living situations, including frequent moves, and, especially, patterns of parental intrusiveness that involve stimulation for which the baby is not prepared. For example, a six-month-old baby is playing, and the parent picks it up quickly from behind and plunges it in the bath. Or a three-year-old is becoming frustrated in solving a problem, and a parent taunts or ridicules. Such practices excessively stimulate and also compromise the child's developing capacity for self-regulation."

Sroufe goes on to say that medicating a child doesn't address these deeper issues: "Putting children on drugs does nothing to change the conditions that derail their development in the first place. Yet those conditions are receiving scant attention. Policy makers are so convinced that children with attention deficits have an organic disease that they have all but called off the search for a comprehensive understanding of the condition."[17]

ADHD: It's Not All in the Genes

This is not to say that organic factors don't have a role in the development of ADHD symptoms. But it's when adverse environmental conditions interact with genetic vulnerabilities that ADHD symptoms may arise. One study found a relationship between a variation of a serotonin transporter gene (5-HTTLPR) and caregiver intrusiveness (as opposed to nurturance) in producing ADHD symptoms in a group of institutionalized preschoolers.[18] Another study showed that the DRD4 seven-repeat allele (a version of one dopamine receptor gene that has been associated with the ADHD diagnosis) increases a child's susceptibility to engage in "sensation seeking" as a response to lower qualities of parenting such as anger, rejection, and/or negative regard of the child by the parent.[19]

Having a child diagnosed with ADHD does not mean that you are a child abuser or a poor and neglectful parent. However, these studies should wake us up to the fact that ADHD is not some sort of inborn genetic flaw that turns children into family menaces, but rather that psychosocial factors play an important role in the genesis of hyperactivity, inattentiveness, and impulsivity. When a child experiences clear symptoms of depression or anxiety, parents and mental health professionals are usually quick to begin looking for events in the child's life that might explain the symptoms rather than rushing immediately to a medication that will stop the symptoms (although medications can, and in many cases should, be an important part of treating mood and anxiety disorders). The same thing ought to happen when a child displays symptoms of hyperactivity, inattentiveness, and/or impulsivity. If more attention were focused on the impact of adverse life experiences in contributing to ADHD, there would be less of an urge to make the symptoms go away with a pill and much more willingness to employ nondrug strategies to bolster the child's social and emotional life and to create positive life experiences that will benefit everyone in the family.

CHAPTER EIGHT

Reason #5 for America's ADHD Epidemic: We Let Our Kids Consume Too Much Junk Media

It was bound to happen. New research now reveals that humans have a shorter attention span than a goldfish. The average attention span for people has fallen in the past fifteen years from twelve seconds at the start of the millennium to eight seconds in 2015 (goldfish can hold it together for about nine seconds).[1] Now, try this little experiment. Go online to YouTube and watch an episode from the 1956 television comedy *The Honeymooners* called "A Dog's Life."[2] As you watch, count the number of scene changes, camera changes, physical movements, sound shifts, situation shifts, and emotional shifts (*Spoiler alert:* The action takes place in one room for the first eleven minutes). Then boot up the movie trailer for the 2016 feature film *Nerve*, about a high school senior who enters an online reality video game of truth or dare (minus the truth).[3] Repeat your counting procedure as before. Can't do it? Too fast? Several years ago media experts began to speak of "jolts per minute" as a way to measure changes that occur on the screen from one moment to the next. The Center for Media Literacy in Malibu, California, defined a *jolt* as "the moment of excitement generated by a laugh, a violent act, a car chase, a quick film cut—any fast-paced episode that lures the viewer into the program."[4] With today's turbo-paced media, it makes more sense to talk about jolts per second. Still with me?

I have another question: Could any of this have to do with a disorder for which the first two words of its name consist of *attention deficit*? Well, not according to the ADHD community. In fact, the International Consensus

Statement on ADHD that was signed by over eighty ADHD experts specifically denied any role that media might play in the origin of the disorder when they lambasted critics of ADHD who claimed "that any behavior problems associated with ADHD are merely the result of problems in the home, *excessive viewing of TV or playing of video games*, diet, lack of love and attention, or teacher/school intolerance."[5] We've already seen in this book how research supports a link between ADHD and school accountability rules as well as a link between ADHD and adverse conditions in the home. In this chapter, we'll take up the question of whether the rise of media in our culture (such as television, video games, the Internet, texting, and mobile apps) has anything to do with the rapid expansion of ADHD diagnoses in the past several years. The short-attention-span answer is that it does. Starting with studies in the early 1970s that examined the first introduction of television into rural communities in Canada (studies that concluded TV had a negative impact on children's behavior and cognitive abilities), there have been a growing number of investigations into the links between media and learning, executive functioning, behavior, and ADHD.[6]

How Our Brains Get Hooked on Media

First, however, I think it would be helpful to stop for a moment and take a look at what media actually does to our nervous systems. In 1927, the Russian physiologist Ivan Pavlov (famous for the salivating dogs experiments) wrote about "the orienting response." This is defined as an organism's immediate reaction to any change in the environment short of the "startle reflex."[7] When an organism encounters a new stimulus such as a sudden noise or a bright flash of light, it will pay attention to that stimulus before it can even identify the source. From an evolutionary point of view "the orienting response" was vital in alerting humans to any potential threat from their surroundings (a predatory animal, a hostile tribe, inclement weather), so that they could mobilize their resources to engage either in fighting the threat or getting the hell out. Starting in the 1950s (although there were glimmerings of this as early as the turn of the last century) scientists began to conceptualize another nervous system response they termed "habituation," which is the tendency of an organism after repeated exposures to the same stimulus to become less and less responsive to it.[8] It's a little bit like the story of "The Boy Who Cried Wolf," in which the shepherd's false cries of danger, at first met with quick and decisive action by the villagers, were later, after repeated false cries by the boy, ignored by the villagers (much to the detriment of the boy and his flock).

These primitive biological responses are exactly what the creators of television shows and commercials have exploited over the past five decades. They've used changes in camera angles, shifts in scenes, accents of color, modulations of sound, and scenarios involving strong emotions *to grab people's attention* so that they would buy the products advertised on their shows (this being, of course, the bottom line for all the media's manipulations). Over time, as viewers became habituated to the usual smoke and mirrors, the media producers had to up the ante and deliver louder noises, quicker bursts, more flashy sights, and more emotionally compelling content. When consumers became habituated to these new changes, the producers would jack up the stimulation even more, and on and on it went until we finally arrive at the adrenaline-pumping standards of today's media world. This is why 1950s sitcoms strike us as so slow and static compared to the high thrills and chills of today's movie trailers and MTV music videos.

But there's another series of events going on in our nervous systems that has a huge impact on our responses, and not just to television and video games but to social media, the Internet, smartphone apps, and texting. Whenever media stimulates us, it essentially delivers rewards to our nervous system. The reward centers in our brain become activated by a wide range of technological triggers: Facebook likes, Internet hits, ring tones signaling an incoming text message, blog traffic stats, retweets, and other digital pleasures. These stimuli target *the dopaminergic pathways of the brain*, especially in an area called the *ventral striatum*, and an area within it named the *nucleus accumbens*, which is sort of like a relay station for processing rewarding stimuli in the brain. These are the pleasureful hits that we get from our social media contacts; our video game points and badges; our insatiable hunger for news, gossip, and information on the Internet; and our driving need for other forms of media entertainment. Behavioral psychologist Susan Weinschenk puts it very well when she writes: "With the Internet, Twitter, and texting you now have almost instant gratification of your desire to seek. Want to talk to someone right away? Send a text and they respond in a few seconds. Want to look up some information? Just type your request into google. Want to see what your colleagues are up to? Go to LinkedIn. It's easy to get in a dopamine induced loop. Dopamine starts you seeking, then you get rewarded for the seeking which makes you seek more. It becomes harder and harder to stop looking at e-mail, stop texting, or stop checking your cell phone to see if you have a message or a new text."[9] Scientists have detected striatal dopamine release during the playing of video games, and have evidence of a reduction in the number of dopamine receptors and transporters (the vehicles of dopamine transmission in the synapses of brain cells) in people with Internet addiction.[10] These and other studies suggest that intense use of media may deplete the dopamine available for optimal brain functioning.

The New Disorder in Town: AMDD (Attention to Media Deficit Disorder)

It's just a hop, skip, and a jump from these findings to America's ADHD epidemic. Reports on the causes of ADHD frequently make reference to dysregulation of dopamine pathways and abnormalities in the brain's striatum. There are echoes of the studies just cited in reports that have linked striatal dopamine transporter and receptor abnormalities and reduced striatal dopamine activity to ADHD.[11] To complete the picture, a number of studies now link ADHD directly to media use. A group of 1,323 middle childhood participants were assessed over a thirteen-month period, and both television viewing and playing videos were associated with subsequent attention problems.[12] Another study linked Internet addiction to ADHD along with other psychiatric conditions like depression and social phobia.[13] Finally, a meta-analysis of forty-five empirical studies looking at media use and ADHD-related behaviors of children and adolescents revealed a small but significant relationship between ADHD and media use.[14] Dimitri A. Christakis, the director of the Center for Child Health, Behavior and Development at the Seattle Children's Hospital, wrote: "For many years, my laboratory has been exploring what we call the overstimulation hypothesis: the notion that overstimulating the developing brain in the first years of life will condition it to expect high levels of input and will lead to shorter attention spans later. We have found that exposure to rapidly paced television programs in the first three years of life increases the risk of attentional deficits at school age. We also found that cognitive stimulation during that same period in terms of reading, singing, and playing with children decreases the risk of attentional deficits. Simply put, there are things that we can do for children that maximize their genetic potential. Unfortunately, we are not doing them."[15]

Saving Children from Today's Media Menace

The most recent statistics available on media use among all children and adolescents in the United States (a 2010 report based on 2002 data) reveals that *the average child between the ages of eight and eighteen spends about seven hours per day using media*. Nearly two thirds of the television portion of this media diet involved violent scenes, including violence in children's programming.[16] Christakis noted that young children are spending 30 percent of their waking hours in front of a screen (and this statistic was recorded before the advent of touchscreens and apps).[17] Even the American Academy of Pediatrics (AAP), recognizing that our lives now are immersed in a digital world, has relaxed its original standards (which were "no TV for kids under two," and no more than two hours of media for older children). They now suggest that parents "monitor" their children's "media diet."[18] Media writer Jordan Shapiro agrees that it is time to change the guidelines, saying: "Screens are now a ubiquitous part of our lives. It is a technology that has been completely integrated into the human experience. At this point, worrying about exposure to screens is like worrying about exposure to agriculture, indoor plumbing, the written word, or automobiles. For better or worse, the transition to screen based digital information technologies has already happened and now resistance is futile. The screen time rhetoric that accompanied the television—when this technology was still in its formative age—is no longer relevant."[19]

Whether you agree with this point of view or not (and I don't), the rise in the ubiquity of media in our culture seems to have gone in tandem with the rise in the numbers of children and adolescents diagnosed with ADHD. As we've seen, there are clear neurological mechanisms that appear to link them. Fortunately, researchers have provided parents with a few ideas about to how to handle this media dilemma. Studies suggest, for example, that *violent* media has the biggest negative impact on attention and behavior. Chronic exposure to violent media appears to adversely affect prefrontal areas of the brain controlling emotion and inhibition.[20] Also, studies reveal that *educational* media may not have the same negative effects on attention and behavior in young children that both *violent* and *entertainment* programming seem to have.[21] Finally, there are suggestions, as noted earlier, that when young children engage in family literacy activities (such as shared reading, library visits, and pleasure reading) or engage in singing, dancing, and free play, it reduces hyperactive behaviors and the amount of television watched. (I provide other suggestions for lessening the negative impact that media has on children in Strategy #38: Limit Entertainment Media.)[22] But we should stand back for a moment and take stock of what is happening to our children in this media wasteland. Fifty years ago, Canadian professor and media futurist Marshall McLuhan spoke of a generation of kids whose worldview would no longer be based on plodding, one-step-at-a-time thinking, but rather on instantaneous flashes of immediate sensory data.[23] This time has now arrived. What McLuhan may not have seen in his crystal ball, however, was the millions of children in his "electronic village" who would end up being labeled as having ADHD and medicated with powerful schedule II drugs, simply because they were responding in a biologically programmed way to a major cultural shift.

CHAPTER NINE

Reason #6 for America's ADHD Epidemic: We Focus Too Much on Our Kids' Disabilities and Not Enough on Their Abilities

Imagine for a moment that the world has been magically transformed into a culture of flowers. In this new society, some of us are petunias, some are begonias, and still others are tulips. Let's just say that in this world of flowers, the psychiatrists are the roses. Visualize with me a scene in which Psychiatrist Rose sees her first patient. It happens to be a calla lily. Psychiatrist Rose begins her diagnostic workup by taking a chlorophyll biopsy and sending it to the lab. Then she measures Calla Lily's vital characteristics, including his yellow spadix, his white spathe, and his green stem. Finally, she administers the RNRSF, which is the Rose Normality Rating Scale for Flowers, which asks questions like, "On a scale from 1 to 5, how do you feel about being rained on?" and "Have you ever caused vomiting, bloating, or diarrhea to an animal that's taken a bite out of you?" Three days later, Psychiatrist Rose gets the chlorophyll biopsy back from the lab and meets with Calla Lily in her garden bed waiting room. "Well, I've got some bad news and some good news," she informs the lily. "According to my diagnostic criteria, you have Petal Deficit Disorder, or PDD. We're not sure what causes it. We think it's a chemical imbalance of some type. It may be genetic and you might actually pass it on to your children. The good news is that our local herbicide representative has just dropped off some free samples of a new drug called Petalin, and if you take it regularly you can learn to live a successful and productive life on a bed of sandy loam somewhere." The shocked

Calla Lily took the Petalin samples quietly and went off to live a new life as a disordered flower.

The Myth of the Normal Brain

This story may seem strange or silly to you because *a calla lily is just what it is*, one variety among a huge diversity of flowers. It's not supposed to have petals. It has other features that make it unique. But in this little vignette the lily is seen as coming up short because it doesn't meet the criteria that Psychiatrist Rose has for a flower, which presumably include having lots of petals, being fragrant, and coming in a variety of attractive colors. There's a paradox here concerning diversity in our own people-populated society. On the one hand, we value biodiversity, which provides humanity with aesthetic pleasure, food, and healing substances, among many other benefits, and we celebrate cultural diversity, which gives our world new ideas, original patterns of behavior, and compelling traditions of many kinds. On the other hand, it seems that when it comes to differences among human brains, we turn to the book of the rose psychiatrist—*The Diagnostic and Statistical Manual* (DSM)—and look for defects, deficits, and dysfunctions instead of assets, possibilities, and gifts.

Now, you might argue that we actually do need to have certain standards in judging neurological capacity. I'll agree with you that standards are important in some areas. There is, for example, a block of metal in the basement of the Bureau of Weights and Measurements outside of Paris enclosed by three glass bell jars to protect it from anything that might mar its surface. This is the standard kilogram to which all other kilograms in the world must be compared. But, please note: There is no human brain in any vat in the Smithsonian or the National Institute of Mental Health, or anywhere else, that represents the "normal brain" to which all other brains must be compared. And if there is no standard or normal brain in existence, then how are we to say which brains in our world are normal and which are abnormal?[1]

The ADHD community likes to flaunt the thousands of studies that have been done to "prove" that ADHD exists. As noted earlier, I do agree that many of these studies show differences between the brains of children and adolescents that have been diagnosed with ADHD and those that are considered typically developing or so-called "normal" (and what does that even mean now?). But have they really found something called ADHD stamped somewhere on these children's brains? Of course not. As we noted in chapter 2, there are no biological markers for this disorder. Yes, scientists have discovered that the brain structures and processes of some kids labeled ADHD may be different from those of typically developing children (although, please remember what has been said up to this point in the book about how many of those brain differences have likely been caused by environmental factors). Still, we're talking about *differences* here, not disorders.

The ADHD World: Awash in a Sea of Negativity

The response from the community of ADHD believers has been clear: This is a real disorder. A "fact sheet" available on the Web site of ADHD guru Russell Barkley provides a laundry list of negatives related to ADHD. According to Barkley, children with ADHD manifest some of the following deficits:

- Impaired response inhibition
- Poor impulse control
- Poor capacity to delay gratification
- Excessive task-irrelevant activity
- Poor sustained attention
- Low persistence of effort to tasks
- Impaired working memory
- Delayed development of internal language and rule following
- Difficulties with regulation of emotions, motivation, and arousal
- Diminished problem-solving abilities
- Diminished ingenuity and flexibility in pursuing long-term goals

In terms of their future outcomes, according to Barkley's fact sheet, people with ADHD are more likely than the general population to

- Be undereducated in adulthood
- Experience difficulties in work adjustment
- Be underemployed
- Change jobs more frequently
- Have a greater turnover of friendships and dating relationships
- Be more prone to marital discord and divorce
- Be more apt to speed while driving and have more traffic citations, traffic accidents, and license suspensions[2]

Presumably this litany of negatives applies only to those individuals who have not taken their medications, have not attempted any evidence-based nondrug interventions, and have spent most of their time around people who see them largely in terms of their negatives.

Keep in mind that the term ADHD actually consists of three negatives: *deficit, hyperactive,* and *disorder.* As such, it takes its place in the history of special education amid a long line of disabling terms: *feebleminded, imbecile, idiot, retarded, hyperkinetic, minimally brain damaged.* A look at the pioneers of special education in the twentieth century reveals a checkered history of negative stereotypes and low expectations. This roll call includes eugenicist Henry H. Goddard, who coined the diagnostic term *moron* in 1910; neuropathologist Samuel Orton, who, in 1925, asked teachers to refer students to him "who were considered defective or who were retarded or failing in their school work"; neuropsychiatrist Alfred A. Strauss, who in the 1940s at Wayne County Training School in Michigan worked out the psychopathology of "minimal brain injury"; and psychologists Samuel Kirk and William Cruickshank, who "invented" the term *learning disability* in 1963 in a Chicago hotel room.[3] No one consulted the children themselves about the dehumanizing terms used to describe them, and the psychological consequences of such negative labels have been in many cases devastating. In one study, speaking of his ADHD, a child reports: "It's like a disease eating on you, you know, like you try to behave but it keeps on going on in your head to stop you behaving, and I always got in trouble for it."[4] Speaking of ADHD labeling, Italian clinical psychologists Antonio Iudici and Elena Faccio write: "Following diagnostic labeling, children will learn to use the attitude of 'disengagement' and irresponsibility that adults have implemented against them. For example, in the case of success or 'appropriate' behavior, diagnosed children will award the credit to their medications; if they fail, they will think that the disease is stronger than what they can do."[5] Labeled kids are routinely herded into remote classrooms or to trailers in back of the regular school building and taught in "special classes" using outdated materials, rote learning techniques, and externally controlling behavior modification programs.[6]

Diversity, Not Disability

As a special education teacher in the 1970s in Montreal, Canada, and in northern California in the United States, I taught kids with labels like "educationally handicapped," "learning disabled," and "behaviorally disordered," who I soon discovered possessed many positive attributes. My kids were artists, storytellers, athletes, dramatists, and musicians, and displayed many other talents. Yet in my classroom *they were defined by what they could not do instead of what they could do.* I finally came to the realization that if a child was having difficulty with learning, behavior, or motivation, what she needed more than anything else was to be surrounded by adults who saw *the best* in her, not *the worst.*

So in the 1980s I entered graduate school and completed my doctoral dissertation on the *strengths* of children who had been labeled as "learning disabled."[7] Over the past several years, I've extended my interest in a strength-based approach to learning to include children and adolescents diagnosed with ADHD. In fact, I've discovered a new movement that I believe provides a more positive context in which to think about kids diagnosed with ADHD than the disease-ridden, disorder-plagued medical model used by virtually every researcher, clinician, and professor in the ADHD community. This new approach is called *neurodiversity.* It originally emerged from the autism rights community as members of that group declared that they *were not disordered but different.*[8] The first use of the word came in a 1998 article in *The Atlantic,* when New York journalist Harvey Blume wrote: "Neurodiversity may be every bit as crucial for the human race as biodiversity is for life in general. Who can say what form of wiring will prove best at any given moment?"[9] One of my advocacy priorities has been to apply neurodiversity to other "disorders," including ADHD.[10] What makes neurodiversity a better model than the deficit-oriented medical model is that it acknowledges *both the challenges and strengths* possessed by these kids.

The ADHD Advantage

There's been a steady growth in the literature over the past two decades suggesting that children, adolescents, and adults with the ADHD diagnosis manifest a number of positive attributes, skills, strengths, and traits. A professor of creative studies at the University of Georgia, Bonnie Cramond, compared the traits of creative people with the warning signs of ADHD and found that, except for the terms used (positive for creative people, negative for people diagnosed as ADHD), they were practically identical.[11] The spontaneous artist, for example, became the impulsive dilettante, the divergent writer was reduced to the distractible plodder, and the musician brimming with vitality was regarded as the hyperactive scatterbrain. In one study, individuals with ADHD outperformed a control group of non-ADHD subjects on the Unusual Uses Task, which is a measure of divergent thinking (an important component of creative behavior).[12] A more recent study found that adults identified as having ADHD showed higher levels of original creative thinking on the Abbreviated Torrance Test for Adults and higher levels of real-world creative achievement compared to typically developing adults.[13] In a study of adolescents, a group identified as having ADHD displayed an enhanced ability to overcome the constraining influence of examples (for example, they were able to come up with their own wild ideas even when given examples that might have swayed them to think more conventionally with respect to the models provided).[14] A study of twelve- to thirteen-year-old children concluded that kids diagnosed with ADHD scored higher on tests of verbal creative thinking and nonverbal originality.[15] Perhaps most telling is a study of creativity in ADHD-diagnosed children showing that they had lower scores on the Torrance Test of Creative Thinking—Figural (nonverbal) when they were under pharmacological treatment (taking methylphenidate) but higher scores when they were not taking the drugs.[16]

Other studies have shown links between ADHD and entrepreneurship. There are many examples of successful businesspeople who have been diagnosed with the disorder, including billionaire business mogul Richard Branson, brokerage pioneer Charles Schwab, IKEA founder Ingvar Kamprad, JetBlue founder David Neeleman, and world-renowned economist Diane Swonk.[17] A recent study of French small firm owners suggests a link between ADHD symptoms and an entrepreneurial orientation.[18] Kinko's founder Paul Orfalea, who has been diagnosed with ADHD, says: "Because I have a tendency to wander, I never spent much time in my office. My job was going store to store, noticing what people were doing right. If I had stayed in my office all the time, I would not have discovered all those wonderful ideas to help expand the business."[19] Martha Denckla, a research scientist at the Kennedy Krieger Institute, notes that while ADHD-identified kids may not particularly excel in academic learning, they tend to be *good incidental learners*.[20] That's exactly what I found in my teaching. These kids are good at paying attention to things they're not supposed to be paying attention to, and often, it is precisely this manner of perceiving that leads to discovering new things. As thirteen-year-old Matthew Kutz, a student identified as having ADHD, puts it: "Being ADD means you see things other people miss. When you see a peach you see a piece of fruit. I see the color, the texture, and the field where it grew. . . . Being ADD, when I read a book about marine life my mind allows me to travel with the fish and imagine life beneath the sea. Or I can read a book about astronomy and dance among the stars."[21] Some educators now regard "off-task" behaviors in school as contributing to learning and understanding the world around us.[22] In addition, research has documented how irrelevant but novel stimuli actually improved the performance of children diagnosed with ADHD.[23]

Why ADHD Is Still in the Gene Pool

In fact, the symptoms of ADHD, while dysfunctional in certain social contexts like the traditional teacher-directed classroom, may have been advantageous not just to wandering businessmen and starstruck youngsters, but also to prehistoric humans. This might help explain why genes for so-called inattention, hyperactivity, and impulsivity might have been adaptively selected for in the evolution of humanity.[24] In a hunter-gatherer society, the advantage would belong to the individual who could

- Be constantly on the move in looking for food, shelter, and other essentials (hyperactivity)
- Continually monitor all the stimuli in their environment for clues as to what might be harmful or helpful for survival (distractibility)
- Respond quickly to a sound or sight in his surroundings that might signal the attack of a predator (impulsivity)

In other words, the three classic warning signs of ADHD, regarded as disabling by the ADHD community, might have been precisely what humanity needed to survive, multiply, and evolve over the course of tens of thousands of years. There is some support for this hypothesis in studies that track the distribution of genes in different populations. In one study, the presence of a gene sometimes associated with ADHD (the seven-repeat allele of the dopamine DRD4 gene) was discovered to be higher among hunter-gatherer populations in Brazil compared to those who were agriculturists.[25] While this theory is still up for debate, it raises the broader issue that the symptoms of

ADHD, while viewed as a disability within the narrow scope of classwork, homework, chores, and schedules, is an advantage when looked at against the broader background of humanity's history. We've also seen in this chapter how it serves as a positive quality in today's complex world where ADHD-related traits have helped people achieve success in the arts, business, economics, and other fields. Isn't it time that we stopped using the gloomy term ADHD, with its three negatives, and started writing, researching, and thinking about these children, adolescents, and adults in terms of their strengths and abilities?[26]

Reason #7 for America's ADHD Epidemic: Too Many People Have a Vested Economic Interest in Seeing It Continue

Millions of people regard ADHD as an established scientific fact. However, if you pierce through the crust of outward respectability you'll discover that there's a complex network of significant economic interests that keep the so-called objective reality of this disorder afloat. Beneath the research studies, the clinical data, the testimonials of respected authorities, and the support of governmental agencies, universities, and other esteemed institutions, there are complex financial forces at work that feed the ADHD blob, propel its introduction into new markets (such as adult ADHD, ADHD in young children, and new markets abroad), and promise to maintain and even expand its presence into the foreseeable future. In this chapter, we take a look at some of these underlying relationships and see what we can conclude about their influence in the labeling and medicating of millions of children in the United States and worldwide.

Drugging Kids Down on the Pharma

The single most significant economic factor driving the growth of ADHD worldwide is the active role of giant pharmaceutical companies in aggressively marketing drugs used to treat ADHD, including brands such as Vyvanse, Concerta, Adderall, and Strattera. According to the business intelligence firm GBI Research, the market for ADHD drugs in 2013 amounted to almost $12 billion, with a total of sixty-eight new "therapies" (the industry's Orwellian term for drugs) for ADHD currently in the process of development for potential future approval by the Food and Drug Administration (FDA).[1] The cost of these drugs is not cheap. Prices for one hundred pills at a middle dose range start at $140 for Ritalin and go up to as high as $635 for Strattera. Troublingly, there are drugs that seem to be marketed to appeal especially to the needs and tastes of young children.[2] Methylin from the company Alliant, for example, comes in a grape-flavored syrup, along with a marketing message: "Give 'em the Grape!"[3] Adzenys is a chewable candy-flavored amphetamine for children just approved by the FDA from Neos Therapeutics.[4]

The single biggest factor that has made ADHD drug marketing so potent a force in our culture relates to a key decision by the FDA in 1997 (finalized in 1999) to allow pharmaceutical companies to advertise their products directly to consumers through television, magazines, the Internet, and other media channels.[5] This direct-to-consumer marketing has had the unintended consequence of profoundly reshaping the doctor–patient relationship. According to Joe Dumit, professor of anthropology at the University of California, Davis, "these ads often portray active consumers-become-patients, who paid attention to the TV or Web site and recognized a risk that their doctors missed or misdiagnosed. Consumers can self-diagnose online or even by listening to symptoms as defined in the ad, and increasingly they are arriving at their doctors' offices with demands rather than questions. Doctors, in turn, because of the multiple pressures of limited patient time, keeping up with rapidly changing information, and the constraints of health maintenance organizations and insurance, are quite vulnerable to these demands."[6] Evidence suggests that direct-to-consumer advertising increases sales of drugs, and although in some cases this helps avoid their underuse, in many other instances it leads to overuse.[7]

ADHD Drug Marketing: The Not-So-Hidden Persuaders

Ads promoting ADHD drugs have been designed by marketers to tug at the very heartstrings of parents. A 2009 ad for Concerta from the drug company Janssen, for example, shows a curly headed boy doing his schoolwork and underneath, the text reads: "If your child struggles with attention deficit hyperactivity disorder (ADHD), Concerta can help them get on the path to success." Another ad from Shire, the makers of Adderall, shows a child's crayon drawing of "My Family," where the mother and father both have frowns and the child is depicted only with the top half complete and the bottom half a mass of squiggles. The caption reads: "The disruption of ADHD affects more than their grades."[8] Another advertisement for Adderall shows a mother hugging her young son with the text promising: "Finally! Schoolwork that matches his intelligence. Family hours that last for hours. Friends that ask him to join the group. A trusted solution for ADHD."[9] Shire has subsidized a comic book for children diagnosed with ADHD called "Medikidz Explain Living with ADHD" that goes out to doctors' offices, presumably to be distributed to newly diagnosed pint-size patients.[10]

Proponents of direct-to-consumer marketing of ADHD drugs say that this media approach provides valuable information to parents about ADHD and ensures that more people who need it will receive treatment. Implicit in this reasoning, however, is the assumption that the information provided will be accurate. But as Jonathan Leo, professor of neuroanatomy at Lincoln Memorial University, and Jeffrey Lacasse, professor of social work at Florida State University, point out: "If the advertisements are inaccurate, then the doctor-patient relationship is greatly complicated, as an explanation by a physician that differs from the information disseminated by the advertisements would be met with resistance and confusion by the patient."[11] And many times, those claims do turn out to be fraudulent. Shire Pharmaceuticals, for example, was fined $56.5 million in 2014 for claiming in advertisements that its product Adderall XR was clinically superior to other drugs because it would prevent poor academic performance and "normalize" its recipients to the extent that they would be indistinguishable from their non-ADHD peers.[12] *New York Times* reporter Alan Schwarz, author of *ADHD Nation: Children, Doctors, Big Pharma, and the Making of an American Epidemic,* in a piece for the newspaper titled "The Selling of Attention Deficit Disorder," notes: "The Food and Drug Administration has cited every major ADHD drug—stimulants like Adderall, Concerta, Focalin and Vyvanse, and nonstimulants like Intuniv and Strattera—for false and misleading advertising since 2000, some multiple times."[13] Drug companies have strong ties with many Web sites that purport to deliver objective information about ADHD to parents and those who suspect they have adult ADHD. According to one study, thirty-seven of the top fifty-seven Web sites on ADHD (as ranked by Google and Yahoo!) were run by pharmaceutical corporations, and the quality of the information on these sites was judged to be poor with a strong bias toward biogenetic explanations of ADHD.[14]

The Big Payoff in Promoting ADHD Drugs

Another strand in this tangled web of economic influence is the financial support that drug companies give, sometimes without public knowledge, to individuals and groups that are key players in the research, diagnosis, and treatment of ADHD. The parent advocacy group Children and Adults with Attention-Deficit/Hyperactivity Disorder (CHADD), for example, which was instrumental in helping get ADD (as it was then called) designated as a handicapping condition under federal disability laws in the 1990s, was secretly taking money from pharmaceutical companies for years before disclosing its financial connections after a 1995 PBS broadcast revealed its underhanded dealings with drug companies.[15] It now regularly reports the amount it receives each year from Big Pharma. In the 2008–2009 fiscal year, for example, it took in $1,174,626 from Eli Lilly, Johnson & Johnson's McNeil division, Novartis, Shire US, and UCB, spending $330,000 on its annual conference, $114,950 on its twentieth-anniversary gala, and $187,747 on a salary for its chief executive officer.[16] Between 2006 and 2009, Shire alone paid CHADD $3 million to have CHADD's bimonthly magazine, *Attention*, distributed to doctors' offices nationwide.[17]

The doctors who do the diagnosing and prescribing of ADHD and its many drugs are another key link in the marketing chain employed by big pharmaceutical firms. Drug companies typically hold "professional development" seminars for doctors where the benefits of the firm's new products are touted. *New York Times* reporter Schwarz described one such meeting sponsored by Shire to promote Adderall XR, in which a psychiatrist from Denver paid by the company to speak proceeded to give inaccurate information about ADHD and Adderall XR to the seventy-five doctors attending. According to Schwarz's report, the doctor told his colleagues to educate their patients on the lifelong nature of the disorder, despite evidence that many, if not most, individuals cease to meet the criteria for ADHD after adolescence (as noted in chapter 4). He also claimed that stimulants were not drugs of abuse (despite the fact that they are restricted by the federal government because of their abuse potential), and that side effects of Adderall XR were "generally mild" despite clinical evidence of insomnia, significant appetite suppression, and mood swings.[18]

Big Pharma also influences doctors' decisions about ADHD drugs through the frequent contacts that physicians have with company sales representatives. One salesman interviewed in Schwarz's report, Brian Lutz, a Shire representative who sold Adderall XR between 2004 and 2009, said he met individually every two weeks with around seventy psychiatrists in his Oakland, California, territory, adding up to *about thirty to forty sessions with each psychiatrist each year.* Lutz told Schwarz that if he was asked by a doctor about side effects or about potentials for abuse he downplayed them, referring the physicians to the small print on the drug's box. While feeling that he never lied about the product to the doctors, he regretted his role in promoting the drugs, saying: "We sold these pills like they were cars, when we knew they weren't just cars."[19]

Even more troubling is evidence showing that the very scientists who have engaged in legitimating ADHD and its various drug treatments through their so-called objective research have themselves been subsidized by drug companies. In 2008, a Senate investigation revealed that Joseph Biederman, Timothy E. Wilens, and Thomas J. Spencer, three of the most prolific and highly respected researchers in the ADHD community, had been substantially subsidized by drug companies and failed to report much of their income.[20] Big Pharma paid $1.6 million to Biederman alone in speaking and consulting fees. Their research was then used by the pharmaceutical companies in their marketing and promotional efforts. As Schwarz observed specifically in regard to Biederman's research: "Those findings typically delivered three messages: The disorder was underdiagnosed; stimulants were effective and safe; and unmedicated ADHD led to significant risks for academic failure, drug dependence, car accidents and brushes with the law."[21] The three researchers were eventually punished by their institutions, Harvard Medical School and Massachusetts General Hospital, for violations of conflict of interest policies through their nondisclosures.[22] Maintaining transparency regarding his own involvement with drug companies, Russell Barkley, arguably the single most respected and trusted researcher in the ADHD world and author of the bestselling book *Taking Charge of ADHD*, disclosed during a 2009 PowerPoint presentation his own financial relationships with Eli Lilly, Shire, Medice, McNeil, Janssen-Ortho, Janssen-Cilag, and Novartis.[23] Finally, and perhaps most shocking of all, the very organization that has established the criteria for ADHD in its *Diagnostic and Statistical Manual* (DSM), the American Psychiatric Association, itself receives significant funding from drug companies.[24]

Making a Living off ADHD

While drug companies represent the primary force promoting the current epidemic of ADHD diagnoses, it is by no means the sole economic engine driving the pandemic forward. The ADHD bandwagon represents a cash cow for many interests in the economy, including individuals marketing some of the following:

- ADHD products
- ADHD camps
- ADHD-oriented schools
- ADHD coaching services
- ADHD tutors
- ADHD-friendly counseling agencies
- Law firms helping parents of ADHD-diagnosed kids negotiate the special education maze
- Clinics, hospitals, and community mental health agencies with ADHD centers
- Nonprofit organizations representing ADHD interests
- Psychological and medical subspecialty practices in ADHD
- Medical journals, which benefit from advertising of ADHD drugs

Another huge financial beneficiary of ADHD is public education. In 1975, Congress passed the Education for All Handicapped Children Act, which mandated that children with special needs had the right to receive an appropriate education in "the least restrictive environment."[25] Children diagnosed with ADHD symptoms were not originally eligible for services in this bill. But in 1990, the advocacy group CHADD heavily lobbied Congress to make ADHD a handicapping term in its reauthorization of the bill, retitled Individuals with Disabilities Education Act (IDEA). However, in the face of strong opposition from many education and civil rights groups that believed that another stigmatizing label would only harm children, *Congress refused to certify ADD as a disability eligible for federal funds and school services.*[26] What many people don't realize is that ADD/ADHD essentially slipped in through the back door the very next year via a letter from the U.S. Department of Education that was quietly circulated to state school superintendents specifying three ways in which children with attention deficit disorder could qualify for special education services in public schools under existing laws.[27] Finally, in the face of continued pressure from CHADD and other ADHD lobbying groups, Congress put the words for ADD and ADHD into the law when IDEA was itself reauthorized in 1997. As journalist Melina Sherman points out:

> The iteration of IDEA that was passed in 1997 legislated ADHD into existence by recognizing it as a learning disorder eligible for a host of free federal special education services. ADHD children would now be able to receive counseling, physical therapy, diagnostic and prescription services, rehabilitation, and more. Most prominently featured among these services was the development of Individualized Education Programs, which gave ADHD children the right to attend special classes tailored to their unique needs as well as separate schooling, a reduced number of homework assignments, and extra time on tests.[28]

This opened the floodgates to children diagnosed with ADHD being served in schools across the nation and in effect gave employment to many of the half million special education teachers in the United States, who currently earn a median yearly salary of $56,800.[29] And these teachers in turn needed training from colleges and universities plus instructional materials for their classrooms, so another beneficiary of the ADHD epidemic is the textbook industry that publishes ADHD materials, grabbing a chunk of the $14 billion in revenue from textbook sales every year. Other individuals and organizations that gain from the growth of ADHD include

- Manufacturers of structured curriculum and behavior-modification programs
- Authors of behavior rating scales (the Conners rating scales, for example, have sold untold millions of copies over the years)
- Computer apps for ADHD
- ADHD posters, smiley stickers, and behavior charts (to reward good performance)
- A host of ADHD gizmos, including timers to keep kids on schedule

A new generation of so-called brain training computer games and programs, including Lumosity, Cogmed, and ACTIVATE, are also entering the market hoping to deliver the same sort of benefits to kids diagnosed with ADHD as those produced by medications.[30] Also, new ways of assessing ADHD are being developed, including *The Quotient ADHD System*, purchased from BioBehavioral Diagnostics by education giant Pearson, which uses a series of performance tasks and psychological questions to diagnose ADHD. Like the pharmaceutical giants, they have come under scrutiny about their advertised claims from the FDA.[31]

Nurturing Potentials Versus Realizing Profits

The fact that people make money from ADHD is not the issue here. Many people who earn their living wholly or in part because of the presence of ADHD in our society are doing excellent work on behalf of children and adolescents (special education teachers, for example). However, when livelihoods are connected to ADHD, people who receive this support are more likely to resist suggestions that the disorder may be flawed. Yet, the real problem with financial interests related to ADHD comes when people sell, market, and promote products and services, not because they wish to help children and adolescents realize their full potential but because they wish to realize their own potential to make a profit. We haven't even mentioned the sector of society that stands to gain the most financially from the ADHD myth: the shareholders of stocks in giant pharmaceutical companies and global education corporations, who see their share prices rise with every ADHD drug prescription that a doctor writes out and every ADHD assessment or curriculum program that a psychologist or school administrator purchases. When profits are driving the rise in ADHD diagnoses and medication use, we must begin to seriously question the "scientific" explanations for these increases. In this case, the idea of ADHD, already suspect because of the issues discussed in earlier chapters of this book, stands accused of running rampant through our culture at least in part because of human greed.

How the ADHD Experts Defend Their Disorder (And Why Their Arguments Tend to Be Pretty Lame)

The ADHD powers-that-be do not take criticisms of their disorder lying down. In a series of statements, interviews, broadcasts, journal articles, books, and blog posts, clinicians, scientists, doctors, psychologists, and parent advocates who support the ADHD myth have generated a full-throated defense of their position and sought in various ways to discredit those who ask too many questions about the reality of ADHD. In this chapter, I examine their arguments and discuss why their responses have been, to quote the chapter subtitle, pretty lame. I'll do this by giving names to the various strategies they have used to counter the critics' reasoning and evidence, providing examples of how they have done this, and exploring the holes in their defense.

The Ad Hominem ("Attack the Man") Defense

I'll start with the very crudest of refutations, that being, if you haven't got a very good response to a set of arguments, then attack the person or persons making them rather than the ideas they put forth. In the International Consensus Statement on ADHD, signed by more than eighty ADHD professors, clinicians, and researchers, there is the statement: "The views of a handful of nonexpert doctors that ADHD does not exist are contrasted against mainstream scientific views that it does, as if both views had equal merit."[1] Here we see the critics derided as "nonexpert doctors." Presumably, an "expert doctor" would be one who accepts the reality of ADHD, so essentially nothing is advanced here beyond the idea that those doctors who do not believe in the reality of ADHD are different from those who do. Then, to turn the knife in a bit, the phrase "as if both views had equal merit" is added at the end. This is the sort of phrase a person might use toward an adversary as a putdown ("So you say that Republicans are better than Democrats, as if your views had equal merit to mine, harrumph . . ."). The consensus statement also brands critics of ADHD as "fringe doctors." I guess that would include such critics of the neurobiological basis of ADHD as L. Alan Sroufe, professor emeritus at the University of Minnesota School of Education and Human Development; Peter Conrad, the Harry Coplan Professor of Social Sciences at Brandeis University; and Eric Taylor, the former head of the Child and Adolescent Psychiatry Department at King's College, London.

The Big Switcheroo Defense

The switcheroo gambit seeks to defuse an argument, once again, not by engaging with the actual facts presented but through the distraction of simple contradiction. So, for example, against the evidence presented in chapter 7—that family difficulties can contribute to ADHD symptomology—ADHD advocates respond by claiming that it's the other way around: ADHD children create troubled families. Another instance of the Big Switcheroo defense occurred when an article appeared in the medical journal *Pediatrics* in 2004 suggesting that early television exposure leads to subsequent attention problems in children.[2] Soon after, a "research commentary" appeared in CHADD's magazine *Attention* stating that: "Early behavior problems may lead to more television viewing, rather than more television viewing causing later attention problems."[3] The Big Switcheroo strikes again.

The Straw Man Defense

A straw man argument is when someone seeks to discredit an opposing point of view by transforming that perspective into one or more simple statements that are clearly and obviously wrong (and in some cases not even part of the debate) and then proceeds to refute these patently weak arguments as if they were grappling with the more complex and nuanced criticisms in the original view. For example, on the Web site WebMD, in a feature called "ADHD Myths and Facts—Topic Overview," one "myth" is given as: "ADHD is caused by bad parenting. All the child needs is good discipline."[4] Now, to my knowledge, no critic of the ADHD consensus has actually made such an argument. In fact, this particular straw man seems very close to comments I've heard from griz-zled Depression Era disciplinarians about ADHD to the effect that: "All the kid really needs is a good slap on the side of his head." Refuting the simplistic statement that "ADHD is caused by bad parenting" avoids a more complex argument (given in chapter 7) that adverse factors such as physical abuse or trauma in a child's home environment can impair neurological development and be linked to ADHD symptoms.

The Authority Defense

The time-tested authority defense says "Authorities hold my position. So there!" Such an argument was consistently used in the Middle Ages as a way of arguing about scientific and philosophical questions ("Aristotle said it, so it must be true"). A good example of this flawed defense within the ADHD community is given in the Consensus Statement on ADHD: "All of the major medical associations, and government health agencies recognize ADHD as a genuine disorder because the scientific evidence indicating it is so overwhelm-ing." However, just because a medical association says it's so does not make it true. The American Psychiatric Association classified homosexuality as a mental disorder until 1973, and a task force of the American Psychological Association met with CIA officials during President George W. Bush's admin-istration to advise them on effective ways to bolster the legal and ethical justi-fication for torturing individuals suspected of being terrorists.[5] Since when does being an authority equate to representing truth?

The Scare Defense

The particular mode of argument known as the scare defense has been em-ployed with varying degrees of success by politicians for millennia. It basi-cally says: "If you follow the arguments of my critics, then bad things will happen to you or your loved ones." It is a particularly reprehensible means of arguing because it seeks to exploit the deeper fears, anxieties, and worries that all humans experience to one degree or another, and it does this primarily as a means of achieving the arguer's own particular agenda. In this case, ADHD authorities argue that the criticisms being advanced against ADHD may do positive harm to children and adolescents by influencing parents not to get their children properly diagnosed and medicated. This is tantamount to withholding life-saving medicine from a sick person or keeping food from a starving child. In a statement given in reaction to Richard Saul's book, *ADHD Does Not Exist*, Ruth Hughes, chief executive of CHADD, said: "This book adds to the stigma of ADHD and hinders the diagnosis and treatment of thousands of people who legitimately do have ADHD, and whose lives would be significantly improved with treatment."[6] Another statement of this argument is given by Zeigler Dendy, a former special educator, school psychologist, and author on books about teaching children with a diagnosis of ADHD: "I just hope people don't say these kids don't need treatment or that they don't need medicine, because then our kids will develop gaps in learning."[7] And Ned Hallowell, co-author of the best-selling ADHD book *Driven to Distraction*, writes about his concerns with media critical of ADHD: "I do wince at the articles, though, because I fear people will be scared away from getting the help that they might need."[8] Not articulated in these views is the idea that people might actually *benefit* from hearing a variety of viewpoints about ADHD and thus be in a better position to make an informed decision about their own health care needs or the needs of their children.

The Restatement-of-the-Obvious Defense

The restate the obvious way of reasoning argues that we know ADHD exists because we can see the symptoms of ADHD with our own eyes. ADHD expert Ned Hallowell uses this type of defense when he writes:

> *ADHD is a shorthand term for a collection of symptoms that most assuredly do exist. One may quarrel with the shorthand term, as I certainly do, but no one with eyes to see and ears to hear would contend that there are no children or adults who meet the diagnostic criteria for ADHD as laid out in the DSM-5. In fact, there are millions of children and adults who meet the definition of ADHD. To say, then, that it does not exist is like saying that the nose on your face does not exist. You may not want to call it a nose, but whatever you call it, it's there.*

The problem with this defense is that it doesn't tell us anything that we don't already know. The DSM-5 criteria include descriptions of symptoms that very clearly exist. That doesn't prove that a neurobiological clinical entity called ADHD is causing those symptoms. I was explicit in pointing this out in chapter 1 by saying I'm well aware of the presence of inattentive, hyperactive, and impulsive children in our society. As Hallowell points out, this fact is as obvious as the nose on your face. To my knowledge, there are no critics of ADHD who deny that these symptoms exist. The important questions are: Why do these symptoms exist? What explanation can we give for them? What do we do about them? What is up for debate, in other words, are the many assumptions made by ADHD experts that involve placing millions of children under one label (ADHD), arguing that the symptoms are due to biogenetic factors, and asserting that these symptoms can best be treated with psychoactive medications.

The Weak Analogy Defense

Another response to ADHD criticisms involves using analogies to defend the existence of ADHD. The best, and in my opinion the most humorous, example of this defense occurs in the International Consensus Statement on ADHD at its conclusion when it states (after its use of a straw man argument): "To publish stories that ADHD is a fictitious disorder or merely a conflict between today's Huckleberry Finns and their caregivers is tantamount to declaring the earth flat, the laws of gravity debatable, and the periodic table in chemistry a fraud." The implication here is that the concept of ADHD is as solid as the law of gravity. It's not clear on what basis this judgment was reached. But what is clear is that to my knowledge there is no debate about the law of gravity outside of a select group of physicists who are still trying to reconcile the gravitational force with the other three key forces in nature (electromagnetic, strong nuclear, and weak nuclear), while there *is* quite a heated debate about ADHD. Where there's smoke, there's fire. And to say that ADHD is as undebatable as the law of gravity is to turn a blind eye to a multitude of arguments (many of them presented in this book) for why ADHD may not be as valid a construct as its experts claim.

The issues I've raised in this book about the spurious nature of the ADHD story are not cut-and-dried answers that authoritatively disprove the existence of this disorder. Instead, I've tried to raise questions about the assumptions that underlie the widespread presence of the ADHD diagnosis in our culture. The best approach to countering my views or the views of other critics of ADHD should not be the weak defenses described in this chapter but rather measured discourse with respect to the ideas themselves. This is where the battle concerning ADHD should be fought, not in broad generalities, sweeping conclusions, and fallacious reasoning. Many of the claims made in this book come not just from medical research but also from sociological analysis, anthropological surveys, psychodynamic critiques, economic analyses, and other legitimate sources of inquiry. A truly fruitful debate on the question of ADHD's existence will ultimately be built on the foundations of multiple perspectives and a diversity of viewpoints about how children grow, learn, and attend to the world around them.[9]

The Value of Multiple Perspectives in Improving a Child's Behavior and Attention Span

The humanistic psychologist Abraham Maslow once wrote: "I suppose it is tempting, if the only tool you have is a hammer, to treat everything as if it were a nail."[1] This, unfortunately, seems to be the situation with ADHD and its most vehement supporters. By linking ADHD to causes that are said to be neurobiological in origin, ADHD practitioners have drastically limited the number of tools they can make use of to help the millions of children who are experiencing difficulties with behavior and attention. By turning restless children into medical patients, it has *de facto* made *medicine* the most important weapon available to defeat hyperactivity, impulsivity, and inattention—medicines that include powerful psychoactive drugs like Ritalin, Adderall, Concerta, and Strattera. To be fair, the ADHD community also allows into its selective circle of treatments one primary nondrug approach to the problem. Reaching back to 1950s behaviorism, when B. F. Skinner and his reinforcement model of learning held sway in American psychology, many ADHD experts (though not all) strongly advocate behavior therapy as an effective treatment, which often translates into giving restless children smiley face stickers, points exchangeable for toys and privileges, and other external reinforcements to shape their behavior. Outside of indoctrinating parents, teachers, and children in the fundamentals of the ADHD myth, plus a little cognitive therapy thrown in for good measure, that's pretty much all that's available for worried parents to use with their restless, inattentive, and/or impulsive children. Not a very big tool kit.

If the ADHD powers-that-be had incorporated as part of its core set of beliefs findings from sociology, psychodynamic psychology, psychoanalysis, family systems theory, anthropology, human ecology, developmental psychology, and other fields of inquiry, it would have dramatically expanded the range of tools available to help these children thrive. In such an interdisciplinary setting, ADHD-identified children would no longer have to be viewed solely in terms of their deficient behavior and medication-starved brains. Of course the ADHD community will be quick to say that it certainly *does* pay close attention to the child's social life, his developmental needs, his emotional state of being, his family situation, his cultural diversity, and other factors that make up an overall approach to the child's problems. However, each of these components remains secondary to the essential biological core of the disorder.

Developmental psychology, for example, is important to ADHD researchers and clinicians primarily insofar as it advances a better understanding of how this neurobiologically based disorder varies in the presentation of symptoms and requires different forms of assessment and treatment from infancy to adulthood. The emotional, social, educational, and familial dimensions are important only insofar as they represent aspects of the child's life that are impaired by this biogenetic disorder. The cultural dimension is important insofar as parents from different cultures may be more or less inclined to accept or reject the diagnosis and drug treatment that doctors recommended. Figure 1 presents a graphic representation of how ADHD experts have essentially made

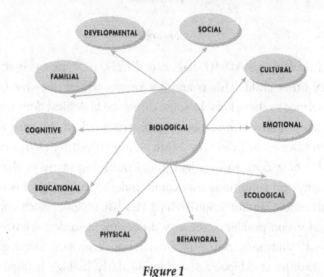

Figure 1

neurobiology the hub around which the other domains (to which I've added behavioral, cognitive, creative, ecological, and physical domains) revolve.

All that's required to change this limited neurobiological point of view and vastly expand the number of tools available to help ADHD-diagnosed kids is to replace this biocentric model with a child-centered model that incorporates biology as simply *one* of the domains important to a child's well-being (Figure 2). When we give equal potential weight to each of these domains of the child's life, we open up opportunities for a wide range of nondrug strategies that can be used to help children diagnosed with ADHD, including the 101 strategies described in this book.

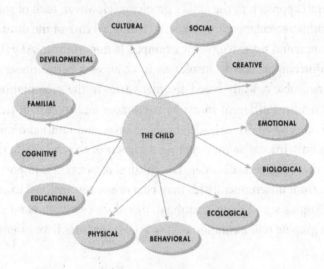

Figure 2

Each child with an ADHD diagnosis differs, in some cases significantly, from every other child. This is another reason why a one-size-fits-all label does a disservice to these kids. In some cases, the biological *does* represent the most important issue with respect to a particular child. Richard Saul, in his book *ADHD Does Not Exist: The Truth About Attention Deficit and Hyperactivity Disorder*, does an excellent job of outlining many of the biogenetic and other physical conditions that could underlie the symptoms of hyperactivity, inattention, and/or impulsivity.[2] His list includes such conditions as hearing and vision problems, sensory processing disorder, seizure disorders, fetal alcohol syndrome, schizophrenia, mood disorders, Asperger's/autism spectrum disorder, and bipolar disorder. Similarly, biology is important when a child is allergic to specific foods or has been provided with insufficient nutrition. For other children, the most important factor may be developmental, as, for example, in the case of a child whose brain matures two to three years later than a typically developing child. Still other children may be helped most by focusing on the educational domain, particularly if they are especially sensitive to active learning and need a dynamic curriculum to keep their attention. The familial and emotional components may be most relevant for a child who is traumatized by physical abuse or other forms of stress at home.

Having a wide range of both theoretical and practical perspectives makes room for the tremendous diversity researchers see in children diagnosed with ADHD. Researchers have been trying for decades to come up with better ways of differentiating kids who have different issues with respect to ADHD, but all they have come up with are crude subtypes and confusing co-morbidities that mix and match symptoms with other disabling conditions. In reality, however, children come in all the colors of the rainbow. In fact, one ADHD researcher has started to move the field in the right direction by suggesting that attentional capacity, executive functioning, and other symptoms of ADHD represents a *spectrum* (much like autism) of behaviors that extends from highly functioning to severely impaired.[3] In reality, for the more than six million children in America who have been diagnosed with ADHD, there are more than six million reasons for their unique behaviors. The best overall approach to these problems, then, is a comprehensive spectrum of, let's not call them "treatments," which again evokes the medical model, but rather, *solutions* to help these kids achieve success in school and life.

The 101 strategies I outline in this book provide a good starting point to this project. Of course, I'm not suggesting that parents use *all* 101 strategies. I've provided a questionnaire and a chart below to help you narrow down the strategies that would be most likely to succeed with your particular child. So, for example, if your child or teen has a low sense of self-worth, I've suggested a number of emotionally-based strategies that can help her affirm her unique capabilities in life. For the child who is a highly physical learner and climbs walls if there's nothing more interesting to do, I've indicated several options, including sports that work best for restless kids, hands-on ways to learn new things, and martial arts. Finally, although the book has the word *child* in the title, most of the strategies in Section III apply equally well to *adolescents*. To help parents evaluate which strategies are most appropriate to their child's or teen's developmental level, I've provided an age range for each strategy (there are no recommendations for children under the age of four because I have strong reservations against children this young being diagnosed with ADHD).

Read over the items in this questionnaire and check the ones that seem to apply to your child or you. Then go back over the items you checked and underline or copy down the strategies listed for those items. This will provide you with a good place to start in implementing an overall plan to help your child or adolescent.

Questionnaire to Choose the Best Strategies for Your Child or Teen

DOES YOUR CHILD

- _____ Consume more entertainment media (through TV, computer, smartphone, tablet, video games, Internet) than you think is good for him or her? (Strategy #38: Limit Entertainment Media)
- _____ Fidget a lot at school and/or wiggle at home during meals and/or homework time? (Strategy #1: Let Your Child Fidget, Strategy #10: Build, Borrow, or Buy Wiggle Furniture)
- _____ Enjoy doing things that involve creative expression (such as painting, music, dance, theater)? (Strategy #2: Channel Creative Energies into the Arts, Strategy #16: Use Music to Focus and Calm, Strategy #20: Nurture Your Child's Creativity)
- _____ Have trouble sleeping through the night? (Strategy #77: Make Sure Your Child Gets Sufficient Sleep)
- _____ Eat a lot of junk food? (Strategy #30: Limit Junk Food)
- _____ Display more hyperactivity, distractibility, and/or impulsivity shortly after eating? (Strategy #15: Remove Allergens and Additives from Your Child's Diet)
- _____ Run off without having breakfast or eat a breakfast high in carbohydrates but not protein? (Strategy #13: Provide a Balanced Breakfast)
- _____ Stress you out quite frequently? (Strategy #12: Take Care of Yourself)

- _____ Enjoy being on the computer? (Strategy #40: Use Online Learning as an Educational Resource, Strategy #47: Identify Mobile Apps That Can Help Your Child, Strategy #54: Consider Neurofeedback Training, Strategy #83: Utilize the Best Features of Computer Learning, Strategy, #84: Let Your Child Play Video Games That Engage and Teach, Strategy #85: Get Ready for the Thrills and Chills of Augmented and Virtual Reality, Strategy #97: Have Your Child Create a Blog, Strategy #100: Show Your Child Work-Arounds to Get Things Done)

- _____ Seem especially sensitive to colors (e.g., has strong opinions for and against certain colors)? (Strategy #96: Use Color to Highlight Information)

- _____ Appear to have poor self-esteem? (Strategy #21: Hold a Positive Image of Your Child, Strategy #23: Encourage Your Child's Interests, Strategy: #25 Celebrate Successes, Strategy #31: Empower Your Child with Strength-Based Learning, Strategy #33: Teach Your Child How His Brain Works, Strategy #75: Enhance Your Child's Self-Esteem, Strategy #82: Help Your Child Become Self-Aware)

- _____ Have poor study skills? (Strategy #1: Let Your Child Fidget, Strategy #34: Eliminate Distractions, Strategy #44: Let Your Child Engage in Spontaneous Self-Talk, Strategy #72: Suggest Effective Study Strategies)

- _____ Have a good imagination? (Strategy #2: Channel Creative Energies into the Arts, Strategy #20: Nurture Your Child's Creativity, Strategy #79: Teach Your Child to Visualize)

- _____ Enjoy playing games? (Strategy #80: Play Chess or Go with Your Child, Strategy #84: Let Your Child Play Video Games That Engage and Teach)

- _____ Appear to lag behind his classmates in age and/or maturity? (Strategy #26: Make Time for Your Child to Play, Strategy #89: Support Your Child's Late Blooming)

- _____ Have an increase in symptoms when there is a change in routine? (Strategy #24: Establish Consistent Rules, Routines, and Transitions)

- _____ Enjoy sports? (Strategy #4: Enroll Your Child in a Martial Arts Class, Strategy #35: Promote Daily Exercise, Strategy #49: Find a Sport Your Child Will Love, Strategy #94: Lobby for a Strong Physical Education Program in Your Child's School)

- _____ Spend a lot of time sitting at home? (Strategy #5: Make Time for Nature, Strategy #35: Promote Daily Exercise)

- _____ Enjoy it when the family is doing things together? (Strategy #6: Hold Family Meetings, Strategy #45: Engage in Family Exercise and Recreation, Strategy #57: Make Time for Plenty of Humor and Laughter, Strategy #58: Spend Positive Time Together)

- _____ Have difficulty learning through traditional lectures, worksheets, and textbooks at school? (Strategy #9: Encourage Hands-On Learning, Strategy #36: Foster Good Home–School Communication, Strategy #40: Use Online Learning as an Educational Resource, Strategy #56: Provide Opportunities for Learning through Movement, Strategy #59: Discover Your Child's Multiple Intelligences, Strategy #99: Encourage Project-Based Learning at Home and in School)

- _____ Not have many friends and/or have interpersonal difficulties with peers or siblings? (Strategy #81: Have Your Child Teach a Younger Child, Strategy #93: Help Your Child Develop Social Skills, Strategy #98: Work to Enhance Your Child's Social Network)

- _____ Seem to show entrepreneurial skills or interests? (Strategy #78: Activate Positive Career Aspirations, Strategy #95: Support Your Child's Entrepreneurial Instincts)

- _____ Enjoy being around animals? (Strategy #88: Find an Animal Your Child Can Care For)

- _____ Have problems with his or her teacher at school? (Strategy #36: Foster Good Home–School Communication, Strategy #53: Work to Promote Teacher–Child Rapport)

- _____ Say things like "I can't do it, it's just the way I am" and "My ADHD keeps me from being good [or smart]"? (Strategy #60: Help Your Child Develop a Growth Mind-Set)

- _____ Get along well with older adults in his or her world? (Strategy #48: Match Your Child with a Mentor, Strategy #66: Provide Positive Role Models)

- _____ Have tantrums or outbursts when things don't go his or her way? (Strategy #42: Teach Emotional Self-Regulation Skills, Strategy #43: Teach Your Child Mindfulness Meditation, Strategy #46: Share Stress Management Techniques)

- _____ Do his or her studying at home and/or school in a closed room without good lighting or windows? (Strategy #62: Provide Access to Natural and Full-Spectrum Light)

• ____ Become motivated when something is new or different from the routine? (Strategy #39: Promote Flow Experiences, Strategy #50: Provide a Variety of Stimulating Learning Activities, Strategy #65: Pep Up Each Day with at Least One Novel Experience, Strategy #70: Employ Incidental Learning)

• ____ Enjoy hanging around with kids younger than he or she is? (Strategy #81: Have Your Child Teach a Younger Child)

• ____ Not respond well to externally controlling behavior modification programs? (Strategy #68: Co-Create an Internally Empowering Behavior Mod Program with Your Child, Strategy #74: Use Time Out in a Positive Way, Strategy #91: Create a Positive Behavior Contract with Your Child)

• ____ Hang around locations where he or she might have contact with environmental toxins (such as lead)? (Strategy #76: Avoid Exposure to Environmental Contaminants)

• ____ Tend to have a mind that wanders, attention that drifts, and/or a penchant for daydreaming? (Strategy #7: Teach Your Child Focusing Techniques, Strategy #43: Teach Your Child Mindfulness Meditation, Strategy #54: Consider Neurofeedback Training)

• ____ Display symptoms of depression, anxiety, or other signs of emotional distress? (Strategy #64: Consider Family Therapy, Strategy #90: Consider Individual Psychotherapy for Your Child)

• ____ Have chronic problems adjusting to his or her regular public school classroom settings and teachers year to year (Strategy #86: Consider Alternative Schooling Options)

• ____ Have difficulties organizing himself or herself in regard to schoolwork, bedroom space, or other areas of life? (Strategy #22: Provide Appropriate Spaces for Learning, Strategy #101: Teach Your Child Organizational Strategies)

• ____ Enjoy being physical around the house and/or at school? (Strategy #1: Let Your Child Fidget, Strategy #4: Enroll Your Child in a Martial Arts Class, Strategy #10: Build, Borrow, or Buy Wiggle Furniture, Strategy #26: Make Time for Your Child to Play, Strategy #49: Find a Sport Your Child Will Love, Strategy #56: Provide Opportunities for Learning through Movement, Strategy #87: Have Your Child Learn

Yoga, Strategy #94: Lobby for a Strong Physical Education Program in Your Child's School)

• _____ Start acting up when he or she feels bored or under stimulated? (Strategy #50: Provide a Variety of Stimulating Learning Activities)

• _____ Have difficulty relaxing or feel stressed-out at different times of the day? (Strategy #7: Teach Your Child Focusing Techniques, Strategy #43: Teach Your Child Mindfulness Meditation, Strategy #46: Share Stress Management Techniques, Strategy #55: Use Touch to Soothe and Calm)

• _____ Frequently become forgetful of things he or she was told or read or was supposed to remember? (Strategy #37: Strengthen Your Child's Working Memory, Strategy #41: Show Your Child How to Use Metacognitive Tools; Strategy #80: Play Chess or Go with Your Child)

AS A PARENT DO YOU

• _____ Focus a lot of attention on your child's difficulties, deficits, and/or dysfunctions? (Strategy #3: Emphasize Diversity Not Disability, Strategy #21: Hold a Positive Image of Your Child, Strategy #25: Celebrate Successes)

• _____ Notice that your child seems better at certain times of the day? (Strategy #8: Discover Your Child's Best Time of Alertness)

• _____ Get stressed out from your child's behaviors on a regular basis? (Strategy #12: Take Care of Yourself)

• _____ Spend a lot of time telling your child what to do and how to do it? (Strategy #14: Give Your Child Choices)

• _____ Have a hard time with the conventional medical model approach to helping your child or want to explore other cross-cultural approaches? (Strategy #11: Consider Alternative Healing Options)

• _____ Feel a bit shaky about your parenting skills? (Strategy #19: Take a Parent Training Course, Strategy #92: Engage in Positive Niche Construction)

• _____ Have difficulty talking with your child about things that are important to him or her? (Strategy #18: Use Effective Communication Skills)

• _____ Have a great relationship with your child? (Strategy #27: Be a

Personal Coach to Your Child, Strategy #28: Build Resilience in Your Child)

• _____ Have concerns about your child being made fun of as a special education student at school? (Strategy #32: Support Full Inclusion of Your Child in a Regular Classroom)

• _____ Want to rule out other potential causes (other than ADHD) of your child's behavioral and/or attentional difficulties? (Strategy #71: Rule Out Other Potential Contributors to Your Child's Behavior)

• _____ Have problems getting your child's attention for chores, meals, and other daily activities? (Strategy #29: Give Instructions in Attention-Grabbing Ways)

• _____ Wish you had some better strategies for disciplining your child? (Strategy #19: Take a Parent Training Course, Strategy #52: Provide Immediate Behavioral Feedback, Strategy #61: Use Natural and Logical Consequences as a Discipline Tool, Strategy #67: Discover and Manage the Four Types of Misbehavior)

• _____ Think that dietary changes might result in significant improvements in your child's behavior and attention span? (#13: Provide a Balanced Breakfast, Strategy #15: Remove Allergens and Additives from Your Child's Diet, Strategy #30: Limit Junk Food, Strategy #63: Cook with Foods Rich in Omega-3 Fatty Acids)

Strategies Categorized by Type of Approach

As an additional help in tailoring strategies to your child's needs, I've organized the 101 strategies in this book according to which domains of a child's life (see Figure 2, page 80) are addressed. Note: Some strategies are listed in more than one category.

BEHAVIORAL

(strategies that improve your child's outward behaviors)

• Strategy #14: Give Your Child Choices
• Strategy #24: Establish Consistent Daily Rules, Routines, and Transitions
• Strategy #29: Give Instructions in Attention-Grabbing Ways
• Strategy #52: Provide Immediate Behavioral Feedback

- Strategy #61: Use Natural and Logical Consequences as a Discipline Tool
- Strategy #67: Discover and Manage the Four Types of Misbehavior
- Strategy #68: Co-Create an Internally Empowering Behavior Mod Program with Your Child
- Strategy #74: Use Time Out in a Positive Way
- Strategy #91: Create a Positive Behavior Contract with Your Child

BIOLOGICAL
(dietary strategies that affect your child's biochemistry)

- Strategy #13: Provide a Balanced Breakfast
- Strategy #15: Remove Allergens and Additives from Your Child's Diet
- Strategy #30: Limit Junk Food
- Strategy #63: Cook with Foods Rich in Omega-3 Fatty Acids

DEVELOPMENTAL
(strategies that are sensitive to your child's unique patterns of development)

- Strategy #5: Make Time for Nature
- Strategy #26: Make Time for Your Child to Play
- Strategy #89: Support Your Child's Late Blooming

COGNITIVE
(strategies that improve the way your child thinks)

- Strategy #7: Teach Your Child Focusing Techniques
- Strategy #17: Teach Your Child Self-Monitoring Skills
- Strategy #33: Teach Your Child How His Brain Works
- Strategy #37: Strengthen Your Child's Working Memory
- Strategy #41: Show Your Child How to Use Metacognitive Tools
- Strategy #42: Teach Emotional Self-Regulation Skills
- Strategy #43: Teach Your Child Mindfulness Meditation
- Strategy #44: Let Your Child Engage in Spontaneous Self-Talk
- Strategy #46: Share Stress Management Techniques
- Strategy #51: Teach Goal-Setting Skills

- Strategy #54: Consider Neurofeedback Training
- Strategy #60: Help Your Child Develop a Growth Mind-Set
- Strategy #79: Teach Your Child to Visualize
- Strategy #80: Play Chess or Go with Your Child
- Strategy #101: Teach Your Child Organizational Strategies

CREATIVE
(strategies that provide ways in which your child's exuberant energies can be channeled)

- Strategy #2: Channel Creative Energies into the Arts
- Strategy #20: Nurture Your Child's Creativity
- Strategy #39: Promote Flow Experiences
- Strategy #65: Pep Up Each Day with at Least One Novel Experience
- Strategy #95: Support Your Child's Entrepreneurial Instincts
- Strategy #97: Have Your Child Create a Blog

CULTURAL
(strategies that are sensitive to your child's broader cultural setting)

- Strategy #11: Consider Alternative Healing Options

ECOLOGICAL
(strategies that modify the environment in such a way as to enhance your child's ability to succeed at school and in life)

- Strategy #5: Make Time for Nature
- Strategy #8: Discover Your Child's Best Time of Alertness
- Strategy #10: Build, Borrow, or Buy Wiggle Furniture
- Strategy #16: Use Music to Focus and Calm
- Strategy #22: Provide Appropriate Spaces for Learning
- Strategy #26: Make Time for Your Child to Play
- Strategy #30: Limit Junk Food
- Strategy #34: Eliminate Distractions
- Strategy #38: Limit Entertainment Media
- Strategy #47: Identify Mobile Apps That Can Help Your Child

- Strategy #50: Provide a Variety of Stimulating Learning Activities
- Strategy #62: Provide Access to Natural and Full-Spectrum Light
- Strategy #71: Rule Out Other Potential Contributors to Your Child's Behavior
- Strategy #76: Avoid Exposure to Environmental Contaminants
- Strategy #77: Make Sure Your Child Gets Sufficient Sleep
- Strategy #83: Utilize the Best Features of Computer Learning
- Strategy #85: Get Ready for the Thrills and Chills of Augmented and Virtual Reality
- Strategy #88: Find an Animal Your Child Can Care For
- Strategy #96: Use Color to Highlight Information
- Strategy #92: Engage in Positive Niche Construction

EDUCATIONAL

(strategies that improve your child's performance at school)

- Strategy #1: Let Your Child Fidget
- Strategy #9: Encourage Hands-On Learning
- Strategy #31: Empower Your Child with Strength-Based Learning
- Strategy #32 Support Full Inclusion of Your Child in a Regular Classroom
- Strategy #36: Foster Good Home–School Communication
- Strategy #40: Use Online Learning as an Educational Resource
- Strategy #56: Provide Opportunities for Learning through Movement
- Strategy #59: Discover Your Child's Multiple Intelligences
- Strategy #70: Employ Incidental Learning
- Strategy #72: Suggest Effective Study Strategies
- Strategy #73: Provide Your Child with Real-Life Tasks
- Strategy #84: Let Your Child Play Video Games That Engage and Teach
- Strategy #86: Consider Alternative Schooling Options
- Strategy #94: Lobby for a Strong Physical Education Program in Your Child's School
- Strategy #99: Encourage Project-Based Learning at Home and in School
- Strategy #100: Show Your Child Work-Arounds to Get Things Done

EMOTIONAL

(strategies that improve the way your child feels)

- Strategy #2: Channel Creative Energies into the Arts
- Strategy #3: Emphasize Diversity Not Disability
- Strategy #21: Hold a Positive Image of Your Child
- Strategy #23: Encourage Your Child's Interests
- Strategy #25: Celebrate Successes
- Strategy #28: Build Resilience in Your Child
- Strategy #31: Empower Your Child with Strength-Based Learning
- Strategy #42: Teach Emotional Self-Regulation Skills
- Strategy #46: Share Stress Management Techniques
- Strategy #64: Consider Family Therapy
- Strategy #66: Provide Positive Role Models
- Strategy #75: Enhance Your Child's Self-Esteem
- Strategy #78: Activate Positive Career Aspirations
- Strategy #82: Help Your Child Become Self-Aware
- Strategy #90: Consider Individual Psychotherapy for Your Child

FAMILIAL

(strategies that help create a positive family climate within which your child can prosper)

- Strategy #6: Hold Family Meetings
- Strategy #19: Take a Parent Training Course
- Strategy #24: Establish Consistent Rules, Routines, and Transitions
- Strategy #25: Celebrate Successes
- Strategy #45: Engage in Family Exercise and Recreation
- Strategy #57: Make Time for Plenty of Humor and Laughter
- Strategy #58: Spend Positive Time Together
- Strategy #64: Consider Family Therapy

PHYSICAL

(strategies that make use of your child's physical nature to improve his behavior and attention span at home and school)

- Strategy #1: Let Your Child Fidget
- Strategy #4: Enroll Your Child in a Martial Arts Class
- Strategy #9: Encourage Hands-On Learning
- Strategy #26: Make Time for Your Child to Play
- Strategy #35: Promote Daily Exercise
- Strategy #49: Find a Sport Your Child Will Love
- Strategy #55: Use Touch to Soothe and Calm
- Strategy #56: Provide Opportunities for Learning through Movement
- Strategy #87: Have Your Child Learn Yoga
- Strategy #94: Lobby for a Strong Physical Education Program in Your Child's School

SOCIAL

(strategies that improve the way your child relates to other people)

- Strategy #18: Use Effective Communication Skills
- Strategy #27: Be a Personal Coach to Your Child
- Strategy #48: Match Your Child with a Mentor
- Strategy #53: Work to Promote Teacher–Child Rapport
- Strategy #81: Have Your Child Teach a Younger Child
- Strategy #93: Help Your Child Develop Social Skills
- Strategy #98: Work to Enhance Your Child's Social Network

Unlike psychoactive medications, these strategies have no negative side effects, and in fact, most of them are good for *all* kids, not just those who have the ADHD label. Try a few strategies and see if they produce positive results. If they do, incorporate them into your child's life on a regular basis and continue to introduce more strategies over time. You'll likely see that you're enriching not just your child's life, but the life of your whole family. Good luck and have fun!

SECTION III

*101 Ways to Improve
Your Child's Behavior and Attention Span
without Drugs, Labels, or Coercion*

Let Your Child Fidget
(Ages 4–18)

"Stop wiggling!" "Keep your hands to yourself!" "Spit out that gum!" "Don't fidget!" These are phrases frequently heard as harried teachers and parents supervise kids sitting at their desks doing schoolwork or slouching over kitchen tables doing their homework. Now comes new research suggesting that such behaviors as foot tapping, gum chewing, leg swinging, chair tilting, and finger rapping aren't so bad after all. Scientists divided children aged ten to seventeen into two groups, those who had been diagnosed with ADHD and those who were typically developing. They fitted actometers to their ankles as a means of recording their leg movements (a good measure of fidgeting). Then the subjects engaged in a computerized task requiring close attention to detail and clear cognition. They were shown an arrow on the screen and had to push a button indicating which direction it pointed to. The arrow was flanked by several other arrows pointed in different directions (requiring more focused concentration to keep from getting confused). Results indicated that ADHD-identified kids performed better on the task when they were fidgeting, but the same was not true for typically developing children.[1] Julie B. Schweitzer, a professor in the Department of Psychiatry and Behavioral Sciences at the University of California, Davis School of Medicine, and one of the researchers in this study, suggested that constant movement probably increased the mental arousal for these kids in the same way that psychostimulants do.[2]

Schools are beginning to recognize the benefits of fidgeting and are building it into the school day. At Quaker School in Horsham, Pennsylvania, teachers keep boxes of "fidget tools" available, including Silly Putty and Koosh balls (brightly colored balls with hundreds of tiny filaments on them) to use whenever they want.[3] Scott Ertl, a former elementary school teacher, developed Bouncy Bands, a special bungee cord that fits between the legs of a school desk or chair that students can bounce their legs against.

At home you can put a bounce into your child's homework sessions by keeping some of these "fidget widgets" around the house. Other fidgeting tools include a tennis ball, chewing gum, a hand grip exerciser (the kind used in fitness programs), pipe cleaners to twist around, a string of beads, a large bolt and nut (for screwing in and out), paper and pencil for doodling (research suggests doodling can also aid in comprehension and focus) and other small objects that your child can safely and quietly manipulate while he works.[4] The key word here is *quietly*. Steer clear of objects that make clicking, tapping, or rattling sounds that could disturb others in the house (unless your child is working alone in a room with good sound insulation). Allowing your child to fidget while he works creates a win–win situation: Your child is better able to focus and you have one less thing to worry about!

FOR FURTHER INFORMATION

Therapy Shoppe: P.O. Box 8875, Grand Rapids, MI 49518; 1-800-261-5590; therapyshoppe.com. Sells a wide variety of hand fidget tools plus other practical therapeutic supplies to therapists, teachers, and parents.

STRATEGY #2

Channel Creative Energies into the Arts
(Ages 4–12)

In chapter 8 I detailed some of the links that exist between ADHD and creativity. In a sense, your child's inattention and/or hyperactivity and impulsivity is simply undirected energy in his body and/or mind that needs to be directed toward a meaningful goal. There are several things you can do at home to help your child channel his creative energies through *the arts*. First, locate an area of the house where you can set up a "make-a-mess corner." Supplies might include finger paints; modeling clay; paint, brushes, an easel; drawing paper, colored pencils; and collage materials, such as old magazines, wallpaper samples, colored cloth, paper, and/or glue. Make sure the creativity corner is in a part of the house where messes can be easily cleaned up, perhaps by covering the floor with newspaper, an old sheet, or a plastic tarp or by putting the creativity corner in the basement or garage. Here are a few other ideas:

- Obtain an empty appliance box and create a puppet theater with your child. Purchase some simple puppets at a toy store or make your own out of old socks, and let your child put on puppet shows with her friends.
- Save hand-me-down clothes and put them in a sturdy container for use as a costume box. Let your child dress up and put on special skits, plays, or dances dressed up as she wishes.
- Create a musician's corner stocked with simple percussion instruments and home audio equipment with recording capabilities. Your child can tape her own performances or play her favorite music.

Finally, for kids with special aptitudes and strong motivation, consider music lessons, dance classes, or art programs where they can develop their talents in a more formal way. But don't push your child into these activities; be led by your child's own interest in pursuing formal study, and try to keep a respectful distance from her creative work unless she invites you to become involved.

At school, push for a strong arts program that includes classes in music, dance, theater, and the visual arts. These programs are all too often the first to be cut when there is a budgetary problem, yet for your child they may represent the courses in school where she achieves her greatest successes. Encourage your child's teacher to incorporate the arts into regular class-room activities. When I taught in the public schools, I had a regular "choice time" during the day when students could draw, make art projects, listen to music, or be creative in other ways. Teachers should also bring the arts into the curriculum by having students role-play history lessons, draw pictures illustrating math problems, and create raps and songs about characters in literature. By providing your child with expressive arts materials and an appropriate setting for using them at home, as well as advocating for the arts at your child's school, you can serve essentially as a "patron of the arts" and help your child's creative energies move toward goals and projects that will give him the deep satisfaction of being creative and successful.

FOR FURTHER INFORMATION

Susan Schwake, *Art Lab for Kids: 52 Creative Adventures in Drawing, Painting, Printmaking, Paper, and Mixed Media—for Budding Artists of All Ages* (Beverly, MA: Quarry Books, 2012).

STRATEGY #3

Emphasize Diversity Not Disability
(Ages 4–18)

I think the biggest problem I have with the label Attention Deficit Hyperactivity Disorder is that there is nothing in the description that gives any indication of the *positive qualities* of the child or adolescent being labeled. This can have devastating consequences. Ever since publication of the book *Pygmalion in the Classroom* fifty years ago (in which teachers were fooled into thinking a certain group of kids would excel in the coming year and the teachers' expectations actually made it happen), studies have shown that expectations play a huge role in how a child turns out in school and life.[1] When a child is labeled as having ADHD, parents, teachers, specialists, and others tend to engage in a *disability discourse* about the child that emphasizes his problems more than his possibilities. Imagine if Leonardo da Vinci were a student diagnosed with ADHD in today's classroom. Here's a possible dialogue during a conference to discuss his IEP (Individualized Education Program):

School Psychologist: "Well, I ran him through some tests, but his attention was all over the place."

Learning Specialist: "I'm concerned that he occasionally writes backwards. As you probably know, this is a soft sign for neurological dysfunction."

Classroom Teacher: "Yes, I've seen those reversals in my classroom. He never seems to get any work done. He'll start one thing and then lose interest. He's always doodling in the margins of the worksheets I *give him. And when he's not doing that, he's looking out the window daydreaming."*[2]

As they talk, nobody seems to recognize little Leonardo's greatness, and even his strengths are turned into problems. As education professors Patricia Cahill Paugh and Curt Dudley-Marling note with respect to kids with special needs, "Deficit construction of learners and learning continue to dominate how students are viewed, how school environments are organized, and how assessments and instruction are implemented."[3]

The concept of neurodiversity (discussed in chapter 9) provides us with a way out of this negative spiral. We should be regarding kids labeled ADHD as if they were fragile flowers, amazing buds, exquisite blooms, and exotic orchids. When you talk with your child about ADHD, try to avoid the clunky machine metaphors that ADHD experts use to explain the disorder (for example, "Your engine runs too fast"), and instead, speak to your child about the wonderful diversity of animals, plants, trees, sea life, birds, and other organisms in the world (*National Geographic* is a terrific magazine to use for this purpose), and then tell him that it's the same with human beings and brains (see also Strategy #33: Teach Your Child How His Brain Works). Remind him that all beings have strengths and weaknesses and a key to success in life is learning how to maximize one's strengths and minimize one's weaknesses. Diversity is essential to the well-being of the world, and your child's diversity is one important part of that richness!

FOR FURTHER INFORMATION

Thomas Armstrong, *The Power of Neurodiversity: Unleashing the Advantages of Your Differently Wired Brain* (Cambridge, MA: Da Capo, 2010).

STRATEGY #4

Enroll Your Child in a Martial Arts Class
(Ages 5–16)

A common sight on many playgrounds around the country these days is children practicing their karate, judo, and tae kwon do moves. Inspired by a flurry of movies featuring superheroes such as Bruce Lee, Chuck Norris, and Jean-Claude Van Damme, today's kids from ages five to sixteen seem intent on practicing martial art techniques that have their origins in Asian traditions dating back several hundred years. Now it appears that martial arts are a wonderful vehicle for developing self-control, concentration, and social competency with children who've been diagnosed as having ADHD.[1]

Karate and other martial art disciplines help children with attention and behavior problems in several ways. First, they train children to control their boundless supply of energy. For kids who seem to be at the mercy of their own seemingly uncontrollable behaviors, these sports offer a chance to begin directing physical and mental energy in an intentional and focused way. Second, martial arts empower kids to feel good about themselves by enhancing their capacity to defend themselves, improving their physical coordination, and developing a skill that is highly valued within their peer group. Third, they promote respect for others through the ritual courtesies (such as bowing, waiting for one's turn) and ethical values that each art employs. Finally, they give kids an acceptable way of handling aggressive feelings without hurting themselves or anyone else.

There are many differences among the wide range of martial arts taught in this country. Some of the main traditions are the following:

- *Karate* (a Japanese word meaning "empty hand"). Stresses defensive blocks and the use of kicking and striking motions.
- *Judo.* A Japanese art (but derived from the Chinese word meaning "gentle way") that places emphasis on throwing one's opponent and using pressure on different points of the body to disable an individual.

- *Aikido* (Japanese for "mind-meeting way"). Teaches defensive techniques similar to those of judo but with less emphasis on making physical contact with one's opponent.
- *Tae kwon do.* A Korean form of karate that concentrates on kicking motions.
- *Kenpo.* An Americanized version of Asian martial arts that combines traditional skills with modern boxing techniques.
- *Tai chi chuan.* A Chinese martial art (literally Supreme Ultimate Boxing) that in most Westernized versions teaches specific slow bodily movements without contact with an opponent as a means of enhancing well-being.
- *Karobics.* A contemporary combination of karate, tai chi, and aerobics.

To find a suitable martial arts class for your child look first for low-cost children's classes taught through community and fitness centers, after-school programs, or recreational centers. (A comprehensive nationwide list of martial arts organizations is provided at usadojo.com/kata/organizations.asp). There are also many excellent programs available through private businesses that often operate as storefront enterprises. You can find out about these programs by flipping through the yellow pages under "martial arts instruction." Make sure the instructors are certified by a reputable national or international organization. Take some time with your child to observe a lesson or two so that you both feel comfortable with the setting. Don't hesitate to ask the instructors questions or share any concerns you might have. Once your child has enrolled, help keep his interest high by regularly giving him a chance to show you what he's learned, go together to observe adult demonstrations of martial arts, and encourage him to stick with it when he feels bored or discouraged. Once he begins to see how martial arts is positively transforming his whole attitude toward himself and others, he may never want to quit!

FOR FURTHER INFORMATION

Mike Massie, *Martial Arts Drills and Games for Kids: Over 50 Exciting Drills and Games for Kids That'll Keep Your Students Training Through Black Belt* [Kindle] (Bellevue, WA: Amazon Digital Services, 2012).

STRATEGY #5

Make Time for Nature
(Ages 4–18)

Perhaps I'll sound like a grizzled and wistful old man when I say this (I'm sixty-six years old), but when I was a child I used to spend hours every day with friends running in fields, playing in parks, and spending time during the summer splashing around in a handful of Minnesota's eleven thousand lakes. Increasingly kids today are not having this same sort of experience. Much of a child's leisure time now is spent indoors in front of a video screen with a smartphone, tablet, television, computer, or video game console. According to a recent poll by The Nature Conservancy, an organization dedicated to protecting the world's natural resources, only 10 percent of kids polled reported spending time in nature on a daily basis, while 88 percent indicated that they're online every day.[1] We're all aware of the impact of a sedentary lifestyle on obesity in children.[2] Less well known, however, is the impact that this nature deprivation is having on the behavior and attention spans of our kids, especially those who have been diagnosed with ADHD. A number of studies now reveal that when ADHD-identified children and adolescents spend time in nature, their symptoms decrease and the rate of decline is directly proportional to the "wildness" of the nature setting (for example, the woods are "wilder" than a city park).[3]

When planning a vacation, consider going on a hiking and camping expedition before you book that trip to Disneyland or Walt Disney World. You don't need to pack up your kids and head to the Grand Canyon to get this green effect. One study suggested that even twenty minutes spent in a park can increase attention span in kids diagnosed with ADHD.[4] If you don't have a park nearby, then scoot your child out to the backyard, to a friend's yard, or to a nearby field to organize a sandlot ball game with kids in the neighborhood. Even a simple walk in an area where there are trees can be a step in the right direction. And don't let winter interfere with your plans. As the Norwegians say: There's no such thing as bad weather, just bad clothing. Richard Louv, author of *Last Child in the Woods: Saving Our Children from Nature-Deficit Disorder*, thinks that time in nature, while not a panacea, should become a regular nondrug alternative to help decrease ADHD symptoms. He says: "A walk in the woods would be the ideal treatment: it's not stigmatizing, has no serious side effects, and it's free."[5]

FOR FURTHER INFORMATION

Richard Louv, *Last Child in the Woods: Saving Our Children from Nature-Deficit Disorder* (Chapel Hill, NC: Algonquin, 2008).

Richard Louv, *Vitamin N: The Essential Guide to a Nature-Rich Life* (Chapel Hill, NC: Algonquin, 2016). More than 500 activities for connecting children and adults with nature.

STRATEGY #6

Hold Family Meetings
(Ages 4–18)

A family meeting is a regularly scheduled coming together of all family members to discuss issues of mutual importance. Such meetings function as a place where parents and children alike can share positive experiences, express feelings, plan fun things to do together, establish family rules, settle conflicts, deal with recurring issues, and solve problems in a cooperative way. Parents and children function as equals in a family meeting. This democratic structure helps ensure that parents aren't perceived as tyrants, and provides children with opportunities for problem solving, decision making, consensus building, and many other skills important for getting along with others.

Family meetings work by having members agree to meet at a regularly scheduled time (usually once a week) for a set length of time (twenty to thirty minutes is recommended for younger children, one hour for older kids). At the first meeting, a chairperson should be appointed. A parent usually can take on this role initially to model the behaviors for their kids. But the chairperson's role should rotate every week so that each family member has the opportunity to experience being a facilitator. A "scribe," or secretary who is responsible for writing up a summary of the meeting, should also be appointed, and this role should also rotate each week (very young children who haven't developed writing skills yet can keep records using a voice recorder app on a tablet or smartphone). The basic structure of a meeting looks something like this:

- Summarize previous meeting (that is, the reading of minutes)
- Discuss old business
- Bring up new business
- Summarize the meeting and any decisions made

The minutes of the meeting can be posted during the week on the kitchen bulletin board so that family members have a reference point for the decisions and agreements made.

In a family meeting, decisions and agreements are usually made by consensus rather than majority rule. Consensus means that family members need to work actively to find a cooperative solution to family issues. Any agreements made through a family meeting are effective until the next meeting. If parents or children are dissatisfied with the results of the agreement at any time during the week, they need to postpone their dissatisfaction until the meeting. A special "meeting book," however, can be set up where family members can record their feelings and put issues of concern on the agenda for the next meeting.

It's very important, especially at the early stages of holding family meetings, to encourage the involvement of the kids. Parents can easily overwhelm the meeting with their advice, lecturing, ideas, and judgments. Make a conscious effort to hold back at the start and let your children propose suggestions, bring up issues, and plan events. Be sure that the family meeting is upbeat and proactive. If all you do at the meeting is bring up problems, make criticisms, and dole out consequences for misbehavior, your children are likely to lose interest fast. Start your meetings on a positive note by sharing positive experiences and complimenting or appreciating other family members for things that happened during the week (see also Strategy #25: Celebrate Successes). End your meetings with a fun activity such as a game, a sport, or a movie (see also Strategy #45: Engage in Family Exercise and Recreation).

Above all, keep the focus on the family. If you have a child who's been diagnosed with ADHD, then it's likely he's used to being singled out for disruptive or disturbing behaviors. Try very hard not to make family meetings a time of focusing on his problems. If your ADHD-diagnosed child's behaviors keep showing up frequently on the meeting agenda, remember to frame his problems as a family issue, seek out his advice in coming up with solutions, put in enough agenda items related to other family members so that he doesn't feel picked on, and give him regular experiences of serving as chairperson and secretary. As your child begins to experience himself more as an equal in the family meetings, his own inner powers of self-control and self-discipline are likely to be activated and used to help solve not only his own difficulties but those of other family members as well.

FOR FURTHER INFORMATION

Elaine Hightower and Betsy Riley, *Our Family Meeting Book: Fun and Easy Ways to Manage Time, Build Communication, and Share Responsibility Week by Week* (Minneapolis, MN: Free Spirit, 2002).

STRATEGY #7

Teach Your Child Focusing Techniques
(Ages 6–18)

The ability to attend to one's immediate environment is a capacity that has probably existed from the very beginning of the evolution of life forms. After all, an organism that failed to be attentive to its environment was all too often eaten up by a predator and thus could not pass its genes on to the next generation. In today's society, demands on a person's attention have become increasingly complex. For the child diagnosed with ADHD, such demands have more to do with teacher and parent instructions than with avoiding extinction.

Nevertheless, the development of attention does represent a kind of survival skill for these kids—at least in terms of their successful adaptation to the society around them. Can this ability be trained? The answer is a solid yes. For thousands of years, human beings have learned to control attention using specially designed meditative techniques. Yogis, shamans, and other practitioners have trained their minds to shut out distracting thoughts, to develop mental tranquility, and even to control autonomic functions like heart rate and skin temperature (see also Strategy #43: Teach Your Child Mindfulness Meditation).

Current research suggests that focusing exercises or meditative techniques can be successfully used to help children labeled ADHD.[1] Here are some strategies to help you get started:

- *Ask your child to focus his attention exclusively for a given period of time on a single object somewhere in the house and describe what he is experiencing.* This will require him to pay close attention to colors, shapes, reflections, shadows, textures. Using a candle as an example, you might say: "What do you see? Feel the wax. Do you notice the orange part?"
- *Play an attention game.* Similar to the staring games that children sometimes play, this activity involves staring at an object with total focus. The last person to stop looking wins the game. Objects to look at might include a picture, a favorite toy, a tree, or a cloud.
- *Focus on inner images as a way to train concentration.* You might suggest that your child picture her favorite place, her best friend, or her favorite color. Limit the activity to no more than three minutes to start with and then gradually extend the time (see also Strategy #79: Teach Your Child to Visualize).

If these activities make your child anxious or confused or are perceived as an obligation or chore, then stop doing them. However, if your child thinks they're fun and shows increasing levels of capability over time, then it's probably worthwhile to continue.

Training attention has sometimes been compared to housebreaking a puppy. You place the puppy on the newspaper knowing he will wander off. When he does, you pick the puppy up and place him back on the newspaper. If he wanders off again, you continue to place him on the newspaper repeatedly until he finally learns where to go. The mind can wander like a puppy dog. Many professionals and parents of children labeled ADHD testify to the fact that these kids' minds often wander as relentlessly as their bodies. Sometimes this is an asset—it makes for wonderful creativity and the formation of new and innovative ideas. But when the time comes for relatively uncreative tasks like doing a spelling test or remembering to take out the garbage, then the ability to focus on the job at hand may turn out to be quite important to your child's successful adaptation to life.

FOR FURTHER INFORMATION
Deborah Plummer, *Focusing and Calming Games for Children: Mindfulness Strategies and Activities to Help Children to Relax, Concentrate, and Take Control* (London: Jessica Kingsley, 2012).

STRATEGY #8

Discover Your Child's Best Time of Alertness
(Ages 7–18)

Spring fever. The afternoon siesta. The Monday blahs. The ways in which we mark time are crucial to our behavior and ultimate well-being. The field of *chronopsychology* studies the effects of our inner time-sensitive biological rhythms on the physical, cognitive, and emotional dimensions of our lives. And because these built-in rhythms affect the human attention span, what we learn from chronopsychology may be quite helpful for youngsters who've been identified as having attention deficits. It may, in fact, be possible to identify when your child's best times of day are in terms of focused attention, problem-solving ability, and memory skills.

The most important inner timekeepers that all humans experience are the circadian rhythms, which occur in twenty-four-hour solar and twenty-five-hour lunar cycles. During these cycles, there is a fluctuation in the efficiency of neurotransmitter molecules that chemically regulate normal rest and activity cycles. Studies suggest that children diagnosed with ADHD have altered circadian rhythms that affect their sleep patterns and result in atypical patterns of alertness and inattention during the day, including daytime sleepiness (see Strategy #77: Make Sure Your Child Gets Sufficient Sleep). Most typically developing children show a pattern of being more attentive in the morning, but this may be different for some children diagnosed with ADHD, and by adolescence, there is definitely a shift for most teens into "eveningness" (a propensity to be more alert later in the day).

One suggestion to help monitor your child's best time of alertness is to keep a diary over a period of a week or longer (and have your child's teacher do the same, if possible) to identify his best times of alertness (you can also have your child or teen keep his own alertness diary). If he seems to be most alert in the morning, this would be the ideal time for test taking, note taking, worksheet learning, and other types of seatwork, while evening may be the worst time of the day for doing homework. In such a case, you may want to suggest that your child do assigned schoolwork in the morning before going off to school. On the other hand, if you discover that your child is more of an owl, or night person, then she may be hitting her stride in attention and learning only after school gets out. In that case, carrying over school tasks not completed into the evening may be entirely appropriate. In addition, if you discover that your child's teacher is scheduling the afternoon period with tests, lecture, drill, and seatwork, and your child is having difficulty paying attention, then it may be wise to confer with the teacher and/or a school administrator about loosening up that time period to allow for more open-ended activities like art, physical education, and project-based learning. In any case, it may be very important to your child's success in school, and in life, if you and he can discover those special islands of alertness during the day and year when he is especially good at buckling down and getting things done.

Encourage Hands-On Learning
(Ages 4–12)

"Put that toy away!" "Stop fiddling with the pencil sharpener!" "Can't you learn to keep your hands to *yourself*?" Do these comments sound familiar? If you have a child, or have ever taught a child, then you're probably all too familiar with these or similar phrases. And if that child has been diagnosed with ADHD, then you've possibly experienced more than your share of stories along this line. Yet for all the trouble such behaviors seem to cause, behind these annoyances lies an important need for your child: to have direct hands-on experience with the world.

From my contacts over the years with parents and teachers who have worked with children identified as having ADHD, it's apparent to me that many of these children have an even greater need for hands-on learning than most kids. Here are a few socially appropriate ways for ADHD-identified kids to satisfy the need to explore, work, build, and solve problems with their hands so that they don't end up becoming a hands-on nuisance!

- *Give your child something to do with his hands while he's involved in stationary activities.* If your child has to sit for long periods in a car on a trip, for example, make sure he has materials to keep his hands busy. Some possibilities include small puzzles (Rubik's Cube), miniature action figures, yarn for making cat's cradles or other string forms, and an Etch-A-Sketch or other simple drawing device (see also Strategy #1: Let Your Child Fidget, for more ideas).
- *Provide opportunities for tactile stimulation.* Some teachers have created a "tactile tub" consisting of a small plastic wading pool filled with any one of a number of substances, including water, oatmeal, sand, cornmeal, shredded paper, plastic foam packing beads, or flour, among other possible ingredients. This environment provides plenty of tactile

stimulation as kids scoop up the material, rub their hands in it, and use if to form islands, castles, or other fantasy creations.

- *Supply three-dimensional building materials for free play.* Examples include Lego blocks, an Erector set, Lincoln Logs, D-Stix, Tinkertoys, simple wooden blocks, pattern blocks, plastic connector beads, origami, clay, and playing cards for building castles. Provide an open space where your child can work on ongoing projects without having to take the structure down between play sessions.
- *Use manipulative materials to help your child learn academic subjects.* There is a wide range of hands-on materials that teach math concepts in concrete ways, including Cuisenaire Rods, Dienes blocks, Unifix Cubes, Geoboards, Tangrams, and Number-Blox. To learn science concepts, kids can do hands-on science experiments. Even reading can become hands-on if you provide special books: pop-up books, scratch-'n'-sniff books, touch-'n'-feel books, books kids can take apart and put back together in a different way, and plastic or magnetic letters for creating words and sentences.

One parent allowed her child to finger-paint the shower walls with shaving cream (it's so easy to wash off). Another let her child paint the sidewalks with water on a hot day (it evaporates in the heat). In these and other ways, you can keep your child from becoming too touchy, help him grasp new material, and provide strategies that allow him to get a good grip on life!

FOR FURTHER INFORMATION

The Editors of Klutz Press, *Kids Travel: A Backseat Survival Kit* (Palo Alto, CA: Klutz, 1994).

Build, Borrow, or Buy Wiggle Furniture
(Ages 4–16)

Kids who are allowed to fidget, use squeeze balls, or wiggle at home or in school may be better able to concentrate on their work (see Strategy #1: Let Your Child Fidget), but there can be difficulties connected with some of these ideas. The child who constantly tilts his chair on two legs may be in danger of tipping over like our Fidgety Phillip from chapter 2. The rigid design of some school furniture may inherently limit a student's ability to move without banging his shins or calves. The stiff wood, metal, or plastic seats and backs of chairs may encourage slouching and result in poor posture that could have a negative impact on a child's spinal column. In response to these and other challenges, there is a growing movement in education to provide children with ergonomic furniture that allows them greater freedom to spin, stand, twirl, and/or bounce while engaged in their schoolwork or homework.

At Mary Lee Burbank School in Belmont, Massachusetts, teacher Katie Caritey's second-grade classroom has two standing desks, where kids can work either sitting or standing. The kids love them. Comments from students include these:

- [The standing desks] "help me concentrate without even thinking about what others are doing."
- "Being able to stand or swing my legs helps me calm down my brain so I can think better."
- "When I get to school in the morning, my brain is tired and not ready for learning yet. When I sit at the standing desk, it wakes up my brain and helps me get ready for thinking."[1]

Each day Caritey chooses kids to use the standing desks who are especially energetic or having trouble completing their work. Research supports her strategy. In one study, students with hyperactivity and attention issues used stability balls (large durable plastic balls that one can sit on) in the classroom over a period of twelve weeks. Results indicated increased levels of attention, decreased levels of hyperactivity, and increased time on task while engaged with their schoolwork.[2] In another study, kids diagnosed with ADHD were allowed to sit at swivel chairs they could spin around in while engaged in a series of cognitive tasks such as remembering and repeating a set of numbers to researchers. The children did better when they were on swivel chairs than when they were seated on a standard chair. It is interesting that students without the ADHD diagnosis performed worse on the swivel chairs.[3]

In addition to the equipment already mentioned, there is a wide range of furniture types that can provide students (or children at home) with opportunities to move, such as:

- Hokki Stools (they swivel while kids work)
- Pedal desks (children can keep their feet in motion)
- Disc 'O' Sit cushions (preinflated plastic discs that can be stacked and sat on)
- Kneeling chairs (kids sit on a low seat with pads for kneeling)
- Howda chairs (legless chairs that allow students to sit close to the floor and rock)
- Webble Active Footrests (plastic rockers to fit your feet into)

Parents don't need to spend a lot of money to give their kids wiggle-friendly furniture for homework sessions. Possibilities that can fit any budget include an old office swivel chair, a cast-off rocking chair, an exercise bicycle in the garage, or a standing-desk that you can build yourself for only $22 (time.com/money/3589580/standing-desk-ikea-hack). Keep in mind that when you're giving your child new and creative ways to work out the wiggles, you're also providing her with the opportunity to demonstrate her best efforts to succeed in school and life.

FOR FURTHER INFORMATION

Moving Minds by Gopher: http://www.moving-minds.com; 1-855-858-8551. An online source of ergonomic furniture, stability balls, standing desks, and other active seating solutions for home and school.

Consider Alternative Healing Options
(Ages 8–18)

Treatments used for ADHD since its inception in the early 1970s have largely been based on a 350-year-old Western medical tradition that regards drugs and surgical interventions as the primary means of treating physical, mental, and emotional symptoms and their underlying causes. While this tradition has been crucial in saving lives, reducing suffering, and extending the lives of hundreds of millions of people, there are other medical traditions, some of them thousands of years old, that may also be valid ways of managing a child's symptoms of hyperactivity, inattentiveness, and impulsivity. In the 1990s, the U.S. Congress established an Office of Alternative Medicine at the National Institutes of Health (now called the National Center for Complementary and Integrative Health), which has been evaluating evidence, doing research, disseminating information, and training physicians in the use of practices derived from many of these traditions. Only recently, however, have researchers started investigating the use of alternative healing approaches in treating ADHD. A 2003 survey indicated that 50 percent of all children with an ADHD diagnosis were being treated using complementary and alternative medicine therapies, but only 11 percent of parents were communicating to their physicians that they were doing so.[1] Even when they communicate with their doctors, a 2013 study suggested that fewer than 50 percent of the doctors were interested in learning more.[2]

Many parents come from cultural traditions that have been using alternative medical approaches in their families for generations, while other parents have become aware of these traditions more recently through friends or mass media. Some of the major alternative healing traditions to consider are

- *Traditional Chinese Medicine.* A twenty-five-hundred-year-old tradition. In this system, ADHD is said to be due to, among other things, a disharmony between the two primary life principles, *yin* and *yang*, and deficiencies, imbalances, or overactivity of the life force (*qi*) in its connections between the heart, spleen, liver, gallbladder, and/or kidneys. Treatments include acupuncture, herbs, physical movements (*qi gong*), dietary modifications, and lifestyle changes.[3]

- *Ayurvedic medicine.* A tradition founded in India whose origins are said to go back as far as 5000 BCE ADHD is viewed as caused by the impairment or weakening of rational thinking (*dhee*), the retaining power of the mind (*dhriti*), and memory (*smriti*), resulting in improper contact of the senses with their objectives in the world. Treatments include herbs, diet, aromatherapy, massage, and yoga.[4]
- *Chiropractic.* Founded by American healer D. D. Palmer in the 1890s; spinal manipulations, massage, and nutritional supplements are used to manage ADHD symptoms.[5]
- *Homeopathy.* Founded by German physician Samuel Hahnemann in the late eighteenth century. Based on the idea of "like treating like," practitioners use repeated small doses of certain medicinal herbs associated with hyperactivity and other ADHD symptoms to treat the patient.[6]

Consult with your child's doctor before initiating any alternative and/or complementary treatments because there may be potentially harmful ADHD drug–alternative treatment interactions (especially when material substances are to be ingested or injected). At the same time, use of ADHD drugs together with alternative approaches may be more powerful than drugs alone. If possible, work with a physician who specializes in the emerging field of pediatric integrative medicine.[7] If you aren't working with a doctor, then make sure to find a fully licensed and certified practitioner in one or more of these alternative healing options who has experience working with children and adolescents diagnosed with ADHD.

FOR FURTHER INFORMATION
National Center for Complementary and Integrative Health: 9000 Rockville Pike, Bethesda, MD 20892; nccih.nih.gov. Provides information on finding a medical doctor who specializes in complementary and integrative health in your area.

STRATEGY #12

Take Care of Yourself
(Ages 18–88)

Over the years many parents have called, written, or spoken with me in person about the anguish they've suffered as a result of having a child with special needs. Sometimes this pain occurs as a result of attempts by the parent to motivate others—especially the schools—to understand and accept their children. As one parent put it in an online computer message: "You see, I have a dream that I wake up one day and I don't have to explain why my child is the way he is anymore to anyone." At other times, the frustration stems more from direct conflicts with the child. No parent has expressed this sense of heartache better than a Louisiana mother who wrote me and said, "To be honest, I wish I could trade in this child. By ten a.m., this child has worn me down. I am very unhappy. If this were a husband, I would probably divorce him."

In all the controversy surrounding appropriate ways of helping children diagnosed with ADHD, the needs of their parents can all too often be ignored. Yet research suggests that these parents are themselves victims—victims of the system that refuses to understand their children, victims of their children's unpredictable behavior, and victims of other stresses that make effective parenting especially difficult. Notwithstanding the comments I made in chapter 7 about how parental stress contributes to ADHD symptoms, a number of studies also point to the high stress levels involved in parenting a child with an ADHD diagnosis.[1]

These findings suggest that parents of kids diagnosed with ADHD may require as much help as their children in coping with stress. Such parents need to discover strategies for taking care of themselves and getting support from their environment if they are to be of much help to their children. A calmer, happier, and more secure parent is in a much better position to respond appropriately to a child's difficult behaviors than one who is angry, anxious, or insecure. In learning effective ways of taking care of themselves, parents also model important self-help skills for their children. Finally, when parents focus attention on their own needs, they liberate themselves from the tendency to dwell exclusively on their child's problems. They begin to see that the world doesn't revolve around their child's "disability" and that simple realization can provide a much-needed distance in what might be a stormy parent–child relationship. Some activities you can do to reduce your own stress levels include these:

- Watch fun movies
- Read for pleasure
- Listen to relaxing music
- Spend time in nature
- Go out for romantic dinners with your spouse
- Attend your local house of worship
- Get together with friends
- Play or watch sports
- Meditate
- Do yoga or tai chi
- Go out for nights on the town (such as plays, musicals, concerts)
- Take a bubble bath
- Schedule fun trips, cruises, or vacations
- Garden

Be sure to schedule several of these or similar activities each week so that you have a way of recharging your batteries on a regular basis.

Another important strategy for taking care of yourself is to establish an effective support system. Research suggests that parents who experience greater levels of social support (from extended family and community sources) see greater behavioral improvements in their children as they go through parent-training programs.[2]

Tap family resources such as grandparents or friends of the family in getting support. Sometimes just knowing that you can call a relative or friend to get a word of encouragement, sympathy, or advice helps reduce the burden you might feel in a difficult situation with your child. Community resources are also available to support parents. Some towns have a parental stress hotline you can call for immediate advice. Also, many communities have special parenting centers that offer classes, counseling, and other resources for struggling parents (see Strategy #19: Take a Parent Training Course). Finally, consider professional help in dealing with your stress levels. By making *you* the focus of attention for a change, you'll discover inner resources to enrich not only your experience as a parent but your experience as a whole person.

FOR FURTHER INFORMATION

Mark Bertin and Ari Tuckman, *Mindful Parenting for ADHD: A Guide to Cultivating Calm, Reducing Stress, and Helping Children Thrive* (Oakland, CA: New Harbinger, 2015).

Martha Davis, Elizabeth Robbins Eshelman, and Matthew McKay, *The Relaxation and Stress Reduction Workbook*, 6th ed. (Oakland, CA: New Harbinger, 2008).

STRATEGY #13

Provide a Balanced Breakfast
(Ages 4–18)

When I was a child, Sunday morning breakfast usually consisted of some devilishly delicious sweet rolls my mother had baked in the early morning hours. Sunday afternoons were spent sleeping them off (sometimes in church!), or just feeling vaguely restless or irritable. Science now supports the idea that a sugar-laden high-carbohydrate breakfast of sweet rolls, syrupy pancakes, waffles dripping with jam, or even toast and butter, make it more likely that a child will have difficulties paying attention in the hours to come.[1]

Eating these carbohydrate-rich foods raises the levels of the neurotransmitter serotonin in the brain, causing the eater to feel sleepy, restless, irritable, or inattentive. Sudden surges of serotonin can also throw off levels of other neurotransmitters such as dopamine and norepinephrine. Protein, however, increases the level of amino acids, and these serve to block many of the effects of serotonin.

To help ensure that children's school days will be free of these attentional and mood shifts, provide your child with breakfasts that have a good balance of complex carbohydrates (for example, cereals, bread, pasta), protein (such as milk, yogurt, cheese, eggs, lean meat, fish, poultry), and fruit (like juice, fresh fruit, canned fruit). The chart below offers a few examples of what might constitute a poor breakfast on the one hand, and a good breakfast on the other:

"WANDERING ATTENTION" BREAKFASTS	"FOCUSED ATTENTION" BREAKFASTS
hash browns and ketchup, grapefruit juice	boiled egg, a whole wheat muffin with almond butter, milk
sugary cereals without milk, water	granola and milk, an apple
pancakes or waffles with syrup, apple juice	multigrain pancakes with applesauce, walnuts, and yogurt, hot or cold herbal tea with honey
sweet rolls and/or Danish, high fructose juice	bean burrito with salsa, banana smoothie
muffins, commercially—sold frozen orange juice	scrambled eggs, freshly—squeezed orange juice
candy, soda	oatmeal with nuts and raisins, 2 percent milk
toast and butter, coffee with sugar	vegetable omelet with cheese, a drink of 1/4 fruit juice combined with 3/4 sparkling water

For kids who are resistant to the good food items listed in the chart, try jazzing up the meal by varying the appearance and ingredients of the breakfast. To serve oatmeal, put grapes on the top for eyes, the end of a banana for the nose, and a few walnuts (or a dribble of yogurt) for the mouth to create "Oatmeal Man." Another way to encourage your child to eat more nutritious foods is by allowing him to make choices about what he wants for breakfast. If he's old enough, get him involved in preparing his own meals. You might find that he begins to channel some of his frenetic energies into cooking.

FOR FURTHER INFORMATION

Missy Chase Lapine, *The Sneaky Chef: Simple Strategies for Hiding Healthy Foods in Kids' Favorite Meals* (Philadelphia: Running Press, 2007).

Missy Chase Lapine, *The Sneaky Chef to the Rescue: 101 All-New Recipes and "Sneaky" Tricks for Creating Healthy Meals Kids Will Love* (Philadelphia: Running Press, 2009).

Give Your Child Choices
(Ages 4–18)

Few children diagnosed with ADHD are ever given the opportunity of having an important say in the decision-making process that will affect their educational futures. Many children are not even given a chance to attend special school meetings at which their educational placement is being discussed. More to the point with children diagnosed as having ADHD, few if any of these kids have the opportunity to have an important say in whether they're to be medicated or in what other treatment approaches might be used to help them (I know of no research study on psychoactive medications that has allowed children to have any role at all in their medical management).

This loss of choice can have devastating consequences. Some children will respond with rage. However, many more children will die a slow, quiet spiritual death as they find their personal voice ignored and their dignity forgotten. Externally, it will appear as if the child has lost motivation, become withdrawn, or is depressed (which will be interpreted by doctors as a *co-morbid factor*), but essentially what has happened is that her inner flame has gone out. Her passion has been extinguished. Regrettably, many ADHD-oriented programs add insult to injury by providing these children with phony choices. One popular ADHD book advises parents of inattentive children to say something like this: "Johnny, look at me! You have a choice! Either you clean this room up right now or you will have to go to time out." That's not a choice! That's an adult dictating to a child the terms of his future behavior.

When parents and teachers empower ADHD-diagnosed children with choices, the children no longer need to manipulate their environment to get what they want. Many of the undesirable behaviors shown by these kids are, at a deeper level, attempts by them to exert some type of control over their surroundings. The act of choosing itself serves as a calming and stabilizing force for some kids. The ability to choose is like a muscle. It gets stronger through use.

You can help your child exert his "choice muscles" in several ways. At school, he should be allowed to attend important school meetings where his educational objectives are being charted, and he should be given the opportunity to ask questions, make comments, and have his ideas respected and included in the discussion. In the classroom, teachers should provide these kids with opportunities all through the day for making choices. Such choices might include the following:

- What math problems to work on ("You can do the problems on page 54 or page 55.")
- What book to read ("You can read *Tom Sawyer* or *Huckleberry Finn*.")
- What type of homework to do ("You can write an essay or do a tape-recorded interview with an expert on the subject.")
- What sort of long-term project to engage in ("You can do a photo essay, a diorama, a mural, or a play about the Civil War this term.")

Also, parents and teachers should have educational materials available with choice built into them. For example, the Choose Your Own Adventure reading series allows kids to stop at different points in the story and make choices about what the hero should do. Their choices lead them to any one of a number of story endings. Computer programs also allow kids to make choices. In one free mobile app, The Oregon Trail, children have the opportunity to take a computer journey across the country, deciding what they'll take along, and when confronted with obstacles on the way, how they'll deal with each problem in turn.

At home, let your child choose the time, place, and method for doing chores or homework assignments. If you do use rewards and punishments in shaping your child's behavior, at least let your child be involved in deciding which ones they'll be so he will feel like a partner in his own rehabilitation (see Strategy #68: Co-Create an Internally Empowering Behavior Mod Program with Your Child, Strategy #74: Use Time Out in a Positive Way, and Strategy #91: Create a Positive Behavior Contract with Your Child). Involve your child in making family decisions about where to go for dinner or how to spend a weekend or where to take a summer trip. And when it's time to go to bed, don't give him the false choice of "my way or the highway." Instead, offer him a real choice: "Do you want to go to bed in your blue PJs or your red PJs?" This approach maintains your child's dignity, allows him to flex his choice muscles, and does it all while keeping the "to bed or not to bed" question off the negotiating table. Remember that by giving your child the opportunity to make lots of little choices while he's young, you make it much more likely that he'll make the right decisions later on in life when the big decisions roll around!

FOR MORE INFORMATION

John Holt, *How Children Learn* (Cambridge, MA: Da Capo, 1995). A classic book that carries an important message about respecting children's dignity and supporting their ability to make good choices in their learning at home and school. Illustrates how adult efforts at authoritarian control can leave children baffled, confused, and defeated.

STRATEGY #15

Remove Allergens and Additives from Your Child's Diet
(Ages 4–18)

Over the past twenty years scientists have discovered a lot about the relationship between diet and the symptoms of ADHD. While the field is still dogged by controversy and much remains to be done in terms of future studies, there is a consensus emerging that diets that eliminate food additives and/or specific food allergens (wheat, nuts, milk, and soy) have a small but significant aggregate effect on improving ADHD-related behaviors in children and adolescents and may have an even greater impact on a small group of kids diagnosed with ADHD.[1]

The best way to tell whether a specific food additive or allergen is contributing to your child's ADHD symptoms is to set up what's called an elimination diet to test the impact of specific foods or additives on attention and/or behavior. This begins with the creation of an *oligoantigenic* diet. This is a diet which restricts the child's intake to a small selection of foods that have been proven to have little role in creating allergic or behavioral reactions. For a sample list of these foods go to: livestrong.com/article/96514-oligoantigenic-diet-list. Then, over a period of days, foods are slowly introduced into the child's diet one at a time while the parent or doctor monitors him for flare-ups in the symptoms of ADHD as well as the potential onset of physical symptoms such as irritability, fatigue, stuffy nose, dark circles under the eyes, puffiness around the eyes, abdominal pain, and/or headaches. To implement what is popularly known as the Feingold diet, you also need to eliminate specific preservatives, food dyes, artificial flavors, flavor enhancers (such as monosodium glutamate), and foods containing salicylates, which is a chemical found in many plants (such as bananas, pineapples, and dates). Once culprit foods or additives are discovered through these flare-ups, they can be removed from the diet, though some experts recommend rotating them on and off the diet for the foreseeable future.

Naturally, an intervention of this magnitude requires the cooperation of the entire family. It's especially important that you consult with your child to make sure that she is willing to go along with the sacrifices that might be necessary to make the effort a success. Otherwise this diet becomes an externally controlling force that she might well attempt to sabotage. Depending on her age, she can be involved in learning about the different additives and/or allergens, discovering how to read the ingredients section of packaged foods, and exploring creative cooking ideas that are additive free. If your child is older and enjoys writing or keeping statistics, she might want to be involved in the monitoring process as well. You might even make a game of it called "Catch the Culprit." Also, make sure to get support from other families participating in the same or a similar diet. Organizations such as the Feingold Association can put you in contact with participating families and supply you with a list of common food and additive triggers, shopping guides, creative recipes, and information regarding what to watch out for in popular restaurants and fast-food establishments. Changing your child's diet can involve a big commitment of time (and some scientists have speculated that it is the family cooperation that often is the real factor in behavior change), but remember this: What may be eating your child could be what your child is eating! (See also Strategy #30: Limit Junk Food, for an approach to diet that is much easier to implement.)

FOR FURTHER INFORMATION

The Feingold Association of the United States: 11849 Suncatcher Dr., Fishers, IN 46037; 1-631-369-9340; feingold.org.

Use Music to Focus and Calm
(Ages 6–18)

"Music hath charms to soothe the savage breast," goes the old saying. But does this apply to the ADHD breast as well? I think it does. Many parents of kids who've been diagnosed with ADHD have told me that their children have trouble attending to words (teachers' instructions, parents' directives) but not to music. In fact, they even suggest that for some of these kids, music serves as a real asset in helping calm and focus.

New research indicates that learning a musical instrument, especially one that involves keeping time with a group, may improve executive function skills.[1] In one study, students learned gamelan music, an Indonesian ensemble style that includes a lot of rhythm and synchronization, and after one year they had improved their attention on cognitive tests. The lead researcher noted: "It is possible that music practice could become a non-pharmacological intervention for problems such as ADHD (attention deficit-hyperactivity disorder)."[2] Another study suggested that music can increase dopamine neurotransmission in the brain.[3]

Researchers indicate while some kids who have been diagnosed with ADHD will experience a positive effect in focusing better with music as a background, for some it will be a distraction.[4] Because of this differential effect, I would suggest that you experiment with your child, allowing him to study or engage in other home tasks with his preferred music for a few days and then without the music for the same period of time. Then you can compare the results, including a look at the productivity and accuracy of work completed, attitudes and feelings that came up, and things you and your child or teen might have noticed about the beneficial or detrimental aspects of the music. See if different types of music make a difference in the results. For school settings, you could approach a teacher and suggest a similar experiment. In my own special education classes, I let students listen to their favorite music on headsets as long as they were making progress. Music was not allowed if it seemed to be distracting or disturbing individual students in any way. In historical times and still today in some cultures, music is prescribed to treat emotional and physical illness much as today's physicians prescribe medicine. For your child's attentional and behavioral difficulties, music may well turn out to be the good medicine you've both been seeking.

FOR FURTHER INFORMATION

Don Campbell, *The Mozart Effect for Children: Awakening Your Child's Mind, Health, and Creativity with Music* (New York: William Morrow, 2002). While focusing mainly on classical music and children's songs from birth to age ten, this book points to the powerful impact that music can have on perception, emotional well-being, language development, learning, and attention.

STRATEGY #17

Teach Your Child Self-Monitoring Skills
(Ages 7–18)

A big part of the lives of many children who have been diagnosed with ADHD involves other people monitoring their behavior. The physician uses rating scales to evaluate their symptoms. The teacher uses behavior checklists and test results to keep track of their performance. Parents use verbal feedback and sometimes a bit of yelling thrown in for good measure to let them know how the cow ate the cabbage. But the reality of the situation is that we want children and adolescents to be able to monitor their *own* behavior and performance so that they can internalize how they are doing at any given moment in time without having someone always telling them what to do. Fortunately, there are a number of simple strategies that parents and teachers can impart to kids to help them look at their own attention, behavior, and/or academic performance, thus giving them the ability to modify how they act, learn, and attend to outside demands.

One principle of behavioral therapy is a simple rule: If you ask someone to count a specific behavior they wish to eliminate or acquire, they begin to change their behavior. A teacher might have a child who regularly falls out of his chair at school keep track of the number of times he does this each day, write the number on a piece of paper, and give her the slip of paper at the end of the day. In this way, the child becomes the "owner" of his own behaviors and usually wants to decrease the number each day. Other tools that children can employ to take ownership of their own behaviors include checklists, rating scales (the very ones used by parents and teachers to rate them), and graphs (where they can keep track of their behaviors throughout the day, week, or month). To set up a self-monitoring program, sit down with your child and establish together a specific behavior that you want to see him increase or decrease, pick a way to monitor the behavior, fix intervals of time (for example, every five minutes during a homework session) for "check-ins" when he will evaluate how he's doing, and finally, a time when you can assess together the improvements that have occurred over a longer stretch of time.

Technology provides more sophisticated tools for engaging in self-monitoring. The timer feature on smartphones, for example, can be set to beep at periodic intervals. The child can monitor a behavior (such as, "Have I been paying attention to my homework?") during a study session. Similarly, the field of personal informatics has joined up with wearable technology to create devices like the MotivAider, which looks like a beeper and can be clipped on a belt or waistband. The user thinks of a word, phrase, or image that relates to the behavior she wants to eliminate or cultivate (for example, "Stay focused on my work"). and then programs the device to vibrate at selected intervals. When the vibration is felt, the user automatically thinks of the message. Self-monitoring pays dividends in terms of performing well in school. One study of elementary school children diagnosed with ADHD concluded that both self-monitoring of their attention and keeping track of their academic performance improved their ability to stay on-task in studying spelling words and increased their spelling test scores.[1] Other studies have shown similar positive results.[2] More important, self-monitoring empowers kids to take responsibility for their own actions, thus leading to greater levels of growth and maturity.

FOR FURTHER INFORMATION

I-Connect: www.iwillgraduate.org. Web-Based Solutions to Self-Management and Support Connections for High School Students. Online support site for an Android app (I-Connect) that provides customizable self-monitoring options (for example, "Am I on task?") with cuing as a sound, a flashing light, or a vibration. Collects data over time that can be analyzed and interpreted with a teacher, parent, or other mentor.

Use Effective Communication Skills
(Ages 4–18)

When confronted with the disruptive behaviors of a child, some parents have an almost irresistible impulse to nag, cajole, threaten, lecture, confront, judge, criticize, or ridicule in response. Research shows, in fact, that parents of kids diagnosed with ADHD in particular tend to use significantly more commanding and negative statements and fewer neutral and positive communications with their children than the parents of typically developing children.[1] However, such communications rarely have the intended effect of better-behaved children. More often, they worsen an already fractured parent–child relationship. That's why the development of more positive communication patterns between parent and child represents a major component in the effort to improve a child's behavior and a parent's peace of mind.

Positive discipline experts H. Stephen Glenn and Jane Nelsen suggest that the basis for a successful parent–child relationship is formed from "dialogue based on firmness with dignity and respect." They counsel parents to *avoid* five basic communication barriers to the development of closeness and trust with their kids:

- *Assuming.* "I didn't tell you that because I knew you'd get angry."
- *Rescuing.* "Now, remember to take your homework with you to school."
- *Directing.* "Pick up your clothes."
- *Expecting.* "I thought I could count on you to behave."
- *Adultisms.* "You know better than that!"

Instead, they suggest parents can *improve* their relationships with their kids immeasurably by employing five communication builders:

- *Checking.* "What were you thinking I wanted you to do?" (Not delivered in a sarcastic way.)
- *Exploring the what, why, and how.* "What could you do differently?" "Why were you so angry at me?" "How did that happen?"
- *Encouraging.* "I would really appreciate it if you could pitch in and get the garage cleaned up."
- *Celebrating.* "I think you did a terrific job on your homework assignment."
- *Respecting.* "I'd love to hear your ideas for solving this problem."

These positive communications help parents enter into the world of their children or adolescents to determine what feelings, motivations, and intentions might be underlying their misbehaviors. In addition, these patterns of communication honor children for behavior that is positive. Instead of closing off dialogue through the five *barriers* to communication, the *builders* help open up meaningful talk between parent and child, talk that might well prevent the need for an *if-then* ultimatum and instead lead to the peaceful resolution of conflicts.

A major key to developing positive channels of communication with your child or teen involves the use of active listening. This means putting your full attention into listening to your child's or teen's concerns, feelings, and needs, and letting him know that you hear and understand him. If your child comes bursting into the room in tears, for example, active listening means being able to make eye contact with your child, use a builder communication ("What's going on? Why are you so upset?"), listen carefully to his words ("Billy hit me, and then Mary said I was a crybaby"), and then reflect back to him what you've heard and that his feelings are okay ("It sounds like Billy and Mary have been treating you badly. That must have been really upsetting for you.").

Another important communication skill involves the use of "I" messages. When you precede a communication with the word *I*, you personalize it so that your child doesn't feel judged or commanded by an arbitrary and impersonal third force ("I'm really upset with you for hitting your sister" rather than "You've just broken rule number four of the household that says no hitting"). Parent-training experts Don Dinkmeyer and Gary D. McKay recommend that "I" messages include three components: *a clear description of the behavior, the feeling it creates in you,* and *the consequences of the behavior.* They use a simple formula for remembering how to phrase "I" messages:

1. When: "When you muddied up the kitchen floor . . .
2. I feel: . . . I felt angry . . .
3. Because: . . . because I had spent the whole morning cleaning and polishing it for the party this evening!"

This kind of communication allows children to see directly how their actions have an impact on the environment, and more important, it does this without blaming or judging.

Finally, pay attention to nonverbal communication. Make sure that your nonverbal message matches your verbal one or your child may become confused (for example, telling your child that "breaking the end table is not a big deal" while your face turns red with anger). It may take some fine-tuning on your part, but in the end your efforts to develop positive communication patterns with your child are likely to be richly rewarded with a closer parent–child relationship and one that has fewer kinks and more links in it (see also Strategy #19: Take a Parent Training Course).

FOR FURTHER INFORMATION

Don Dinkmeyer Sr., Gary D. McKay, and Don Dinkmeyer Jr., *The Parent's Handbook: Systematic Training for Effective Parenting* (Fredericksburg, VA: STEP, 2008).

Haim G. Ginott, *Between Parent and Child: The Bestselling Classic That Revolutionized Parent-Child Communication* (New York: Harmony, 2003).

H. Stephen Glenn and Jane Nelsen, *Raising Self-Reliant Children in a Self-Indulgent World: Seven Building Blocks for Developing Capable Young People* (New York: Harmony, 2000).

STRATEGY #19

Take a Parent Training Course
(Ages 18–88)

Parenting is hard work. Parenting a child with an ADHD diagnosis may be even harder according to several studies that chronicle the difficulties faced by families who have a child or children identified as having ADHD. But whether it's the child provoking the parent or the parent who is aggravating the child, clearly there needs to be a change in what clinicians call the *coercive cycle* that exists in many ADHD households. This cycle refers to a negative family pattern in which a child's behavior (not following a parent's request or demand) provokes a negative response from the adult (yelling, criticizing, punishing), which in turn creates more problem behavior by the child, and so on, until a certain point is reached at which either the child accedes to the parent's request or the parent gives up and accepts the child's attitude. This then sets in motion a chronic pattern of negative interactions that lead to poor outcomes for the child in terms of aggressive behavior, disrupted social skills, impaired peer relationships, and subpar academic performance. Research reveals that conflict is high in families with children who have been diagnosed with ADHD, and that in these families parents use more negative and ineffective strategies with their kids (such as power assertions, punishments, inconsistency) than parents of typically developing children.[1] Parents of ADHD-diagnosed kids also feel less self-efficacy in their ability to help their children, less welcomed by their children's schools and teachers, and less able to spend time and energy to help their kids with academics compared with parents of children not diagnosed with ADHD.[2]

Fortunately, research also suggests that parent training can help turn around such negative interactions. The best parenting programs focus on the underlying issues that impede good communication between parent and child. The Centers for Disease Control and Prevention (CDC) suggests that optimal parenting programs provide some of the following features:

- Teaching parents active listening skills
- Helping children recognize, identify, and label emotions
- Reducing negative communication patterns (sarcasm, criticism, etc.)
- Providing positive attention for children's appropriate behaviors
- Engaging in activities with the child that are positive, playful, creative, and free-flowing

The CDC also notes that the best parenting training formats include a component in which parents can interact directly with their children *during the training class* and receive feedback (not simply listen to lectures, do role-play, or practice new strategies with their children at home).[3]

You can find parenting training classes in a number of settings, including community parenting centers, university extension courses, clinics and hospitals that focus on ADHD issues, religious organizations, private franchised businesses, charities that sponsor courses, and individual parenting experts who do workshops and ongoing classes (see below for a Web site that can help you find a class). Pick a parenting class that focuses on positive parenting strategies and empowering children to succeed rather than a class that puts emphasis primarily on sending kids to time out, giving them rewards for good behavior, and engaging in other forms of externally controlling or positively coercive parenting. Positive parenting is the most important activity that can contribute to the betterment of our world. Make sure to get the help you need to become the very best parent you can be!

FOR FURTHER INFORMATION

National Parenting Education Network: npen.org/professional-development/parenting-education-networks-organizations-and-programs-by-state. Includes the directory Parenting Education Networks, Organizations, and Programs by State.

Nurture Your Child's Creativity
(Ages 4–16)

One of the most pronounced features of children and adolescents who end up with an ADHD diagnosis is that they're out-of-the-box kids. They don't look at the world in the same way as the more disciplined and organized kids or adults in our society do. They daydream, come up with wild ideas, do unique things, have original opinions about things, and exude more vitality and energy than the average child. A big question should be, Why do we label *these* kids as the disordered ones and not the children who are overly conscientious and anxious to win the approval of teachers and administrators? People who are slavishly obedient to adult authority are a much greater threat to society than those who are more rebellious and independent (do I need to give examples?).[1]

Although I presented quite a bit of evidence in chapter 8 for the creative abilities of kids diagnosed as ADHD, a number of experts in the field have claimed that kids with the diagnosis are no more creative than other kids and in some cases even less so because of their lack of focus.[2] Whether your child scores higher than average on a creativity test is really not the issue here. In fact, the truly creative person will be more likely to do *worse* on these tests, by having trouble fitting into the regimented format of standardized testing and the test examiner's rigid protocols (tests must be conducted in exactly the same way as they were when originally validated). The real focus should be on what you can do to validate your child's creative nature and how you can help him expand it. In many cases, kids diagnosed with ADHD are just like vessels brimming with vital energy looking for places to flow. Here are some guidelines for supporting your child's creative process:

- *Nourish your own creativity.* Your child looks to you as a role model, so get out those paints, musical instruments, clay, or collage materials and be creative alongside your child or teen.
- *Avoid judgments, criticisms, and comparisons.* These are the deadly

enemies of creativity that can stop it in its tracks; even praise can destroy creativity (the child will create things just to please you and to get more praise).

- *Honor your child's individuality.* Accept your child's creations even if they seem flawed or incomplete to you; creativity is more of a process than a finished product.
- *Don't force your child to do something "creative."* Pushing your child to produce is likely to backfire; creative people sometimes go through long periods of stagnation or inactivity before inspiration kicks in.
- *Provide the resources your child needs.* If your child enjoys scribbling with crayons on a sketchpad, don't overwhelm her with a professional artist's array of materials; listen to her needs and provide her with what she needs and asks for (maybe a larger box of crayons or bigger sheets of paper).

Childhood is a time of curiosity, inventiveness, and creativity for all kids. Honoring and encouraging the creative development of kids diagnosed with ADHD, who think in original, unusual, or innovative ways, are among the best things you can do for them!

FOR FURTHER INFORMATION

Bobbi Connor, *The Giant Book of Creativity for Kids: 500 Activities to Encourage Creativity in Kids Ages 2 to 12—Play, Pretend, Draw, Dance, Sing, Write, Build, Tinker* (Boulder, CO: Roost Books, 2015).

STRATEGY #21

Hold a Positive Image of Your Child
(Ages 4–18)

The German poet Goethe once said, "Treat people as if they were what they ought to be and you help them to become what they are capable of being." This means that we ought to hold in our mind's eye the most positive vision possible of our kids. One of the biggest problems I have with the ADHD myth is that it creates an image of the child based on disease, damage, and deficit—not on asset, affirmation, and advantage. That's why I recommend that parents and professionals avoid using terms like *the ADHD child* to describe a child who's experiencing learning or behavior problems. If a child is having trouble at home or in school, the last thing he needs is to be saddled with a new label. What he requires most of all is to be surrounded by adults who see the best in him.

Proponents of the ADHD myth sometimes say that the use of the ADHD label itself is liberating for many parents and children. Having a name to put to something that has been troubling them for years offers a means of controlling and to some extent triumphing over that confusion. It's not unusual for a parent to say, "I used to think that my child was crazy . . . that *I* was crazy . . . that my child was lazy and unmotivated. . . . Now I realize it's all because he's ADHD!" I would agree that the use of the term *ADHD* is a step up from informal labels like "stupid," "crazy," "brat," "nincompoop," and "menace to society." However, I believe there are further steps up the label ladder that we can take in constructing more positive images of these kids.

I realize some parents might have difficulty initially creating a positive image of their child. If you've had to endure years of tantrums, power struggles, defiance, and other difficulties, then positive traits might not easily come to mind. However, I'd like to invite you to reframe some of the negative terms you might be using to describe your child into positive terms that can serve as "hope magnets" toward which your child can be pulled. Here are some examples:

INSTEAD OF THINKING OF YOUR CHILD AS	THINK OF YOUR CHILD AS
hyperactive	energetic
impulsive	spontaneous
distractible	creative
a daydreamer	imaginative
inattentive	a global thinker with a wide focus
unpredictable	flexible
argumentative	independent
stubborn	committed
irritable	sensitive
aggressive	assertive
attention deficit disordered	unique

Remember that a *hyperactive* child is an *active* child. The energies that many kids labeled ADHD possess represent a valuable natural resource that, properly channeled, can really make a difference in the world!

FOR FURTHER INFORMATION

Robert Rosenthal and Lenore Jacobson, *Pygmalion in the Classroom: Teacher Expectation and Pupils' Intellectual Development* (Carmarthen, UK: Crown House, 2003). Describes the famous education experiment in which teachers' expectations increased students' intellectual growth.

STRATEGY #22

Provide Appropriate Spaces for Learning
(Ages 4–18)

Children diagnosed with ADHD who are often on the move or who have a wider attentional focus may need a learning space that is larger or more flexible than that of the average child. Many of these kids have to learn in overcrowded classrooms that allow for little flexibility and under conditions that may even worsen hyperactive symptoms. When animals are crowded into cages for long periods of time, symptoms of stress—including aggression and hyperactivity—occur at epidemic levels. Similar results can be observed in human populations.[1] Rutgers University professor Carol S. Weinstein commented: "Nowhere [but in schools] are large groups of individuals packed so closely together for so many hours, yet expected to perform at peak efficiency on difficult learning tasks and to interact harmoniously."[2]

Crowding isn't the only problem in providing appropriate spaces for learning. School and home spaces may trigger or worsen symptoms of hyperactivity if they are *underarousing*. Classroom design expert Anita Olds describes some of the problems in many schools: "The barrenness and homogeneity of the physical parameters of classrooms can deaden arousal and interfere with children's capacities to stay alert and attentive. Cold, shiny tile floors, multiple chairs and tables of identical design and hard finish, dull-colored walls lacking recesses or changes in texture, ceilings of uniform height, which dwarf the size of the room's occupants, and fluorescent lights, which spread a constant, high-powered glare over all activities indiscriminately, all contribute to feelings of boredom, listlessness, and dislike for the settings in which learning takes place" (see also Strategy #10: Build, Borrow, or Buy Wiggle Furniture and Strategy #62: Provide Access to Natural and Full-Spectrum Light).[3] In a bland classroom space such as this, children diagnosed with ADHD may find it necessary to create their own stimulation through fidgeting, daydreaming, socializing, or wandering around to meet their higher arousal quotas.

At school, these kids should have their own desks or learning areas marked out for them. At home, your child should have his or her own private study area. It might be a desk in a corner of the bedroom or a special nook in a basement or study. Make sure, though, that it's comfortable and relatively free of major distractions such as a television or social chatter (see also Strategy #34: Eliminate Distractions and Strategy #72: Suggest Effective Study Strategies). Classrooms should have a variety of study spaces to accommodate the needs of kids' different energy states. Learning-styles consultant Rita Dunn had her students studying in a number of innovative spaces, including a math tub (a free-standing bathtub that one can lie in only while doing math work), a reading teepee, a couch, a tent, and a rocking chair. In some schools I've worked in, parents have volunteered their time to create special multileveled lofts, where kids can snuggle into private spaces to study. To provide more variety in classroom spaces, Olds suggests some of the following additions: pillows, plants, soft furniture, kid-size furniture, mobiles, murals, carpets, canopies, and wall dividers. The same type of variety should exist in a child's home study areas. Make sure your child has a role in designing these areas. The space in which your child does his learning should be considered almost sacred—in the sense that he is giving birth to new ideas. Let's treat these areas with respect, then, and give our children the space they need in which to learn.

FOR FURTHER INFORMATION

Kids' Rooms: Simple Projects for Designing Child-friendly Spaces in Your Home (Stockholm: Bonnier Books, 2007).

STRATEGY #23

Encourage Your Child's Interests
(Ages 4–12)

Some ADHD researchers have suggested that children diagnosed with ADHD have a motivation deficit.[1] I believe that such a label, like ADHD itself, is misleading. Kids diagnosed with ADHD don't have a motivational deficit. They have motivations toward other goals—ones that are considered unimportant by ADHD experts, and they're not always motivated by the things that authorities *want* them to be motivated by. The rewards that drive so-called normal kids—praise, a letter grade on a report card, a weekly allowance—aren't always effective with kids diagnosed with ADHD. These kids are more likely to go their own way and be driven by inner motivations and interests.

What then are these interests? Unfortunately, there is virtually nothing in the ADHD literature on what actually interests these kids. Why don't we know if kids diagnosed with ADHD love lizards, astronomy, rocks, music, field trips, carpentry, or a thousand other things? It's because ADHD proponents are much more focused on what ADHD kids *aren't* interested in: lectures, textbooks, worksheets, boring routines, endless instructions, rote skills, and so forth. Apparently these are the things ADHD professionals consider most important in life; why else would they claim that noninterest in them qualifies children for a neurologically based motivation disorder?

The chart of 105 activities below represents only a small fraction of the full range of possibilities for interests, but it can nevertheless help you to begin to focus in on what motivates *your* child.

The best way to discover your child's interests is to observe him during times when no one is telling him what to do. What are the things that fill him with enthusiasm, excitement, interest, and passion? What are the activities that most absorb his energies and attention? Once you've discovered what they are, work delicately to help preserve these interests by providing resources that can help draw them out or extend them into other directions. A

WHAT'S YOUR CHILD INTERESTED IN?

action figures	drawing	photography
airplanes	eating	pictures
aquariums	ecology	playhouse
art	electricity	playing
astronomy	electronics	poetry
balloons	finger paints	puppets
balls	fishing	puzzles
baseball	football	radios
baseball cards	gardening	reading books
bicycling	geography	rubber stamp sets
biographies	hiking	running
birds	history	science fiction
blocks	hockey	Scouts
board games	insects	seashells
boats	jungle gym	secret codes
the body	kites	sewing
bubbles	Lego blocks	singing
cards	lizards	skateboarding
carpentry	machines	skating
cars and trucks	magic	sky watching
cartoons	magnets	soccer
cheerleading	make-believe	stamp collecting
chemistry set	makeup	storytelling
clay	map reading	stuffed animals
clocks	marbles	swimming
clothes	martial arts	talking
coin collecting	math	telephoning
coloring	microscopes	television
computers	miniature soldiers	telling jokes
cooking	money	traveling
dancing	movies	tree climbing
digging	music	video games
dinosaurs	musical instruments	water
dolls	other cultures	weather
drama	pets	writing

mother of a twelve-year-old son diagnosed with ADHD, for example, helped fuel his interest in animals by bringing into the house a turtle and some hermit crabs that he could care for and study.

It's important not to overwhelm a child's interests with too much adult "help." Many times, children prefer to engage in hobbies and activities by themselves and might resist adult interference, however well intentioned. Regard your child's interests—no matter how trivial they may seem or how far removed from the practical world they are—with a sense of honor and respect. It's far more likely that your child's personal interests will lead him to a successful future than that ADHD drugs or behavior modification programs will. One parent related to me how her distractible and fidgety daughter from age nine to age eleven created an imaginary world of "weepals." There were 164 of these fanciful creatures in all—and for each one she gave a special name, personality, and set of unique characteristics. She even created houses and furniture for them. By the age of twenty-three she had translated this interest into a successful career coordinating several departments of a law firm! So then, what interests *your* child?

FOR FURTHER INFORMATION

Monica McCabe Cardoza, *Child's Play: Enriching Your Child's Interests, from Rocket Science to Rock Climbing, Stamp Collecting to Sculpture* (New York: Citadel, 2003).

STRATEGY #24

Establish Consistent Rules, Routines, and Transitions
(Ages 4–16)

If there is one maxim that everyone involved with ADHD can agree on—doubters and believers alike—it's that children with this alphabet soup label need consistency and reliable structures in their daily life. Researchers at the Institute of Human Development at the University of California, Berkeley, have identified three primary parenting styles that bear a striking similarity to the fairy tale "Goldilocks and the Three Bears." One parenting style provides too much control, one provides too little, and the third consists of just the right amount of structure in a child's life.[1] They are

- *The authoritarian style* (the "rigid brick wall family"). Parenting expert Barbara Coloroso identifies this type of family as consisting of dictatorial parents who demand blind obedience from their kids. Such families combine high expectations, robotic consistency, and high control with low levels of warmth and communication.
- *The permissive child-rearing style* (the "jellyfish family"). These parents are essentially the opposite of authoritarian parents. They project high warmth and communication but have little control, offer inconsistent or no daily routines, and provide few clear expectations for their kids.
- *The authoritative parenting style* (the "backbone family"). This optimal parenting approach combines the best aspects of the first two patterns. These parents provide clear and consistent rules and expectations within the context of a caring and loving family.

Research suggests that children who are raised in backbone families show the greatest independence, leadership, social responsibility, originality, self-confidence, and achievement orientation. Kids from rigid brick wall families, on the other hand, tend to be obedient but less independent or confident of themselves, whereas children in jellyfish families are the worst off of all: They lack social responsibility, aren't particularly independent, are low in self-confidence, and have high anxiety.

All children need clear limits and consistent boundaries. But children who themselves are inconsistent in their behaviors need them even more. If a child who already feels like a cue ball caroming around on a pool table has to live in a family where meals are haphazard, rules are inconsistently enforced, and events arise without warning, then he's likely to bounce clear off the billiard table. Consequently, a primary responsibility for parents and teachers of kids who already have behavior difficulties is to provide a safe and protected space at home and at school, an environment with consistent rules, regular routines, and efficient transitions to help clear a steady path through the day. Some of the following suggestions can help accomplish these goals:

- See that your child gets up at about the same time every morning, has regularly scheduled meals with family members, and goes to bed about the same time every evening (see also Strategy #77: Make Sure Your Child Gets Sufficient Sleep).

- Create a special daily and/or weekly calendar with your child where he can write or draw in events that are coming up. Keep this calendar in the child's bedroom where he can frequently see it. A number of computer apps are also available that do this, including Cozi and HomeRoutines.

- When unpredictable events are brewing on the horizon, prepare your child for them with a few words ("Today when I pick you up at school, we won't be going home. We're going to the airport to welcome Grandma for a visit"). It might be helpful to suggest that your child visualize the new event so that when it comes it won't be so upsetting to his daily routine.

If your child's life has been unstable up until now and/or rules have been inconsistently enforced, he may initially respond to the "new consistency" with irritation, anger, or other negative feelings. However, when your consistency is accompanied by a sense of respect and caring for your child, you can rest assured that you're providing him with the backbone he'll need to make his own way in the world as an adult.

FOR FURTHER INFORMATION

Michele Borba, *The Big Book of Parenting Solutions: 101 Answers to Your Everyday Challenges and Wildest Worries* (San Francisco: Jossey-Bass, 2009).

Barbara Coloroso, *Kids Are Worth It!: Giving Your Child the Gift of Inner Discipline* (New York: William Morrow, 2002).

Celebrate Successes
(Ages 4–18)

Think back to a typical day with your child or teen. Did you remind him three times to clean up his room? Did you yell at him for taking that toy away from his sister? Did you put him in time out for sassing you? The days and nights of parents who have a child diagnosed with ADHD can be filled with stressful events like these and many more besides. But what about the things that your child has done *right* during the day? Did these events pass by silently, without acknowledgment? If so, then this strategy can help you catch those positive occurrences and let your child know that you saw them and value the effort that it took to achieve them.

There are a number of ways in which you can celebrate successes whenever you "catch your child being good" or when you see that your child has done something meriting special recognition. Here are a few suggestions:

- During family meals, mention something positive that you saw your child or teen doing during the day.
- Take photos of your child or teen displaying something made or done that she feels proud of and post them (with her permission) on a "celebration bulletin board."
- When your child or adolescent achieves something of great significance, take the family out to a restaurant and have a celebration dinner.
- Let your child or adolescent have a party with his friends at your home to celebrate milestone events (winning a prize, receiving an award at Scouts, getting good grades, being mentioned in the news, graduating).
- Write a letter to your child or teen letting him know that you saw and appreciated the positive things he did that day or week, and then list them.
- Make personalized success certificates that you can give to your teen or child in recognition of positive accomplishments (customize them to include the positive event).

- Bake cupcakes and when your child has done something special, stick a lit candle in one of them and present it to your child, perhaps with a song (how about "Happy Victory to You"?).
- Make a video of your child narrating her own success story that she can illustrate with props.
- Before bedtime, review with your child the positive things she's done during the day.

No event is too small to be celebrated. If you've asked your child or teen to take out the garbage and he does it only for his bedroom, then celebrate what he *did* do rather than rail against him for forgetting the other rooms. See the positive side of things that may initially look negative to you. So, if your child or adolescent plays a lot of video games, instead of complaining and telling him to do something else for a change, show some interest in his scores and celebrate with him when he reaches a certain level of mastery. These interventions may seem trivial to you, but they have a cumulative effect over time. Ultimately, they will empower your child to feel good about himself and will help foster the kinds of attitudes and behaviors that you want your child or teen to display for the rest of his life.

FOR FURTHER INFORMATION

Jenny Rosenstrach, *How to Celebrate Everything: Recipes and Rituals for Birthdays, Holidays, Family Dinners, and Every Day In Between* (New York: Ballantine Books, 2016).

STRATEGY #26

Make Time for Your Child to Play
(Ages 4–10)

Children for the most part have stopped playing in our culture and the consequences of this trend can be devastating to society. Children no longer spend dreamy hours playing make-believe, running in the fields pretending that they're pirates, climbing trees, turning cardboard boxes into castles, and playing submarine captain in the bathtub. Instead, they're indoors watching television, surfing the Internet, and texting their friends. One outcome of this drastic change in children's leisure time behavior is the growing incidence of attention deficit hyperactivity disorder. When children play, according to neuroscientist Jaak Panksepp, they exercise their frontal lobes and establish important neural connections to the limbic system or emotional brain.[1] These are the areas of the brain most at risk in children labeled ADHD. Panksepp has indicated that play facilitates the inhibition of behaviors (a positive development) and that ADHD drugs actually reduce playfulness in both rats and children.[2]

Let me clarify what I mean when I say *play*. I'm not talking about soccer competition, video games, educational games, or play that has rules largely made up and supervised by adults. I'm talking about child-initiated play that includes such things as imaginative journeys, make-believe scenarios, creative products like mud pies, active rambling on playground equipment, and rough-and-tumble play in natural settings. These are the activities that help grow a child's brain and that lead to cognitive, social, and emotional development. Moreover, when children play, they do the very thing that highly creative people like Albert Einstein, Isaac Newton, and Nobel Prize–winner Barbara McClintock did when they played with ideas.[3] Children need plenty of time to engage in imaginative play, rough-and-tumble play, and creative play using whatever materials the child can lay his hands on. Here are some guidelines for facilitating an environment in which your child can engage in free play:

- You can and should be playful with your child to let him have a role model from which to create his own patterns of play.
- Don't tell your child how to play; at the most, take part in a play scenario that your child has created and has invited you to engage in, but don't hog the spotlight and, above all, don't control the action!
- Have materials around the house and yard that lend themselves to child-initiated play, including cast-off clothes for dress-up; art materials; cardboard boxes; a backyard fort; old magazines for cut and paste; and a variety of toys, dolls, and miniature figures (action figures, soldiers, buildings, trees).

• Give your child access to a park, nature setting, or playground where she can spontaneously engage in playful behaviors, either alone or with friends (see also Strategy #5: Make Time for Nature).

Most important, give your child the *time* to play. So many kids these days have their daily schedules filled with classes, tutors, piano lessons, soccer practice, and other activities that leave no extra time for free unstructured play. By giving your child several hours of playtime every week (free from technology), you can help her develop the neurological connections that lead to mature behaviors in thinking, attending, socializing, and emotional self-regulation.

FOR FURTHER INFORMATION
David Elkind, *The Power of Play: Learning What Comes Naturally* (Cambridge, MA: Da Capo, 2007). One of the nation's most renowned developmental psychologists provides critical information on what constitutes real play and how to foster it in the home, school, and broader community.

STRATEGY #27

Be a Personal Coach to Your Child
(Ages 8–18)

A few years back, when ADHD for adults became a major trend, a new type of specialist emerged in the ADHD community called an ADHD coach. The coach was there to encourage, motivate, help set goals, provide resources, offer strategies, and in other ways do what an athletic coach does for a sports team: support the effort while staying out of the game. The coaching model offers an opportunity for parents who are willing to spend a little extra time to help their kids be successful. By being a coach for your child, you can detach yourself somewhat from your parenting role—where you feel personally responsible for clothing, feeding, and disciplining him—and offer expertise to help him come up with his own solutions to whatever life puts in his way.

The job description for being a successful ADHD coach to your child includes the following duties (using homework as an example). You can

- *Help your child come up with motivating strategies.* "What type of ideas or feelings might help motivate you to finish your homework?"
- *Assist your child in setting realistic goals for himself.* "How many word problems do you think you can do in an hour?"
- *Think of resources that might be useful to your child.* "I know some sites on the Internet you might check out for information to help you with your assignment."
- *Help develop time-management skills.* "If you use a timer you can keep track of how long you have left to work."
- *Suggest work-arounds to help your child meet a goal.* "If you use the Dragon NaturallySpeaking computer program we gave you, you can save time getting down your ideas for the book report you have to write." (See also Strategy #100: Show Your Child Work-Arounds to Get Things Done.)
- *Aid your child in identifying his strengths and how to use them.* "You love taking pictures with your phone, so what about using a few photos to go along with this essay you're writing?"
- *Prompt your child to think about the expectations that others have for him.* "What exactly did your teacher tell you about how to do the assignment?"
- *Ask your child to consider what he might have done differently.* "What do you think you could have done on that homework assignment that you got a D on last week to turn it into an A or B project?"
- *Encourage your child to do his best.* "I've seen you do incredible things with other assignments your teacher has given to you, so I know you can ace this one too."
- *Celebrate accomplishments.* See Strategy #25: Celebrate Successes.

Remember, just as you wouldn't do your child's homework for him, it's important that you help him work out *his own* solutions to the difficulties and questions that come up regarding such issues as doing schoolwork, completing household obligations, getting along with peers, forging a better relationship with his teacher, and saving his allowance for a special goal. And don't forget, as a coach you're also part of his cheerleading squad, so be positive, radiate lots of energy, and believe in your child's capacity to become victorious in whatever challenges he faces.

FOR FURTHER INFORMATION
Nikki Grant, *Life Coaching for Kids: A Practical Manual to Coach Children and Young People to Success, Well-being and Fulfilment* (London: Jessica Kingsley, 2014).

STRATEGY #28

Build Resilience in Your Child
(Ages 7–18)

The great inventor Thomas Edison, who many people believe would have been diagnosed with ADHD had he grown up in twenty-first-century America, once completed a series of ten thousand experiments on a particular invention he was trying to develop. All of them had failed to produce the anticipated results: "I have not failed," said Edison. "I've just found 10,000 things that won't work."[1] Edison went on to receive more than one thousand patents for his inventions. His dauntless energy and spirit epitomize a key psychological trait that gives people the ability to face difficulty without flinching: *resilience*. Resilience is the ability to maintain a positive and proactive attitude regarding oneself and one's place in the world even in the midst of severe adversity.

Many ADHD-diagnosed kids go through a lot of adversity in their young lives. They have interpersonal problems with teachers, peers, and parents, difficulty with schoolwork and chores, and challenges in organizing, attending to, and directing their daily activities. It's perhaps not surprising that a recent study concluded adolescents diagnosed with ADHD have lower levels of resilience than typically developing teens.[2] However, the good news is that individuals can change dramatically from having a maladaptive attitude to having one that is resilient. While life events themselves have a strong bearing on the development of resilience, according to some research the most important factor in developing resilience in a child or adolescent is *having at least one stable and committed relationship with a supportive parent, caregiver, or other adult in their life.*[3]

You can be that person. But to maximize the likelihood that your child will become one of those lucky individuals who have a resilient attitude, there are a number of strategies you can use in your interactions with him. You can build resilience in your child by helping him:

- *Reframe negative events into positive learning opportunities.* Not think to himself, "Life sucks, I got put on detention in school last week," but instead realize, "I learned two ways I can stay out of detention from some kids who were in there with me."
- *Differentiate between things he can control and those he can't.* To think, "Okay, I got an F on that exam last week. I can't change that, but if I study hard, I can improve my grade next time."
- *View difficult tasks as challenges rather than setups for failure.* Not to think to himself, "I know my teacher has it in for me," but instead believe, "I'm going to show my teacher that her first impressions of me were wrong."
- *Regard setbacks as temporary rather than a permanent state of affairs.* Not to feel, "I'm just a troublemaker," but instead realize, "I looked bad when I started that fight, but it'll blow over and things will get better, I just know it."
- *Make the decision to see himself as an actor rather than a victim.* Not to think to himself, "That bully is going to beat the crap out of me after school today," but instead respond, "I'm taking some friends of mine with me when I leave school today so that bully knows I have friends who've got my back."

When talking with your child, use some of the communication strategies listed elsewhere in this book (Strategy #18: Use Effective Communication Skills) and gently guide him in the right direction in terms of suggesting things he might say to himself after suffering a negative life event, whether it be a breakup with a girlfriend or a bad score on an important test. If you practice these strategies along with him, you'll be providing good role modeling that will encourage him to become more resilient in response to the life challenges he's already gone through as well as those that are inevitably up ahead.

FOR FURTHER INFORMATION
Kenneth R. Ginsberg, *Building Resilience in Children and Teens: Giving Kids Roots and Wings*, 3rd ed. (Elk Grove Village, IL: American Academy of Pediatrics, 2014).

STRATEGY #29

Give Instructions in Attention-Grabbing Ways
(Ages 4–16)

A common problem that can vex parents of kids who've been diagnosed with ADHD is giving a child instructions ("Take out the garbage," "Do your homework") and not having the child follow them. Whether the erring child didn't hear (as kids often claim), forgot (another good excuse), or as ADHD experts assert, failed to comply because of some central processing deficit is a moot point (although, see Strategy #37: Strengthen Your Child's Working Memory). What really matters is finding a way to get kids to follow instructions. There are in fact many better ways of grabbing a child's attention that can be enjoyable for both parent and child.

A key principle in developing attention-grabbers is to make them vivid and compelling. According to Tony Buzan, author of *Use Both Sides of Your Brain*, people are more likely to attend to and remember something if it:

- moves (kinetic)
- is colorful
- is imaginative
- is exaggerated in some way
- is novel
- has multisensory features
- is absurd

Based on these elements, here are some suggestions the next time you give your child instructions or tell her something important:

- *Sing the instructions to her.* The parents of world-famous pianist Arthur Rubinstein did this when other methods failed to reach the young prodigy.
- *Speak in visual metaphors.* One mother who was constantly reminding her child to turn off the lights when leaving the room had success when she told him to "turn on the dark."
- *Use physical signals.* For taking out the garbage, create a prearranged gesture—like holding your nose and saying "Pee yew!"—as a cue for her to do her assigned chore.
- *Employ photos as pictorial cues.* Take a photo of your child's room when it's clean. Then, the next time you want her to clean her room, simply show her the photo or have it on her plate at the breakfast table as a reminder.
- *Engage your child or teen in the creation of attention-getting devices.* She might, for example, want to draw her own pictures (such as a garbage can, a messy room with an arrow pointing to a clean room, a properly set table) that anyone in the family can then show her if she's forgotten to do a task.
- *Touch your child while giving instructions.* This acts to "ground" the child in her body and makes it more likely she will pay attention.
- *Engage your child in a physical action.* Before you say something to her, throw a beanbag or a ball saying, "Catch!" and then quickly follow up with the important information.

There's no reason why you should have to be a "parrot parent" endlessly squawking the same instructions over and over again to your attention-challenged children. If anything, parents (and teachers) should be more like peacocks, proudly displaying a colorful plumage of strategies for winning a child's recognition.

FOR FURTHER INFORMATION

Eric Jensen, *Brain Compatible Strategies: Hundreds of Easy-to-Use Brain-Compatible Activities that Boost Attention, Motivation, Learning, and Achievement* (Thousand Oaks, CA: Corwin Press, 2004). Strategies for grabbing the brain's attention.

STRATEGY #30

Limit Junk Food
(Ages 4–18)

For almost fifty years a small but committed group of parents have felt very strongly, despite denials from ADHD experts, that food was a major contributor to their children's hyperactivity or ADHD symptoms. Many of them rallied behind support for the Feingold Diet, allergy-free diets, or other ways of modifying food intake for their kids (see Strategy #15: Remove Allergens and Additives from Your Child's Diet). However, little attention during that time was ever focused on the impact of the plain old junk food millions of children were consuming daily from McDonald's, Burger King, Hardee's, KFC, Wendy's, Jack in the Box, Carl's Jr., and other fast-food outlets. It turns out that by simply eliminating or cutting way back on your child's intake of these highly processed, high-fat foods, you may be doing quite a bit to alleviate ADHD symptoms in your child.

A number of international studies over the past five years point to a link between the consumption of junk food and ADHD. A study of school-aged children in Tehran, Iran, found a link between a fast-food dietary pattern and ADHD.[1] Korean researchers studying the diets of elementary school children between the ages of seven and twelve concluded that there was a connection between a "snack food" diet and ADHD, and conversely, that a "traditional-healthy diet" (low fat, high carbohydrate, high intake of fatty acids and minerals) was associated with lower odds of having ADHD.[2] And an Australian study suggested that a Western dietary pattern with higher intakes of total fat, saturated fat, refined sugars, and sodium and deficient in omega-3 fatty acids, fiber, and folate was associated with an ADHD diagnosis in adolescents.[3] Curiously, there seems to be a noted absence of research from the United States, leading one to question whether the fast-food industry, whose corporate headquarters are mostly situated in the United States, might have had any influence on directing research agendas.[4]

Parents who still want to take their kids to fast-food outlets would do well to support their children in choosing healthy foods that are on the menu. Instead of a double cheeseburger, fries, and a malted milk, choose a grilled chicken salad, apple slices, and an ice tea. However, the scarcity of truly healthy foods on most fast-food chains' menus should be a wake-up call for parents to stop these junk food visits and begin a practice of more often eating nourishing food at home. A McDonald's Happy Meal may turn out to be an unhappy meal for your child and your family when the ADHD symptoms start to kick in.

FOR MORE INFORMATION

Eric Schlosser, *Fast Food Nation: The Dark Side of the All-American Meal* (Boston: Mariner, 2012).

STRATEGY #31

Empower Your Child with Strength-Based Learning
(Ages 7–18)

One of the things I discovered from my years as a special education teacher is that when it comes to helping kids with special needs, the schools tend to focus the lion's share of their energy on remediating weaknesses, not on harnessing strengths. If the student is weak in reading and has auditory sequencing difficulties, for example, then he most likely spends his time blending phonemes (the sound units like *nn*, *uh*, and *tuh* that make up words like *nut*) using some of the following strategies: filling out phonemic awareness worksheets, practicing decoding skills while reading in a group or to the teacher, or playing a phonics board game with classmates. Whatever strengths the student has (let's say, musical ability) would be beside the point and used only perhaps as a reward for completing his phonics worksheets (allowing him to listen to his favorite music).

On the other hand, if the schools really took strength-based learning seriously, then they would be more creative about their learning methods and use the student's musical capabilities to help him learn to read. How could they do this? In several ways. First, they could use musical lyrics to his favorite songs as the texts for him to use in his practice reading. Second, teachers could treat each of the forty-four phonemes in the English language as a musical sound, or a sound from nature, and have fun with the student putting together these sounds in creative ways. Third, they could have him work on a computer program that slows the phoneme sounds down (so that they actually have a musical quality) and then asks him to blend or combine the different sounds together. Not many schools currently engage in this type of strength-based learning. As part of your advocacy for your child at school, this is something you can and should talk to your child's teachers about (strength-based learning is an up-and-coming trend in education). But you can also use this strategy in helping your child complete his schoolwork at home. The chart below gives you some suggestions for how you might go about doing this.

IF YOUR CHILD IS WORKING ON THIS SKILL OR SUBJECT	AND ONE STRENGTH OF HIS HAPPENS TO BE	THEN CONSIDER THIS LEARNING STRATEGY
spelling word list	artistic ability	propose that he make pictures out of the words on the list (put spokes in the loops of the word *bicycle*)
vocabulary word list	dramatic expressiveness	suggest that he act out the meanings of the different words on the list
an essay on what he did during the summer	loves horses	encourage him to write about the horse breeding farm he visited during the summer
memorizing the times tables	athletic ability (basketball)	have him recite the times facts ($2 \times 3 = 6$) while he shoots baskets
studying for a history exam	good social skills	recommend that he get a group of his classmates together to form a study group
understanding a science concept	hands-on ability	suggest that he create a hands-on model or experiment to illustrate the concept

While speaking about their ADHD-diagnosed son, Shelley and Andy Raffino of Chicago observed: "We spent so much time trying to fix our son's weaknesses that we never focused on his strengths. The constant negativity, pressure and medication destroyed Robbie's confidence."[1] Make sure that you don't make the same mistake. Use your child's strengths to help him develop in his areas of greatest need.

FOR FURTHER INFORMATION

Thomas Armstrong, *Neurodiversity in the Classroom: Strength-Based Strategies to Help Students with Special Needs Succeed in School and Life* (Alexandria, VA: ASCD, 2012).

STRATEGY #32

Support Full Inclusion of Your Child in a Regular Classroom

(Ages 7–18)

To many parents of children who've been diagnosed with ADHD, the idea of getting special education services from the local public school system sounds all too tempting. It simply makes intuitive sense that if a child is having trouble in a regular classroom environment, he ought to be removed from that environment and placed in another setting where he *can* succeed. Then, when he's "better," he can be placed back in the regular program. That's the theory, anyway.

The truth of special education, however, is something altogether different. Special education exists as its own self-contained universe with its own special tests, special texts, special materials, special jargon, and special *problems.* Your child has every chance of entering a world where he will be defined according to his *disability*, not his *ability*. Like a prison, the special ed classroom could be the place where your child learns special misbehaviors from the school's real troublemakers. Kids in regular classrooms might then begin looking at your child as a freak, a "'tard," or worse. Teachers in regular programs may begin to see your child as a "disabled" learner instead of a student with a bright future. Instead of being surrounded by teachers and learning experiences that seek to draw out the best in your child, the special education classroom could spend most of the time concentrating on your child's weak points. How many adults would like to have their own personal limitations highlighted six hours a day, five days a week?

Let me hasten to say that not all special education classrooms are like this. Many special ed programs are taught by highly committed teachers who teach to a student's strengths, who use state-of-the-art learning strategies, and who work intensively to get the child back into a regular classroom environment as soon as possible. But in general, parents of children diagnosed with ADHD are well advised to think in terms of *full inclusion* in the regular classroom for their kids.

The advantages of your child being fully included in a nonlabeling, nontracked classroom (as opposed to a separate classroom containing only special education students) are many. First, your child will be exposed to positive role models for behavior from the other students. Such contact may be instrumental in helping your child develop important social skills if this area has been a problem in the past. Second, your child has a much greater chance of not being singled out as a special ed kid (one child in a special education classroom commented that the "ed" in *special ed* referred to "extra *dumb*"). Instead, your child will function as a "normal" person—a nonlabel most kids desperately desire to have during their growing-up years. Third, your child will be exposed to the same subject matter as everyone else instead of taking a separate curriculum in a special ed class. This means he will be less likely to fall behind his peers if he is removed from the regular classroom. Finally, he will encounter a rich diversity of learning styles and backgrounds among his peers instead of being in a group where everyone shares the same or a similar label.

Make sure, though, that your child's school provides plenty of support for full inclusion, including extra support personnel, and a curriculum that is based on differentiated learning (learning that is tailored to the needs of each individual child). Not having this support is almost as bad as not receiving any services at all. In a society like ours that is becoming increasingly diverse, it's especially important to provide kids with the message that differences are good! In a truly inclusive classroom, your child's differences can be celebrated along with those of everyone else.

FOR FURTHER INFORMATION

William Henderson, *The Blind Advantage: How Going Blind Made Me a Stronger Principal and How Including Children with Disabilities Made Our School Better for Everyone* (Cambridge, MA: Harvard Education Press, 2011).

STRATEGY #33

Teach Your Child How His Brain Works
(Ages 7–18)

ADHD experts advocate telling newly diagnosed children about what ADHD is, how it affects them, how it's treated, and how they can thrive in spite of it. One of the components of this reeducation plan often includes a description of how the ADHD brain works. Unfortunately, these explanations too often leave a great deal to be desired. Of particular concern is their heavy emphasis on machine metaphors. In one book written for ADHD-diagnosed kids titled *Otto Learns About His Medicine*, Otto is a young car who visits an engine specialist and receives a special additive that allows his engine to run at the correct speed.[1] Other machine metaphors used by ADHD advocates include the cockpit of a jet plane, a train that's going too fast, a VCR (that requires you to hit the pause button every thirty seconds), and a Ferrari with weak brakes.[2] There are a couple of problems with using machine analogies for the so-called ADHD brain. First, even if it's not included in the explanation, there's an underlying sense in these analogies that there's something wrong with the machine, therefore, it must be broken. Keep in mind that many of our insults use similar metaphors ("His elevator doesn't go all the way to the top floor").

Second, emerging research in neuroscience suggests that the brain isn't a machine at all; it's more like a rain forest. According to Nobel Prize–winning biologist Gerald Edelman: "The brain is in no sense like any kind of instruction machine, like a computer. Each individual's brain is more like a unique rainforest, teeming with growth, decay, competition, diversity, and selection."[3] Edelman's theory of what he terms "neural Darwinism" has been called by the late neurologist and essayist Oliver Sacks, "the first truly global theory of mind and consciousness, the first biological theory of individuality and autonomy."[4]

This sort of explanation is much more likely to appeal to children, especially those who love nature. The firing of neurons inside the brain can be likened to lightning in the rain forest (when we have great ideas, after all, we have "brainstorms"). The ebb and flow of neurotransmitters in the synapses between brain cells can be compared with the sea tides. The dendrites, or branches that reach out of neurons to connect with other neurons, can be analogized to the trees and branches of the rain forest. The incredible resilience of the brain—its ability to recover from injury, insult, or damage—can be equated with the way a forest immediately begins repopulating itself after a fire.

Moreover, a rain forest is filled with diversity, which is a good way to talk about the diversity of brains and the value of diversity to humanity because there are great treasures hidden away in the rain forest (like healing herbs) just as there are great treasures hidden away in your child's own brain forest. Finally, you can talk about neuroplasticity and how the brain's dendrites or branches literally grow in response to positive learning experiences (just as rain makes the trees grow). As one middle school student put it after learning about the neuroplasticity of the brain: "I imagine neurons making connections in my brain when I study. I feel like I'm changing my brain when I learn something, understand it, and review it."[5] This "brain forest" metaphor provides a much more realistic analogy to the brain and one that allows for a deeper understanding of the most amazing and incredible organic formation in the universe.

FOR FURTHER INFORMATION

JoAnn Deak, *Your Fantastic Elastic Brain* (San Francisco: Little Pickle Press, 2010). This children's book doesn't use a rain forest analogy but is still an excellent picture book on how the brain works through neuroplasticity, for ages four to eight.

JoAnn Deak and Terrence Deak, *The Owner's Manual for Driving Your Adolescent Brain* (San Francisco: Little Pickle Press, 2013).

Eliminate Distractions
(Ages 7–18)

Sometimes it's great to have a brain firing off in different directions, making connections, noticing things, blazing away in all its glory. This type of functioning, after all, is an important feature of the creative mind. On the other hand, there are times when one needs to be able to focus on the task at hand. For your child that might mean taking out the garbage, doing math problems, reading a book, or cleaning his room. Consequently, when extraneous things get in the way of getting things done, learning how to deal with distractions can become a valuable skill to develop, especially if your child has a highly distractible brain. Here is a procedure to help your child or teen learn how to handle distractions that keep him from doing tasks that require focus. Using the sample chart below as a guide, have your child write at the top of a piece of paper the specific task he'll be working on. (*Note:* you can work together on this.) Then fill in each column:

- *Things liable to distract me.* This list might include a ringing cell phone, the sound of the television, the background noise of people talking, a favorite toy beckoning to be played with, pop-ups on social media, family members coming into the room.
- *How I'll know I'm distracted.* These are the "warning signs," the internal physical or outer behavioral cues your child or teen can learn to recognize as indicators that he's off task. Examples are emotional or bodily sensations, physical actions like getting out of his chair or going into the kitchen for something to eat, and mental fantasies that lead him astray. (See also Strategy #17: Teach Your Child Self-Monitoring Skills.)
- *How I'll deal with the distraction.* This is the most important column and is where your child devises an action plan of ingenious strategies, such as reciting a mantra like "I will stay focused" or putting on some

at-the-ready earplugs, to shut down the influence of the distractions once he's recognized the warning signs.

• *Things that could help me focus.* In this column your child lists things that could help him focus on the task at hand, such as turning up the brightness on the computer screen or removing himself to a quieter room. Note that your child may list things that as a parent you regard as distractors, but give him the opportunity to demonstrate that they either work or don't work for him.

TASK TO FOCUS ON: WRITING A TERM PAPER ON MY COMPUTER

THINGS LIABLE TO DISTRACT ME	HOW I'LL KNOW I'M DISTRACTED	HOW I'LL DEAL WITH THE DISTRACTION	THINGS THAT COULD HELP ME FOCUS
pop-ups on my computer	when I go onto Facebook and start posting things	turn off the pop-up feature on my computer while I'm writing	making the font I use blue and bold
my baby sister screaming	when I start getting angry (feeling hot in my face and chest)	put on some headphones	Some low-volume music that relaxes me

Some tips for your child to keep in mind when working on eliminating distractions and staying focused on a project include these:

• *Keep the task simple.* If there are twenty-five math problems to do, break the assignment down to five problems at one sitting.
• *Choose the specific time you plan to do the task.* While experts often recommend doing the required tasks first before recreation or other activities, your child may have a different tempo or style for doing things, so let him determine the time, but then suggest that he use some sort of device (a clock alarm) to signal to him that it's time to get started.
• *Use technology tools to help eliminate computer distractions.* There are a number of computer apps that shut down parts of the computer screen or temporarily prevent access to distracting sites (like social media), including WriteRoom, Isolator, Camouflage, Dropcloth, Minim-Other, Swept Away, and SelfControl.

• *Put away anything liable to cause distractions before you begin.* That means shutting down computer programs liable to compete for your attention, putting a bedsheet over any enticing-looking toy or gadget that might steal the focus, or closing the curtains if outside events might take precedent over the task.

While multitasking may be something your child claims to do very well (and popular opinion seems to support this view), research suggests otherwise. Performance suffers when people divide their attention and attempt to take on several tasks at the same time, and this is particularly true of kids with an ADHD diagnosis.[1] By using these distraction-elimination tips, children can move from one learning triumph to the next and find success in anything they put their focused mind to!

FOR FURTHER INFORMATION

David A. Greenwood, *Overcoming Distractions: Thriving with Adult ADD/ADHD* (New York: Sterling, 2016). Written for adults, it nevertheless includes a number of strategies for handling distractions that could be useful for older children and teens and also offers parents a picture of how to deal with distractions once their kids reach adulthood.

STRATEGY #35

Promote Daily Exercise
(Ages 4–110)

Here's something that doesn't make sense to me. Doctors with the aid of drug companies are writing millions of prescriptions for powerful and expensive psychoactive medications to use with children who are hyperactive, inattentive, and/or impulsive. Yet there's another available remedy that's free, that is not controlled by the Food and Drug Administration, and that has a variety of other health benefits besides decreasing symptoms of ADHD. What is this miracle treatment? *Exercise.* Yes, a simple activity that children *used* to do all the time in playgrounds, backyards, fields, forests, sports centers, and schools, but now do much less frequently because of school cutbacks on recess, increased time spent on media, fewer and less challenging playgrounds (due to fears of litigation), and overscheduling of a child's day in after-school courses, tutors, lessons, and other "enrichment" activities.

A growing number of studies over the past few years have revealed the power of exercise to reduce ADHD symptoms in children. One of the most recent and best-run scientific studies randomly assigned children diagnosed with ADHD and typically developing children to either a before-school physical exercise group where they played active games, or a sedentary classroom-based intervention where they did art projects. Each session lasted thirty-one minutes for the two groups and the daily program lasted twelve weeks. Results suggested that the exercise intervention reduced ADHD symptoms both in the school and in the home.[1] In another study, seventeen children with ADHD symptoms in grades kindergarten through third grade took part in a continuous moderate-to-vigorous exercise program for twenty-six minutes a day for eight weeks. The vast majority of the kids showed overall improvement in behavior according to parent, teacher, and program staff ratings.[2] "There is an increasingly compelling amount of information supporting exercise as a treatment for ADHD and also as an aid to enhance learning," says Jordan D. Metzl, a sports medicine physician at the Hospital for Special Surgery in New York City. "Rather than push drugs on our kids as a first-line treatment, we should be encouraging them to move before, during, and after school."[3]

There are a number of ways you can encourage your child or adolescent to engage in regular exercise:

- *Support involvement in sports that involve continuous movement.* Soccer and basketball are better in this regard than baseball and football; having to be always on the move pumps out more protective brain chemicals than having to wait your turn in a game. (See also Strategy #49: Find a Sport Your Child Will Love.)
- *Make use of community resources.* Locate your community's nearest playgrounds, exercise centers, sports fields, hiking trails, and other spaces where your child or adolescent can put in some regular exercise time. (See also Strategy #5: Make Time for Nature)

- *Suggest that your child or adolescent work out before he goes to school.* Even a run around the block a few times can get the heart pumping and the blood flowing through the brain to create a state of mind that will help him pay better attention in the classroom.
- *Schedule regular walks and hikes as a family.* If you build in time for the whole family to hike in the woods, walk around the lake, or jog along a trail, you'll help instill a habit that has the potential to stay with your child for the rest of his life. (See also Strategy #45: Engage in Family Exercise and Recreation.)

More than anything else, parents need to get their kids off the couch, away from the computer, and onto the treadmill, bicycle, race track, soccer field, hiking trail, and/or other setting where active aerobic activities happen. Not only will their ADHD symptoms decrease, they'll also strengthen their cardiovascular system, lower their risk for most major diseases, and boost their all-around physical, emotional, and mental health. Can ADHD drugs produce the same benefits?

FOR FURTHER INFORMATION

John J. Ratey with Eric Hagerman, *Spark: The Revolutionary New Science of Exercise and the Brain* (Boston: Little, Brown, 2013).

STRATEGY #36

Foster Good Home–School Communication
(Ages 6–18)

Parents of kids who have been diagnosed with ADHD often feel intimidated about getting directly involved with their child's school because they've had bad experiences themselves with teachers when they were growing up or, more frequently, because teachers have complained about their children, taken away their privileges, put them on detention, and/or yelled at them for misbehavior. To these parents, school doesn't seem like a very friendly place at

all. In fact, research suggests that parents of students who have been diagnosed with ADHD perceive the school as less welcoming and teachers as more
demanding than parents of kids who are typically developing.[1] Yet research
also indicates that positive parental involvement in a child's education at home
and school is associated with higher academic achievement, better behavioral
outcomes, and more engagement and motivation in school.[2] Consequently,
forging a positive partnership between the home and the school can be one of
the best things you can do to secure your child's success in the classroom and
assure positive outcomes later on in life. Here are a few suggestions for doing
this:

- *Attend school functions on a regular basis.* Parent–teacher conferences, back-to-school nights, and other school events provide opportunities to become acquainted with your child's teachers and get a feel for
  the kind of school atmosphere your child is exposed to on a daily basis;
  ask if you can visit your child's classroom while it's in session; even
  better, volunteer to work in the classroom or help out at school in some
  other way.
- *Communicate with your child's teacher frequently.* Whether you
  communicate by e-mail, text, phone, or a visit to school, the more often
  you can touch bases with the teacher and other school staff, the better
  able you are to advocate for your child's needs (for example, you can let
  the teacher know how your child learns best and what works best for
  him as far as eliciting positive behavior).
- *Consider asking for a daily report card from the teacher.* Studies suggest that there are positive outcomes from having the teacher keep tabs
  on specific positive goals for the child throughout the day (fewer outbursts in class, higher scores on pop quizzes, more hand-raising, etc.)
  and then communicating that information to the parent, who can arrange suitable rewards with the child at home for meeting those goals.[3]
- *Nip school problems in the bud before they have a chance to get out of
  control.* Many schools have home–school collaboration programs,
  which may include conjoint behavior problem-solving sessions; Web
  sites that provide access to your child's daily schoolwork, homework
  assignments, test results, and grades; and other structures that make
  parents co-partners in their students' learning at school.

Above all, have a positive proactive attitude when communicating with the school about your child (see also Strategy #53: Work to Promote Teacher–Child Rapport). Federal law gives parents the legal right to make sure that their children with special needs receive an appropriate education based on an Individualized Education Program (IEP). But this process will work more smoothly if you're warm and flexible with school staff rather than angry and demanding, an attitude that is likely to make teachers more defensive and less willing to cooperate. By engaging in a friendly collaboration with your child's teachers you can ensure that she develops the sense that home and school are on the same page and, at the same time, on her side.

FOR FURTHER INFORMATION

National Parent Teachers Association (PTA): 1-800-307-4782; info@pta. org. There are more than twenty thousand PTA units nationwide.

STRATEGY #37

Strengthen Your Child's Working Memory
(Ages 7–18)

It's late afternoon and you tell your ADHD-diagnosed son: "Please take out the garbage, do your homework, and then come downstairs and help set the dinner table. Okay?"

"Sure, Mom," he responds.

An hour later you wonder where he is, so you go upstairs and find him in his bedroom playing a video game. "What did I ask you do?" you say, impatiently tapping your foot.

"Uh, something about the garbage?" he replies with an innocent smile on his face.

You might be inclined at this point to believe that he's *choosing* to do the video game and *choosing not* to do the other tasks. However, in reality it may be something entirely different: a failure of his working memory. Working memory is our ability to hold information temporarily in our brain while we're doing other things. In this case, the multitask instructions you gave your son essentially "slipped out of his working memory" before he even got to the garbage can. New research suggests that a big reason many kids labeled ADHD are inattentive and distractible has to do with their difficulties with working memory.[1]

You can help your child develop his working memory in a number of ways. Here are some tips:

- Play games that require working memory like Concentration, Battleship, and chess (see also Strategy #80: Play Chess or Go with Your Child).
- Sing memory songs that keep adding elements to the lyrics as they go on, such as "The Twelve Days of Christmas" or "My Aunt Came Back," which adds physical movements as well (see a demonstration at youtube .com/watch?v=ysZvMtnion8).
- Place small objects on a tray and let your child look at them for five seconds, then withdraw them and see how many he can remember; increase or decrease the number of objects as needed, and over time increase the memory load.
- Give your child a series of numbers, spoken out loud, then have him repeat them back to you.
- Have your child enroll in a computerized brain-training program such as Cogmed Working Memory Training (cogmed.com) or Interactive Metronome (interactivemetronome.com).

Research on working memory suggests that children will make more progress if they continually push against their limits to remember items.[2] Also, studies conclude that people can hold only about four things at a time in their minds (it used to be seven), so don't tax your child with too long a list of instructions. Keep in mind too that your child may have an excellent *long-term* memory and remember the names of every doll she ever owned or every baseball player that ever played on her favorite team, but still have difficulties with short-term or working memory. By helping your child mentally practice remembering things, you can help her do a better job of following directions at home and school.

FOR FURTHER INFORMATION
Tracy Alloway and Ross Alloway, *The Working Memory Advantage: Train Your Brain to Function Stronger, Smarter, Faster* (New York: Simon & Schuster, 2014).

STRATEGY #38

Limit Entertainment Media
(Ages 4–18)

The statistic is stark and sobering. Today's kids are spending an average of seven hours a day on entertainment media through their involvement with television, computers, phones, and other electronic devices.[1] The impact of this trend on children and adolescents diagnosed with ADHD was detailed in chapter 8, but it stands repeating that screen time for these kids is associated with attention problems, learning difficulties, negative attitudes toward school, poor grades, and long-term academic failure.[2] It's important to understand that these results apply only to violent and/or entertainment media and not to the kinds of educational media that are covered elsewhere in this book (see Strategy #40: Use Online Learning as an Educational Resource, Strategy #47: Identify Mobile Apps That Can Help Your Child, Strategy #83: Utilize the Best Features of Computer Learning, and Strategy #84: Let Your Child Play Video Games That Engage and Teach). Here are a few guidelines to help reel in the rampant entertainment media consumption of your ADHD-diagnosed child or teen:

- *Establish "screen-free zones," including your child's bedroom.* Bedroom access to television, computers, and videos is associated with less sleep (a problem for many kids diagnosed with ADHD), higher media use, and consequent attention problems.[3]
- *Discourage engagement with any violent media.* The research is clear that consuming violent media in any form is associated with higher levels of aggression in all children and adolescents, and studies suggests that kids diagnosed with ADHD may be particularly vulnerable.[4]

- *Watch entertainment media with your child and discuss it together.* Because it's futile to try to ban it outright (children's curiosity will lead them to go elsewhere for their media consumption), spend time with your child watching entertainment, and even violent media, and talk about the content. This will engage both the emotional brain and the prefrontal cortex and make viewing a learning experience for both of you.
- *Engage in literacy-related and other nonmedia activities as much as possible as a family.* Replace TV time with reading time, video game playing with board game playing, and Internet cruising with trips to the library to find out more about the world (see also Strategy #45: Engage in Family Exercise and Recreation).

Rather than being seen as the "mean parent" who won't let her child watch anything good on TV or play any cool video games, it's better to work toward being the "media facilitator" who helps kids evaluate, think about, and learn from the media they consume every day.

FOR FURTHER INFORMATION

Common Sense Media: commonsensemedia.org. This site assists parents with media issues and provides ratings of TV shows, movies, video games, apps, and Web sites.

STRATEGY #39

Promote Flow Experiences
(Ages 4–18)

Several years ago I received a letter from a mother/physician who wrote about a quarrel she had with friends who kept telling her that her child probably had attention deficit disorder: "When I . . . began pointing out to people that my child is capable of long periods of concentration when he is watching his favorite sci-fi video or examining the inner workings of a pin-tumbler lock,

I notice that the next year's definition states that some kids with A.D.D. are capable of normal attention in certain specific circumstances. Poof! A few thousand more kids instantly fall into the definition." Actually, what she was probably referring to when she mentioned her child's ability to concentrate for long periods of time was evidence from the field suggesting that ADHD-diagnosed kids and adults often engage in a process of *hyperfocus*.[1] That is, they spend too much time focusing on the things that interest them! While most ADHD experts tend to regard hyperfocus as another negative sign of the disorder, it actually bears a very close resemblance to a highly positive psychological phenomenon called *flow* (although perhaps these experts are referring more to an externally similar but very different phenomenon called "time sucking"; a good example of this is a person who spends hours a day in a mindless stupor watching TV or cruising the Internet).

Flow is a word coined by psychologist Mihály Csíkszentmihályi to describe a state of attention that occurs when the challenges of a task are neither too difficult nor too easy but just right (another "Goldilocks and the Three Bears" phenomenon! See Strategy #24: Establish Consistent Rules, Routines, and Transitions).[2] In this state, an individual feels totally absorbed in an activity, enjoys it for its own sake, stays focused sometimes for hours at a time, and upon finishing the task feels refreshed rather than exhausted. Csíkszentmihályi studied highly skilled individuals, such as artists, rock climbers, and surgeons, and they all reported the same type of total focus while engaged in their craft. He also noted that children enter flow states all the time. While you can't force a child to have a flow experience (that would immediately shut down the child's intrinsic joy of learning), you can help prepare an environment that will favor the occurrence of a flow experience. Here are some suggestions:

- *Provide your child with plenty of time to enjoy the activities that give him the most pleasure.* This could be in art, sports, music, nature, science, reading, writing, or any of a thousand other pursuits.
- *Have tools and resources available that can facilitate your child's engagement in that highly enjoyed activity.* Examples include paints for art, access to a basketball court for sports, a piano for music, a magnifying glass for nature, or a microscope or telescope for science.
- *Pursue your own flow states.* By engaging in things that give you a lot of joy, you will inspire your child to follow your example.

* *Remember not to push, judge, or turn the experiences your child has into a competition with other kids.* These actions will destroy any chance of having a flow experience.

Keep in mind that your child will let you know when he's entered a flow experience by the twinkle in his eye, the smile on his face, and his reluctance to stop whatever he's doing. The great Italian educator Maria Montessori called this type of total absorption in a learning activity "the great work." You owe it to your child and to yourself to allow him this opportunity to experience the joy of learning firsthand.

FOR FURTHER INFORMATION

Mihály Csíkszentmihályi, *Finding Flow: The Psychology of Engagement with Everyday Life* (New York: Basic Books, 1998).

STRATEGY #40

Use Online Learning as an Educational Resource
(Ages 10–18)

Until recently, schools controlled the gateways of knowledge and allocated educational content to their students in bite-size nuggets that took the form of textbooks, slide shows, lab experiments, lectures, and other finite parcels of knowledge. Now in the twenty-first century, students have direct access to an entire universe of learning online. More than one in four students now take at least one distance education course; that's a total of 5.8 million students. To name only three available resources for online learning, MIT has made more than two thousand of its courses available free of charge to consumers (ocw.mit.edu/OcwWeb), the Khan Academy includes a library of more than sixty-five hundred short video lessons that span a wide range of subjects (khanacademy.org), and the Monterey Institute's National Repository of Online Courses (montereyinstitute.org/nroc) provides access to an entire online high school curriculum free of charge for the individual learner.

Such access to learning has obvious advantages for older kids diagnosed with ADHD. There is more opportunity for students to choose courses and topics that interest them and to select teachers who are less likely to bore them. If they don't pay attention the first time around, there's always the opportunity to play a lecture or lesson back as many times as needed to get it right. Instead of having to show up for class early in the morning without having gotten enough sleep, students can choose their best times of alertness during the day to study online. If the student gets bullied at school, studying online at home or another nonschool location avoids the painful and destructive impact of this type of intimidation Always late for school? Not a problem with online learning; the student can set his own schedule. Got the fidgets? Be as antsy as you want in an online learning environment at home.

Of course, there are some potential drawbacks to keep in mind as well. If your child or teen already has trouble disciplining himself to do his school homework, then it's likely he may have the same difficulty setting his own hours for online study (to help him overcome this hurdle, see Strategy #17: Teach Your Child Self-Monitoring Skills, Strategy #72: Suggest Effective Study Strategies, and Strategy #101: Teach Your Child Organizational Strategies). There's also a greater potential for distractions in the home environment (some online learners solve this by going to a library to study; see also Strategy #34: Eliminate Distractions). But if the freedom involved in online learning outweighs the restrictions that school places on your child's or teen's learning style, then keep the following tips in mind:

- If you choose a degree-granting program, make sure that it has received accreditation from a major national credentialing association.
- Consider doing online learning as a *supplement* to your child's or adolescent's current schooling situation (many elementary, middle, and high schools already are doing this with what are referred to as "blended learning" programs and "flipped classrooms").
- If self-discipline is a big issue, consider hiring an ADHD coach to help your child or adolescent with organizational skills, time management strategies, goal setting, and study tips (you can find one through the Professional Association of ADHD Coaches at paaccoaches.org; or you can be a coach yourself, see Strategy #27: Be a Personal Coach to Your Child).

Online learning isn't for everyone, but for an ADHD-diagnosed child or adolescent who's motivated enough to want to give it a try, online education might provide them with a new way to learn free of the restrictions that a brick-and-mortar school can place on the different drummers and out-of-the-box learners among us.

FOR FURTHER INFORMATION

Kevin J. Fandl and Jamie D. Smith, *Success as an Online Student: Strategies for Effective Learning* (New York: Routledge, 2016).

STRATEGY #41

Show Your Child How to Use Metacognitive Tools
(Ages 10–18)

Metacognition means literally "thinking about thinking." This concept has become an important focus for educators over the past few years because it has the advantage not just of teaching students content (like science, math, and literature) but of giving kids the tools they need to look at and change their own learning and thinking processes to help them master new material. The old (modified) adage "Give a Student a Fish, and You Feed Her for a Day. Teach a Student to Fish, and You Feed Her for a Lifetime" applies here. For kids diagnosed with ADHD, metacognition is an important dimension of the prefrontal executive functions viewed as key in managing behavior and attentional capacities. Here are a few tools that your child or adolescent can learn how to use:

- *Cognitive organizers.* These are "concept maps" typically represented in visual form as diagrams, charts, checklists, graphs, timelines, conceptual maps, or other displays that help concretize both the process and the content of learning. One great app that uses a cognitive organizing process called *mind-mapping* is Kidspiration (for older students and adults there's a separate program called Inspiration). Students create a central hub that represents a key topic being explored and then brainstorm all the ideas that come to mind by placing them as spokes around that central theme. For examples of other cognitive organizers, see *The Teacher's Big Book of Graphic Organizers* in "For Further Information.")

- *Think-alouds.* This is a process of externalizing one's mental processes by speaking them out loud so that one can more fully recognize them and change them as necessary; for proofreading a story a think-aloud might sound something like this: "First I need to read it all the way through, then I should highlight any mistakes in yellow, then correct the yellow parts, and finally print out the final draft." It will help a great deal if you engage in your own think-alouds to show your child or teen how it's done, and then let her create her own versions for solving a math problem, figuring out a procedure at home, or thinking about other issues that don't have immediate answers. You can also encourage your child or teen to talk out loud when reading a book ("Hmmm . . . I wonder why the author made this character so mean . . .").

- *Thinking journals.* This might take the form of a simple spiral notebook where your child writes down answers to simple metacognitive questions that relate to situations at school or home, such as these:

  How might I have done _____ better? [last night's homework]

  What did I learn from _____? [the fight I had with Ronnie last week]

  What could I do differently the next time I _____? [try to repair my bicycle tire]

  What are some other ways of doing _____? [the long-division problems my teacher assigned]

- *Mental problem-solving kit.* This is a series of steps that your child or adolescent can go through to help solve any problem, big or small.

  1. Define the problem.
  2. Identify several potential solutions.
  3. Evaluate each alternative.
  4. Choose a solution.
  5. Implement the solution.
  6. Evaluate the results.

Put the steps on a card and then practice two or three examples before turning your child loose and letting him try it on his own.

You can also help your child or teen develop metacognitive skills by playing board games or card games and asking her to share her strategies for winning. Try suggesting to your child or adolescent, after a misbehavior or problem has occurred, that he reflect on ways the issue might be avoided or resolved in the future. By helping your child engage in these simple thinking exercises, you're equipping him with the mental muscles he needs to solve the many problems and challenges he's likely to meet in the future.

FOR FURTHER INFORMATION

Katherine S. McKnight, *The Teacher's Big Book of Graphic Organizers: 100 Reproducible Organizers That Help Kids with Reading, Writing, and the Content Areas* (San Francisco: Jossey-Bass, 2010).

Donna Wilson and Marcus Conyers, *Teaching Students to Drive Their Brains: Metacognitive Strategies, Activities, and Lesson Ideas* (Alexandria, VA: ASCD, 2016).

STRATEGY #42

Teach Emotional Self-Regulation Skills
(Ages 4–18)

It's early morning and the family is having breakfast together. Rachel grabs a fresh blueberry out of brother Jason's bowl. Jason slugs his sister. Rachel shouts out, "Mom!" and then starts to cry. Jason gets up from the table and tips over the chair on purpose. Dad asks Jason to pick it up. He refuses, runs into the living room, and starts to jump up and down on the sofa yelling at the top of his voice, "Rachel is a crybaby! Rachel is a crybaby!"

What we're witnessing here is a classic example of emotional dysregulation. This small incident might have ended with Jason laughing at the theft or with him saying "Dad, Rachel stole my blueberry," or with him asking Rachel why she did that, or with him telling Rachel that it was okay but he wants one of her raspberries in trade. Instead, Jason was unable to regulate his feelings about having something of his (however small) taken away, and his emotions escalated and spun out of control.

Statistics suggest that 25 to 40 percent of children diagnosed with ADHD have problems with emotional regulation and that this failure to handle feelings in an appropriate way can lead to family conflict, peer difficulties, and antisocial behavior. On a biochemical level what happens is that the hypothalamus and amygdala (parts of the emotional brain) begin firing and sending signals to the rational prefrontal cortex asking it to help control (inhibit) the out-of-control feelings. This fails to occur.[1] To assist your child in better regulating his own emotional states here are a few strategies you can use:

- *Talk with your child about his feelings at the time they happen, and ask him to name the emotions.* Kids can't control their emotions if they don't know that they're having them or what they are. You can get a How Are You Feeling Today? poster displaying thirty emotions by Jim Borgman at amazon.com/Feeling-Today-Fantasy-Poster-Borgman/dp/B000MYM5D4.
- *Help your child identify kinesthetic red flags that might alert him to a potential emotional escalation.* A flushed face, squinting eyes, and tight muscles between the shoulder blades are some common bodily reactions. This awareness can help him to stop the intensification of emotion in its tracks.
- *Go over scenarios of past escalations with your child and help him discover what he might do differently next time.* The chart below may be useful in developing a range of potential strategies for appropriately regulating emotions whenever they occur in the future.

LEARNING TO HANDLE MY EMOTIONS

TRIGGER	HOW THAT MADE ME FEEL	WHAT I DID IN RESPONSE	WHAT I COULD DO IF IT HAPPENS IN THE FUTURE
My brother stuck his tongue out at me.	angry	punched him	Tell him I'm mad and walk out of the room.
I got an F on my math test.	angry and ashamed of what others would think	tore the test up and threw the pieces at the teacher	Take three deep breaths and then make an appointment to meet with the teacher to talk about how I could do better next time.
Jane told me in class that I'm not invited to her party.	sad and upset	put bad words on her locker with a Magic Marker	Tell her that it makes me sad to hear her say this and ask her why I wasn't invited.
I found out that I made the varsity soccer team.	really happy and excited	started running around the field punching my team members on the arm	Run around the track a few times as "victory laps" until I'm exhausted.

Finally, help your child recognize emotions in *others* so he can gain a better understanding of how to respond when *they* begin to react to something he's said or done. By following these guidelines, you'll be giving your child a set of tools that will help him short-circuit future tantrums, stop fights, limit pouts, decrease antisocial behaviors, and prevent other forms of acting-out behavior that impair the quality of his life and yours.

FOR FURTHER INFORMATION

Lauren Brukner, *How to Be a Superhero Called Self-Control!: Super Powers to Help Younger Children to Regulate their Emotions and Senses* (London: Jessica Kingsley, 2015). For ages four to seven.

Lauren Brukner, *Stay Cool and In Control with the Keep-Calm Guru: Wise Ways for Children to Regulate their Emotions and Senses* (London: Jessica Kingsley, 2016). For ages seven to fourteen.

Sheri Van Dijk, *Don't Let Your Emotions Run Your Life for Teens: Dialectical Behavior Therapy Skills for Helping You Manage Mood Swings,*

Control Angry Outbursts, and Get Along with Others (Oakland, CA: Instant Help/New Harbinger, 2011).

Teach Your Child Mindfulness Meditation
(Ages 5–18)

At first glance it might seem as if getting your ADHD-diagnosed child to meditate would be like asking a live butterfly to pose for a still-life watercolor painting. But the great attraction of mindfulness meditation is that the meditator doesn't have to keep his body or mind still but simply *become aware* of everything going on inside the mind and outside in the world. Mindfulness meditation emerged originally from the tradition of Theravada Buddhism in Southeast Asia, but the practice was adapted for nonreligious use in the late 1970s by American scientist Jon Kabat-Zinn at the Stress Reduction Clinic at the University of Massachusetts Medical School. After the success of his stress reduction program, the practice spread and became the focus of a number of books, programs, and research studies that have increased exponentially since that time.[1] Several research studies provide preliminary evidence that mindfulness meditation can improve self-regulation of attention, decrease behavior problems, improve executive functioning, and reduce parental stress in children and adolescents diagnosed with ADHD.[2]

The cornerstone of mindfulness meditation is the breath. Meditators are asked to focus their attention on the inflow and outflow of air in the nostrils or the up and down movements of the stomach muscles with each breath. Naturally, the mind isn't going to remain focused on the breath for long and it will wander all over the place and experience many other things both internally (ideas, feelings, images) and externally (perceptions of sounds, sensations of air or clothing on one's body, light on one's closed eyelids). The main idea is to simply notice the distractions and return to the breath. A thirty-minute session may involve becoming distracted and going back to the breath *hundreds* of times. Awareness is the key. The younger the child, of course, the shorter the session should be, but even a minute or two can help. In fact, as a parent, you can periodically ask your child during the day to become aware for a few seconds of the sounds around him, or the tingling in his fingertips, or his breathing, and that will help improve attention and awareness. Here are some other tips to help you get started:

- *Get a book, video, or audio CD to provide guidance on meditation.* There are now literally hundreds of resources available for learning mindfulness meditation and some excellent ones too for teaching children how to meditate (see "For Further Information" below).
- *Meditate with your child.* The idea of standing by while your child meditates is simply silly. You need to model the process for your child and also reap the benefits of meditation so the two of you can share your experiences.
- *Build in other focusing components to meditation sessions.* Elsewhere in this book I've provided other activities you can incorporate into your meditation sessions to vary them and find new ways to engage your child or adolescent (Strategy #7: Teach Your Child Focusing Techniques, Strategy #46: Share Stress Management Techniques, Strategy #79: Teach Your Child to Visualize, and Strategy #87: Have Your Child Learn Yoga).

Above all, don't force your child to meditate. Make it easy for her to get started. The traditional postures for meditation are the lotus position (sitting on a cushion with one leg folded over the other) or sitting in a chair. But if your child wants to lie on the floor and notice shadows on the ceiling, that's great. Or build in some chanting (animal sounds are good with younger kids). However you do it, you'll be helping your child or adolescent become aware, and this awareness, more than anything else, will produce the true benefit by increasing attention and softening behavior.

FOR FURTHER INFORMATION

Amy Saltzman, *A Still Quiet Place for Teens: A Mindfulness Workbook to Ease Stress and Difficult Emotions* (Oakland, CA: Instant Help/New Harbinger, 2016).

Eline Snel, *Sitting Still Like a Frog: Mindfulness Exercises for Kids (and Their Parents)* (Boston: Shambhala, 2013). Includes a sixty-minute audio CD of guided exercises read by Myla Kabat-Zinn.

STRATEGY #44

Let Your Child Engage in Spontaneous Self-Talk
(Ages 4–10)

Observe young children at play and you'll notice them often side by side fully engaged in an activity and talking out loud to no one in particular. Russian psychologist Lev Vygotsky referred to this phenomenon as *private speech* and regarded it as the beginning of a process of internalizing language as self-talk.[1] He observed that when children get older, this private stream of words becomes internalized as inner speech. The parallel chatter of youngsters at play is replaced by the silent mind chatter of adults at work. Using such silent self-talk to direct the mind toward specific goals is one of the key features of verbal activity in humans.

Studies suggest that children with ADHD symptoms engage in more out-loud spontaneous speech compared to typically developing children, and more important, that they perform just as well on schoolwork tasks as so-called normal children *when they are allowed to talk while they are studying.*[2] Researcher Sydney Zentall's work at Purdue University indicates that kids who are diagnosed with ADHD are *less* likely to talk when they are *asked* to do so. But when they're not *supposed* to be talking, they talk quite a bit.[3] In a traditional classroom, this spontaneous talk may be regarded by teachers as off-task or disruptive behavior (and even used to confirm the diagnosis of ADHD). However, by understanding that these kids need to use their natural self-talk capabilities to help them process information more effectively, parents and teachers should be encouraged to make sure that these types of behaviors are regarded not as disruptive but as a positive educational strategy (this process developmentally leads them toward a time when they will eventually develop internal self-talk).

At home, provide your child with a secure study space away from rooms where others might be distressed by out-loud verbalizations. That way she can be allowed to talk to her heart's content. At school, teachers should give children diagnosed with ADHD the opportunity to work on their studies in a separate space where they won't disturb other members of their class with their spontaneous self-talk. Silence may be golden for some kids, but for the child identified as ADHD, spontaneous self-talk may be their ticket to a more successful learning experience.

STRATEGY #45

Engage in Family Exercise and Recreation
(Ages 4–104)

If the humdrum of family life is propelling you and your kids into negative patterns of interaction, then integrating family exercise and recreation into your daily routine is a surefire way to pull out of it and start having fun again. Spending leisure time together as a family provides many benefits for kids diagnosed with ADHD. In fact, many of the strategies in this book come together in family exercise and recreational activities (Strategy #35: Promote Daily Exercise, Strategy #57: Make Time for Plenty of Humor and Laughter, and Strategy #58: Spend Positive Times Together). In addition, your child has the opportunity to work on social and communication skills as part of cooperating with family members to create a memorable experience. Here are some activities and outings to consider:

- *In-home family recreation.* Physical games, dramatic role-play, sing-a-longs, special-day celebrations, family art sessions, party games
- *Backyard family games.* Touch football, tag, horseshoes, badminton, croquet, Twister
- *Good weather activities.* Picnics, barbecues, walks in the park, kite flying, bicycling
- *Day trips.* Going to an aquarium or zoo, the beach, a children's museum, an amusement park, a music concert, a movie theater

- *Multiday vacations.* Hiking expeditions, visits to state or national parks, historical tours, road trips to new places, family camps, sports museums

To make sure that old negative patterns don't creep into the new activities, here are a few recommendations to keep in mind:

- Keep a calendar posted listing the upcoming trips and activities (you can title it Coming Attractions).
- The day before the event, go over the itinerary or planned activity and help your child anticipate any potential difficulties that might arise and how he might deal with them.
- When picking a game or activity involving special skills, make sure that your ADHD-diagnosed child has those skills or learns them before the start of the event.
- For trips and vacations, pick places where there are a variety of things to do. For example, a trip to a lake where your child could swim, fish, sail, water ski, explore the ecology, or hike along the trails would be a much better choice than a guided tour to a historical site where there are rules and restrictions such as staying in groups, not touching exhibits, and not interrupting the guide's talk.

It's important, of course, to establish some basic ground rules for proper behavior during family exercise and recreational activities, but make sure that while you're engaged in an event, there's a lot of flexibility built in for family members to goof off, laugh, take breaks, embrace the unexpected, and most important, have fun!

FOR FURTHER INFORMATION

FamilyFun magazine: parents.com/familyfun-magazine. Part of the Parents magazine group of publications, it offers eight issues per year, a digital edition, and online features.

STRATEGY #46

Share Stress Management Techniques
(Ages 4–18)

When I taught children with attention and behavior difficulties, I frequently noticed how *tense* many of these kids were as they wrestled with math problems, struggled to learn the rules of a new game, or grappled with any new learning task. It was almost as if these kids were bursting at the seams with energy and it took all their effort and resolve—expressed in muscular tension—to hold that energy in. Add to this the frustrations they experienced from not fitting in; problems with peers out on the playground; and criticisms they received from siblings, parents, and other teachers, and what you're looking at are students who are under a great deal of *stress*.

While there are many ways of relieving stress included elsewhere in this book (see, for example, Strategy #35: Promote Daily Exercise, Strategy #43: Teach Your Child Mindfulness Meditation, and Strategy #87: Have Your Child Learn Yoga), one important tool involves the use of quick physical relaxation exercises that a student can learn and use whenever he feels under pressure at home or at school. These exercises provide an immediate relief from muscular tension, offer a channel for discharging excess energy, supply a means of allaying anxiety, and give the child a way to focus attention on something solid and specific—the physical body—to help ground awareness in the here and now.

When teaching your child relaxation methods, it may be helpful to use picture metaphors in describing the specific physical movements he should engage in when doing the exercises. Some of the following scenarios may be helpful. Your child can do most of these exercises seated in a comfortable position or while lying on a carpeted floor.

- *The Balloon.* Take a deep breath as if you were a balloon blowing yourself up large; then slowly let the air out of the balloon. Repeat two or more times.

- *The Robot/The Rag Doll.* Make your body as stiff as a robot's for several seconds, then make it as limp as a rag doll's for several seconds. Repeat two or more times.
- *The Cat.* Lying facedown on the floor, begin to stretch like a cat; stretch arms, legs, arch the back, yawn—just like a cat. Repeat two or more times.
- *The Elevator.* Imagine that you're in a cozy elevator. You feel it slowly descending, and as it does, you feel more and more relaxed.
- *The Honey Jar.* Try this one standing up. Imagine that you're swimming in a jar of honey; you need to move very slowly.

Make sure to do these exercises with your child first (or have a sibling or friend there as a support), and then gradually withdraw as he becomes competent in using them. You may find that your child wants to modify them or develop his own unique exercises. The more these activities become a part of your child's life, the more likely he is to use them.

Physical relaxation needn't always consist of formal techniques. According to author and pediatrician T. Berry Brazelton, your child can develop his own self-comforting methods to deal with stressful events. "When ADHD children start building toward a crisis," says Brazelton, "they need a way to withdraw from the stimulation and regain control. If he already has such a pattern . . . point this out to him and help him use the pattern *before* the crisis occurs. If he doesn't have a way to comfort himself, you'll need to teach one." Ways to relax include

- Throwing a ball against a wall
- Listening to music
- Playing with pets
- Spending time with favorite relatives or friends
- Gazing at clouds or other natural phenomena
- Taking a walk
- Spending time in a secret place (a fort or a tree house)
- Taking a nap
- Playing with a favorite toy
- Daydreaming

(See also Strategy #42: Teach Emotional Self-Regulation Skills.)

Life has never been as stressful as it is for kids in this complex world. But, by teaching your child to use stress management strategies, you're empowering him with techniques that he can use for the rest of his life.

Lawrence Shapiro and Robin Sprague, *The Relaxation and Stress Reduction Workbook for Kids: Help for Children to Cope with Stress, Anxiety, and Transitions* (Oakland, CA: Instant Help/New Harbinger, 2009).

STRATEGY #47

Identify Mobile Apps That Can Help Your Child
(Ages 8–18)

A mobile app is a computer program designed to run on a smartphone or tablet. As of June 2016, there were 2.2 million different apps available for free or purchase that ran on the Android operating system (Google) and about 2 million apps that ran on Apple's iOS devices. It's been estimated that such apps have been downloaded over a hundred billion times since 2008.[1] Within that vast collection of apps are a broad range of programs designed to address almost every aspect of an ADHD-diagnosed child's life. There are apps for paying attention, for monitoring one's mood, for managing time, for keeping track of homework assignments, for helping with organizational skills, for assisting with self-monitoring of attention and behavior, and for many more skills besides. Parents need to keep up with the dazzling array of programs coming out every month. This section provides an introduction and overview to some of the best apps that are currently out there as of fall 2016 to help with ADHD-related issues. (*Note:* prices may change over time.)

- *Keep track of homework.* myHomework—enter homework assignments by subject or due date, for upper elementary and high school level (Apple; free)
- *Organizational skills.* Corkulous—a virtual cork board that kids can

use to pin to-do lists, brainstorms, notes, and other data (Apple; $4.99); Evernote—store articles, photos, handwritten notes, and/or data for easy retrieval later on (Apple, Android; free for lite version)

- *Time management.* Time Timer—a virtual sixty-minute clock face showing in red the amount of time left to work on a task (Apple; $4.99); 30/30—create specific tasks and set the amount of time you need to finish each one (Apple; free)
- *Note taking.* SoundNote—students can take notes in class, and if they have difficulty keeping up, they can write a word, hit the audio button, and listen to the missed portion of the lecture by tapping on that word again (Apple; $4.99)
- *Working memory.* Flashcards Deluxe—students create their own flashcards or download premade sets from a library of over four million cards; flashcards can be removed once learned and difficult cards can be set to be replayed more often (Android, Apple; $3.99)
- *Self-monitoring skills.* StayOnTask—the user sets an audio/visual signal to appear randomly during study periods to remind her of her task at hand (Android; free)
- *Emotional self-regulation.* How Would You Feel If . . .—the app asks this question followed by one of fifty-six different life situations designed to begin discussions on handling emotions; for example, "How would you feel if your favorite football team lost?" (Apple $3.99; Android $1.99)
- *Goal-setting skills.* EpicWin—create goals, then blow them up when you achieve them! (Apple; $1.99)

This list of apps is just a beginning. To keep up with the ever-increasing collection of helpful programs for ADHD-related issues, check in periodically with the online magazine *ADDitude* (additudemag.com), which regularly features the top apps that support children and adults diagnosed with ADHD or LD (learning disabilities).

FOR FURTHER INFORMATION
Android Apps on Google Play: https://play.google.com/store/apps?hl=en.

Apple Apps Store: https://itunes.apple.com/us/genre/ios/id36?mt=8.

Match Your Child with a Mentor
(Ages 8–16)

Kids need older role models to help them surmount many of the challenges and obstacles that life presents. Mentors can also inspire youth to acquire the positive qualities needed for success in the adult world. This is why the elders of indigenous cultures have for millennia been putting older children and adolescents through rites of passage to separate them from their parents, isolate them in challenging environments, and integrate them back into the culture as full-fledged adults. While the ancient practices of traditional societies for the most part no longer have a place in today's modern world, kids who struggle with attention and behavior issues have an even greater need for this kind of adult-supervised direction.

Informal mentoring programs, where middle school and high school kids are matched with college students, adult volunteers, or older retirees, can make a big difference in normalizing behavior and creating focus and direction in a such a young person's life. Eye to Eye is a national coalition of mentoring groups that matches kids diagnosed with ADHD and learning disabilities with college students who have a similar diagnosis. Research conducted at Columbia University's Teachers College reveals that 88 percent of students who go through the Eye to Eye program feel better about themselves, 93 percent report that their mentor was the kind of student they wanted to be, and 86 percent reported that "being a part of Eye to Eye got me to think about what I am good at."[1] Mentoring programs for kids diagnosed with ADHD have also been associated with improvements in academic performance and school attendance.[2]

Mentoring is different from tutoring, which focuses almost exclusively on developing school-related skills. Instead, mentors spend time hanging out with their mentees, talking about hopes, fears, life goals, and anything else that comes up, as well as sharing mutual interests and activities. Marcus Soutra, a photographer who was diagnosed with ADHD and dyslexia in childhood, shares how his school "matched me up with a 25-year-old commercial photographer who became my mentor. My mentor didn't have learning or attention issues. Yet we bonded over our common interest in photography. We got to know each other. He let me use his camera and darkroom. When we met, we talked about how to take the best shots, how cameras worked and our favorite photographs. Working with him helped me find success outside of school. I'll never forget selling my first photo—it sure made up for all those poor grades on spelling tests!"[3] Although Soutra's experience was with a non-ADHD-identified individual, he suggests that there is a benefit to having someone as a mentor who shares your diagnosis. He writes: "It's important for your child to have someone in her life who can relate to her struggles with learning and attention issues. That can be anyone—a friend, a family member or an older classmate. Your child can even have more than one mentor."[4] Look for a mentoring program through your child's school (school-based mentoring includes an academic focus as well), your town's community center, or through national organizations such as Eye to Eye or Big Brothers Big Sisters.

FOR FURTHER INFORMATION

Big Brothers Big Sisters of America: 2202 North Westshore Blvd., Suite 455, Tampa, FL 33607; 1-813-720-8778; bbbs.org.

Eye to Eye: 1430 Broadway, Floor 6, New York, NY 10018; 1-212-537-4429; info@eyetoeyenational.org. A coalition of youth mentoring programs run by and for those with learning differences (including ADHD).

STRATEGY #49

Find a Sport Your Child Will Love
(Ages 6–16)

The mother of Olympic swimming champion and ADHD-diagnosed Michael Phelps once recalled being told by a teacher: "Your son will never be able to focus on anything." Instead, he found joy swimming and could sit for hours at a swimming meet waiting for the chance to compete in a race lasting only a few minutes. His mother said that the swimming pool is Michael's sanctuary, a place where he can burn off excess energy and concentrate on winning an event for himself and his teammates.[1] His positive example suggests that sports can serve as a key factor in helping many kids diagnosed with ADHD thrive. Research supports this conclusion. In one study, children identified as having ADHD were divided into two groups. One group engaged in a ninety-minute athletic activity twice a week for six weeks. The other group received education on behavior control. Compared with the behavior group, the sports group showed greater improvement in attention, social skills, and cognitive function.[2] In another study, a group that engaged in swimming activities showed greater ability to inhibit impulsive behaviors when compared with a control group.[3]

While any sport that captures your child's interest can prove to be the right one for his needs, experts generally agree that individual sports tend to work better for kids with an ADHD diagnosis. Group sports usually have more rules and require more social skills in coordinating actions with team members (although soccer may be an exception because of its popularity with kids and all the running that's involved). Here are a few examples of individual sports that could be winners for your child:

- *Tennis.* There's little downtime and plenty of rallying
- *Swimming.* With one's head in the water much of the time distractions are kept to a minimum
- *Gymnastics.* Teaches discipline and focus
- *Wrestling.* Has a minimum of rules with an emphasis on instincts and strategy
- *Track and field;* Running events are great at burning off excess energy
- *Archery.* Trains concentration and builds self-confidence

Here are some tips to keep in mind when thinking about a sport for your child:

- Let your child try several sports first to find the one or ones that he likes the best.
- Deemphasize the competitive aspects of the sport if your child has a hard time losing; highlight the more fundamental benefits (exercise, discipline, focus, self-confidence).

- Whenever possible, see that your child plays sports with others at roughly his own skill level to avoid frustration, although better players can also be role models and teach valuable skills.
- Support your child in the sport he chooses to participate in even if it concerns you (many kids diagnosed with ADHD, for example, love extreme sports like snowboarding, surfing, rock climbing, and scuba diving; just make sure he's with highly competent certified instructors or mentors).

Remember that the real purpose of a sport is to have fun and get fit. By encouraging your child to become involved in a sport, you'll be providing him with a positive way to channel his energies and develop the self-confidence he needs to succeed in life.

FOR FURTHER INFORMATION

Joel Fish and Susan Magee, *101 Ways to Be a Terrific Sports Parent: Making Athletics a Positive Experience for Your Child* (New York: Touchstone, 2003).

STRATEGY #50

Provide a Variety of Stimulating Learning Activities
(Ages 4–10)

You might think, "My kid is already stimulated. Too much as a matter of fact. If anything, he needs *less* stimulation!" In the 1950s, educators also thought this was true and designed stimulus-free classrooms for hyperactive kids, believing it would help calm them down. Current thinking on the matter, however, has it exactly the reverse. It's now believed that many kids who are labeled ADHD may in fact be *under aroused*. These kids appear to require a higher dose of stimulation than the average person, and if they don't get it, they try to create it by making their *own* stimulation (through hyperactive and impulsive behaviors). This helps explain why psychostimulants such as Adderall are so effective with many of these kids.

The most exciting implication of this research is that stimulation *from the learning environment* can also help optimize the arousal state of children and teens diagnosed with ADHD. Researchers have demonstrated that when stimuli such as color, light, music, and animals are added to a classroom, these students become more focused.[1] Not all stimulation is beneficial, however. High levels of talking in a classroom setting, for example, can be distracting and result in higher activity levels.

One of the key researchers in this field, Sydney Zentall of Purdue University, suggests that home and school environments for hyperactive kids should be exciting, novel, and stimulating places of learning—not boring, repetitive, worksheet wastelands. Quoting from one of her "hyperactive heroes," Friedrich Nietzsche, Zentall points out that "habit is a great deadener," and that kids identified as ADHD hate restrictions on activities and repeating things over and over again.

Schools need to provide more stimulation for these students. Instead of reading a dull history textbook and answering the questions at the back of the book, for example, they might build replica artifacts used during that historical period, interview people in the community who are experts in that era, keep journals of what it might have been like to live at that time, listen to music of that epoch, draw murals, create dioramas, or put on a play that reenacts the period. As one mother of a child diagnosed with ADHD said to me, "Justin, a hyperactive child who has problems with ideas on paper, can quite easily become Mariano Vallejo, a nineteenth-century Californian. He can also get fellow actors to produce a creditable performance."

Stimulating learning activities should also become a central feature in the home. Engage your child in multisensory activities, including some of the following possibilities:

- Put natural food coloring in bread dough and make sculptures that can be eaten after they're baked.
- Purchase a rubber stamp set and let your child create her own messages, signs, and compositions.
- Buy a stopwatch and time different activities (try walking around the house, standing on one foot, threading a needle).

- Place diluted dishwashing liquid in a sink or a bowl and use various implements (straws, hollow cans, plastic tubing, wire loops) to dip into the solution and blow bubbles with.
- Put a variety of significant objects into a time capsule (such as a plastic food-storage container) and then bury it ceremoniously in the backyard.
- Obtain an empty appliance box and turn it into a house, car, mountain, post office, store, or anything else, using art materials.
- Take a walk and look for only round things, or any other category that you care to dream up, such as dogs, red things, things that look broken, or tall things.

Using the theory of optimal stimulation as a framework, it stands to reason that the closer to optimal stimulation the child is, the less need there will be to create stimulation through psychostimulant medication. That such drugs are being used to help kids adjust to boring, routine-ridden, repetition-plagued classrooms says more about the sad state of many schools than it does about the so-called deficits of these kids (see chapter 6). The theory of optimal stimulation challenges us all to create vital educational environments where every child can reach his or her true potential.

FOR FURTHER INFORMATION

Susan K. Perry, *Playing Smart: The Family Guide to Enriching, Offbeat Learning Activities for Ages 4–14* (Minneapolis, MN: Free Spirit, 2001).

STRATEGY #51

Teach Goal-Setting Skills
(Ages 7–18)

We often tell our kids that we want them to achieve their dreams, but rarely do we give them detailed instructions on how exactly to reach them. Goal setting is one of the executive abilities associated with the prefrontal lobes and one of the last functions to fully mature in the brain in late adolescence and early adulthood.[1] For children and adolescents who have been diagnosed with ADHD, developing goal-setting skills may be a crucial intervention to help them succeed in school and life. Kids identified as having ADHD too often set goals that are unrealistic ("I want to be an NBA basketball star") or too quickly set them without sufficient reflection as to the consequences ("I plan to get wasted tonight").

People don't reach their goals merely by wishing and hoping that something magical will happen to bring them what they feel they want or deserve. They do it by envisioning what they want, carefully planning how they intend to get it, and then engaging in very specific things that gradually lead them toward their objectives. Parents and teachers should teach goal-setting as a set of skills just like reading or math. Here are some tips on how to guide your child through the steps of successful goal setting and achievement:

- Ask your child or adolescent to list two or three things he'd like to have, do, or accomplish over the next month or two (short-term goals are best to start with; later on, you can shift the focus to long-term goals).
- Make sure the goals are precisely defined. *Not*: "I want to have a lot of money" *but* "I want to save up $75 to take my girlfriend to a nice restaurant."

WHAT GOAL I WANT TO ACCOMPLISH	HOW I PLAN TO ACCOMPLISH MY GOAL	WHAT GOOD THINGS WILL HAPPEN WHEN I ACCOMPLISH MY GOAL?
80 percent on my next math test	study thirty minutes after dinner every weekday until the test	It will raise my grade in math from a C to a B.
not fight with my sister for the next seven days	think of all the qualities I like in my sister; write down how fights in the past started and ways to avoid them in the future	My sister and parents will be happier, and they won't yell at me.
save up enough money to buy a build-it-yourself solar powered robot kit	save my allowance and do odd jobs mowing people's lawns	I'll feel proud of myself; my friends will come over to see the robot I built.

- Tell your child or teen to write down specific actions that will lead toward the achievement of that goal. *Not*: "I plan to get a job" *but* "I will apply for an after-school job at Macy's and JCPenney."
- Have him set a deadline by which he plans to achieve the goal; he may not reach it on that date, but it gives him something to shoot for and he can always readjust the date later on.
- Ask him to write down any obstacles that might get in the way of reaching the goal and how he plans to overcome those obstacles.

The chart below provides some examples of a goal-setting process that you can use in helping your child or adolescent reach his objectives.

To raise the probability that the goal will be reached, here are some suggestions you can give your child or teen:

- Suggest that he write the goal down in large print and put it (along with photos, images, and/or affirmations like "I Can Do It!") on his background computer screen or on a piece of poster board next to his bed or desk; this will keep the goal firmly in his mind as he goes about achieving it.
- Talk about his goal pursuit with family members and friends who are

WHAT MIGHT GET IN THE WAY OF MY ACCOMPLISHING MY GOAL?	HOW I PLAN TO OVERCOME THE OBSTACLES TO ACCOMPLISHING MY GOAL	WHAT I PLAN TO DO WHEN I ACCOMPLISH MY GOAL
if I watch TV instead of studying	put a reminder on the TV set telling me not to watch it but to study	I'll reward myself with an ice cream sundae.
losing my temper and getting angry at my sister	notice when I start to get mad at her and take three deep breaths	My sister will let me use her new iPad for a day if I do this.
if I spend my allowance on candy, comics, and sodas	when I receive my allowance I'll put it in a piggy bank; I'll have to break the bank to get the funds	I'll buy the robot and have a lot of fun putting it together.

likely to support him in achieving it (and caution him to stay away from those who might seek to discourage him or put down his efforts).

- Find someone who has achieved a similar goal to talk to about what she did that led to her success.

By following these guidelines, your child or adolescent can begin to achieve small goals at first and then go on to larger objectives in the future. The actual process of setting goals may be more important than the goals themselves. As motivational expert Zig Ziglar once pointed out: "What you get by achieving your goals is not as important as what you become by achieving your goals."[2]

FOR FURTHER INFORMATION

Beverly K. Bachel, *What Do You Really Want?: How to Set a Goal and Go for It! A Guide for Teens* (Minneapolis, MN: Free Spirit, 2016).

STRATEGY #52

Provide Immediate Behavioral Feedback
(Ages 6–16)

When I was a special education teacher I had a student named Ralph who was prone to impulsive actions like falling down hysterically on the ground and rolling around on the floor. One day I brought a camera to school and took a picture of Ralph in one of his "moments." Later on, after he had calmed down, I showed the picture to him and was amazed at the impact it had. He seemed to look at the photo as if the boy depicted there was someone else. Gradually, though, he began to realize that the person on the floor really was him. I could see little lights go on inside of his head as he started to connect himself to his behavior. He never threw a tantrum again.

This experience made me realize the importance of providing immediate feedback to kids with behavior and attentional problems. Many of these children go in and out of control without ever becoming aware of the consequences of their actions, without realizing how their actions look to other people, and without experiencing themselves as the "prime mover" of their behavior. As a result, they find it very difficult to change their behavior. By providing immediate feedback to these kids, we can give them a means of owning or taking responsibility for their actions.

Here are a couple of ways that parents can give kids immediate and frequent experiences of feedback so that they can start to get a real sense of themselves and their impact on the environment.

- *Quantify your child's behaviors.* Identify one of your child's problem behaviors (falling out of his chair) and then count the number of times during the day that this behavior occurs. At the end of the day, present the figure to your child in a matter-of-fact way. It's important to give the feedback in a nonjudgmental fashion so that your child's defenses aren't aroused.
- *Use technology to catch behaviors on the fly.* Take photos or video of your child when he is demonstrating a behavior you'd like to eliminate. Make sure to show him the photo or play back the videotape as soon after the behavior as possible so that he can more easily connect what he sees on the screen or in the photo to his recent actions. You can also use audiotape or digital recording (for recording insults or swearing), a behavior diary (to write down specific actions and words used), or a full-length mirror to let your child see for himself what his actions look like the moment he is engaged in them.

Ultimately, these activities are designed to confront out-of-control kids with a way of observing and then taking charge of their own actions. Although no words may pass between you two (and you must avoid at all costs any sermonizing as a follow-up to your feedback), when you present your child with accurate, objective, and nonjudgmental feedback, essentially you're asking him, "Is this the way you want to come across to the world?" Many kids, seeing themselves perhaps for the first time, will want to respond, through their responsible actions, with a resounding no!

Work to Promote Teacher–Child Rapport
(Ages 4–18)

It goes without saying that teachers are vital to your child's success in school. But it goes even further: a teacher can affect your child's entire life. American writer Henry Adams famously said, "A teacher affects eternity; he can never tell where his influence stops."[1] Now there is research to support this view. One study found that a preschooler's chances of being referred for special education later on in elementary school are affected primarily by a negative and stressful relationship with his preschool teacher rather than any lack of engagement with the curriculum or other demographic risk factors.[2] In Strategy #3: Emphasize Diversity Not Disability, we looked at the famous Pygmalion in the Classroom study, which concluded that teachers' positive expectations for their elementary school students increased intelligence test results by the end of the year.[3] At the secondary level, high school students with teachers who have high expectations for them are far more likely to graduate from college several years later than those for whom teachers have lower expectations.[4] Add to these studies research findings that teachers from kindergarten to twelfth grade have lower expectations for kids diagnosed with ADHD than typically developing kids (a bit higher if they are on meds) and it becomes clear that a major task for parents of ADHD-identified children is to serve as a strong advocate for their kids' positive qualities, traits, and strengths to his teachers at school.

There are several ways in which you can increase the chances that your child's teacher(s) will view your child or adolescent in a positive light and have a warm and supportive relationship with him that leads ultimately to positive dividends later on in school and life, even if their current relationship is stormy or stressful. Here are a few ideas:

- *Bring evidence of your child's strengths to the first parent–teacher conference of the year.* Share photos of your child's accomplishments, interests, and strengths (such as the FFA award for his prize pig, an art work, or an intricate Lego structure he built in his bedroom).

- *Work cooperatively with your child's teacher during the year.* Don't be seen by the school as "the demanding mother" but rather as the helpful advocate who provides positive information regarding some of the best ways in which to reach your child and help him learn. Listen to the teacher and ask what you can do at home to help her efforts. Volunteer in the classroom to show your support. (See also Strategy #36: Foster Good Home–School Communication.)

- *Encourage your child to get along with his teacher, even if the relationship is strained.* Suggest to him that working things out now is an important life skill that will help him deal with people he regards as difficult later on as an adult.

- *Meet with your child's teacher (and include your child or teen) as soon as any conflict arises.* Use any problem-solving programs or procedures provided by the school to help resolve the issue.

- *When positive things happen in the classroom, express appreciation to the teacher.* Write a note, make a phone call, send an e-mail, or give a small token of thanks, and encourage your child to do the same (avoid expensive gifts that will cause your child to be branded as the teacher's pet and possibly bullied).

The best thing you can do for your child to help ensure a positive relationship with his teacher is to equip him with the appropriate strategies and skills provided in this book so that when he goes to school, his teacher will smile brightly and welcome him into the classroom with positive expectations.

Consider Neurofeedback Training
(Ages 7–18)

Developments in technology and neuroscience are opening up new vistas for people with disabilities. People with quadriplegia can now operate a computer cursor using only their thoughts. People with a range of disorders from migraines and depression to anxiety and post-traumatic stress disorder (PTSD) are being helped to cope with their symptoms through neurofeedback or the systematic training of their brain waves. Now children and adolescents diagnosed with ADHD are seeing improvements in their symptoms through this technology.

The human brain generates very small amounts of electrical current that can be measured on an electroencephalogram (EEG). These currents vary in amplitude according to the state of mind of the individual. For an adult in a quiet resting state, most of the EEG record will consist of *alpha* waves from the back of the head that repeat themselves at about ten hertz (a hertz is an international unit of frequency equal to one cycle per second). More rapid rhythms associated with a state of focused and alert attention in the central and frontal portions of the brain occur at eighteen to twenty-five hertz and are referred to as *beta* waves. Rhythmic slow waves at frequencies between four and seven hertz—called *theta* waves—are normal in infants and young children but tend to decrease during the elementary school years. These waves are also associated with daydreaming, hypnogogic imagery (dreamlike images that occur between sleeping and waking), creativity, and a "wide" focus of attention.

Neurofeedback programs have been designed to assist ADHD-diagnosed children and adolescents in producing less *theta* and more *beta* brain waves, thus improving their ability to focus and concentrate. Kids watch video displays and play video games that involve different challenges while being hooked up to sensors attached to their scalp or arm that measure their brain waves. In one program, as long as a child is producing *beta*, bright colors advance around a wheel accompanied by tones going up the musical scale. In another program, the trainee has to produce *beta* waves to keep a digital airplane or bird above a certain line on the computer screen.

Neurofeedback training has many attractive features for inattentive kids. It works like a video game, has bright colors and sounds, provides immediate feedback, and offers rewards for a job well done. But does it work? For years, many ADHD experts worked hard to deride neurofeedback as an "unscientific and unproven" intervention for ADHD.[1] In the past five years, however, a number of well-designed studies have shown measurable signs of improvement in attention, focus, and behavior in children who've undergone neurofeedback training.[2] One recent study which appeared in the journal *Pediatrics* found greater and quicker improvements in symptoms among ADHD-diagnosed schoolchildren who underwent forty sessions of in-school neurofeedback training compared with two other groups of ADHD-diagnosed kids, one that served as a control group and the other that engaged in cognitive training. These results held up six months after the training ended.[3]

There are certain guidelines that parents should keep in mind when considering a neurofeedback program for their children. First, consider this as an *adjunctive* treatment to be used with other approaches and not as a foolproof method of "curing" ADHD. Steer clear of any practitioner who claims 100 percent remission of symptoms or makes other excessive claims about the effectiveness of neurofeedback. Second, neurofeedback training may not be appropriate for your child if he is clinically depressed, suffers from seizure disorders, is under seven years of age, or has psychotic episodes. Third, work with a practitioner who is clinically certified and has plenty of experience working with kids with attention problems. Ask about prior experience—some neurofeedback technicians claim to be certified after only three days of training. Finally, remember that the neurofeedback program doesn't create the results, the child does. Children do different things to create the changes in brain waves. Some children visualize, others get physical feelings or think specific thoughts. It's what kids do with their mind that helps create the new behaviors—the program merely serves as a medium for change.

FOR FURTHER INFORMATION

International Society for Neurofeedback and Research: 1350 Beverly Rd., Suite 115, PMB 114, McLean, VA 22101; certify.bcia.org/4dcgi/resctr/search.html. Web site includes a database in which you can find a certified practitioner in your area.

STRATEGY #55

Use Touch to Soothe and Calm
(Ages 4–12)

As a teacher of children with special needs, I often found myself in situations where a child was out of control: throwing a tantrum, fighting with another student, or simply driven to distraction. At such times, I almost instinctively found it necessary to reach out and touch the child—often just lightly on the shoulder—as a way of making contact and sending a message of reassurance. Princeton anthropologist Ashley Montagu wrote that touch is a strong human need, stimulating the release of endorphins in the brain that have a pain-relieving effect similar to that of morphine.[1] For thousands of years, the "laying on of hands" has been regarded as a potent method of physical and emotional healing. We can learn to use its powerful influence in sensitive ways to help lessen the effects of some of the more disturbing behaviors experienced by children who've been identified as hyperactive or ADHD.

Kids diagnosed with ADHD can benefit from touch in many ways. First, as we've seen in this book, many ADHD-diagnosed children have high needs for stimulation, and that includes tactile and bodily stimulation as well. You can see this in the way many of these kids interact with their environment: touching the walls and furniture of a room as they pass through it, knocking roughly up against their friends and enemies, fidgeting restlessly while seated at their desks. These kids appear to be trying to provide themselves with adequate physical stimulation. Sensitive and safe forms of nonsexual touch from parents and teachers can help meet some of these needs.

Second, many of these kids have experienced chronic stress, whether from school problems, peer conflicts, or parent–child tensions, and have developed uncomfortable muscular kinks that impair learning and attention. Touch can serve as a way of helping dissolve those tensions and free up constricted muscular energy that can then flow in the child's body in a more natural way. Finally, studies indicate that touch and massage improve behavioral outcomes and positive emotional outlook in children and adolescents with an ADHD diagnosis.[2]

There are many ways of providing nourishing touch experiences for your child, including back rubs, hugs, foot massages, and light back scratching. But first, make sure to get your child's consent for a massage. Nothing could be more annoying, uncomfortable, and even potentially abusive than a parent who insists on touching a child without permission. If you massage your child, make sure that your hands are warm. Press gently yet with strength. Older kids may not feel comfortable with formal massage yet may welcome opportunities for tickling, wrestling, or other indirect ways of making body contact. At school, where physical contact with children is complicated by teachers' fears of sexual molestation charges, a simple touch on the shoulder may be enough to reassure a distraught child or help a distracted student focus.

Light physical contact can also be worked into academic experiences. For example, students might spell words on each other's backs. And students can even be taught to give themselves self-massage in areas of tension (for example, "palming, or massaging the muscles surrounding the eyes by placing the hands gently over the eyes and gently rubbing to relieve eye strain) or press special energy points (associated with the Traditional Chinese Medicine practice of acupressure) to help focus and ground awareness. Touch, after all, is simply human energy, and when we learn to apply it in nourishing ways with kids whose energies are off-track, we can help them find a place of calm within themselves and assist them in moving with confidence into the world.

FOR FURTHER INFORMATION

Mary Atkinson, *Healing Touch for Children: Massage, Acupressure and Reflexology Routine for Children Aged 4–12* (London: Gaia, 2009).

STRATEGY #56

Provide Opportunities for Learning through Movement
(Ages 4–18)

During one of my education workshops on learning styles a teacher shared the story of a boy in her fourth-grade classroom who was quite hyperactive and couldn't seem to focus on the material she was trying to teach him. One day, she asked him to water the plants while she went on with her teaching and was surprised to learn afterward that he managed to absorb a great deal of her lecture material while doing the chore. This suggests that many children—among them, children diagnosed with ADHD—need to move in order to learn. Unfortunately, virtually all children these days are expected to learn under classroom conditions where they must sit quietly at their desks for long periods of time (even, I'm very sorry to say, in preschool!). It's understandable, then, why many of these kids squirm, wiggle, and show other signs of ADHD-related behavior.

Movement activities should be a regular part of the academic program at school. Here are some strategies teachers can use:

- Role-play history lessons or act out reading passages
- Learn spelling words by standing up on the vowels and sitting down on the consonants
- Master the times tables by counting while moving in a circle and skipping on every third, fourth, or fifth number (and on up to ten or twelve)
- Create an algebraic equation by having class members form a group equation where each child represents a different mathematical symbol ($2x + 1 = 5$)

At home, there are many ways to provide channels for learning through appropriate physical movement, including some of the following:

- During homework sessions, allow your child to lie on the floor if that feels more comfortable or to find some other posture (such as standing up) that helps get the job done.
- Permit him to get up frequently and move around while reading if that seems to be his style; he may get more done in short bursts than in long, drawn-out struggles to get him to sit still and finish his work.
- Let your child read and/or study while in a rocking chair, hammock, or on a porch swing, swivel chair, or stationary bike (see also Strategy #10: Build, Borrow, or Buy Wiggle Furniture).

Above all, keep in mind that your child's ADHD symptoms sometimes become a problem when the environment around him fails to provide an appropriate place for movement. Once you've begun to accept your child's need for motion, you can set out to provide him with some truly moving learning experiences.

FOR FURTHER INFORMATION

Carla Hannaford, *Smart Moves: Why Learning Is Not All in Your Head* (Salt Lake City, UT: Great River, 2007).

Rae Pica, *Moving and Learning Across the Curriculum: More Than 300 Activities and Games to Make Learning Fun*, 2nd ed. (Clifton Park, NY: Delmar, 2006).

STRATEGY #57

Make Time for Plenty of Humor and Laughter
(Ages 4–18)

Several years ago I was doing a workshop for a group of teachers on ADHD strategies and one teacher raised her hand and shared that she'd been the comedian Carrot Top's teacher when he was a child. She said that Carrot Top (real name: Scott Thompson) would act quite silly during class time but that she found a surefire way to get him to stop. She told him that if he could act appropriately during class she would give him a fifteen-minute block of time at the end of the class session to do a comedy routine. It worked like a charm! While Scott Thompson hasn't been diagnosed with ADHD, many individuals who ultimately became famous comedians and entertainers have been, including Jim Carrey, Whoopi Goldberg, Woody Harrelson, Suzanne Somers, Tom Smothers, Howie Mandel, and (extending the definition of entertainer a bit) James Carville. A lot of kids diagnosed with ADHD are the "class clowns," and their sense of humor is often seen as a behavior problem and another indication of their disorder.

However, humor and laughter play an important role in life and health. People who laugh have less of the stress hormone cortisol in their blood.[1] Laughter also triggers release of the brain's natural painkillers, the endorphins.[2] Neuroscientist Jaak Panksepp, who was the first researcher to discover laughter in laboratory rats, suggests that playful laughter is a positive evolutionary development that, if given more opportunity to express itself through rough-and-tumble play, could reduce the symptoms associated with ADHD.[3]

Here are some ways that you can inject more humor and laughter into your family's daily schedule:

- *Scan joke books, read the funny papers, and look for hilarious things in the news to share together as a family during meal times and at other points during the day.* Research suggests that most laughter happens as a response to other people laughing, so leave time for everybody to have their chuckle before moving on to the next joke.[4]
- *Get a few props together and put on funny skits together as a family.* Or use the kind of prompts that improvisational troupes employ (for example, select a place, a character, and a situation, and improvise a scene using those elements).
- *Use humor to soften parent–child communications.* Clinical psychologist and former president of the National Attention Deficit Disorder Association Peter Jaksa shares the story of how a parent's usual command for a child to come to dinner—"Ginny, it's time for dinner!"—wasn't working but that changing it to "It's time to eat, Pete!" produced positive results.[5]

- *Don't try to fake it.* Insincere laughter is processed by a different part of the brain than genuine laughter.
- *Be clear that obscene humor or humor that disparages others is off-limits.* If your child happens to slip up and do this anyway, use it as an opportunity to teach him about why it's considered inappropriate and degrading to others.

They say that laughter is the best medicine, so make sure that you and your family get a regular dose of the jollies every day without fail.

FOR FURTHER INFORMATION

The Humor Project Inc., 10 Madison Ave., Saratoga Springs, NY 12866; 1-518-587-8770; https://www.humorproject.com. Promotes the importance of humor and laughter in education, medicine, and daily life; offers conferences, a newsletter, a speaker's bureau, and resources such as books and DVDs.

STRATEGY #58

Spend Positive Time Together
(Ages 4–18)

Parents are truly a child's first teachers. Nature maintains the dependence of children on parents for several years after birth so that parents can help mediate a child's adaptation to the environment. If that relationship includes a lot of yelling, arguing, fighting, and other negative interactions, then the child's adaptation to life will be compromised. On the other hand, a positive relationship between parent and child prepares the child for full and active participation in the world. This positive relationship is forged from all the little moments that parents and children spend together: moments of playfulness, creativity, respect, problem solving, wonder, silliness, curiosity, and delight that the parent and child mutually share. If these moments are absent, the child is left without a beacon to light her way through life.

It's understandable, then, that children instinctively crave positive contact with their parents. Citing a study of twenty-five hundred fifth graders, author Zig Ziglar writes, "The one thing that upset children the most was spending too little time with their parents."[1] Ziglar points out that "for a child, love is spelled T-I-M-E." When a group of boys diagnosed with ADHD were asked to select their favorite rewards for positive behavior from a list that included games, television, toys, and candy, time spent with parents led the list.[2] Unfortunately, in many households where time is stretched thin by working parents and a faster pace of life, positive time between parents and children is a scarce commodity. And for families in which a child has already experienced behavior difficulties, much of this precious time can be wasted in negative interactions.

Don't wait for the positive times to happen: make them happen by scheduling them into your day. For busy parents, this may involve having a special time with your child before breakfast or after dinner on weekdays. But make sure it happens regularly even if for only a few minutes at a time. Some of the positive things you can do together with your child include these suggestions:

- Reading a book
- Going for a walk
- Playing a board game
- Listening to music
- Telling funny jokes
- Looking at family photos
- Drawing pictures
- Playing catch
- Singing songs
- Taking a car ride
- Going to the zoo
- Having a conversation
- Going out for dinner
- Cooking something together
- Building something
- Repairing something in the house
- Playing one-on-one basketball
- Going on a picnic

- Visiting a historical site
- Doing a puzzle
- Engaging in a craft project
- Watching TV and talking together about what you see
- Playing with pets
- Doing card tricks or magic tricks
- Writing a collaborative story
- Visiting a museum
- Playing a sport (bowling, tennis)
- Doing a science experiment
- Looking at your child's collection (sports cards, coins, stamps, dolls)
- Phoning a relative
- Putting on music and dance
- Meditating or praying
- Learning something new
- Going miniature golfing
- Looking up information on the Internet
- Planning a trip
- Playing educational video games
- Telling stories
- Reading magazines together and talking about them
- Making things with clay
- Riding bikes
- Creating music with instruments
- Playing with toys
- Doing volunteer or charity work
- Solving brainteasers

In addition to the suggested activities, plan on being available for special events in your child's life, including teacher conferences, soccer games, the school play, music recitals, and celebration times like birthdays and graduation (see also Strategy #25: Celebrate Successes). Also consider daily events such as meals and bedtime as regular opportunities for positive contact with your child. At mealtimes talk about the day's news, relate good things that happened during the day, or share funny jokes or stories. At bedtime (for younger kids), read a favorite book or tell a bedtime story, listen to your child talk about things he did during the day, and end with I-love-yous and reassuring hugs and kisses. By providing your child or teen with a safe and loving parent relationship, you're helping install shock absorbers in your child that have a lifetime guarantee.

FOR FURTHER INFORMATION

Cynthia L. Copeland, *Family Fun Night*, 2nd ed. (Kennebunkport, ME: Cider Mill Press, 2016). Tips and advice for setting up weekly family time, as well as hundreds of practical ideas for spending quality time together, with an emphasis on "unplugged" activities.

STRATEGY #59

Discover Your Child's Multiple Intelligences
(Ages 4–18)

I taught a remarkable group of kids during my five years in special education classrooms. Among them was a boy who held the national swimming record for breaststroke in his age group; a girl who was a model for a national department store chain; a boy whose science fiction sagas had us all wondering what he would think of next; a girl who was being investigated by parapsychologists for psychic abilities; several students with superior artistic skills; and kids who were natural leaders, mechanical wizards, musicians, and mathematicians. What they all had in common was difficulty with the traditional classroom model of workbooks, lectures, and standardized tests, a difficulty that revealed itself in learning, behavior, and/or attention problems.

What I discovered in my years of working with these kids was that each one of them was a learner—but that each student learned in a different way. While pursuing my doctorate in psychology, I began to understand why and how they learned differently. In 1986 I was introduced to the theory of multiple intelligences developed by Harvard researcher Howard Gardner, who criticized the idea of I.Q. intelligence and suggested that there are at least eight separate intelligences.[1] The chart below lists them and describes the best way of teaching kids who have proclivities in each one (keep in mind that *all* kids have *all* eight intelligences and they combine in different ways to make each child unique).

NAME OF INTELLIGENCE	CAREERS INCLUDE	CHILDREN LEARN BEST IN THIS WAY THROUGH
WORD SMART	writer, editor, professional speaker, lawyer	reading, writing, speaking, memorizing
NUMBER/LOGIC SMART	scientist, mathematician, computer programmer, data analyst, physician	logical problem solving, analyzing numerical data, interpreting statistics, creating hypotheses
PICTURE SMART	artist, architect, graphic designer, illustrator, film editor	drawing, visualizing, working with visual media
BODY SMART	athlete, dancer, actor, craftsperson	hands-on learning, role-play, drama, learning by moving
MUSIC SMART	composer, conductor, disc jockey, sound engineer	rhythmic learning, listening to music, creating songs
PEOPLE SMART	manager, marriage counselor, union leader, politician	communicating with others, cooperating, collaborating
SELF SMART	psychotherapist, life coach, entrepreneur	personal reflection, goal setting, affective learning
NATURE SMART	marine biologist, veterinarian, farmer, forest ranger	being outdoors in nature, caring for plants and/ or animals, thinking ecologically

Once a child enters school, there tends to be an emphasis on only two of the intelligences: *word smart* and *number/logic smart* (reading, writing, math, and science). If a child has natural strengths in these areas, then he'll probably do quite well in school. If he has difficulties with linguistic and logical intelligence, however, then he may well end up with an ADHD diagnosis, even if he possesses high levels of ability in one or more of the other six intelligences.

A person with an inclination toward *body smart* seems to be at high risk for the ADHD label. This child needs to learn about things by touching them, by moving around, by building with his hands, and in other ways getting physical with the learning process. If this student has to spend several hours sitting quietly in a classroom listening to lectures, filling out worksheets, and reading textbooks, he's likely to respond to this confining scenario with restlessness, fidgeting, inattentiveness—in short, the symptoms of ADHD.

At school, these kids need to study literature by acting out the characters, learn history by creating dioramas of famous historical events, master mathematics by jumping up on every seventh number to learn multiples of seven, and acquire their science knowledge by engaging in hands-on experiments. At home, these kids should be able to do their homework standing up or sitting in a rocking chair; quench their curiosity about the world by visiting museums, observatories, and libraries; and in other ways be able to learn by wandering around.

FOR FURTHER INFORMATION

Thomas Armstrong, *In Their Own Way: Discovering and Encouraging Your Child's Multiple Intelligences* (New York: Tarcher/Perigee, 2000).

Thomas Armstrong, *Multiple Intelligences in the Classroom*, 3rd ed. (Alexandria, VA: ASCD, 2009).

Thomas Armstrong, *You're Smarter Than You Think: A Kid's Guide to Multiple Intelligences* (Minneapolis, MN: Free Spirit, 2014).

STRATEGY #60

Help Your Child Develop a Growth Mind-Set
(Ages 7–18)

"I can't do that, it's too hard!" "Joey made me goof up!" "Teacher doesn't like me and that's why I'm flunking!" These are three of the million excuses I used to hear in my special education classes from my students. Rather than face a challenge head-on, a challenge they actually had the capacity to meet successfully, many of these kids would instead look to forces outside of themselves to explain away their difficulties. This is understandable given the cycle of failure that many of these kids had been through. After repeated low grades from teachers, rejection from peers, and criticism from parents and siblings, many of these kids felt like giving up. Scientists have coined a term to describe this phenomenon: *learned helplessness*.

Studies suggest that children and adolescents diagnosed with ADHD are more likely to experience learned helplessness than typically developing kids.[1] But new research suggests that they can undo this crippling state of mind by adopting a positive mental outlook. Stanford University psychologist Carol Dweck discovered that when people believe intelligence is innate and inborn ("I simply wasn't born with a lot of smarts")—a condition she calls a *fixed mind-set*—they exhibit less self-control and perform more poorly on academic coursework compared to those who believe that personal effort or willpower ("I can do it if I try hard enough") is largely responsible for success in life. This latter perspective she calls a *growth mind-set*.[2]

At home there are several things you can do to help your child develop a growth mind-set. First, spend time talking with him about the reasons for his successes and failures in school. You might make a list of all the reasons he comes up with for doing well or poorly in his classwork. Then go over the list together, examining each reason and highlighting the ones he has most control over. Encourage him to create a positive attributional statement such as "I do well when I work hard" or "Good things happen when I try." Perhaps he can even make a poster with his positive statement on it to keep near his study area.

Second, share stories with him of individuals who tried hard and succeeded in life. Good examples include Helen Keller, who despite being deaf and blind became a world-famous author, and Thomas Edison, who was hyperactive as a child (it was Edison who said, "Genius is 1 percent inspiration and 99 percent perspiration"). Read literature together that reinforces the value of persistence, effort, and initiative, including the fable of the ant and the grasshopper, the tale of the tortoise and the hare, the stories of John Henry and the Little Engine That Could, or for older kids and teens the biographies of people who overcame difficulties through positive effort to succeed such as Stevie Wonder, Oprah Winfrey, Marlee Matlin, and Stephen Hawking.

Finally, when you see your child showing good effort, let him know it! Be a cheerleader for your child and you can help him activate his own inner cheerleader. Then sit back and watch his grades and motivation rise.

FOR FURTHER INFORMATION

Mary Cay Ricci, *Mindsets in the Classroom: Building a Culture of Success and Student Achievement in Schools* (Austin, TX: Prufrock Press, 2013).

Mary Cay Ricci and Margaret Lee, *Mindsets for Parents: Strategies to Encourage Growth Mindsets in Kids* (Austin, TX: Prufrock Press, 2016).

STRATEGY #61

Use Natural and Logical Consequences as a Discipline Tool
(Ages 7–18)

Joey is playing roughly with his toy truck and breaks it. Mom comes into the room and yells, "How many times have I told you to be gentle with your things? Go to your room!" Joey runs off crying while Mom picks up the toy and throws it in the garbage. A half hour later, Mom comes into Joey's room and says, "I hope you've learned your lesson! Tomorrow we'll go to the mall and get you another truck if you're good the rest of the day."

Has Joey learned his lesson? Probably not. More likely, Joey has learned to associate breaking things with anger toward Mom for punishing him, and gratefulness toward Mom for getting him a new toy. There's nothing in the "lesson" that helps Joey relate the manner in which he plays with toys to their breaking and subsequent loss. In the above scenario, Joey appears to have been disciplined. However, if you look up the word *discipline* in the dictionary, you'll see that it's derived from the Latin word *discipulus*, meaning "a learner." In other words, *real* discipline implies that a learning experience has taken place. Joey has only learned that if he breaks another toy, he'll be sent to his room and then be taken to the mall to buy a new one.

The use of natural or logical consequences, on the other hand, is much closer to the true meaning of the word discipline. Natural consequences refers to things that happen as a result of the natural flow of events. In this case, the natural consequence of Joey playing roughly with the toy is that the toy breaks. A further natural consequence of the toy breaking is that Joey no longer has a functioning toy. In this case, nature supplies its own consequence and Mom really doesn't have to do anything at all, other than to say something like "Gee, Joey, I'm sorry your toy broke," help him see the relationship between his actions and the result (delivered in a nonjudgmental way) and leave it at that. No yelling, no punishment, and no new toy.

Logical consequences are a little bit different. These refer to events created by a parent that are logically related to the child's actions. So, if Joey had been playing roughly with his *sister's* toy truck and broke it, then Mom might arrange a logical consequence that required Joey to buy his sister a new one using his allowance money.

The use of natural consequences is the preferred approach of the two because the impersonal forces of nature do all the disciplining. Logical consequences, on the other hand, seem to work best primarily with behavior motivated by a need for attention. If you're locked in a power struggle with your child or your child seeks revenge for some perceived wrong, he's apt to interpret your efforts to arrange a "logical" consequence as another example of how you're out to get him. And if he already feels angry or hurt, he's likely not to care what consequences you may concoct for him, logical or otherwise.

To apply natural consequences, child discipline guru Rudolf Dreikurs recommends that parents simply ask the question, "What would happen if I didn't interfere?" If the toy is lost, there is no toy. If the child misses dinner, he becomes hungry. These are inevitable consequences that don't require the intervention of the parent. Of course, if the child is likely to hurt himself with no parental interference (such as playing out in traffic), then immediate action in the form of logical consequences may be warranted (being put in the backyard where it's safer, for example).

To create effective logical consequences, according to parenting expert Jane Nelsen, parents need to apply the criteria of the 3 Rs: Is the proposed consequence *related, respectful,* and *reasonable?* If the child is sent to bed for throwing a tantrum, the consequence is not *related* to the child's original behavior. If the parent tells a child who just broke a toy, "There! I hope you're satisfied with what you just did!" there's no real *respect* for the child. And if the child marks up her desk with graffiti and she has to clean every class member's desk as a result, then that's not *reasonable.* Remember that the real purpose of discipline is not to "teach your kid a lesson!" but to help your child or teen learn new and more positive behaviors for living more responsibly in the world.

FOR FURTHER INFORMATION

Rudolf Dreikurs and Loren Grey, *The New Approach to Discipline: Logical Consequences* (New York: Plume, 1993).

Provide Access to Natural and Full-Spectrum Light
(Ages 4–18)

Unless we've been on an extended hiking or camping trip, it's hard for us in the modern world to envision what it must have been like for people living in the era before the advent of the electric light. For hundreds of thousands of years humans evolved under conditions where the sun and a little fire and lightning were the only available sources of light. When it got dark, people went to sleep. Our circadian rhythms or daily wake-and-sleep cycles developed under those natural conditions. Now, however, people work and study into the night hours with electric lighting, and increasingly the glare of computer screens, as a customary part of their lives. Recent studies have confirmed that this intrusion of artificial light into the dark hours of the evening may contribute to a variety of human ills including depression, diabetes, obesity, cardiovascular problems, cancer, and now, ADHD.

A study published in the scientific journal *Biological Psychiatry* in 2013 revealed a link between high solar intensity (SI; defined as kilowatt hours of sunlight per square meter per day) and a lower prevalence of ADHD. A map displaying the incidence of ADHD diagnoses in the United States shows that the lowest rates of ADHD diagnoses are in the Southwestern states, which receive more days of sunlight than any other part of the country. On the other hand, some of the highest rates of ADHD are in the Southeastern states, which typically receive more cloudy and rainy weather. The study suggested that sunlight alone could be responsible for 34 to 57 percent of the variance in ADHD diagnoses across the different parts of the country.[1] At the same time, other studies have indicated that evening exposure to the "blue spectrum light" emitted by many computers, tablets, and smartphones suppresses melatonin, a hormone that is important in maintaining the body's natural circadian rhythms, which leads to sleep problems, a frequent occurrence among kids diagnosed with ADHD, and this exposure also contributes to poorer concentration during the daylight hours.[2] (See Strategy #77: Make Sure Your Child Gets Sufficient Sleep.)

What do these findings mean for parents (and teachers) of children and adolescents diagnosed with ADHD? Here are a few suggestions for actions to take in view of these reports:

- Make sure your child spends as much time as possible outdoors in natural light, particularly during the morning hours.
- Have your child or teen avoid working with computer screens two to three hours before going to bed.
- Use dim red lights for night-lights. Red light has the least influence on shifting circadian rhythms in humans.
- Place your child's or teen's study area near a source of natural light, and for evening study, install full-spectrum lighting. These bulbs better approximate the spectrum of natural light than conventional incandescent or fluorescent lighting; they can be purchased from a variety of online sources.
- Encourage your child's school to investigate the possibility of modifying classrooms for better access to natural light, and installing full-spectrum lighting in strategic areas of the school (for example, areas where high-stakes tests are given).

Scientists are only beginning to understand the role that natural and artificial light plays in children's and adolescents' learning, attention, focus, and behavior. But these initial findings suggest that parents take a proactive role in ensuring that their kids spend less time in artificial lighting environments and more time taking in the healthful benefits of the sun's rays during the day.

FOR FURTHER INFORMATION

Full Spectrum Solutions: P.O. Box 1087, Jackson, MI 49204; 1-888-574-7014; www.fullspectrumsolutions.com. Sells a wide range of full spectrum lighting sources, light therapy boxes, and commercial light applications.

STRATEGY #63

Cook with Foods Rich in Omega-3 Fatty Acids
(Ages 4–18)

You've probably been hearing a lot about omega-3 fatty acids and their potential to help kids and adults diagnosed with ADHD. The reason for this publicity is the number of well-designed studies in recent years that have demonstrated a clear link between consumption of these nutrients and improvements in ADHD-related symptoms. One study found lower levels of omega-3 fatty acids in the blood of children identified as having ADHD when compared with typically developing kids. The researchers then engaged in a meta-analysis of several studies that gave omega-3 supplements to ADHD-diagnosed kids and discovered that these supplements reduced hyperactivity on both teacher and parent rating scale reports, and that they reduced inattention on parent reports.[1] In another study conducted in the Netherlands, forty boys between the ages of eight and fourteen who had been diagnosed with ADHD, and thirty-nine typically developing boys, ate 10 grams (about one-third ounce) of margarine every day. Half of the boys ate margarine enriched with 650 milligrams of omega-3 fatty acids and the other half ate plain margarine (the placebo). After sixteen weeks, all the boys who ate the enriched margarine (both ADHD and typically developing) had improved attention compared to the placebo group, when measured on parent rating scales and functional MRI brain scans of cognitive control.[2] To understand why these interventions worked, it helps to know that the brain is made up of mostly fat (60 percent of it). This fat, known as white matter, helps form the myelin sheathing that insulates the axons conducting electric impulses through a brain cell. This fatty white matter also protects the cell's membrane, keeping it healthy and flexible. If the cell membranes become stiff, neurotransmitters like dopamine and norepinephrine can't pass as easily between them. Unfortunately, the body isn't able to make omega-3 fatty acid, so it must be obtained from the diet. There are three types of omega-3 fatty acids: ALA, EPA, and DHA. ALA is found in vegetable oils, the other two are in marine oils. EPA and DHA have the biggest impact on healthy brain functioning.

So how does this research affect you as a parent? It suggests that you ought to be including more omega-3 fatty acids in your child's diet. Here are some recommendations:

- *Use cooking oils that are high in ALA omega-3 fatty acids.* Canola oil, sunflower oil, flaxseed oil, and cod liver oil
- *Eat foods high in ALA omega-3 fatty acids.* Brussels sprouts, kale, mint, parsley, spinach, watercress, walnuts, pumpkin seeds, and chia seeds
- *Eat fish that contain high levels of EPA and DHA omega-3 fatty acids.* Halibut, herring, mackerel, oysters, salmon, sardines, trout, and fresh tuna
- *Buy foods that have been enriched with omega-3 fatty acids (look for a label on the package).* Eggs, margarine, milk, juice, soy milk, yogurt, bread, cereal, flour, pasta, peanut butter, oatmeal, packaged pizza, and flour tortillas
- *Discuss with your physician the pros and cons of giving your child omega-3 fatty acid supplements.* There can be a bleeding risk at high dosage levels, and supplements are not as likely to be readily absorbed or to be in the proper ratio with omega-6, another fatty acid, as are the oils found in natural foods.

Unlike elimination diets (Strategy #15: Remove Allergens and Additives from Your Child's Diet), which require major changes in your child's eating patterns, this strategy can be easily and seamlessly integrated into your family's regular meal schedule, especially with so many readily available foods that are enriched with omega-3 fatty acids. By initiating this simple shift in your food-buying habits, you can be making a major difference in your child's ability to focus and behave appropriately at home and school.

FOR FURTHER INFORMATION

William Sears and James Sears, *The Omega-3 Effect: Everything You Need to Know About the Supernutrient for Living Longer, Happier, and Healthier* (Boston, MA: Little, Brown, 2012).

Consider Family Therapy
(Ages 4–18)

In family systems theory, each member of a family is seen as an interconnected part of the whole and each member influences and is influenced by every other member. Problems that arise in individuals within the family are not seen as the unique problem of that person but rather as a problem in the family system. In this context, ADHD-related symptoms in a child may represent a response to some kind of tension existing in the family matrix: between mother and father, between father and *his* father, between siblings, or through some other family combination.

Regrettably, the identification of one member of the family as ADHD makes it all too easy for a family system to continue not to deal with deeper systemic problems because the problem has been effectively projected onto the child. This process is referred to by family therapists as *scapegoating*. Family therapy pioneer Murray Bowen points out, "Parents can go from one physician to another until the 'feared' defect is finally confirmed by diagnosis. Any defect discovered in physical examination, laboratory tests, and psychological tests can facilitate the projection process."[1] In this perspective, then, an ADHD diagnosis may serve to mask deeper family difficulties.

The research is clear that families with ADHD-identified kids are not trouble free. As discussed earlier in this book, there appear to be higher levels of marital distress, parental psychopathology (including depression and anxiety), and other life stresses in such families.[2] While the child's ADHD symptoms may exacerbate these difficulties, as we saw in chapter 7 it's also true that family problems work in the other direction and fuel a child's inattention, hyperactivity, and/or impulsivity. Because of this, the use of family therapy can serve as an important potential intervention for many families who have an ADHD-diagnosed child. Some family therapists accept the ADHD diagnosis and work on helping families cope with the difficulties associated with having a restless, inattentive, or impulsive child in the house. They may provide practical assistance in setting limits, developing effective communication, and enhancing self-esteem. Other family therapists will treat the entire family as "the patient" and attempt to discover family patterns, rules, secrets, myths, conflicts, alliances, or other interactions in the family that may be contributing to the ADHD symptoms of one family member. Depending on the therapist and the goals of therapy, family therapy may last a few sessions or go on for several years.

It's especially important to remember that if you decide to consider family therapy as an option, this does not mean that your child's difficulties are your fault or that you have failed as a parent. What family systems theory emphasizes is that ADHD symptoms do not reside solely within your child but are part of a larger web of relationships that include not only you and your spouse, but also your parents and other significant relatives of the present and past. Family therapy, then, offers the possibility not only for the healing of your child but also for the healing of yourself and others in your family.

FOR FURTHER INFORMATION

American Association for Marriage and Family Therapy: 112 South Alfred St., Alexandria, VA 22314; 1-703-838-9808; aamft.org/imis15/AAMFT/Content/Directories/Find_a_Therapist.aspx. The Web site includes a database in which you can find a therapist in your area.

Pep Up Each Day with at Least One Novel Experience

(Ages 4–18)

It's often been said that children and adolescents diagnosed with ADHD need clear routines and structure, which is very true (see Strategy #24: Establish Consistent Rules, Routines, and Transitions). But research also suggests that these kids get bored more easily than typically developing children. So if the family schedule consists of always doing the same things day after day, week after week, month after month, there may not be enough excitement to fuel your child's arousal system, and this could lead to flare-ups in hyperactivity, distractibility, and/or inattentiveness.

Research indicates that ADHD-diagnosed kids are especially attracted to novelty. Brain scan studies suggest that the novelty-seeking areas of the brain light up more for children identified as ADHD than for typically developing kids when unusual or rare stimuli are flashed on a screen.[1] As noted earlier in this book, kids with an ADHD diagnosis are more likely to have a dopamine receptor gene called *DRD4*, which is associated with risk taking or novelty seeking.[2] Studies also reveal that when children identified as having ADHD are engaged in an activity and something irrelevant pops up unexpectedly while they're doing it, their performance on the original activity improves.[3]

Here are ten ways in which you can build in wacky, oddball, crazy, loony, out-of-the-ordinary experiences and situations into your regular family schedule:

- Get a book on optical illusions (*Magic Eye, Xtreme Illusions*, etc.) and spend time enjoying the visual distortions.
- Change the schedule of daily events around occasionally (have dinner in the morning and breakfast at night).
- Rearrange a few pieces of furniture in the house for a day without

letting anyone know in advance (put the dining room table in a bedroom, and an end table in the kitchen).

- Have an "Opposite Day" when people do and say things that are the opposite of what they'd normally do or say (say "bye" when you greet someone, and "hello" when you leave).
- Keep a boredom box filled with things to have fun with (a Slinky, Rubik's cube, "x-ray" glasses, neon wands, Silly Putty, hand buzzer, etc.).
- Order novelty toys on the Internet (see "For Further Information" below) and have fun sharing them with each other.
- Read out loud and discuss things in books filled with fabulous facts (try *The Guinness Book of World Records, Ripley's Believe It Or Not!,* or *5,000 Awesome Facts (About Everything)*).
- Have a strange clothing day, where family members put on weird costumes to wear around the house.
- Change the titles and plots of familiar books you read to your child (*Goodnight Sun, The Rat on the Bat*).
- Do something as a family that you've never done before (visit a new town, meet a new person, play a new game, eat a new food, listen to a new style of music).

Spread the activities out over a period of weeks and months, thinking of ways you can amaze and delight not only your ADHD-diagnosed child but all the other members of the family as well, and let your child or adolescent also come up with surprises of his own.

FOR FURTHER INFORMATION

Oriental Trading: 1-800-875-8480; orientaltrading.com. Novelties for celebrations, special events, learning new things, crafts, and having fun.

STRATEGY #66

Provide Positive Role Models
(Ages 4–18)

What do Winston Churchill, Steven Spielberg, Thomas Edison, Jim Carrey, and Curious George all have in common? They represent examples of ADHD behaviors seen in a positive light. And for kids labeled ADHD who may tend to look at themselves in a negative way, it's particularly important to learn about individuals—both real and fictional—who are admired by others for the healthy ADHD-like traits they embody. Learning more about these figures can cause kids to identify with them and this can help fuel a positive mind-set and an affirmative attitude about life.

A look back through history reveals a stunning array of individuals who, were they transplanted into contemporary public schools, might well have been candidates for an ADHD diagnosis. Here's a short list: Sarah Bernhardt, Will Rogers, Orville Wright, Ludwig van Beethoven, Leonardo da Vinci, Louis Armstrong, Nikola Tesla, William Randolph Hearst, Enrico Fermi, Huey Long, Ignace Jan Paderewski, François Truffaut, Vincent van Gogh, John Keats, Charles Darwin, Mary Baker Eddy, Florence Nightingale, and Friedrich Nietzsche.

One needn't look only at historical examples, however, to find positive role models for kids diagnosed with ADHD. Many current celebrities have either been diagnosed or self-identify as having that label, including Olympic swimmer Michael Phelps, actor Channing Tatum, film director Steven Spielberg, and recording artist Justin Timberlake. Another good source for positive ADHD role models is relatives, friends of the family, and teachers who were hyperactive in childhood and achieved success in the community. Sometimes these positive connections occur within the nuclear family. Author James Evans, in his autobiographical work *An Uncommon Gift*, writes about how his hyperactivity was dealt with inside of his own family matrix. "My hyperkinesia . . . was a novelty to most people, and was accepted by my parents as healthy. . . . My parents assumed that I would grow out of my energetic stage, just as my father had done."[1] It's this notion of okay-ness and the feeling of connectedness to successful adults that makes such a huge difference in a young person's developing sense of competence and self-esteem.

You can help your child discover positive role models in a number of ways:

- Go to the library and look up the biographies or autobiographies of eminent individuals who struggled with behavior or attention problems in childhood.
- Research the family tree for relatives who were particularly restless yet successful in their careers.
- Read children's books that include characters modeling positive ADHD-like traits (Curious George, Ramona Quimby, Pippi Long-stocking).
- Watch TV shows or movies that include characters embodying ADHD-like qualities (Bart Simpson, Scooby Doo, The Minions, Percy Jackson, Robin Williams in *Good Morning, Vietnam*).
- Read cartoon strips that feature energetic and unpredictable characters ("Dennis the Menace," Peppermint Patty in "Peanuts," "Calvin and Hobbes," "Garfield").

Your child may even want to do a school project featuring one or more of his favorite "hyperactive heroes." By focusing on successful individuals who were also hyperactive, distractible, or impulsive as children or adults, your child or teen may soon begin to believe a very important truth: "If they can be successful, then so can I!"

FOR FURTHER INFORMATION

Judy Brenis, *ADHD Heroes* (CreateSpace Independent Publishing Platform, 2014).

STRATEGY #67

Discover and Manage the Four Types of Misbehavior

(Ages 4–18)

Kahlil Gibran, in his well-known poem about children, says, "Your children are not your children / They are the sons and daughters of life's longing for itself." By this, Gibran means, among other things, that children are not parents' property, but rather have their own independent lives and destinies. As separate human beings, children are deserving of our deepest respect. These watchwords are especially important when considering appropriate discipline methods for managing children's misbehaviors.

An approach to discipline that embodies this kind of respect for children has its origins in the work of Alfred Adler, an Austrian psychiatrist who was at one time a disciple of Sigmund Freud. Adler and his colleague Rudolf Dreikurs, an American psychiatrist, believed that all children's behavior was bent on achieving two goals: to feel a sense of belonging and to be significant. Children who misbehave are trying to reach these two objectives, but they mistakenly believe that they can attain these goals by engaging in activities seen as troublesome or disturbing by those around them. An important first step in helping children learn more appropriate ways of behaving resides in discovering the real reasons behind a child's misbehavior and then dealing with the underlying need.

Dreikurs suggested that instances of misbehavior are apt to fall primarily into one of four types:

1. *Children misbehave to gain attention.* When children misbehave in this way, they're trying to feel significant and establish a sense of belonging by *drawing attention* to themselves. ("You haven't been paying enough attention to me! I want you to notice me and care about me!")
2. *Children misbehave to achieve power.* Here children are trying to

feel important and connected to others by *asserting* themselves in a strong way. ("I can do *what* I want, *where* I want, *when* I want! So there!")

3. *Children misbehave to seek revenge.* Here, children want *compensation* for the hurt of feeling deprived of importance or a sense of belonging. ("So you don't think I matter much, do you? Well, I'll show you a thing or two!")

4. *Children misbehave to assume an attitude of inadequacy.* In this case, children are reacting to a perceived loss of importance and belonging by simply *giving up*. ("Nothing I do makes any difference to you! Well, you can just forget about it! I'm not doing anything anymore!")

A specific instance of misbehavior can outwardly look like any of these four types. So, for example, when Susie knocks the flowerpot off the table, she could be saying "Pay attention to me!" or "I'm more powerful than you!" or "That's what you get for punishing me!" or "I don't care anymore!" You'll need to do some problem solving to get at the underlying issue, including a look at your child's past misbehaviors (is there a pattern?), a sizing up of the current situation (what events led up to this misbehavior?), and your own parental intuition.

Once you've identified the type of misbehavior, you need to take practical steps to deal with it. Each of the four types requires a somewhat different approach. Here are some possible responses:

- When the issue is *attention*, you might ignore the behavior or do something unexpected (sing a funny song in response to a child's attention-getting whining).
- If the underlying motive is *power*, then you might need a cooling-off period followed by a problem-solving session to resolve the struggle.
- If your child seeks *revenge*, then curbing the urge to retaliate and welcoming cooperation might be ways you could handle the problem.
- If your child misbehaves because of *feelings of inadequacy*, then teaching her skills in the area of perceived inadequacy, as well as setting up opportunities for her to experience success, can go a long way toward moving her in a more positive direction.

Some parents might think, "Well, my child is misbehaving because he has ADHD, not because of these other things, and so he basically just needs medication and behavior modification to control his medical condition." But just because your child has a diagnosis of ADHD doesn't mean that he's any less human or any less subject to the same need to feel significant and have a sense of belonging as any other child. Once you realize that medication, rewards, and punishments don't really get to the heart of a child's misbehavior and that all children seek and deserve respect and encouragement, then your relationship with your child will likely improve dramatically.

FOR FURTHER INFORMATION

Rudolf Dreikurs and Pearl Cassell, *Discipline without Tears: A Reassuring and Practical Guide to Teaching Your Child Positive Behavior* (New York: Plume, 1999).

Jane Nelsen, *Positive Discipline* (New York: Ballantine, 2006).

STRATEGY #68

Co-Create an Internally Empowering Behavior Mod Program with Your Child
(Ages 7–18)

When I was a special education teacher in northern California, I taught a group of ten boys who had been referred to my class because school administrators concluded that their behavior and learning problems made it difficult for them to remain in a traditional classroom. The centerpiece of my behavior management system in the classroom was a behavior chipboard, which was prominently displayed on a wall at the front of the room. It consisted of a large sheet of plywood to which I'd affixed ten horizontal rows of pegs, six pegs to a row. On the left side of each row of pegs was a student's name. On each peg was a round piece of tag board or "chip" with a hole cut in the middle so it could slide easily onto the peg. Each morning the students would come into the room and see that they had all six chips next to their name. During the day, however, they knew that if they broke any of the posted class rules (such as no fighting, no throwing things, no bad language), they would have chips removed from the board. A chart next to the chipboard explained that if a student had six chips left at the end of the day he'd be entitled to a reward.

I was proud of my chipboard, not only because I had crafted it myself but because it represented in my mind the quintessence of classroom control—a virtue that had been impressed on me many times by my supervisors during my special education career. As you might guess, problems began to arise with the behavior chipboard almost from the start. If some of the boys lost chips early in the day it would cast an emotional pall over the rest of the morning and afternoon because they had no hope of getting them back until the next day. This would cause them to act up, resulting in further loss of chips, more emotional turmoil, and so on in a vicious downward spiral. After seeing this wasn't working, I decided to change things a bit so that a student could "earn his chips back" through positive behavior. This helped for a while. However, the boys eventually began to complain about why they weren't getting chips back on the board when so-and-so got *his* chips back up. As the weeks passed, the chipboard became the focal point of a battle of wills—mine and the students'.

Eventually, I decided to discard the chipboard. But before I did so, I shared with the class the reasons for my dissatisfaction and heard their complaints as well. I also told them that before I could throw the board away we would need to develop some ground rules for being together in the classroom. So we talked for days about rules and the consequences of breaking or keeping them. Some students wanted to institute much more severe consequences than the ones we had (including being paddled, starved, isolated, and beaten), and suggested more lavish rewards than I could provide (a trip to Disneyland). But after a couple of weeks we developed a list of rules and contingencies that both I and my class felt we could live with, and we posted them on the wall.

I remember vividly the day we stopped using the chipboard and instituted the new plan. It was quite refreshing to see students almost immediately break the rules that they themselves had helped create. It was even more liberating to see them submitting to the consequences they had agreed on for their infractions. The weeks and months that followed were not always easy, but they were free of the sapping of energy that came from trying to control these kids' lives. We all worked together now and we all felt an underlying sense of commitment to our collaborative classroom.

The reason I've gone on at some length to describe this experience is that the ADHD community tends to promote what I'd call "externally controlling behavior modification" programs by which kids are given rewards for good behavior and "response costs" (the withdrawal of awards) for infractions. There's a subtle coercion that works underneath the surface of such evidence-based programs (yes, they do work, but because children want the rewards, not because of their underlying desire to improve themselves). By far the better solution is to use internally empowering behavior modification programs where you co-create the system with your child or adolescent. Here are some steps to make it happen:

Step 1. Discuss together what your mutual concerns are, listen to your child's or teen's view of the matter, and come to an agreement about the nature of the problem and the specific goal(s) you both would like to achieve (see also Strategy #51: Teach Goal-Setting Skills).

Step 2. Negotiate any rewards that will follow after the successful demonstration over a given period of time of the new behavior or resolution of the difficulty; do the same, if appropriate, for any consequences that might follow the failure of this project.

Step 3. Set up a chart on which progress can be marked and viewed by both of you at any time of the day as you embark on the program.

Step 4. When the goal is reached, celebrate the success of the new behavior with a little ritual (see Strategy #25: Celebrate Successes) in which you proffer the reward, or if the goal was not reached, discuss what went wrong, administer the agreed-on consequence, and renegotiate a new agreement.

You can still use the equipment, materials, posters, and reinforcements that ADHD entrepreneurs and experts promote, but now, instead of imposing the program *on* the child or teen, you'll be doing the program *with* the child's or adolescent's active participation. The respect you give your child or teenager will be the key to making this collaborative program work.

FOR FURTHER INFORMATION
Jane Nelsen and Steven Foster, *Positive Discipline for Children with Special Needs: Raising and Teaching All Children to Become Resilient, Responsible, and Respectful* (New York: Harmony, 2011).

STRATEGY #69

Use Aromas to Calm and Center
(Ages 8–18)

The belief that specific aromas have both medical and psychological benefits has been around for thousands of years. Anthropologists speculate that prehistoric cultures created incense from burning gums and resins and did smudging from aromatic plant materials for healing purposes and as offerings to the gods. Ancient Vedic, Greek, Roman, and Persian cultures all employed aromatherapy as part of the healing process.[1] More recently, scientific researchers have published studies suggesting that aromatherapy can be helpful in alleviating anxiety, nausea, stress, sleep problems, and hypertension, though there is still concern about the lack of well-designed research studies in this field.[2] What makes this strategy particularly intriguing for ADHD-related issues is that, according to some studies, children diagnosed with ADHD appear to have heightened sensitivity to odors.[3] Consequently, it seems worthwhile to explore the potential of specific aromas to heighten alertness, calm overactive behavior, reduce stress, and improve overall well-being. Here are a few aromatic oils out of hundreds available that have been regarded as helpful in improving emotional and cognitive functioning:

- Roman chamomile has soothing and comforting effects.
- Lavender is a key oil that is calming and reduces anxiety.
- Patchouli works by soothing the nervous system.
- Frankincense affects the hypothalamus-pituitary-adrenal axis in reducing stress.

- Ylang-ylang increases calmness.[4]
- Peppermint boosts alertness.
- Cedarwood eases stress.

Aromas can be diffused in a number of ways. You can add a few drops to bathwater, put some drops in a boiling pot and inhale the steam, use it in diluted form as a massage oil, put it in an aroma diffuser (available online or through massage supply outlets), or add a few drops to a hot compress. Do not use aromas if your child begins to complain or shows that he doesn't like them (remember, ADHD-diagnosed childrens' and adolescents' ostensibly acute olfactory sense may make them especially sensitive to particular odors). Don't proceed with treatment until you've consulted with your doctor and/or a certified alternative health care professional (such as a naturopath, chiropractor, or herbalist). Unsupervised use could result in improper application, unwanted side effects, or exacerbation of existing health problems. This is still a new area for ADHD, but in conjunction with other complementary healing approaches, it could very well have a salutary effect on your child's or adolescent's ADHD symptoms.

FOR FURTHER INFORMATION

Nick Acquaviva, *Essential Oils: 7 Essential Oils for Children With ADHD: A Holistic Approach to Reducing ADHD Symptoms* (ecase publishing/Amazon Digital Services, 2015).

STRATEGY #70

Employ Incidental Learning
(Ages 4–18)

Most children diagnosed with ADHD are actually very good at paying attention. They're good at paying attention to what they're not supposed to be paying attention to. In the classroom they hear Joey telling Suzy about what happened to Billy during recess. They see the funny drawings that Ed made on the chalkboard before class started (drawings the teacher hasn't even noticed yet). They pay attention to their own inner thoughts: daydreams about being somewhere else besides school—perhaps at an amusement park or camping in the forest. They pay attention to everything except the parent or teacher—who drones on and on much like the adults in the *Peanuts* television specials (they all seem to be saying, *wock-wock-wock-wock*).

We should not be too quick to consider this type of incidental attention as a disorder. After all, most of what we learned during the first five years of life involved just this form of diffused attention. Young children master complex tasks like walking and talking by letting their minds be drawn to what interests them and by absorbing knowledge in incidental ways. The essential rule is, if children aren't paying attention, find out what they *are* paying attention to and then put the material they need to learn smack-dab in the middle of their current field of attention. You might call this the Energizer Bunny Strategy. A boring commercial is lulling us to sleep when suddenly this supercharged mechanical rabbit comes onto the scene from out of nowhere commanding our full attention and, incidentally, advertising the intended product.

At home, you can use incidental learning in getting your kids to attend to and follow through on everyday tasks. Here's a scenario of what this might look like:

> *Mom is telling Mike to take out the garbage. Mike doesn't seem to hear her and goes on playing with his miniature cars and trucks in his bedroom. Rather than wear out her vocal cords, Mom gets down on the floor with him and starts playing with the cars. "This one is a garbage truck, Mike. See, the garbage man is getting out in front of our house. He's saying to his buddy, 'We can't collect the garbage here, Ed, because Mike hasn't brought it out yet.'" Mike looks up at Mom and zooms out of the room in the direction of the kitchen where the garbage is waiting for him.*

In this example, Mom went right into Mike's attentional field—his play world of miniature toys—and wove her instructions into the images of his private world. She used incidental attention to deliver the message. Other ways of using incidental learning include the following:

- Record spelling or vocabulary words against the sound track of your child's favorite music and play it while he is getting ready to go to school.

- Put your child's or teen's homework assignment *for next week* on the bedroom wall *this week* so he can subliminally absorb the information without having to focus on it.
- Engage in a puppet show, where "teacher puppets" deliver the math lesson taught that day in school to "student puppets."

Too often, parents or teachers dismiss the child's failure to comply as a threat, a nuisance, or a symptom of ADHD. If the content of the child's incidental attention is first given some respect, then it may be much easier to move his attention to where you'd like it to be.

FOR FURTHER INFORMATION

Barbara K. Given and Bobbi DePorter, *Excellence in Teaching and Learning: The Quantum Learning System* (Learning Forum Publications, 2015). Written for teachers, this book includes some of the same principles involved in incidental learning to help kids absorb information more quickly and effectively.

STRATEGY #71

Rule Out Other Potential Contributors to Your Child's Behavior
(Ages 4–18)

My pediatrician father often complained to me that doctors "these days" didn't take good histories like they used to (this was in the 1960s). He'd received his medical degree from McGill University, which nurtured the careers of pioneers in medicine like Sir William Osler, Hans Selye (the originator of the concept of stress), and the neurosurgeon Wilder Penfield. My dad felt that pediatricians needed to take their time before making a diagnosis and, in addition to the appropriate medical tests, ask questions about the history of the complaint, past medical history, family diseases, social history (such as parental marital status, sibling relationships), potential allergies, medications taken, and other germane facts. I'm sure that if he could see what was happening to-day with the in-and-out rapidity of current doctor–patient relationships, he'd have a cow.

Sanford Newmark, head of the Pediatric Integrative Neurodevelopmental Program at the University of California, San Francisco, reflects my father's feelings in his concerns about the quick diagnoses occurring now with ADHD and children, saying, "It is often diagnosed without the type of thorough history and examination needed for an accurate assessment. This would involve talking to parents, the child and teachers, as well as reviewing school records and other testing. Instead, many children are diagnosed after a visit of 15 to 20 minutes with a pediatrician or other professional."[1] Another physician, neurologist Richard Saul, created quite a stir in the press with his book title, *ADHD Does Not Exist.* I believe what he was really saying in his book was that there are a wide range of conditions, disorders, and diseases that involve hyperactivity, inattentiveness, and distractibility and that physicians should be looking at the possibility that one or more *other* conditions may be the culprit before labeling a child with a disorder that just happens to be receiving the most publicity and uses the simplest solution—a pill. Here are several of the candidates that Saul suggests a physician investigate and rule out before going on to consider an ADHD diagnosis:

- *Hearing and vision problems.* A child will be inattentive and distractible if he can't hear or see what's going on in school or around the house.
- *Sleep disorders.* Many kids labeled with ADHD have significant sleep problems (see Strategy #77: Make Sure Your Child Gets Sufficient Sleep), which can leave them feeling scattered, unfocused and distractible during the day.
- *Substance abuse.* This applies especially to adolescents whose use of alcohol, marijuana, speed, and other drugs can mimic the symptoms of ADHD.
- *Mood disorders.* Symptoms of bipolar disorder, for example, include hyperactive mania, a lack of concentration, and a mind that moves from one thing to the next very rapidly; it's especially important to identify this disorder (or its melancholy cousin, unipolar depression) and treat it as quickly and effectively as possible to prevent a future major depressive episode.

• *Learning disabilities.* If a child has serious difficulties with reading (dyslexia), writing, mathematics, or other academic skills, these could be causing symptoms of hyperactivity, inattentiveness, and distractibility because of the child's frustrations with school and schoolwork.

Saul also lists several other potential conditions with symptoms that can look very much like those of ADHD: Asperger's disorder, schizophrenia, seizure disorders, fetal alcohol syndrome, obsessive-compulsive disorder, Tourette's syndrome, allergies, pituitary tumor, and heavy-metal poisoning.[2]

To make sure your child receives a correct diagnosis, you should insist he get a *thorough* medical examination from his doctor that includes the components Sanford Newmark described above: talking with parents, the child, his teachers, and other significant individuals, and administering additional medical tests as needed, before making a diagnosis of ADHD. Ideally parents should try to see a *developmental and behavioral pediatrician* if at all possible. These doctors are trained not just to understand the biomedical issues but also to see the child within the context of psychosocial, developmental, and educational concerns. But whatever physician you choose to see, insist on more than just a quick fifteen- or twenty-minute visit followed by a diagnosis and prescription. Keep in mind that the three symptoms of ADHD—hyperactivity, inattentiveness, and/or impulsivity—are the behavioral equivalent of a headache and can mean a variety of things. A thorough medical exam can help rule out other potential contributors to your child's behavior and attention difficulties.

FOR FURTHER INFORMATION

Richard Saul, *ADHD Does Not Exist: The Truth About Attention Deficit and Hyperactivity Disorder* (New York: Harper Wave, 2015).

Society for Developmental and Behavioral Pediatrics: 6728 Old McLean Village Dr., McLean, VA 22101; 1-703-556-9222; info@sdbp.org; sdbp.org/resources/find-a-clinician.cfm. The Web site includes a database in which you can find a clinician in your area.

Suggest Effective Study Strategies
(Ages 8–18)

Recently I read an article in *ADDitude*, a wonderful magazine and online resource that provides strategies and ideas to help children and adults diagnosed with ADHD reach their full potential, which had me thinking about how students study these days quite differently from the way they used to. In the piece, Mary Ann Moon's teenage son and college-age daughter both had been diagnosed with ADHD and had trouble with the traditional method of studying: sitting upright at a desk in a quiet room. Instead, her son listened to his books on audio while lying in bed and throwing a ball against his bedroom wall. Her daughter wasn't a ball thrower, but she needed some low-level ambient noise around to help her focus, so she would listen to radio music and DJ banter while she studied.[1] These two examples might seem to embody sloppy study habits, but for those who understand how the ADHD-diagnosed mind works, such methods turn out to be cutting-edge adaptations that facilitate more efficient modes of thought and comprehension. Each child and adolescent identified as having ADHD is different, so there is no one ADHD-way to study, but here is a list of suggestions to try out. See if one or more of them proves to be a workable strategy that will make your child's or adolescent's study sessions more enjoyable and effective:

- Let your child or teen choose where he wants to study (see Strategy #14: Give Your Child Choices).
- Allow him to fidget as he studies (see Strategy #1: Let Your Child Fidget).
- If he prefers, suggest he study in short bursts over a longer period if it seems to help him get things done.
- Tell him that if he gets bored with a topic, to change tasks, and to return to the first topic when he might be fresher with respect to the subject.
- Suggest some ways he can eliminate distractions while he studies (see Strategy #34: Eliminate Distractions).

- Let him do his homework in a rocking chair, on a stationary bike, or on some other moveable device (see Strategy #10: Build, Borrow, or Buy Wiggle Furniture).
- Let him talk out loud to himself (or others) while he studies (see Strategy #44: Let Your Child Engage in Spontaneous Self-Talk).
- Suggest that he divide his homework assignments into small chunks, prioritize them, and then work on one chunk at a time (the mobile app 30/30 can help with this).
- If he's a social learner, suggest that he study with a friend or create a study group.
- Tell him about tech tools that can make studying more fun and effective (for example, the Livescribe pen, which plays back notes from school written on special paper, speech-to-text apps like Dragon NaturallySpeaking, and mind-mapping tools like MindNode).
- Suggest that he think of a color that helps him study and then to cover his study area with that color, or use a visual image that motivates him to study harder or smarter that he can place in a location where he can see it while he studies (see Strategy #96: Use Color to Highlight Information).
- Let him use time-management tools to help keep track of how much time he has left to work (like the Time Timer app).
- Suggest he use self-monitoring strategies or apps to help keep him on task (try MotivAider; see Strategy #17: Teach Your Child Self-Monitoring Skills).

If your child or adolescent uses one or more of these strategies and you find that he's getting distracted and/or not studying as well as before, talk with him about this. Perhaps together you can tweak the process so it works better; perhaps you'll decide that a particular approach doesn't help at all and you'll need to try something else. Listen to your child's or adolescent's own suggestions for what works, and support him in figuring out the best way to craft a study style that can serve him throughout his school years and beyond.

FOR FURTHER INFORMATION

Eric Jensen, *Student Success Secrets*, 5th ed. (Hauppauge, NY: Barron's Educational Series, 2003). Study strategies for grades six through twelve.

Provide Your Child with Real-Life Tasks
(Ages 5–16)

In my informal survey over the last two decades of teachers' best practices for helping kids diagnosed with ADHD, one item that kept showing up on their lists was "give them something practical to do." They would mention tasks like collecting milk money, watering the plants, or rewinding the film projector. From my own experience in teaching kids with behavior and attentional problems, I can say with absolute certainty that such a child confronted with a choice between doing a worksheet or setting up a computer projector will almost always select the projector task. People out in the real world don't do worksheets but they do set up projectors.

When parents and teachers give children and adolescents with attention and behavior difficulties *real things* to do, rather than artificially contrived assignments, several things happen. First, the child or teen is treated with respect, rises to this higher expectation, and becomes responsible. Second, he's given an opportunity to interact with the real world. Real-life tasks provide the opportunity to discover rules, routines, challenges, and difficulties that are part of being a full-fledged member of society. Finally, he's able to find out what he's good at. As noted child psychoanalyst Erik Erikson observed, kids need to have experiences that make them feel like competent, industrious people or they risk emerging from this important life stage with a sense of inferiority.

There are many real-life jobs and tasks you can offer a child or teen at home or that teachers can provide at school that will help her develop competence, responsibility, and a feeling of membership in society. The following are only a few of the many possibilities:

AT SCHOOL

- Water the plants
- Care for a pet

- Tutor another student
- Take notes to the office
- Straighten the desks
- Sharpen the pencils
- Run the audio-visual equipment
- Collect money for lunch
- Clean the gerbil cage
- Fix a broken machine
- Hand out or pick up student work
- Open and close the windows
- Take attendance
- Be a playground monitor
- Serve as a school mediator to resolve disputes
- Be a student government member
- Do community service
- Reshelve books in the library
- Serve as a lab assistant in science class
- Supervise the computer lab
- Maintain the art supplies
- Help rearrange desks and/or tables and chairs
- Run errands between classrooms
- Serve as a hallway monitor
- Be a "buddy" to a younger child in school
- Read the school announcements over the intercom
- Volunteer in the school cafeteria
- Be a janitor's assistant

AT HOME

- Babysit
- Volunteer in the community
- Fix appliances
- Take care of the yard
- Repaint a portion of the house
- Organize the family's book, music, or movie collection
- Make shelves or other household items

- Cook for the family
- Be the "tour guide" during family outings
- Do special errands
- Teach other family members (such as how to use a computer app)
- Run the household's recycling effort
- Set up a bank account
- Learn CPR and first-aid skills
- Specialize in cleaning tasks (polishing silver, washing the car)
- Put in a garden
- Be the navigator (with map) during family trips
- Take care of pets
- Replace lightbulbs or other consumables
- Plan a family trip
- Set up a sidewalk business
- Preside at a family meeting
- Repair or repaint furniture
- Be the greeter at family parties
- Be responsible for recording TV programs
- Organize a family sports day or games night
- Design greeting cards to send out at holiday time
- Take photos for the family album (or videos for the family archives)
- Help younger siblings with everyday tasks (feeding, toileting)

Make sure the task is not beyond the skill level of your child or adolescent, or he can end up feeling anxious, incompetent, and/or humiliated. If he really wants to do the job, however, help him learn the requisite skills he needs. Some kids have suddenly learned to read, for example, once they realize they need that skill to do something real, like passing a driver's exam or reading a motorcycle repair manual. If your child or adolescent takes to the task and shows a special aptitude for it, you might want to help him find further opportunities to grow in this area. For example, if he enjoys taking care of the gerbil at school, perhaps you could help him get a volunteer job at a veterinarian's office. This kind of real-life experience as a child or teen can pave the way for a real career in adulthood.

FOR FURTHER INFORMATION
Barbara Lewis, *The Kid's Guide to Social Action: How to Solve the Social Problems You Choose—And Turn Creative Thinking into Positive Action* (Minneapolis, MN: Free Spirit, 1998).

STRATEGY #74

Use Time Out in a Positive Way
(Ages 4–11)

When I was a special education teacher and my students misbehaved, I'd often send them to an empty corner of the classroom. Many times this strategy would backfire when students started kicking chairs, throwing spitballs at classmates, smirking and making funny noises from behind the walled enclosure, or refusing to go, forcing me to drag them there. Yet there were also some positive experiences. I especially remember times when students chose *on their own* to go to the time-out area when they felt out of control. It seemed to me that when they actually chose to go to the time-out area—rather than being sent there as a punishment— they seemed to benefit the most.

Time out has been a very popular discipline method used in the ADHD community. One best-selling book (and accompanying video) shows parents of ADHD-labeled kids how to count "1 . . . 2 . . . 3 . . ." and if the child hasn't complied with the parent's command, they must go to the time-out area for five minutes. A typical dialogue might go something like this:

> "Matt, stop poking the dog. That's one." Matt continues poking the dog. "That's two." Matt keeps on poking, not even looking up at the parent. "That's three, take five." Matt doesn't move and is taken to his room yelling.

Unfortunately, using time out as a punitive method with many kids diagnosed with ADHD may actually turn out to be counterproductive. Two prominent ADHD researchers, Thomas and Sydney Zentall, have commented on the use of time outs. According to them, "in general, time-out periods appear to be aversive to hyperactive children. If isolation really has a calming effect on hyperactive children one would expect to see reduced activity during time-out periods. However, [we] . . . observed hyperactive children in time-out environments and noted increased rather than decreased activity levels."[1] This may occur due to the need for many of these under-aroused kids to create their own stimulation in a place (the corner) that has very low levels of stimulation. Even if punitive time out effectively controls a child's behavior in the short run, it may come at a cost to the child's self-respect and sense of dignity.

Child discipline expert Jane Nelsen counsels parents to tell kids that when they feel upset or out of control it can be helpful to have a place they can go to sort things out, to do things to make themselves feel better, or to put themselves in a state of mind that will allow them to go back to the problem and face it in a more constructive manner. Nelsen suggests that the children be the ones to decide when they need to go to a time-out area. She even recommends that parents get a timer that children can set themselves according to the amount of time they feel they need to get themselves together. Places for time out could be anywhere: a bedroom, a special chair, or a bench on the school playground are all suitable. If children associate the words *time out* with punishment, then rename the space something like thinking corner, quiet space, home base, settling-down room, energy place, or chill-out spot.

Because you're changing the purpose of time out from passive punishment (putting the child in a dull or painfully boring place) to the active working out of problems, you can suggest activities that your child do in the time-out area to help him gain control and feel better. Possibilities include

- Visualizing an image that helps them cope (see Strategy #79: Teach Your Child to Visualize)
- Meditating (see Strategy #43: Teach Your Child Mindfulness Meditation)
- Doing physical-relaxation exercises (see Strategy #46: Share Stress Management Techniques)
- Thinking about, writing down, or drawing solutions to their problem

In this redefined space children begin to see the time-out area as a place for renewal, not a place for pain.

To those skeptical about positive time out, Nelsen insists that it really can work if parents give it enough time (three to six weeks) and if they adopt a sincere attitude of encouragement and respect toward the child. "Where did we ever get the crazy idea," Nelsen writes, "that to make children do better we must first make them feel worse?"[2] Positive time out provides kids with a way to get a grip on their own behavior and allows them to take a major role in becoming successful and capable people.

FOR FURTHER INFORMATION

Jane Nelsen, *Positive Time-Out: And Over 50 Ways to Avoid Power Struggles in the Home and the Classroom* (New York, Prima, 1999).

STRATEGY #75

Enhance Your Child's Self-Esteem
(Ages 4–18)

On his Web site, Harvard psychologist Robert Brooks shares a creative writing sample from an adolescent boy diagnosed with ADHD that he'd been seeing in therapy. The teen writes, "Going to school has been like climbing up a steep mountain. Each step is a battle against icy winds. Sometimes I get knocked down. My body is numb. I'm clawing up a steep cliff. I look up and my struggle has hardly begun."[1] This painful description might represent the state of mind for many kids who are diagnosed with ADHD. Perceiving the world in a different way, having a different kind of behavioral and attentional rhythm, struggling with inner conflicts, many of these kids end up being ostracized or taunted by peers, harshly evaluated by teachers, and severely punished by parents for misbehavior. It's no wonder that their sense of self isn't all that rosy.

Studies suggest that ADHD-identified kids have lower self-esteem than their typically developing peers. In one study, children diagnosed with ADHD reported their belief that a core dimension of their "real" selves was persistently "bad," even when they took their medication.[2] In another study of young people's understandings of the diagnosis of ADHD, one youth reported: "ADHD does bad stuff to you. . . . It gives you bad stuff to do and gives you a bad education in school."[3]

Given this state of affairs, it's extremely important to raise the self-esteem of ADHD-diagnosed kids. Unless a child or teen has a positive core of self from which he can move strongly into the world, he won't have the ego strength to withstand the kinds of challenges that life inevitably delivers.

Here are a few specific tips for developing your child's or adolescent's self-esteem:

- Have a success-sharing time during dinner or in the evening where everyone in the family has a chance to talk about at least one positive thing he or she did during the day (see Strategy #25: Celebrate Successes).
- Encourage your child or teen to keep a success-scrapbook containing awards, memorabilia, photos, and pictures of himself doing things he feels proud of, plus anything else that contributes to his sense of self-esteem (but don't prod him to do it if he doesn't want to).
- Suggest that your child or teen create an audio recording where he shares things he likes about himself and/or things he does really well. He can then replay it whenever he feels down and needs moral support.
- Ask your child or teen, "If you could be any animal, which one would you be?" Then suggest that he learn more about his animal and the positive traits that go along with it.
- Draw pictures together as a family depicting favorite activities and scenes of family members doing what they do best; share the pictures and keep them up around the house as reminders of everybody's positive qualities.

Most of these activities can also be incorporated into a classroom curriculum. The teacher might have a "student of the week program" in which the strengths, talents, and gifts of each child are highlighted; have interviews or puppet shows in which students focus on each other's positive qualities; or design writing assignments that prompt students to explore personal attributes ("Write a poem that tells us what you most value about your life").

Self-esteem development shouldn't be about lavishing praise on kids. Research suggests that this can even be harmful to them by setting them up for later disappointment.[4] At its heart, self-esteem education should be about meeting challenges, conflicts, and obstacles successfully. It all begins with a deep-seated belief in the ultimate goodness of your child, or as Spanish cellist Pablo Casals put it: "We should say to each child, do you know who you are? You are a marvel! You are unique!"[5] If this were the message we gave to our kids, and children took that message into their hearts, believed it, and lived their lives on the basis of it, what a wonderful world this would be!

FOR FURTHER INFORMATION

Gershen Kaufman, Lev Raphael, and Pam Espeland, *Stick Up for Yourself: Every Kid's Guide to Personal Power & Positive Self-Esteem*, rev. ed. (Minneapolis, MN: Free Spirit, 1998).

Lisa M. Schab, *The Self-Esteem Workbook for Teens: Activities to Help You Build Confidence and Achieve Your Goals* (Oakland, CA: Instant Help/New Harbinger, 2013).

STRATEGY #76

Avoid Exposure to Environmental Contaminants
(Ages: prenatal through adulthood)

The facts are alarming. U.S. industry produces more than one thousand chemicals known to affect the nervous system and two hundred are considered neurotoxins.[1] You don't have to live near a toxic dump to be affected by these contaminants. According to ADHD expert and clinical professor of psychiatry at Georgetown Medical Center Larry Silver, a number of toxins reside in common household items, including:

- Perfluorinated compounds (PFCs), which can be found in products like Teflon and Scotchgard

- Polybrominated diphenyl ethers (PBDEs), which are fire retardants and are used in clothing, furniture, and bedding
- Phthalates, a group of chemicals that make plastics more flexible, and are used in vinyl, plastic bottles, toys, shower curtains, and raincoats
- Bisphenol A (BPA), an epoxy resin used to line food cans and other containers[2]

Add to these compounds the pesticides found in foods and the heavy metals such as lead that are still in many old homes, and you're looking at a wide range of potential contributors to ADHD symptoms.

The two toxins that have been most conclusively tied to ADHD symptoms are lead exposure and secondhand smoke. The authors of one research report wrote: "Lead exposure is a plausible neurobiological candidate for involvement in ADHD because it disrupts midbrain dopamine and other neurotransmission circuitry. . . . It contributes to what is now an emerging body of literature linking ADHD to lead exposure even at population typical exposures."[3] Lead can be found in contaminated paint, water pipes, dust, soil, and water, especially in and near buildings built before the United States banned lead in residential buildings in 1978. It can also be found in ceramics, china, and porcelain (which can leach into food and water), and in some imported toys and canned goods.

Prenatal smoking has long been seen as a clear cause of ADHD-related symptoms, but more recently secondhand smoke exposure, especially among children under the age of six, has also been implicated in ADHD diagnoses. In one study, the authors wrote: "Our findings suggest that secondhand smoke exposure in children is strongly associated with ADHD independent of other risk factors."[4]

To help protect your child and your family against exposure to these and other contaminants, here are some recommendations:

- If you are a smoker and pregnant, stop smoking immediately; if you currently have children and absolutely must smoke, do it far away from your residence.
- Cover over suspected lead paint surfaces with nonlead paint or with paneling, drywall, or other sealants; do not attempt to chip, sand, or

burn off the paint as this can release lead into the atmosphere; contact your local health department for help in managing removal.

- When possible, buy organic produce, and thoroughly wash all non-organic fresh foods likely to contain pesticides (foods to be especially careful about include: peaches, apples, bell peppers, celery, nectarines, strawberries, cherries, pears, grapes, spinach, lettuce, and potatoes).
- Use green cleaning products that have fewer toxic chemicals.
- Set out sticky traps or bug zappers for pests around the house rather than using toxic remedies.
- Store food in glass containers, avoid nonstick cooking pans, and don't heat food in plastic containers.
- Contact your local water company for information about potential contaminants in your water supply and if in doubt, use a water filter for drinking and cooking.
- Make sure there's plenty of ventilation (open windows if you can) when you clean the house or do renovations, and clean up all trash and dust thoroughly.
- Ask school officials about any environmental hazard projects that may be ongoing at your child's school, and if you're suspicious, press school board and city council members to address the issue immediately.

While there isn't incontrovertible evidence linking most toxic contaminants to ADHD diagnoses (other than lead and cigarettes), future research may uncover new culprits, and it pays to be cautious and proactive regarding the chemicals in our midst, especially since many toxins *have* been linked to other health problems. By maintaining an environmentally healthy home environment (and encouraging your child's school administrators to do the same), you can make sure that your child is protected from toxins that could affect his attention, behavior, and/or overall health.

FOR FURTHER INFORMATION

Debra Lynn Dadd, *Toxic Free: How to Protect Your Health and Home from the Chemicals That Are Making You Sick* (New York: Tarcher Perigee, 2011).

Make Sure Your Child Gets Sufficient Sleep
(Ages 4–18)

It's 9:00 P.M. and fourteen-year-old Jason, who was diagnosed with ADHD at the age of six, is watching TV in his bedroom when his older brother, John, comes in and wants to borrow his iPad to play video games. Jason say no, he needs it to finish a homework assignment and an argument erupts between them. Jason leaves the TV on and starts to work on the assignment using his tablet to convince John that he really needs to study. Now it's 11:00 and Jason gets a text message from a schoolmate that his girlfriend may be seeing another guy. At about the same time, Mom yells, "Lights out!" but Jason, frustrated and angry at the news he's just received, starts playing video poker on his tablet and continues to do so until the early hours of the morning. After three hours of restless sleep, Jason's dad wakes him up by telling him he's going to be late for school. Jason throws on some clothes, rushes past the breakfast table, and barely makes it to his 7:45 class, where he proceeds to fall asleep, earning him a detention.

Jason's story isn't unique. All across the country, and around the world, children and adolescents with and without an ADHD diagnosis aren't getting enough sleep. According to recent guidelines set by the National Sleep Foundation, the average school-age child should be getting somewhere between nine and eleven hours of sleep, and adolescents should be receiving between eight and ten hours of sleep.[1] Studies suggest, however, that 45 percent of children and adolescents are actually getting less than eight hours of sleep per night.[2] The situation is even more troubling when it comes to kids diagnosed with ADHD. First, these kids have a shorter sleep duration than typically developing children and adolescents.[3] Second, a diagnosis of ADHD is associated with a greater likelihood for sleep disturbances, including sleep-onset difficulties, night awakening, trouble with early morning awakening, sleep breathing problems, and daytime sleepiness.[4] Finally, parents of kids diagnosed with ADHD report more problematic evening behaviors during the time period just preceding bedtime, including arguing with siblings, and diffi-culty transitioning into sleep, compared with reports from parents of typi-cally developing children.[5] One study even suggested that adoption of good sleep hygiene habits plus the administration of the hormone melatonin may be adequate to successfully treat sleep initiation problems in children diag-nosed with ADHD.[6] Here are a few suggestions for creating optimal condi-tions that will favor a good night's sleep for your child or teen:

- Set consistent times for going to bed and getting up in the morning; stay with that schedule even on the weekends and holidays.
- Turn off technology devices (TV, computers, tablets, phones) one to two hours before bed.
- Avoid stressful events likely to be arousing before bedtime (such as ar-guments, fights, rough-and-tumble play, vigorous exercise).
- Create a relaxing routine leading up to bedtime that could include reading, listening to music, getting a back rub, meditating, or doing yoga (see Strategy #43: Teach Your Child Mindfulness Meditation and Strategy #87: Have Your Child Learn Yoga).
- Keep the bedroom dim or dark leading up to bedtime, and in the morn-ing, open the blinds or curtains wide to let in natural light; this helps reset the body's inner clock.
- Avoid using bedtime as a reward (being allowed to stay up late) or a punishment (having to go to bed early).
- Avoid heavy meals, caffeine, and (for offending adolescents) drugs and/ or alcohol in the late-evening hours; a light snack before bed (milk, cereal, fruit, or crackers) is fine.
- Make the bed a soothing place, with comfy pillows, smooth sheets, stuffed animals, or other soft paraphernalia that makes your child or teen feel secure.
- Lobby your adolescent's middle or high school to start the academic day later in the morning (adolescents have a sleep cycle unique to that stage of life, causing them to go to bed later and get up later).

Consult your doctor if you notice special problems such as breathing diffi-culties during sleep, restless leg syndrome, chronic insomnia, sleepwalking, frequent nightmares, or other nighttime irregularities, and also about the possibility of taking melatonin as a sleep aid (do not use over-the-counter sleep medications and prescription sleeping pills). If your child is taking psychostimulants, speak with your prescribing physician about changing medications, dosages, or the timing of administration to minimize the stimulant's effect on your child's sleep. Above all, encourage your child or teen to maintain consistency in his sleep–wake routines; over time, the inattention and distractibility that comes from not getting a good's night sleep will dissipate and a bright new day will dawn.

FOR FURTHER INFORMATION

Richard Ferber, *Solve Your Child's Sleep Problems*, rev. ed. (New York: Touchstone, 2006).

STRATEGY #78

Activate Positive Career Aspirations
(Ages 6–18)

It seems critical to me that we help children who've been diagnosed with ADHD see that there are positive futures up ahead for them. Many of these kids suffer through years of frustration in classrooms expecting only to find more of the same once they leave school. Yet it may be that for many of them, the real world might offer a chance to display strengths and abilities that a regimented classroom curriculum never could. Unfortunately, it seems as if the ADHD community too often sends the wrong message to children and adolescents when it broadcasts the results of follow-up studies with children labeled ADHD or hyperactive who grow into adulthood. According to these studies, people with ADHD will have more car accidents, less education, more job instability, more drug abuse, and more criminal behavior than typically developing people.[1] These statistics are troubling not for what they indicate, but for the message they carry to young people diagnosed with ADHD: If you're an ADHD child or adolescent, the chances are better than even you've got a rocky road ahead of you.

This grim future needn't come to pass. The individuals in those studies didn't have the benefit of the kind of broad-based interventions shared in this book, including the faith and trust you have as a parent that your child will prosper in adulthood. What this means is that your child may find his true place in life only when he can get out into the real world and discover a vocation that allows him to do what he does best. In order to ensure that he finds his true vocation, however, you need to begin stimulating his career aspirations from an early age. Let him know that the kinds of traits he possesses are valuable out in the workplace. In terms of the characteristics associated with ADHD-like behavior—need for novelty, frequent changes in tasks, imagination, movement, and spontaneous expression—there are many work roles that fill the bill, including:

- Self-employed entrepreneur
- Freelance writer, artist, or editor
- Airline pilot or train engineer
- Disc jockey or radio announcer
- Traveling salesperson
- Music or dance therapist
- Forest ranger
- Recreational worker
- Itinerant teacher
- Radio, television, or newspaper reporter
- Police officer or firefighter
- Nature photographer
- Building contractor
- Craftsperson
- Artist or sculptor
- Inventor or designer
- Private detective
- Truck, bus, or taxicab driver
- Emergency room physician
- Freelance researcher
- Farmer or ranch worker
- Choreographer or dancer
- Athlete or coach

- Lecturer or workshop leader
- Aerobic or fitness instructor
- Surveyor, cartographer, or architect
- Peace Corps worker
- Fashion model
- Public relations consultant

You can help stimulate career aspirations in your child or teen by introducing him to successful people in the community who themselves were considered hyperactive or diagnosed with ADHD in childhood (see also Strategy #66: Provide Positive Role Models). These individuals can serve as living examples of positive futures for your child and can point the way to specific career goals.

To help fuel career interests, ask your child from time to time what she'd like to be when she grows up. You might even suggest that she draw a picture of what she sees herself doing ten or twenty years from now. Talk with her about her aspirations and take her comments seriously. Don't try to discourage her if she seems to want to take up a vocation you feel is unsuitable or unrealistic. Help feed her dreams while still showing her the wide range of options that are open to her in other areas. Mythology expert Joseph Campbell counseled his students to "follow your bliss . . . and doors will open where you didn't know they were going to be." By helping stoke the flames of your child's personal career ambitions, you're making a significant contribution toward her success in life.

FOR FURTHER INFORMATION

Dale Archer, *The ADHD Advantage: What You Thought Was a Diagnosis May Be Your Greatest Strength* (New York: Avery, 2015).

Kathleen G. Nadeau, *The ADHD Guide to Career Success: Harness your Strengths, Manage your Challenges*, 2nd ed. (New York: Routledge, 2015).

Teach Your Child to Visualize
(Ages 4–18)

A number of years ago I was demonstrating some new techniques for teaching spelling at an upstate New York elementary school classroom and was stymied by an eight-year-old boy named Billy who sat in the front row and refused to stay in his seat during most of the lesson. When I got to the part of the lesson where I have students visualize their spelling words, however, I was amazed to see Billy return to his seat and remain perfectly still while he covered his eyes and "looked" intently at his imaginary words. Not surprisingly, the letters in his mind's eye would not remain stable and I spent a few minutes working with him individually on strategies for making the words stand still. Later on, I realized that something more important than a spelling lesson went on that afternoon. Billy was able to transform his external physical hyperactivity into internal mental motion. And by internalizing his outer activity level, he was able to gain some degree of control over it.

The imagination represents an important potential resource that kids diagnosed with ADHD can draw on to help them learn, attend, and behave. Albert Einstein (himself a behavior problem in his Prussian high school) once said in reference to his own thinking processes, "The imagination is everything." He conducted thought experiments in which he would visualize, for example, what it would be like to ride on a beam of light. These visualizations were key in helping him formulate his special and general theories of relativity. Many other figures in history have used their imaginations to transform society, including the inventor Elias Howe, the author Robert Louis Stevenson, and nuclear physicist Niels Bohr. These thinkers, like many kids labeled ADHD, were daydreamers. The only difference between them was that these eminent individuals used their daydreams productively. With proper guidance, ADHD-diagnosed kids can also thrive through their gift of imagery.

In school, students can place spelling words, times tables facts, math formulas, or other rote material onto imaginary mental screens as a way of memorizing them. Students can also visualize what they've read after reading a story, picture what they've heard after hearing instructions from the teacher, or visualize a historical scene, a mathematical operation, or a science experiment.

At home, children and adolescents diagnosed with ADHD can be assisted in forming their own personalized mental images to help them with focusing, behavior, or social conflict. Some images to suggest to your child or teen might include the following:

FOR CALMING DOWN

- A special place in nature (lake, woods, mountains)
- A favorite trip (amusement park)
- An imaginary journey (to a magical land)
- A secret place (tree house, fort)

FOR FOCUSING

- A favorite color
- A favorite toy
- A special hero
- A favorite movie

FOR RESPONDING TO CRITICISM

- Avoiding flying arrows (of criticism)
- Letting the breeze (of criticisms) pass through you
- Allowing the criticism to fall off your back like water from a duck's back
- Fending off bad words with an imaginary lightsaber
- Putting an imaginary protective white light around you to deal with bullies

The best imagery scenarios for some kids will be unlike any of these suggestions. Let your child create his own mental visualizations as a way of learning something new or for handling stress, conflict, or confusion. Dynamic images such as monster trucks crashing against each other, dinosaurs locked in mortal combat, or space vehicles fighting an interstellar galactic war can, like psychostimulants, actually calm your child or teenager down. Explain to your child or teen that she can summon up her own personal images to help her learn, focus, behave, and manage stress. Not every child will be able to create visual imagery, and for some kids imagery may be too disturbing or agitating to create the desired effect. But for those who have vivid imaginations and a willingness to use their visual minds, success may be just an image away.

FOR FURTHER INFORMATION

Jennifer Day, *Creative Visualization with Children* (Rockport, MA: Element, 2006).

STRATEGY #80

Play Chess or Go with Your Child
(Ages 10–18)

Using a strategy involving a slow-moving board game may seem counterintuitive to many parents of kids diagnosed with ADHD. After all, if a child or adolescent has trouble paying attention or sitting still for long periods of time, how is he going to handle the concentration necessary for a game of chess, which may go on for hours at a time? The answer is that a game needn't go on continuously for hours but can be broken up into smaller chunks of time. People who play chess long-distance often see days go by between moves. But the real answer to why this is a good idea for kids diagnosed with ADHD has to do with the way it improves focus and concentration. In one study, fourteen Lebanese children aged eleven to thirteen were taught how to play chess by an international chess player and trainer. They participated in after-school chess club twice a week for four months (the average time for each session was thirty to forty-five minutes). To deal with the possibility of boredom, the trainer used teaching videos, a behavior chart, and visual cues for remembering the position of the pieces. After four months, the students had improved their concentration and listening skills, and their ADHD symptoms decreased.[1]

In another study, forty-four Spanish children between the ages of six and seventeen took part in an eleven-week chess training program. Researchers found a large effect in decreasing the severity of ADHD symptoms.[2] A further study, in which children learned to play the Chinese logic game Baduk (more commonly known as Go), found that children's executive functioning and brain activity associated with the prefrontal cortex (that is, the area most in need of maturation for kids diagnosed with ADHD) improved.[3]

Here are a few guidelines for introducing chess or Go to your child or teen:

- Teach your child or teen the basic moves and rules of chess (learn them yourself first!) in a series of brief sessions lasting no longer than five minutes each.
- When you start playing games, if your child or teen wants to quit at any time, let him; you can always take up the same game later on (keep the board in a safe location where the pieces can't be jarred or spilled).
- If your child or teen shows no interest in the game, don't push it; chess or Go are not for everyone.
- If your child or teen shows initial interest but then slacks off, gently encourage him to resume but don't pressure him; if he wants to, he'll come back to it someday.
- Let your child or teen choose the conditions that are comfortable to him for playing the game (such as sitting at a table, standing at a counter, lying down on a carpet, sitting on a bed).

Keep in mind that your child or teen may take to the game in a big way and be able to play for long periods of time while he thinks about his next move (a demonstration of hyperfocus or flow). Don't set a limit to the time required for the next move, unless he wants to keep it moving at a fast pace. In such a situation, you can use a timer and agree to a set period of time for each move (say, three minutes). Let yourself be led by your child's or teen's own interest in the game. The important thing is that he play, not to "improve his cognitive functions," but simply because it's a lot of fun!

FOR FURTHER INFORMATION

Murray Chandler and Helen Milligan, *Chess for Children: How to Play the World's Most Popular Board Game* (London: Gambit, 2004).

Have Your Child Teach a Younger Child
(Ages 7–18)

One of the classic images of American education is the one-room schoolhouse. Although there are only few of them left in the country, one educational strategy used in these self-contained educational institutions—cross-age tutoring—remains a potent learning and teaching method. Older kids teaching younger kids provides benefits for both, according to the latest research. And for children who've had learning or behavior problems, cross-age tutoring can offer a means of taking on a more responsible role. Although it may seem as if older tutors have little to gain from the experience of teaching their younger charges, studies provide support for the old Latin dictum *qui docet discit* (one who teaches, learns).[1] In fact, tutors often get *more* out of the experience than the tutees.

Cross-age tutoring seems to help the one who teaches for many different reasons. It requires the child or teen to review basic material that may not have been fully mastered the first time around. Also, tutors must think through the processes they teach before presenting them to their younger tutees. This helps awaken mental processes that can be applied to academic work at their own level. Most important, for kids with behavior and attention problems, cross-age tutoring puts them in the adult role and elicits from them their most responsible social and behavioral skills. It also enhances self-esteem by acknowledging that the tutor is someone who knows something worth teaching.

Encourage your child's school to set up a cross-age tutoring program. If a program isn't feasible for financial or logistical reasons, then talk with your child's teacher and see if an informal arrangement can be made for your child to leave class for twenty minutes during the day to work with a child in a lower grade. Tutoring programs work best when teachers supervise tutors and provide them with simple guidelines in helping younger students, including *avoiding criticism, making the task specific,* and *giving immediate feedback.* Teachers should also think about using other approaches where students teach other students, such as the following:

- *Buddy systems.* Older kids provide informal assistance for younger students in school-related tasks such as how to use the library or a school computer.
- *Peer teaching.* Same-age students teach each other.
- *Cooperative learning.* Small groups of students work together on collaborative projects.

Parents can support cross-age tutoring at home by encouraging their kids to work with younger neighborhood friends or younger siblings. Children or adolescents can help younger kids with their homework or with simple tasks like learning how to ride a bike, draw a picture, or do a cartwheel. These activities offer your child or teen a chance to share his unique gifts and talents with others. The more opportunities he has to experience himself in the role of teacher, expert, or authority, the easier it will be for him to slough off the negative labels that have accumulated over the years due to behavior and attention problems. Cross-age tutoring reminds us that one of the best ways to develop maturity and responsibility isn't by striving to become a model student, but rather by becoming a model *teacher.*

FOR FURTHER INFORMATION

Mary Pippitt, Katharine Davies Samway, and Gail Whang, *Buddy Reading: Cross-Age Tutoring in a Multicultural School* (Portsmouth, NH: Heinemann, 1995).

STRATEGY #82

Help Your Child Become Self-Aware
(Ages 10–18)

I have a hard time with the idea of parents telling their kids that they have ADHD and here's what it is etc. etc.[1] It strikes me as an indoctrination process in which the child is given information that, at least according to this book and the hundreds of references cited, is controversial and frankly debatable.

But the main reason I don't like the spiel given by parents, doctors, and psychologists to children and adolescents about "their ADHD," is that it greatly limits their sense of identity. Now they have a disorder: ADHD. What exactly does that mean? That they are part of the 3 percent . . . no it's 10 percent now . . . no it's more than that . . . of kids who have ADHD? That they have a biogenetic, or is it sociocultural, or perhaps developmental disorder? That they need to take a federally controlled potentially addictive psychoactive drug because, well, let me see, was it to regulate their dopamine, or their norepinephrine, or their frontal lobes?

There's entirely too much up in the air about this "disorder," to be giving children and teens straight talk about what they "have." It's no wonder that research studies suggest kids diagnosed with ADHD have an unrealistic and inflated sense of their abilities (a phenomenon termed by researchers "positive illusory bias").[2] Anyone who has been given a psychiatric label that has three negatives in it (deficit, hyperactive, and disorder) would naturally want to defend themselves against this onslaught by puffing themselves up a bit. But more important, the label ADHD too often keeps them from seeing who they really are. Instead of trapping their identities under the bell jar of an artificial attention disease, we should be helping them understand themselves more deeply as the unique, capable, and interesting people that they are. Here are some suggestions for ways to do this:

- Have them take self-assessment inventories for fun (to understand themselves, not to label themselves). Edutopia (a wonderful education site sponsored by the George Lucas Educational Foundation) provides quick tests of Daniel Goleman's emotional intelligence and Howard Gardner's multiple intelligences on their Web site (www.edutopia.org). See "For Further Information" below for other self-assessment sources.
- Suggest that they keep a diary or personal journal. This journal can be a place where they reflect on life, their feelings about daily events, their interactions with others, and anything else that has meaning for them; make sure they know that no one will look at it, that it's just for their own viewing alone.
- Encourage them to write their autobiography. They can do this in a variety of ways: by writing it, creating a photo montage, making a video, creating an art piece, or presenting a multimedia presentation.

Then they can share it with whomever they want, or no one at all if they wish.

- Use other self-awareness tools discussed elsewhere in this book. Try Strategy #2: Channel Creative Energies into the Arts, Strategy #17: Teach Your Child Self-Monitoring Skills, Strategy #33: Teach Your Child How His Brain Works, and/or Strategy #75: Enhance Your Child's Self-Esteem.
- Don't shy away from discussing ADHD if your child has been diagnosed with it, especially if he asks questions. Provide answers that take in all points of view on the subject, not just the ADHD party line.

Remember that late childhood and adolescence are times of growing self-awareness, and kids are busy constructing an identity that will serve them for good or ill during their grown-up years. By helping your child or teen understand himself thoroughly, beyond limited labels and disabling disorders, you'll be providing him with a foundation on which he can build a stronger sense of self for adulthood.

FOR FURTHER INFORMATION

Here are some additional self-assessments that children and adolescents can take to find out more about themselves and their strengths:

- Gallup's *StrengthsExplorer for Ages 10 to 14* (New York: Gallup Youth Development Specialists/Simon & Schuster, 2007) or Tom Rath's *StrengthsFinder 2.0* (Washington, DC: Gallup Press, 2007). Purchase of either book provides an access code for online assessments.
- Search Institute's *Developmental Assets* Profile (ages eleven to eighteen): search-institute.org/surveys/our-surveys.
- The VIA's Institute on Character's *Survey of Character Strengths*, which can be taken for free online; viacharacter.org.

STRATEGY #83

Utilize the Best Features of Computer Learning
(Ages 7–18)

Elsewhere in this book I've counseled parents to limit the time that your kids spend using media such as computers, tablets, and smartphones for *entertainment* (Strategy #38: Limit Entertainment Media). However, using computer applications for *educational* purposes is one of the best ways to meet the needs of kids who have been labeled ADHD. Most computer learning programs provide instant feedback (quick answers to questions) and immediate reinforcement (often providing bells, badges, or access to higher levels when the user makes the right choices). They allow the child to control her own pace, thus sidestepping problems she may have complying with external authority. The user platform is usually colorful, animated, and graphically interesting. Finally, computer learning programs are nonjudgmental, taking a person from their current level of performance to higher levels of accomplishment in small increments.

It shouldn't be surprising then that research suggests that children and adolescents diagnosed with ADHD do very well in computerized learning programs when compared with more traditional methods of instruction. In one study, children identified as ADHD improved their oral reading abilities and task engagement when using a computerized reading program compared to teacher-directed instruction.[1] In another study, students had increased levels of achievement and better focus on tasks when they were engaged with a computerized math program compared with doing seatwork (workbooks, worksheets, etc.).[2]

These findings suggest that teachers should use computerized instruction rather than lecture and seatwork with children diagnosed with ADHD. Similarly, parents need to provide their kids with access to computers or tablets when doing homework assignments. If you don't have a computer or tablet at home, investigate availability through other sources, such as using a school computer after hours, a computer at the local library, or one at a copy store in your local community. Spend time with your child interacting with the computer program so that you make sure that it interests him, is relatively easy to use, and provides an adequate challenge without being too difficult. Acquire other software applications that teach academic skills; look for titles from ClueFinders, Fun School, Jumpstart, Zoombinis, and School Zone. Do family projects using computers, including playing interactive games, designing greeting cards for holidays using a clip-on art program, and writing family newsletters using a word processing or desktop publishing program. When your child discovers the benefits of computerized learning, you might discover that his learning curve suddenly zooms sharply upward.

STRATEGY #84

Let Your Child Play Video Games
That Engage and Teach
(Ages 7–18)

Yes, it's true: playing video games for pure entertainment is a lot of fun for kids but can lead to attention problems (see Strategy #38: Limit Entertainment Media). But this does not necessarily apply to "serious gaming," which video game pioneer Clark Abt defines as "games [that] have an explicit and carefully thought-out educational purpose and are not intended to be played primarily for amusement."[1] It's also true that kids can sniff out and reject video games that have "an educational purpose," and there certainly are a lot of skill-and-drill programs for sale that are not much more than "electronic worksheets." The real art for video game designers is to develop a game that engages kids and at the same time trains them in developing valuable cognitive skills. Such games have, in fact, been developed recently and are proving to be quite helpful for kids diagnosed with ADHD in developing much needed executive function abilities.

One game called Plan-It-Commander, for example, is a mission-guided video game divided into ten missions and several side missions. As players follow the missions, they are required to solve problems, plan strategies, set goals, manage time, and engage in a number of other higher-order cognitive skills. In a randomized controlled study of eight- to twelve-year-olds (mostly boys) lasting twenty weeks, participants who played the game regularly improved on measures of time management, the social skill of responsibility, and working memory compared with kids in a control group.[2] In another study, kids who played Project EVO, a game designed to improve a child's ability to process multiple streams of information (the player has to steer a character down a river while making decisions about how to respond to objects that appear on the screen), for thirty minutes a day five times a week for four weeks, improved on measures of attention, working memory, impulsivity, and parental reports of the child's executive functioning in daily life.[3]

But the serious game with the greatest appeal for most kids, including those diagnosed with ADHD, is probably Minecraft, in which players are situated in a borderless, randomly generated land with no supplies, directions, or objectives and have to decide what to do and how to do it. They collect materials from the virtual world around them to build items and create whatever their minds can visualize. The greatest attraction of this game is its open-endedness. Here are some comments from ADHD-diagnosed kids who are Minecraft players:

- An eleven-year-old girl said, "Minecraft is lots of fun because you can build a house and it comes with fun stuff like eggs, chickens, animals, bad guys, zombies, and creepers."
- An eight-year-old boy enjoys building with it "because I want to be an engineer when I grow up and I want to be good at it."
- A fifteen-year-old teen commented, "I get to build things as big as I want such as churches, roller coasters. . . . When I was little I used to like to play Legos because it's the same thing as Minecraft."[4]

Minecraft can be adapted to virtually any topic from asteroids to zebras and helps develop focus, creativity, problem solving, collaboration, and a number of other executive functions.[5] Keep in mind that kids diagnosed with ADHD are digital natives. They've never known a world without video games. By choosing *smart* video games for them to play, you'll be helping them develop skills that will transfer over into improved behavior, increased concentration, and better academic achievement in school.

FOR FURTHER INFORMATION
Randy Kulman, *Playing Smarter in a Digital World: A Guide to Choosing and Using Popular Video Games and Apps to Improve Executive Functioning in Children and Teens* (Plantation, FL: Specialty Press, 2014).

STRATEGY #85

Get Ready for the Thrills and Chills of Augmented and Virtual Reality
(Ages 10–18)

Two new technological innovations are emerging on the cultural horizon that can significantly and positively impact the lives of kids diagnosed with ADHD: *augmented reality* and *virtual reality*. Augmented reality is the superimposition of digital information onto one's actual experience of the sensory world. One example of this is the game Pokémon Go, for which users take their smartphones to different locations around their communities (in reality), to catch Pokémon creatures that are situated there (on the screen) superimposed onto the real landscape. Virtual reality, on the other hand, involves a complete immersion in a 360-degree world of its own, determined by the parameters of the particular computer program running it. Each of these technologies offers opportunities for kids who become bored with academics or have trouble paying attention in the classroom to enter into eye-catching and mind-catching worlds that can help them pay attention and learn more effectively.

In the augmented reality application the Guinness Book of World Records, for example, readers see images virtually leaping out of the page in three dimensions (for example an article about sharks seen through an iPad or other tablet or smartphone reveals what appears to be an actual three-dimensional shark coming out of a pool of water on the two-dimensional page). For virtual reality, on the other hand, users need to wear some type of headgear that surrounds their visual field (apparatus may also involve gloves or an omnidirectional treadmill to provide kinesthetic input). Schools are increasingly taking kids on virtual field trips. Students in the San Francisco Unified School District and Polk County Public Schools in Florida, for example, have been using Nearpod VR goggles to visit the ancient pyramids of Egypt, the enigmatic statues on Easter Island, the marine biomes of the Great Barrier Reef, and patriotic landscapes across the United States.[1]

The possible uses of these technologies for kids diagnosed with ADHD, however, go beyond academic enrichment. Virtual classrooms have been designed to both assess and help students cope with virtual distractions (pencils being sharpened, people coming and going, the school bell) while they focus on an academic task.[2] Virtual programs have also been developed that assess and teach safety skills for actions requiring sustained attention, such as driving a car or crossing a road.[3] The potential is great for creating powerful new brain-training programs that sharpen cognitive functions as well as simulations that teach strategies for behaviors such as waiting one's turn, staying with a task, or paying attention to the details of an action.[4] There are, however, a few caveats to keep in mind as these technologies widen their influence:

- Virtual reality could lead to motion sickness or balance issues, so frequent breaks are recommended.
- Augmented reality could create disorientation with respect to the sensory world; the game Pokémon Go, for example, has led some users to walk into traffic, or even fall off cliffs.[5]
- Make sure to choose those programs that have educational or therapeutic value (thrills plus skills) rather than those that just provide thrills and chills.

Finally, don't forget that it's *the real world* that our kids need to adapt to and that the augmented or virtual world is only a tool to help them function more effectively and achieve greater levels of success and accomplishment at home and school.

Consider Alternative Schooling Options
(Ages 6–18)

So many parents have written to me over the past thirty years sharing their stories of sons and daughters with behavior or learning difficulties floundering in public school programs. Many of these parents shared an almost identical three-act scenario:

Act 1: They were contacted by school administrators and told that their child or teen had "a problem."

Act 2: The child or adolescent was tested, identified as ADHD, or some other alphabet-soup disorder, and referred to a special education program.

Act 3: The child or teen continued to have difficulties in special education, and in some cases became even worse, prompting new meetings and tests, and sometimes new labels, as a part of charting the child's or adolescent's educational future.

Most of these parents remained stuck in this Kafkaesque pedagogical drama for the rest of their child's or adolescent's school career. However, a few did not. These parents essentially wrote an Act 4. They took their kids out of the public school system and either put them in a private alternative school or homeschooled them.

Many private schools—especially "for profit" charter schools—tend to sidestep admitting kids with special needs, fearing that they'll lower the school's test scores. However, thousands of private alternative schools exist around the country that honor individual differences in learning. They include Montessori programs, in which students can work at their own pace on learning materials, and Waldorf schools, which embrace a philosophy of education that emphasizes the arts in teaching skills and content. Other alternative schools have been established independently by parents and educators working together to create experiential learning for children in their communities involving student-initiated projects, real-life expeditions, and collaborative learning. If you decide on an alternative school, make sure that you're comfortable with the school's philosophy. Visit the classroom your child would be attending, and check to see that the teachers are certified by the state department of education and/or a recognized educational association.

Some parents have even gone further and homeschooled their ADHD-diagnosed children. Although such an approach requires time and an energy commitment that seems unworkable to some parents, homeschooling parents feel it's worth it. While homeschooling curricula are available for purchase on the Internet, many of these programs are just packaged versions of what a highly traditional academic program at a public school might provide. Authentic homeschooling should optimally be designed around the needs, abilities, and interests of your unique child or adolescent. It's also recommended that you network with other homeschooling parents and together schedule social events so that your child or teen has contact with kids his own age.

Should you decide on an alternative school or a homeschool for your child, you could very well be providing him with a label-free environment in which he can learn in his own way.

FOR FURTHER INFORMATION

Association Montessori International—USA: 206 North Washington, Suite 330, Alexandria, VA 22314; 1-703-746-9919; montessori@amiusa.org; amiusa.org.

Association of Waldorf Schools of North America: 17 Hemlock Hill Rd., Great Barrington, MA 01230; awsna@awsna.org; https://waldorfeducation.org/.

Carolyn Woods, *Homeschooling for the Smart, Energetic, and Easily Bored: Hands-On Learning Methods for Your Gifted, ADHD, or Just Plain Wiggly Child* (Bellevue, WA: Amazon Digital Services, 2014; rev. 2016).

Have Your Child Learn Yoga
(Ages 4–18)

The Roaring Lion. Crab Dance. Lizard on a Rock. Spouting Dolphin. These aren't descriptions of a trip to the zoo, a hike in the woods, or a visit to a beach. They're yoga poses with animal names that children and adolescents can do to help decrease tension, increase attention, and regulate their physiological and mental responses to life events. Yoga (the word is from the Sanskrit and means "union"; it's related etymologically to the word "yoke") is a twenty-five-hundred-year-old set of practices originating in India that emerged from several religious traditions, including Hinduism, Buddhism, and Jainism. While there are many different types of yoga, the kind that Westerners are most familiar with has a nonreligious basis and combines physical *asanas* (postures) with breathing exercises, chanting, and meditation to calm the mind, relax the body, and nourish the spirit. Yoga has become increasingly popular among American children and boasts almost two million youthful practitioners.[1]

Now there's mounting evidence to suggest that the practice of yoga can be beneficial to kids diagnosed with ADHD. In one study, eleven children aged six to ten with attention problems learned yoga practices from a videotape and engaged in deep breathing, physical postures, and relaxation exercises for thirty minutes, twice a week, for a period of three weeks. They showed significant improvements in time-on-task in doing classroom assignments.[2] Another study of children between the ages of five and sixteen who had been diagnosed with ADHD and participated in an average of eight yoga sessions showed improvement in ADHD symptoms on a number of standardized measures.[3] Finally, a German study produced sizable reductions in symptoms of a group of children diagnosed with ADHD who'd practiced yoga. At the end of the study, the group averages for the ADHD scales did not differ significantly from those of a control group.[4]

As a parent, you can enroll your child in a yoga class at a local recreation center, use a video or book to teach (see "For Further Information" below), or

share some simple activities directly with your child. The emphasis should be on having fun. A few enjoyable exercises you can do with your child are these:
5

Roaring Lion. Kneel on the floor with your bottom on your calves, place your hands on your knees, sit up straight, close your eyes, wrinkle up your nose, open your mouth, stick your tongue as far out and down as it will go (as if you're going to lick a bowl of ice cream), inhale deeply, and then breathe out with a powerful roar!

Tree Pose. Stand on one foot with your arms above your head, palms together, and place your other foot against the inside of the inner thigh of the leg holding the weight. As you do this, select a spot on the wall to focus on. This will help you maintain your balance. See how long you can remain in that posture while breathing calmly and evenly.

Frog Hops. Bend down as low as you can, or better yet, crouch close to the floor, take three deep breaths, and then pop up suddenly as high as you can, yelling "RIBBIT, RIBBIT!" Repeat until tired.

Suggest to your child that he do one or more of these (or other) yoga exercises when he's feeling hyperactive, spacy, disorganized, unfocused, or scattered. By concentrating attention on his breath, voice, and body, he can gather together his dispersed energies and use them to study, concentrate, follow directions, and much more.

FOR FURTHER INFORMATION
Lisa Flynn, *Yoga for Children: 200+ Yoga Poses, Breathing Exercises, and Meditations for Healthier, Happier, More Resilient Children* (Avon, MA: Adams Media, 2013).

STRATEGY #88

Find an Animal Your Child Can Care For
(Ages 5–18)

The history of television and film provides us with many heartfelt images of children and their animals: a young Elizabeth Taylor on her horse The Pie in *National Velvet*, Tommy Kirk and his dog Old Yeller, Jon Provost and his dog Lassie, Luke Halpin and his pet dolphin Flipper, and more recently, AnnaSophia Robb and her dog Winn-Dixie. These shows remind us of the tender life-changing moments that animals offer to children. Nowhere can we see the potential benefits of matching children to animals better than in the case of kids diagnosed with ADHD. In a sense, many domestic animals display a number of the same traits as these kids: They often run amok (hyperactivity), jump up and lick you silly (impulsivity), and react quickly to any new stimulus (distractibility). And like many kids diagnosed with ADHD, they possess warmth, naturalness, and a vital instinctual capacity that is a welcome relief from the regimentation of schoolwork, chores, and homework. As one child put it as he watched a therapy horse restlessly prancing around a corral: "He's just like me!"[1]

Research supports the use of animals in helping ADHD-diagnosed children gain greater control and focus over their behavior and attention span. In one study, children with an ADHD diagnosis were divided into two groups. One group received cognitive behavioral therapy plus a canine-assisted intervention (CAI); the other received behavioral therapy without the CAI. After twelve weeks, children who were matched with animals had greater reductions in their ADHD symptoms compared to kids who received only the cognitive-behavioral therapy.[2] A more recent study reviewed research projects that had investigated animal therapy with ADHD-diagnosed kids and concluded the approach had calming, socializing, motivating, and cognitive effects that in turn were associated with a positive impact on several core symptoms of ADHD.[3]

One good way you can integrate animals into your child or adolescent's daily life is by giving him responsibility for taking care of a pet. The Humane

Society has centers where one can adopt a pet for a minimal fee. Having a pet means your child or teen will have to regularly feed, wash, and walk the animal (in the case of a four-legged pet), which will help develop a sense of responsibility. In addition, taking a pet outside may attract neighboring kids, providing opportunities for positive social connections. Playing with the pet will also help burn off excess energy that your child or teen may have stored up, and petting the animal can induce a calming effect. For kids who have difficulties that may get in the way of caring for a pet, it may be helpful to look for a therapist in your area who uses animals with ADHD-diagnosed children. And if these options won't work with your specific setting, think about having your child or teen visit zoos, play with the pets of friends, take charge of a pet being kept at school, or offer to walk the neighbors' animals. Any way you look at it, giving your child or adolescent a chance to connect with animals can provide an important nondrug alternative to help him feel better about himself and succeed in school and life.

FOR FURTHER INFORMATION

Little Parachutes; littleparachutes.com/subcategory.php?sid=89. A Web site that offers an excellent list of children's literature on the theme of pet care, the responsibilities involved, and how to deal with the loss of a pet. The site includes a list of books about owning a pet.

STRATEGY #89

Support Your Child's Late Blooming
(Ages 4–18)

In chapter 4, I focused attention on how we're not letting our kids be kids anymore and how the brains of most children diagnosed with ADHD develop two to three years later than typically developing kids. This means that children diagnosed with ADHD are for the most part what we used to call late bloomers. Nowadays this term has fallen out of favor and taken on a charged meaning for many educators and mental health professionals, who react with scorn at the idea that we should just leave these kids alone because "they'll grow out of it." In my view, there are two extremes to this argument. On the one extreme there are those who say essentially "just leave the late-blooming child alone and he'll catch up with the other kids eventually." On the other extreme are those who say that these kids need early identification and intensive treatment to remediate their deficient skills and behaviors so that they don't fall behind and risk greater failure ahead.[1]

In my view, neither of these points of view are correct. Those who simply say they'll grow out of it and do nothing to help their kids, are failing to support their development. Those who want to intervene early and use drugs and behavior modification to straighten the child out are engaging in what I'd like to call "developmental shock-and-awe." There needs to be a middle ground for kids who develop later than the typically developing child, which offers validation for their different pace and rate of growth but that also provides an enriched environment that supports their physical, cognitive, behavioral, emotional, social, and creative development. I'd like to offer several suggestions to help parents who have late-blooming kids with a diagnosis of ADHD (or those at risk of being so diagnosed):

- Provide your child with a rich learning environment that is geared to his own developmental rhythms, including language arts stimulation, math manipulatives, science explorations, social interactions with a variety of people, art experiences, adventures in nature, and more; these forms of stimulation will directly and positively assist in his neurological maturation due to the brain's neuroplasticity (its ability to rewire itself through environmental stimulation).
- Share with your child images from nature that show different plants and animals maturing at different rates, and let him know that the same thing is true with human beings.
- Don't treat your child like someone two or three years younger; some areas of his brain are developing right on time (or even ahead of time), while others will develop later; your child is neither mature nor immature but rather maturing.
- Tell your child or teen about people of great accomplishment in life who were late bloomers in their childhood or adulthood. Mention Albert Einstein (who didn't start to talk until he was nearly four), Martha

Graham (who didn't start to dance until she was fourteen), Toni Morrison (who didn't write her first novel until she was almost forty), and Grandma Moses (who didn't start seriously painting until she was seventy-eight).

- Avoid using words like *delayed, immature,* or *developmental lag* in your discussions with others, including teachers, relatives, and mental health professionals. Remind them that *neoteny,* or the retention of youthful characteristics into later development, is associated with evolutionary progress (see chapter 4 for a discussion of the importance of *neoteny* to civilization).
- Encourage your child's teacher to use developmentally appropriate multisensory, experiential, interactive, project-based, and hands-on approaches to learning in the classroom and to respect and support your child's late blooming.
- Don't be intimated by those who tell you that you'll harm your child if he doesn't enter an early remediation program or take drugs as a young child to control his symptoms (unless your child also has a diagnosis of mood disorder, in which case early intervention and the use of medications may be warranted to prevent future episodes of depression). Let your family and friends know you're doing everything you can to support your child's or teen's growth according to his own natural rhythms of development. If you have serious concerns about his development, consult your doctor.

Finally, don't expect your child to late bloom into an average, typical, or "normal" individual. In a supportive and enriched environment over time, your child or teen will optimally develop into a mature individual who is uniquely himself with his own challenges, strengths, opportunities, interests, and aspirations. We need to value our late bloomers because they offer society a range of potentialities to which typically developing people don't usually have access.

FOR FURTHER INFORMATION

Robert Kraus (author) and Jose Aruego (illustrator), *Leo the Late Bloomer* (New York: HarperCollins, 1999). For ages four to eight, but a timeless classic that appeals to all age levels.

Consider Individual Psychotherapy for Your Child
(Ages 5–18)

Psychotherapy holds great promise for many children diagnosed with ADHD. Since research suggests that from 25 to 50 percent of children and adolescents diagnosed with ADHD suffer from an anxiety disorder and as many as 60 percent of kids identified as ADHD may have a mood disorder (such as bipolar depression), psychotherapy designed to treat deeper emotional issues may be extremely important to their future well-being.[1] Moreover, because many of these kids end up being criticized by teachers, ridiculed by peers, and/or punished by parents because of their behaviors, they can end up in a cycle of failure in which punishment leads to anger, and anger leads to more inappropriate behavior, which leads to more punishment, and so on in a downward spiral. Furthermore, some of these kids face specific stresses, such as the loss of a parent through death or divorce, domestic or neighborhood violence, illness, or other traumatic experiences. For these stressed-out kids, psychotherapy can provide a way for them to heal emotional wounds. Although many ADHD experts discount the potential effectiveness of psychotherapy on the basis of past studies, more current and better designed research suggests that psychotherapy can be helpful in the lives of kids diagnosed with ADHD.[2]

Depending on the type of therapy and the specific needs of your child, psychotherapy provides several benefits. In psychodynamic therapy, children are helped to look at the emotional conflicts that negatively affect their lives. They can be given a vocabulary for their emotions and be helped to recognize and appropriately express feelings as a way of coping with the many stresses that life inevitably delivers. The medium through which this can occur in therapy may involve words, puppets, drawing, music, drama, storytelling, sand play, or other modalities, depending on the particular training of the therapist.

Other forms of psychotherapy concentrate more on changing specific behaviors or habitual ways of thinking. In cognitive behavioral therapy, the therapist assists the child in learning how to identify his own negative and positive behaviors and shows him ways of shaping new positive behaviors and mental attitudes. Children or adolescents can also participate in group therapy with other kids to learn how to develop important social skills or take part in family therapy (see Strategy #64: Consider Family Therapy).

Regardless of the particular type of therapy you decide is right for your child or teen, make sure that you choose a therapist with solid credentials and specific licensing in her field (see "For Further Information" below). Psychiatrists are medical doctors with several years of specialization in psychiatry and can prescribe medications. Psychologists have a PhD or PsyD in psychology and special clinical training and are also trained in administering diagnostic tests. Other specialties certified to provide psychotherapy include licensed clinical social workers, psychiatric nurses, and marriage and family therapists. Make sure to ask the therapist about her educational background, state licenses held, and affiliations with local and national professional associations. Once you choose a therapist, plan on taking an active role in your child's therapy. This may involve meeting periodically with the therapist to discuss your child's progress and learning what you can do at home to support his growth. It may also involve going into personal psychotherapy yourself. Psychotherapy is not a cure for attention or behavioral difficulties. But when used in conjunction with other strategies, it can provide your child or adolescent with an important source of support on his way to achieving success.

FOR FURTHER INFORMATION

Psychologist Locator: http://locator.apa.org/. Operated by the American Psychological Association (APA), this Web site can lead you to a qualified psychotherapist with a PhD from an APA-accredited program.

Create a Positive Behavior Contract
with Your Child
(Ages 8–18)

Contracts are a part of real life. In a typical contract, an interested party agrees to a set of conditions by which she hopes to gain something, while the other party also perceives gains from the contract and agrees to that set of conditions. Contracts are also used as a behavioral strategy in the ADHD world, but the ones most commonly employed would hardly pass muster in the business world. They usually look like this:

Teacher or Parent: "Here's what I expect you to do." "And here's what'll happen if you don't do it: [punishment]." "And here's what'll happen if you do it: [reward]." "Sign here."

Can you imagine Apple contracting with Cisco Systems on these terms? These faux contracts are in reality reward-and-punishment programs that masquerade as mutually agreed-on contracts, and they do little to develop a child's decision-making, problem-solving, or social skills.

You can help provide your child with a valuable lesson in responsibility by engaging in a process of real-world contracting. Explain to your child or teen that you're concerned about a specific behavior and that you'd like to work out some kind of a solution in the form of a contract. For younger children, you might explain what a contract is by telling them the Brothers Grimm story "The Frog Prince," in which a princess reneges on a verbal contract to let an ugly frog sleep in her bed. For older kids and teens, you can provide examples of the kinds of contracts people engage in during daily life—for example, to buy a house, take out a loan, marry, or begin a job.

Explain that you'd like your child or adolescent to do something for you, but that in return you'll do something for him. Describe the behavior(s) you're concerned about (a messy room, coming home late, forgetting to do homework) and what sort of behavior(s) you'd like to see (clean room, on-time arrival home, remembering to do homework). Ask your child or teen if this description seems accurate, and if not, how *he* sees the situation. Dialogue with him until both of you are in agreement about the nature of the problem and what a good outcome would look like for the both of you. Then let your child or teenager understand that in return for an improvement in the specified behavior, you're willing to do something for him. Ask him what he'd like to receive as a reward (or compensation) for keeping his end of the bargain.

Most kids will have plenty of ideas for rewards and you may find that your child or teen needs to tone down his request to something you'll feel more comfortable with (maybe not a trip to Walt Disney World, but perhaps a family outing to a miniature golf course). Once you've come to an agreement, draw up a contract. Work together on the wording so that it includes the child's or adolescent's own language. You can even ask him what type of paper he'd like it to be on (perhaps a huge sheet or one in his favorite color) and whether he'd like to write or type it up himself. In drawing up the contract, you might want to suggest that it include photos or pictures of what the undesirable and desirable behaviors look like. Include a time frame so that you can at a certain point sit down together and evaluate whether the terms of the contract have been fulfilled. It's preferable to create short-term agreements with quick payoffs (at the end of the day or week) rather than a long-term agreement (end of the month or year). Once the contract is written, make sure it's signed by both parties and prominently posted so that both of you (but not others, unless authorized) have access to it. Then, when the evaluation time rolls around, sit down with your child and assess the results. Did your child or teen do the desired behavior or continue to engage in the undesired pattern? Share any evidence you might have indicating the positive or negative results, and if there is serious disagreement about the outcome, take it to a family meeting (see Strategy #6: Hold Family Meetings).

Some critics might feel that this approach gives too much power to the child. Yet a child who grows up in a family where rules are set down that must be obeyed without question enters adulthood with a passive acceptance of life—a decidedly dangerous attitude during times of change such as ours. On the other hand, a child or adolescent who has the opportunity to take an active role in the management of his own life moves into the world with strength, determination, and confidence. Don't we owe it to our kids to give them this opportunity?

Engage in Positive Niche Construction
(Ages 7–18)

There are two fundamental ways in which parents can help their ADHD-diagnosed kids achieve success. The first way I call Adaptive Success. It involves doing everything you can to help your child or adolescent adapt to the world around him. This may include giving him medications and/or a behavior modification program to control his behaviors so he fits in with classroom and home expectations, or it might involve getting him involved in an intensive remediation program to help him develop skills in reading, math, or other subjects so he will get good grades, score well on tests, graduate, and ultimately land a good job in adulthood. Adaptive Success can also include many of the strategies that have been described in this book to help kids develop the social, emotional, cognitive, and behavioral abilities they need to successfully function in the world. Adaptive Success is vitally important to ensure that your child or adolescent, though different from others in the way he learns, attends, and/or develops, will be able to adapt to the traditions, conventions, rules, and routines that are important in society.

There's a different kind of success, though, that is often neglected by parents, educators, psychologists, and other helpers, which ought to be given equal weight for helping kids diagnosed with ADHD. I call this Actualized Success and it is the flip side of Adaptive Success. I define Actualized Success as helping your child be successful according to his *own gifts and abilities.* Instead of trying to make your child or teen always fit into the surrounding environment, Actualized Success is about *changing the environment to meet the needs of your unique child.* Both of these types of success are important, but parents often need extra help in providing their kids with opportunities to pursue Actualized Success. The way in which parents (and teachers) can do this is given to us by nature. Animals ensure their own thriving in the midst of the pressures of the natural world by engaging in what evolutionary biologists call "niche construction." Birds build nests. Ants create ant hills. Beavers build dams. Bees make hives. Spiders weave webs. In each case, animals are modifying the environment so that it favors the unique strengths that each species possesses (imagine a spider trying to adapt to the conditions of a bee-hive!). We need to do more to help our kids achieve success *on their terms.* This book provides a broad range of strategies to help parents modify their children's environments so that they favor how each child best works and functions in the world. Here are several ways to build a positive niche for your child using strategies from this book:

- Help your child learn how to work around obstacles using technologies and strategies, so he isn't blocked from learning or meeting objectives that are important to him (Strategy #100: Show Your Child Work-Arounds to Get Things Done).
- Work to modify your child's or adolescent's social network to ensure that negative interactions (such as run-ins with bullies and bad relationships with teachers) are less frequent, and positive interactions (such as new friendships and repaired relationships) happen more often (Strategy #53: Work to Promote Teacher–Child Rapport and Strategy #98: Work to Enhance Your Child's Social Network).
- Show your child or teen examples of people with learning and behavior challenges who were able to succeed in life on their own terms (Strategy #66: Provide Positive Role Models).
- Let your child or teen know about careers in the world that make use of his strengths rather than requiring him only to surmount his weaknesses (Strategy #78: Activate Positive Career Aspirations).
- Help your child acquire learning skills in areas of need using strategies that are based on his strengths and abilities, not on his deficits and dysfunctions, and encourage your child's teachers to do the same (Strategy #31: Empower Your Child with Strength-Based Learning).
- Modify environments at home that make it easier for your child to succeed (and encourage your child's teacher to do this as well), such as providing a reading rocking chair or having a bedroom with plenty of natural light (Strategy #10: Build, Borrow, or Buy Wiggle Furniture, Strategy #22: Provide Appropriate Spaces for Learning, and Strategy #62: Provide Access to Natural and Full-Spectrum Light).

By working to create an optimal niche for your child in which he can thrive on his own terms (Actualized Success) and at the same time, acquire skills he needs to adapt to the world around him (Adaptive Success), you'll be giving him the best opportunity to shine in his own way and, at the same time, conduct himself in a way that the world will accept and admire.

STRATEGY #93

Help Your Child Develop Social Skills
(Ages 6–16)

Three kids are quietly playing a game of cards. Eddie walks into the room, quickly pushes one of the kids, and runs away laughing and saying: "Ha! Ha! I got you!" The boys glance up at Eddie and say, almost in unison, "Get lost!" Eddie is confused for a moment, and then runs off in another direction looking for someone else to bother. Eddie is having trouble using appropriate social skills. He'd like to make friends with the boys, but he doesn't know how. His own impulsiveness acts like a bludgeon on the delicately formed social network created by the boys as they play cards. Eddie's situation is a common one for many kids diagnosed with ADHD. Their higher level of energy doesn't always mesh with the social world around them. Emotional outbursts, aggressiveness, and hyperactivity can cause peers to reject them. In one study 52 percent of children with ADHD had been rejected by peers, compared to only 14 percent of randomly selected classmates.[1] This cycle of rejection can create feelings of sadness, anger, and depression, which may in turn fuel more aggressiveness and more negative interactions with peers.

Social skills are not given to us on a silver platter at birth. We learn them by having them modeled for us by parents, siblings, and others, and by practicing them within our own peer group. Kids labeled with ADHD who chronically experience social rejection can greatly benefit from social skills training that helps them master the different components involved in getting along with others, including such skills as taking turns, sharing, cooperating, communicating, dealing with conflict, and abiding by social rules.

There are several ways you can support your child in getting along with peers. First, encourage him to participate in social activities in the neighborhood and community. Noncompetitive and low stress settings like an arts-and-crafts program or a swimming class are generally preferable to highly competitive or high-stress environments like Little League or the community soccer team. It's especially helpful if the activity is supervised by an adult who is sensitive to group dynamics and interpersonal relationships and can help your child over the bumpy spots. Second, encourage your child to invite a friend home for an evening of games, snacks, and/or a movie. A child who has at least one good friendship can weather the storm of difficult peer relations in other parts of his life. Third, do role-playing together using social troubles experienced at school or in the neighborhood as starting points. For example, if your child gets into fights when others tease him, talk with him about some other, nonviolent ways he could respond, and then practice these ideas where one of you plays the teaser and the other plays the teased person. Then switch roles. You can also use puppets to role-play if your child feels inhibited about dramatizing the events himself.

At school, find out if your child's or adolescent's teacher uses some kind of social skills building program, and if not, what sorts of informal activities she uses to help build teamwork, caring, and sharing in the classroom. Remember that social skills are learned, and the more exposure your child has to models of appropriate and healthy social behavior, the more likely that he'll develop his own people skills as he matures.

FOR FURTHER INFORMATION

Pamela Espeland and Elizabeth Verdick, *Making Choices and Making Friends: The Social Competencies Assets* (Minneapolis, MN: Free Spirit, 2006). For ages eight to twelve.

STRATEGY #94

Lobby for a Strong Physical Education Program in Your Child's School

(Ages 6–18)

In 1987 the American Academy of Pediatrics issued a position paper regarding its stand on the use of medications for attention deficit disorder. One of the most telling excerpts from this statement was as follows: "Medication for children with attention deficit disorder should never be used as an isolated treatment. Proper classroom placement, *physical education programs*, behavior modification, counseling, and provision of structure should be used *before* a trial of pharmacotherapy is attempted" [italics added].[1] This clear statement of purpose reveals the importance of strong PE programs in our schools as a key factor in any drug-free approach to treating children who have been diagnosed with ADHD.

Few schools in the United States, however, actually provide the kind of physical catharsis that even typically developing children require every day, let alone those kids diagnosed with ADHD who have even greater needs for physical release. Less than 5 percent of school districts in the country meet recommendations by the American Alliance for Health, Physical Education, Recreation and Dance (AAHPERD) that elementary school students receive 150 minutes of PE per week and secondary students receive 225 minutes of PE per week.[2] Nearly half of U.S. school administrators report having cut significant time from physical education programs and recess to increase time spent in mathematics and reading programs since the passage of the federal education program No Child Left Behind (now called the Every Student Succeeds Act).[3]

Fortunately, there are excellent PE programs throughout the country that serve as models for what high-quality physical education can look like in your child's or adolescent's school. At Madison Junior High School in Naperville, Illinois, for example, the PE program includes a forty-station fitness center with treadmills, stationary bikes, heart rate monitors, and a climbing wall.[4] In the Woodford County Schools in Versailles, Kentucky, the PE coordinator facilitated the installation of seven-hole golf courses at each of the elementary schools, and created a biking program by purchasing confiscated bikes for $5 each and got a local biking club to donate helmets.[5] Most experts recommend that PE programs for kids with ADHD should emphasize individual sports over team sports. Pediatrician Jeffrey L. Alexander points out that "many children with ADHD excel in activities that focus more on individual skills than on teamwork. Examples: wrestling, karate, swimming, fencing, track and field, and tennis"[6] (see also Strategy #49: Find a Sport Your Child Will Love).

You can help establish a strong PE program in your child's or adolescent's school in several ways:

- Serve on a school site council or PTA committee dedicated to improving PE in the school
- Offer to serve as an aide in PE classes or as a volunteer monitor during playground time
- Help build or repair physical education equipment
- Hold fund-raisers to buy needed resources (including having a school-wide fitness fair)

When you support a strong PE program at your local school, you'll help provide your child or teenager with yet another avenue for channeling his hyperactive energies and enhancing his self-esteem.

FOR FURTHER INFORMATION

The 2016 United States Report Card on Physical Activity for Children and Youth: physicalactivityplan.org/reportcard/2016FINAL_USReportCard.pdf.

Support Your Child's Entrepreneurial Instincts
(Ages 8–18)

Has your ADHD-diagnosed child ever shown an interest in starting his own business? Has he ever set up a lemonade stand, created a snow shoveling business, or tried some other business venture? If so, he's in good company. Sir Richard Branson, IKEA's founder Ingvar Kamprad, Kinko's Paul Orfalea, and JetBlue founder David Neeleman are all ADHD-diagnosed individuals who have created wildly successful businesses. More important, these pioneers of business pointed to their ADHD as a critical element that helped them reach their goals. Interviewed by *ADDitude* magazine, Neeleman commented: "If someone told me you could be normal or you could continue to have your ADD I would take ADD. . . . I can distill complicated facts and come up with simple solutions. I can look out on an industry with all kinds of problems and say, 'How can I do this better?' My ADD brain naturally searches for better ways of doing things."[1]

New research supports the idea that ADHD and entrepreneurship make a good pair. In one sample of 10,104 students enrolled in higher education, students with ADHD-like behavior were more likely to have entrepreneurial inclinations.[2] Another study suggested that *it's precisely the lack of sufficient executive functioning ability* plus a propensity toward using intuition and taking risks that makes people diagnosed with ADHD good entrepreneurs.[3] Here are some suggestions for guiding your child's entrepreneurial instincts:

- *Take your child or teen off welfare (that is, stop giving them a "no conditions" allowance).* This will serve as an impetus for him to think of ways he can earn money through his own efforts.
- *Let your child or teen take the lead in deciding what type of business to start, but give him guidance in how he might go about it.* Ask questions such as, How will you advertise your business? How will you determine what to charge? Where will you keep the money you earn? How will you go about making sure your customers are satisfied?

- *Teach your child or teen money-management skills.* Share your own household methods for handling finances and record keeping; if he's old enough, show him how to use money-managing software like Quicken or Mint.
- *Have your child or teen write a business plan for his venture.* Even a plan as simple as "I will ask neighbors if they want their sidewalks shoveled in winter, and lawns mowed in summer" will help him focus on his goals and define exactly what he plans to do and how he plans to do it.
- *Encourage your child or teen to get involved in any entrepreneurial activities going on at her school.* Some schools have Junior Achievement chapters or after-school clubs that help students who are interested in starting their own businesses; if there isn't a program at your child's or adolescent's school, then lobby school administrators to start one.

Finally, even if your child or teen fails in his initial business ventures, let him know that learning from failure is a great way to increase the chances of success in the future. You can ask him to write down the things he learned from the experience, what *not* to do next time, and what strategies will help him to succeed. By fostering your child's or adolescent's business instincts starting at an early age, you'll be helping her develop skills not typically taught in the classroom but vitally important for succeeding in real life.

FOR FURTHER INFORMATION

Junior Achievement USA: One Education Way, Colorado Springs, CO 80906; 1-719-540-8000; juniorachievement.org. Helps young people develop the core competencies of career readiness, entrepreneurship, and financial literacy.

Use Color to Highlight Information
(Ages 4–18)

Children live in a world of color. Their toys are brightly colored. Their picture books are illustrated with vivid hues. Their favorite colors inspire strong personal feelings. But as children proceed through the elementary school grades they confront quite a different world, one dominated, not by color, but by black and white. They write their compositions in black pencil on white paper. They read textbooks full of black words against a white background. They copy words written in white chalk on a blackboard (or increasingly now, black marker on a whiteboard). However, research suggests that kids who have been diagnosed with ADHD may persist in an attraction to color as they progress through school. For these kids, a black-and-white academic world might be a real detriment to learning, and the deliberate use of color in highlighting material could provide an important key to their academic success. In one study, children diagnosed with ADHD had better handwriting and improved behavior when writing on colored as opposed to black or white paper.[1] In another study, girls at-risk for ADHD had decreased off-task behavior and improved problem-solving performance when they used a yellow highlighter pen to emphasize relevant words and units in math word problems.[2]

This research provides support for the idea that parents and teachers should incorporate the meaningful use of color in school activities and homework assignments as much as possible. Provide your child or teen with some of the following resources to use in his work: colored pencils, colored chalk, colored markers, colored paper, and colored transparencies (as overlays for reading written material). Color can be used to highlight specific words, numbers, or text. For example, if the child is studying spelling words beginning with *th*, he might highlight those letters in one color and the rest of the word in another color. In arithmetic, odd numbers might be colored blue and even numbers red, or in learning the times tables every third number might be colored green, every fourth number yellow and so on. Children should be taught to use colored highlighter pens to underline relevant material as they study. With a history assignment, your child or teen might highlight all the significant names in red, the important dates in green, the relevant locations in yellow, and the central ideas in blue. To create a low-stress environment for learning, allow your child to decorate his study area with his favorite color(s). By tuning in to your child's unique hue preferences, you may be helping him move through school, and life, with flying colors.

STRATEGY #97

Have Your Child Create a Blog
(Ages 8–18)

Claire Rose Gammon is a thirteen-year-old girl diagnosed with ADD (inattention without the hyperactivity or impulsivity) who possesses a great passion for fashion design. Her mother suggested that she communicate her interest to others by writing a fashion blog. Claire had been struggling with math and writing and was being bullied and excluded by other girls at school. Her mom thought that creating a blog would give her a chance to engage in writing activities and provide an outlet for expressing herself creatively. Her sister Gabby helped with the blog and soon they were attracting online followers. The girls have put together outfits and posted them on their site, which they call The Trend Sisters (thetrendsisters.wordpress.com). Mom manages the social media part of the blog for safety purposes.

Doing the blog has led to some exciting career opportunities. The two girls have collaborated or engaged in product features with companies such as PromGirl, Supercute Cosmetics, the Frosting Company, Black Tux, and Chalet Cosmetics. Their blogging efforts have also led to several modeling jobs, including one with NASCAR legend Richard Petty. Commenting on how empowering the blog has been to Claire's growth, her mother said: "It's helped her step out of her comfort zone a bit. It's pushed her outside of her box to do what she wants to do. . . . Instead of the ADD controlling her, she's controlling it."[1]

Creating a blog may be just the thing your own ADD or ADHD-diagnosed child or teen needs to do express herself, highlight her interests, gifts, and abilities, and connect with a wider group of friends and followers. Here are some things to keep in mind:

- Major blog sites such as Word Press and Blogger require users to be at least thirteen years old to use their platforms, but for younger kids you can register the blog in your name and involve your child in creating the blog together. Online videos take you through the basic steps of learning to blog, and information on helping kids under thirteen create blogs can be found at kidslearntoblog.com/how-to-start-a-blog-for-kids-under-13.
- There's a large number of blogging sites, Web site–building platforms, zines, and other kid-friendly platforms out there for kids under the age of thirteen to use to express themselves. For examples, see Weebly, Everloop, ClubPenguin, KiddiesKingdom (especially good for very young kids), NationalGeographicKids, Neopets (where kids create their own virtual pets and connect with others about caring for them), Fanlala (good for tweens and teens), My Secret Circle (girls only), Webkinz, and many more.
- Posting on social media sites such as Twitter, Facebook, and Instagram also provides opportunities for personal expression for older kids and teens, but in these cases, the point below should be given special emphasis.
- *Online safety has to be a major priority. Make it clear to your child or teen that they cannot be on any sites that you as a parent cannot personally access.* This should be a nonnegotiable issue. Counsel your child on basic online safety procedures, such as:
  - Avoid communicating with anyone they don't know.
  - Think carefully about what's appropriate and what's not appropriate to post on a blog or Web site.
  - Stay away from anonymous postings.
  - Set privacy features on the blog.

Remember that posting online can be a vital part of your child's or teen's growing sense of self. One study did a content analysis of twenty-five Facebook accounts with ADHD in the title and discovered that a key motivation for posting was the collective construction of a positive group identity.[2] Blogging, Web site building, and posting on social media also represent ways for your child or teen to express her uniqueness, so that, like Claire Rose, she can begin to step out into the world in her best light.

FOR FURTHER INFORMATION

Common Sense Media: commonsensemedia.org. A good resource for addressing parent concerns and providing guidance on social media.

STRATEGY #98

Work to Enhance Your Child's Social Network
(Ages 4–18)

Every child or adolescent exists in the midst of a complex web of social connections (see example below). Some of these relationships are positive, hopeful, and life affirming. Others are negative, depleting, or actively antagonistic. Still others are more ambiguous, with some good features and some bad. Taken as a whole, they represent a system of influences—weak, moderate, and strong—that can make all the difference in the world as to whether your child or adolescent feels supported as a human being, ignored as a nonentity, or actively disliked and considered a nuisance by others.

The first step in enhancing the quality of your child's social network is to become aware of all the relationships in his day-to-day life, both good and bad. To help with this task, create a diagram like the one shown below, putting your child's name in the center. Then map out all the significant relationships in your child's or teen's life at home, school, and in the extended family and community. Remember to include future potential relationships (such as a tutor you could hire, a possible future friend who lives down the street, a baby sister on the way). In drawing arrows from your child or teen to each relationship, choose a blue pencil for those connections that support your child in some way (emotionally, cognitively, socially), a red pencil for those connections that are negative in your child's life, and a standard black pencil for those relationships that appear to be neutral. Once you've mapped out the entire

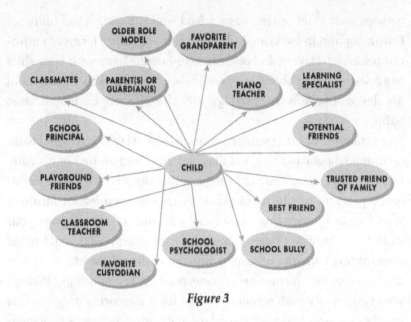

Figure 3

network, start brainstorming a list on a separate sheet of paper of the ways in which you might tweak the system to make it more life-affirming and socially-supportive for your child or teen. Such tweaking can be done in a number of ways (and remember, this is brainstorming, so put down *every* idea that occurs to you, even if it seems impractical):

- *Repairing existing negative relationships.* Let's say your child or teen has a bad relationship with his teacher at school. You can look at the ideas in Strategy #36: Foster Good Home–School Communication and Strategy #53: Work to Promote Teacher–Child Rapport and consider how the relationship might be improved. Or perhaps your child or teenager is always fighting with a sibling; by using conflict resolution strategies you might be able to help resolve disputes (see, for example, the University of Michigan Health Center's advice on sibling rivalry at med.umich.edu/yourchild/topics/sibriv.htm).

- *Lessening the influence of ongoing destructive relationships.* A bully at school may be victimizing your child or teen on a regular basis. In this case, you might inquire to see if there is an antibullying program at your child's school that could work toward alleviating the situation (if not, then lobby school administrators to create such a program). Or perhaps your child or teen has a friend who is having a bad influence (involving him in swearing, substance abuse, or other forms of antisocial behavior). Having an honest face-to-face dialogue with your child or adolescent about choosing friends wisely could make a difference in his choice of friends (see Strategy #18: Use Effective Communication Skills).

- *Strengthening existing positive relationships.* Maybe your child looks up to the school custodian and likes to follow him around in his daily tasks during breaks. You might suggest that the school set up a contingency program in which your child or teen is rewarded for finishing school tasks by spending extra time with him or her. Perhaps your child has a favorite grandmother who lives nearby who could spend time reading with him or helping him out with schoolwork.

- *Encouraging the formation of new positive relationships.* Perhaps your community high school or college has a mentoring program that matches younger kids with secondary and post-secondary school mentors. Such a program could have a significant positive influence on your child or teen. Or maybe there are kids in your neighborhood whom your child or teen doesn't know well but would benefit from befriending. Inviting them to a neighborhood block party could work toward creating new and rewarding friendships.

Finally, see what you can do to strengthen the ties in your immediate neighborhood to increase the chances that community members will begin to support each other, congregate together at playgrounds, parks, and recreational centers, and/or have social gatherings. In a nationwide study, lower neighborhood social support was found to be associated with higher odds of an ADHD diagnosis and higher ADHD severity.[1] By noticing what you can do to improve the quality of your child's *every interpersonal encounter, no matter how small,* you may be able to make a major positive change in the quality of his life.

Encourage Project-Based Learning at Home and in School

(Ages 8–18)

The most difficult environment for kids diagnosed with ADHD is the traditional school classroom in which the teacher lectures, the students take notes, and substantial time is given over to writing papers, filling in workbooks, reading textbooks, taking tests, and waiting for the next teacher instruction. The real difficulty, however, is that *this isn't a good learning environment for anyone*, let alone kids identified as having ADHD. It's just that the kids with the ADHD label happen to be the ones who are honest enough, or alive enough, or sensitive enough, not to want to (or be able to) go along with it! Our greatest educational theorists, including the philosopher John Dewey and the cognitive psychologist Howard Gardner, agree that *project-based learning* is one of the most profound and impactful methods of education *for all kids*.[1] Project-based learning is defined as *experiencing* learning, not just reading about it. It means getting involved with real-life issues (such as ecology, politics, social change, the arts, science), asking probing questions, investigating timely problems, researching topics thoroughly, and then creating projects or outcomes that reflect the acquired new learning. A final outcome for a project could take the form of a video, a poster, a display, a map, a photo montage, a written work, a three-dimensional construction, a multimedia presentation, or manifest in some other way. Here are two examples of project-based learning at work:

- Fourth-grade students in Hannibal, Missouri, received live caterpillars from the University of Kansas and raised them, measured their growth, released them as monarch butterflies, and sent them on their way to Mexico. They then created paper butterflies and sent them to students in Mexico. In the spring when the butterflies returned, the class received their replies from the Mexican students on those same paper butterflies.[2]

- High school students in Danville, California, tested the water quality of the run-off from three different parking lots and discovered that the lot that had been designed to be most ecologically friendly had the cleanest water.[3]

I used Google to search the terms *ADHD* and *project-based learning* and discovered that there was virtually nothing in Google Scholar (where research studies are indexed) on this topic. That tells me that our researchers are focusing the *least* attention on the learning methods that ADHD-diagnosed kids enjoy the *most*. Fortunately, project-based learning *is* alive and well in many of our finest elementary and secondary schools, and kids diagnosed with ADHD are thriving in them. Brown University students Jonathan Mooney and David Cole, who had been diagnosed with learning disabilities and ADHD, summed it up best when they wrote: "Beyond the content or skills learned, we were profoundly affected by our experience with project-based learning. These experiences changed who we are, and they changed our lives. How often can we say that about information given in a lecture? We lived those ideas and skills; we experienced them and integrated them into our lives."[4] Here are a few ways you can bring project-based learning into your own child's or teen's life:

- Encourage your child's or teen's school to incorporate more project-based learning into its curriculum. One book you might recommend they read is the Buck Institute for Education's *Setting the Standard for Project Based Learning: A Proven Approach to Rigorous Classroom Instruction*.[5]
- During holidays or summer vacation when your child or teen might be looking for something to do, ask him what he'd most like to find out about in the world. He may change topics a few times and that's okay. Popular topics might include the local ecology, your family history, outer space exploration, dinosaurs, a social issue like feeding the poor, famous sports records, a historical event like the Civil War, the life of an admired person, a foreign country, a political issue like abortion, creating a collection of bugs (or coins or stamps), learning how food is processed, a favorite animal, a business venture, or any of a thousand other possibilities.

- Provide your child or teen with space somewhere in or around the house that can serve as his project place, and provide (or point him toward) the resources he needs to explore his topic. Include a bulletin board, if he finds it useful, where he can post ideas, images, articles, lists or other documents to help him in his quest.

- Steer a middle path between leaving him completely on his own and taking over the project entirely. Gently guide him in exploring his topic, let him take the lead, but offer your support and suggestions as needed.

The process of engaging in a project is more important than any final product (and if he does a final project, don't evaluate it with either praise or criticism; instead, ask questions about the content of the project). By pursuing a project that fills him with enthusiasm, he'll also be developing his ability to plan, think critically, express himself creatively, communicate to others, make decisions, and take personal and/or social responsibility for things that really matter to him. Such a project is worth more than a thousand worksheets!

FOR FURTHER INFORMATION

Lori McWilliam Pickert, *Project-Based Homeschooling: Mentoring Self-Directed Learners* (CreateSpace Independent Publishing Platform, 2012).

STRATEGY #100

Show Your Child Work-Arounds to Get Things Done
(Ages 8–18)

Many, if not most, of the strategies listed in this book build skills that will enable your child or teen to overcome challenges and strengthen capacities in areas of difficulty. There are times, however, when a person doesn't want to wait around until he develops an ability in order to get something done. The metaphor I have in mind is the person who wastes a lot of energy trying to open a jammed door when there's a door right next to it that's open. I call strategies for finding other *easier* ways to reach a goal *work-arounds*. In the vernacular of education and psychology these are sometimes referred to as assistive technologies or universal design for learning (UDL) strategies.

The idea behind universal design originally came out of urban planning and architecture. One good example of a universal design technology is the curb cut in the pavement of a sidewalk that allows people with disabilities to easily move their wheelchairs across a street. What makes it "universal" is that the curb cut also benefits people with walking canes, kids on skateboards, parents with strollers, and others. A good example of a universal design for *learning* strategy (or work-around) is the spell-checker feature of a word processing program. Instead of having to study hard to be the very best speller in the world, a person can get help by using the spell-checker to spot and correct most misspellings. Another example of a UDL technology is a math calculator. This is an ideal tool for those who have difficulties with basic arithmetic skills but are good at solving higher-order math problems because the calculator can do the lower-order math part for them. There are quite a number of work-arounds you can tell your child or teen about that can help her work around difficulties and assist her in attaining intended goals (some are computer apps and others are nontech). Here are a few:

- *For difficulties with writing, use speech-to-text software.* For people who have trouble getting their ideas down on paper by typing, longhand writing, or printing them, apps like Dragon NaturallySpeaking and Voice Assistant transform the human voice into written text.
- *For difficulties with reading, use text-to-speech software.* Just the reverse of the previous technology, this approach scans text and turns it into synthesized speech sounds. Programs include NaturalReader, TextSpeech Pro, and Audiobook Maker.
- *For difficulties with working memory, use "memory containers."* If your child or teen has difficulty with working memory and forgets things easily, suggest that he create a checklist of all the things he needs to remember (items to take to school, his schedule for the coming week). Or he might record the instructions for homework assignments on his smartphone or use a GPS device if he has trouble remembering directions while driving.

- *For difficulties with notetaking in class, use Livescribe pen.* This technology allows a student to write notes on a specially treated paper and then if there's a problem understanding the notes or the student has left out important information, it has the feature of being able to press down with the pen on a particular sentence and hear an audio recording of the teacher's voice at just that point in the lecture.
- *For difficulties following step-by-step instructions, watch online video lessons.* Use YouTube, Vimeo, or Khan Academy videos that teach step-by-step skills covering a wide range of subjects; videos can be replayed as many times as necessary to master a skill.
- *For difficulties paying attention, use self-monitoring technologies.* Self-monitoring apps like MotivAider allow a person program a device to vibrate at designated or random intervals to serve as reminders while studying or attending a class.

These are just a few examples of how your child or teen can work around chronic difficulties in areas of cognition or behavior while still meeting obligations, requirements, expectations, and standards. Remind your child or teen that it's still important to keep working on those weak areas, but it's nice knowing that you don't have to let your difficulties get in the way of being a good student or a conscientious family member.

FOR FURTHER INFORMATION

Center for Applied Special Technology (CAST): cast.org. A nonprofit education research and development organization that works to expand learning opportunities for all individuals through universal design for learning.

National Center on Universal Design for Learning: udlcenter.org/aboutudl /udlguidelines. Their Web site includes many examples of UDL tools.

STRATEGY #101

Teach Your Child Organizational Strategies
(Ages 7–18)

Many kids with attention or behavioral problems have difficulties with organizational skills. Among the litany of complaints that parents and teachers share are the following: messy bedrooms, forgotten homework, chaotic study skills, missed chores, and skipped deadlines for school assignments. These outer signs of disarray, however, may simply be reflections of an inner disorganization that can be straightened out with some assistance from a patient and at least somewhat organized parent or teacher. Here are some suggestions for helping your child self-organize in several areas of his school and home life.

- *Organize homework assignments in a notebook.* Let your child choose what kind of notebook he'd like to use and let him create art on the front to remind him that this is his homework notebook. Inside the book he can put a calendar for noting deadlines, dividers to separate material by subject matter, pockets for placing "to-do" and "completed" assignments, a pouch (for pencils, pens, and erasers), and plenty of notebook paper for doing assignments.
- *Start the school year off with a few organizational meetings with your child.* For the first few days of school (and periodically thereafter), sit down with your child or teen and review with him his list of assignments, due dates, and the actual homework itself. If your child or adolescent isn't writing down the assignments or forgets to put them in his notebook at school, phone the teacher and ask her to meet briefly with your child toward the end of the day to make sure homework materials are all ready to go home. If your child or teen is confused about which textbooks to bring home, make a colored book jacket for each text that he can illustrate with pictures related to each subject.
- *Provide strategies for organizing home and school space.* Color-code drawers and shelves to remind your child or teenager where clothes

and toys go. He might also want to create a graphic symbol for each drawer—for example, a picture of a pair of pants for the pants drawer. Color-code the clothes bar in the closet so that pants are hung up along the blue segment, shirts along the red segment, and so on. Suggest that your child clean up his room using any of the following categories:

Color (pick up the red things first, then the blue, then the green, etc.)

Size (pick up the smallest things first, the largest things last)

Texture (pick up the smooth things first, the rough things last)

Other (an organizational category of his own devising)

- *Store items in clear plastic boxes so that he can see what goes inside.* Suggest that he organize his school desk by dividing the inside into sections using colored tape: books go over here, pencils in this section, show-and-tell items in this square in the corner, and so forth.

- *Help your child organize household chores.* Create a family chore chart with pictures and names of family members across the top of the chart; then vertically in columns under each name place a series of hooks or pockets. Chores can be put on thick pieces of cardboard and hung from the hooks or placed in the pockets to indicate which individuals are responsible for which chores that day, week, or month. Rotating chores helps keep the experience fresh for your child. Color-code chore tags or paste pictures on them to represent the work involved.

- *Use technology to help your child or teen get organized.* The app iStudiez provides a platform for organizing homework, test dates, deadlines, and other school responsibilities. 30/30 allows kids to set tasks and the time needed to complete them. Due and Home Routines remind kids or teens about assignments or chores and when they need to be done. iRewardChart is the electronic equivalent of a chore chart, which gives points for completed tasks that can be exchanged for rewards.

Make sure your child or teen is involved in helping create these organizational strategies. If methods are simply imposed on him from without, then they'll probably have little impact. Some organizational ideas won't work with your child or teen no matter how long you spend trying to get him to use them. Try out a few of these ideas and see which ones work best. In time, and with proper guidance from you and his teachers, your child or adolescent will discover the organizational strategies that help him manage his life most effectively.

FOR FURTHER INFORMATION

Donna Goldberg and Jennifer Zwiebel, *The Organized Student: Teaching Children the Skills for Success in School and Beyond* (New York: Touchstone, 2005).

NOTES

PREFACE

1   The 1986 edition of my book *In Their Own Way* was revised and expanded as *In Their Own Way: Discovering and Encouraging Your Child's Multiple Intelligences* (New York: Tarcher, 2000).

CHAPTER ONE

1   *The Blob* (1958) was directed by Irvin Yeaworth and starred Steve McQueen in his first major film role. For more information go to en.wikipedia.org/wiki/The_Blob.

2   An adaptation of Virginia Douglas's speech on attention deficits to the Canadian Psychological Association is presented in her "Stop, Look and Listen: The Problem of Sustained Attention and Impulse Control in Hyperactive and Normal Children," *Canadian Journal of Behavioural Science/Revue canadienne des sciences du comportement* 4, no. 4 (October 1972): 259–82. See also Douglas's account of that speech and article in "This Week's Citation Classic," *Current Contents* 44 (October 29, 1984): 16. Retrieved from garfield.library.upenn.edu/classics1984/A1984TN32300001.pdf.

3   The first recognition of attention deficit disorder in American psychiatry is in the *DSM III: Diagnostic and Statistical Manual of Mental Disorders*, 3rd ed. (Arlington, VA: American Psychiatric Association, 1980).

4   The lifting of the U.S. government ban on direct-to-consumer advertising of medications is cited in Alan Schwartz, "The Selling of Attention Deficit Disorder," *New York Times*, December 14, 2013.

5   The medicating of children under the age of four is the focus of the article by Alan Schwartz, "Thousands of Toddlers Are Medicated for A.D.H.D. Report Finds, Raising Worries," *New York Times*, May 16, 2014.

6   For more information on the expansion of ADHD diagnoses beyond American shores see Peter Conrad and Meredith R. Bergey, "The Impending Globalization of ADHD: Notes on the Expansion and Growth of a Medicalized Disorder," *Social Science and Medicine*, 122 (December, 2014), 31-43.

7   Percentages on rates of ADHD diagnoses in children aged five to seven are from U.S. Department of Health and Human Services, Centers for Disease Control and Prevention, National Center for Health Statistics, "Table 35—Health Conditions among Children under Age 18, by Selected Characteristics: United States, Average Annual, Selected Years 1997–1999 through 2012–2014," *Health, United States, 2015: With Special Feature on Racial and Ethnic Health Disparities* (Washington, D.C.: U.S. Government Printing Office, 2015), 157.

8   Information on the diagnostic criteria for ADHD is provided in a fact sheet: "Attention Deficit/Hyperactivity Disorder," American Psychiatric Association, 2013. Retrieved from dsm5.org/documents/adhd%20fact%20sheet.pdf.

9   Information on the key features of the ADHD myth has been taken from several

Notes

Web sites. They include Mayo Clinic, "Attention-Deficit/Hyperactivity Disorder (ADHD) in Children." Retrieved from mayoclinic.org/diseases-conditions/adhd /symptoms-causes/dxc-20196181. National Institute of Mental Health, "Attention Deficit Hyperactivity Disorder." Retrieved from nimh.nih.gov/health/topics/attention -deficit-hyperactivity-disorder-adhd/index.shtml. CHADD, "About ADHD." Retrieved from chadd.org/Understanding-ADHD/About-ADHD.aspx.

10 The consensus statement citing thousands of ADHD studies is Russell A. Barkley, Edward H. Cook, Jr., Adele Diamond, Alan Zemetkin, et al., "International Consensus Statement on ADHD—January 2002," *Clinical Child and Family Psychology Review* 5, no. 2 (June 2002): 89–111.

CHAPTER TWO

1 For an English translation of the German morality tale about Fidgety Phillip see Henrich Hoffmann, *The English Struwwelpeter, or, Pretty Stories and Funny Pictures* (London: Routledge & Paul, 1909).

2 The original text of Still's lectures on children displaying a morbid defect of moral control is found at George Still, "The Goulstonian Lectures on Some Abnormal Psychical Conditions in Children," *Lancet* (1902). Retrieved from archive.org/stream/ b24976295#page/n3/mode/2up.

3 Information on the history of ADHD is taken from Klaus W. Lange, Susanne Reichl, Katharina M. Lange, et al., "The History of Attention Deficit Hyperactivity Disorder," *Attention Deficit Hyperactivity Disorder* 2, no. 4 (December 2010): 241–55.

4 For information about sluggish cognitive tempo, see Alan Schwarz, "Idea of New Attention Disorder Spurs Research, and Debate," *New York Times*, April 11, 2014; and Russell A. Barkley, "Distinguishing Sluggish Cognitive Tempo from ADHD in Children and Adolescents: Executive Functioning, Impairment, and Comorbidity," *Journal of Clinical Child & Adolescent Psychology* 42, no. 2 (2013): 161–73.

5 The 1 to 3 percent estimate HKD used by the International Classification of Diseases was cited in H. Remschmidt and Global ADHD Working Group, "Global Consensus on ADHD/HKD," *European Child and Adolescent Psychiatry* 14, no. 3 (May 2005): 127–37. The American Psychiatric Association's 5 percent figure for ADHD is cited in their "What Is ADHD?," 2015. Retrieved from psychiatry.org/patients-families/ adhd/what-is-adhd. The 11 percent prevalence figure for ADHD is cited in CDC, "Key Findings: Trends in the Parent-Report of Health Care Provider-Diagnosis and Medication Treatment for ADHD: United States, 2003–2011," December 10, 2014. Retrieved from cdc.gov/ncbddd/adhd/features/key-findings-adhd72013.html.

6 Statistics on the rise in ADHD diagnoses and the variations in rates between states are taken from CDC, "Attention-Deficit/Hyperactivity Disorder, Data & Statistics," 2016. Retrieved from cdc.gov/ncbddd/adhd/data.html.

7 Barkley's statement on the variability of ADHD definitions is given in Russell A. Barkley, *Attention Deficit Hyperactivity Disorder: A Handbook for Diagnosis and Treatment*, 2nd ed. (New York: Guilford, 1998), 79.

8 Saul's quotation on ADHD as a disorder defined by its symptoms is in Richard Saul, "ADHD Does Not Exist," *New Republic*, February 14, 2014. Retrieved from new republic.com/article/116625/adhd-does-not-exist.

9 Symptoms of ADHD from the DSM-5 are given in CDC, "Attention-Deficit/Hyperactivity Disorder, Symptoms and Diagnosis." Retrieved from https://www.cdc.gov/ ncbddd/adhd/diagnosis.html.

10   Educator concern about the validity of homework is expressed, for example, in Alfie Kohn, *The Homework Myth* (Cambridge, MA: Da Capo, 2007).

11   The statistic that rating scales are used in 90 percent of ADHD diagnoses is found in Susanna N. Visser, Benjamin Zablotsky, Joseph R. Holbrook, Melissa L. Danielson, and Rebecca H. Bitsko, "Diagnostic Experiences of Children with Attention-Deficit/ Hyperactivity Disorder," *National Health Statistics Reports* 81 (September 3, 2015), cdc.gov/nchs/data/nhsr/nhsr081.pdf.

12   The quotation stating the Conners ASQ may be the most effective diagnostic tool in assessing ADHD is from Ling-Yin Chang, Mei-Yeh Wang, Pei-Shan Tsai, "Diagnostic Accuracy of Rating Scales for Attention-Deficit/Hyperactivity Disorder: A Meta-Analysis," *Pediatrics* 137, no. 3 (March 2016): 1–13.

13   The Conners Abbreviated Teacher Rating Scale was retrieved from altamontepediatrics.com/AbbreviatedSymptomQuestionnaire.pdf.

14   The implication from the Conners rating scale is that fidgeting is a problem behavior, but new research reveals that it may be central to an ADHD-diagnosed person's ability to focus. See T. A. Hartanto, C. E. Krafft, A. M. Iosif, and J. B. Schweitzer, "A Trial-by-Trial Analysis Reveals More Intense Physical Activity Is Associated with Better Cognitive Control Performance in Attention-Deficit/Hyperactivity Disorder," *Child Neuropsychology* 22, no. 5 (2016): 618–26.

15   The circular dialogue between a parent and psychiatrist is from Philip Hickey, "A Critical Thinker's Views on ADHD and the DSM," *National Psychologist*, May 2, 2012. Retrieved from nationalpsychologist.com/2012/05/a-critical-thinkers-views-on-adhd-and-the-dsm/101684.html.

16   Articles on potential biomarkers for ADHD include D. Gilbert, K. Isaacs, M. Augusta, et al., "A Marker of ADHD Behavior and Motor Development in Children," *Neurology* 76, no. 7 (February 15, 2011): 615–21; F. R. Karsz, A. Vance, V. A. Anderson, et al., "Olfactory Impairments in Child Attention-Deficit/Hyperactivity Disorder," *Journal of Clinical Psychiatry* 69, no. 9 (September 2008): 1462–68; and Samuel Cortese, Robin Azoulay, F. Xavier Castellanos, et al., "Brain Iron Levels in Attention-Deficit/Hyperactivity Disorder: A Pilot MRI Study," *World Journal of Biological Psychiatry* 13, no. 3 (March 2012): 223–31.

17   The quotation on the lack of a biomarker for ADHD is in Johannes Thome, Ann-Christine Ehlis, Andreas J. Fallgatter, et al., "Biomarkers for Attention-Deficit/Hyperactivity Disorder (ADHD). A Consensus Report of the WFSBP Task Force on Biological Markers and the World Federation of ADHD," *World Journal of Biological Psychiatry* 13, no. 5 (July 2012): 379–400.

18   For studies on executive functioning impairment in ADHD-diagnosed children, see Douglas Sjöwall, Linda Roth, Sofia Lindqvist, and Lisa B. Thorell, "Multiple Deficits in ADHD: Executive Dysfunction, Delay Aversion, Reaction Time Variability, and Emotional Deficits," *Journal of Child Psychology and Psychiatry* 54, no. 6 (June 2013): 619–27; and Maggie E. Toplaka, Stefania M. Bucciarelli, Umesh Jain, and Rosemary Tannock, "Executive Functions: Performance-Based Measures and the Behavior Rating Inventory of Executive Function (BRIEF) in Adolescents with Attention Deficit/Hyperactivity Disorder (ADHD)," *Child Neuropsychology: A Journal on Normal and Abnormal Development in Childhood and Adolescence* 15, no. 1 (January 2009): 53–72.

19   A key study on the two- or three-year lag in cortical maturation of children diagnosed with ADHD is P. Shaw, K. Eckstrand, W. Sharp, et al., "Attention-Deficit/

Hyperactivity Disorder Is Characterized by a Delay in Cortical Maturation," *Proceedings of the National Academy of Science U S A* 104, no. 49 (December 4, 2007): 19649–54.

20   Information on the maturation of the prefrontal cortex from childhood to adulthood can be found in Elizabeth R. Sowell, Bradley S. Peterson, Paul M. Thompson, et al., "Mapping Cortical Change across the Human Life Span," *Nature Neuroscience* 6, no. 3 (March 2003): 309–15.

21   Sroufe's critique of brain scan studies to validate ADHD is quoted in L. Alan Sroufe, "Ritalin Gone Wrong," *New York Times,* January 29, 2012, SR1.

22   Studies on the impact of trauma on the brain include J. Douglas Bremner, "Traumatic Stress: Effects on the Brain," *Dialogues in Clinical Neuroscience* 8, no. 4 (December 2006): 445–61; and Bruce S. McEwen and John H. Morrison, "The Brain on Stress: Vulnerability and Plasticity of the Prefrontal Cortex over the Life Course," *Neuron* 79, no. 1 (July 2013): 16–29.

23   For information on the genetic basis of ADHD, see an interview with neuroscientist Susan Smalley in Aliyah Baruchin, "Expert Q & A: Nature, Nurture and Attention Deficit," *New York Times,* March 12, 2008.

24   The two studies cited on the paucity of evidence for the genetic basis of ADHD are P. Heiser, M. Heinzel-Gutenbrunner, J. Frey, et al., "Twin Study on Heritability of Activity, Attention, and Impulsivity as Assessed by Objective Measures," *Journal of Attention Disorders* 9, no. 4 (May 2006): 575–81; and Anita Thapar, Miriam Cooper, Olga Eyre, and Kate Langley, "Practitioner Review: What Have We Learnt About the Causes of ADHD?," *Journal of Child Psychology and Psychiatry* 54, no. 1 (January 2013), 3–16.

25   Two studies of gene-environment interactions and ADHD include M. M. Martel, M. Nikolas, K. Jernigan, et al., "The Dopamine Receptor D4 Gene (DRD4) Moderates Family Environmental Effects on ADHD," *Journal of Abnormal Child Psychology* 39, no. 1 (January 2011): 1–10; and J. S. Richards, A. Arias Vásquez, B. Franke, et al., "Developmentally Sensitive Interaction Effects of Genes and the Social Environment on Total and Subcortical Brain Volumes," *PLoS One* 11, no. 5 (May, 2016): e0155755.

26   The study on co-morbidity of ADHD with other disorders in Denmark is Christina Mohr Jensen and Hans-Christoph Steinhausen, "Comorbid Mental Disorders in Children and Adolescents with Attention-Deficit/Hyperactivity Disorder in a Large Nationwide Study," *ADHD Attention Deficit and Hyperactivity Disorders* 7, no. 1 (March 2015): 27–38.

27   A study suggesting that ADHD plus bipolar disorder may represent a distinct clinical subtype is S. Bernardi, S. Cortese, M. Solanto, et al., "Bipolar Disorder and Comorbid Attention Deficit Hyperactivity Disorder. A Distinct Clinical Phenotype? Clinical Characteristics and Temperamental Traits," *World Journal of Biological Psychiatry* 11, no. 4 (June 2010): 656–66.

CHAPTER THREE

1   Bradley's research on psychostimulants is reported in Charles Bradley, "The Behavior of Children Receiving Benzedrine," *American Journal of Psychiatry* 94 (November 1937): 577–85.

2   For a history of medication use for ADHD and its earlier incarnations as a disorder, see Rick Mayes and Catherine Bagwell, *Medicating Children: ADHD and Pediatric Mental Health* (Cambridge, MA: Harvard University Press, 2009).

Notes

3   For the Baltimore County Health Department's survey of medication use, see Daniel J. Safer and John M. Krager, "A Survey of Medication Treatment for Hyperactive/Inattentive Students," *JAMA* 260, no. 15 (October 1988): 2256.

4   Statistics on the growth of medication in the 1990s is given in Gretchen B. LeFever and Andrea P. Arcon, "ADHD among American Schoolchildren," *Scientific Review of Mental Health Practice* 2, no. 1 (spring–summer 2003). Retrieved from srmhp.org/0201/adhd.html.

5   Information about Adzenys is from Meghana Keshavan, "Tasty and Easy to Take, a New ADHD Drugs Alarms Some Psychiatrists," Stat, May 23, 2016. Retrieved from statnews.com/2016/05/23/adhd-drug-concerns.

6   Statistics on the rate and sales of ADHD medication are provided in Luke Whelan, "Sales of ADHD Medications Are Skyrocketing: Here's Why," *Mother Jones*, February 24, 2015. Retrieved from motherjones.com/environment/2015/02/hyperactive-growth-adhd-medication-sales.

7   Lawrence Diller is quoted in Amy Kraft, "Adderall Use Rising among Young Adults," *CBS News*, February 16, 2016. Retrieved from cbsnews.com/news/adderall-misuse-rising-among-young-adults. His book is *Running on Ritalin: A Physician Reflects on Children, Society, and Performance in a Pill* (New York: Bantam, 1999).

8   Stephen Hinshaw is quoted in Whelan, "Sales of ADHD Medications Are Skyrocketing." His book, written with Richard Scheffler, is *The ADHD Explosion: Myths, Medication, Money, and Today's Push for Performance* (Oxford, UK: Oxford University Press, 2014).

9   Information on high-socioeconomic families using ADHD medications to help cope with academic pressures is reported in Marissa D. King, Jennifer Jennings, and Jason M. Fletcher, "Medical Adaptation to Academic Pressure: Schooling, Stimulant Use, and Socioeconomic Status," *American Sociological Review* 79, no. 6 (November 2014): 1039–66.

10 The use of ADHD medications to give nondiagnosed kids from poor socioeconomic backgrounds a leg up in school is reported in Alan Schwartz, "Attention Disorder or Not, Pills to Help in School," *New York Times*, October 9, 2012. Retrieved from nytimes.com/2012/10/09/health/attention-disorder-or-not-children-prescribed-pills-to-help-in-school.html.

11 The data showing the failure of doctors to use behavioral therapy with young children are provided in CDC, "ADHD in Young Children," May 3, 2016. Retrieved from cdc.gov/vitalsigns/adhd/index.html.

12 The diagnosing of children under the age of four is reported in Alan Schwartz, "Thousands of Toddlers Are Medicated for A.D.H.D., Report Finds, Raising Worries," *New York Times*, May 16, 2014. Retrieved from https://www.nytimes.com/2014/05/17/us/among-experts-scrutiny-of-attention-disorder-diagnoses-in-2-and-3-year-olds.html?_r=0.

13 The listing of Adderall and Ritalin as Schedule II drugs is from DEA, "Drug Schedules." Retrieved from dea.gov/druginfo/ds.shtml.

14 New research suggesting that users of ADHD drugs are neither more or less likely to become addicted to illegal drugs later on is reported on in Stuart Wolpert, "Are Children Who Take Ritalin for ADHD at Greater Risk of Future Drug Abuse?" UCLA Newsroom, May 29, 2013. Retrieved from newsroom.ucla.edu/releases/are-children-who-take-ritalin-246186.

15 For reports of ADHD drug abuse and misuse, see Jennifer Setlik, G. Randall Bond, and Mona Ho, "Adolescent Prescription ADHD Medication Abuse Is Rising Along

with Prescriptions for These Medications," *Pediatrics* 124, no. 3 (September 2009): 875–80.

16   Initial research findings from the NIMH showing the superiority of ADHD drugs to behavioral therapy are given in Peter S. Jensen, Stephen P. Hinshaw, James M. Swanson, et al., "Findings from the NIMH Multimodal Treatment Study of ADHD (MTA): Implications and Applications for Primary Care Providers," *Developmental and Behavioral Pediatrics* 22, no. 1 (February 2001): 60–73.

17   Findings from a follow-up study of the MTA showing no differences between ADHD drugs and behavior therapy are in Brooke S. G. Molina, Stephen P. Hinshaw, James M. Swanson, et al., "The MTA at 8 Years: Prospective Follow-Up of Children Treated for Combined Type ADHD in a Multisite Study," *Journal of the American Academy of Child & Adolescent Psychiatry* 48, no. 5 (May 2009): 484–500.

18   James Swanson is quoted in Katherine Sharp, "The Smart Pill Oversell," *Nature* 506, no. 7487 (February 12, 2014): 146–48.

19   Common side effects of psychostimulants are given in S. Punja, L. Shamseer, L. Hartling, et al., "Amphetamines for Attention Deficit Hyperactivity Disorder (ADHD) in Children and Adolescents," *Cochrane Database of Systematic Reviews*, February 4, 2016. Retrieved from onlinelibrary.wiley.com/doi/10.1002/14651858. CD009996.pub2/abstract.

20   Evidence of serious heart problems associated with ADHD drugs is given in William O. Cooper, Laurel A. Habel, Colin M. Sox, et al., "ADHD Drugs and Serious Cardio-vascular Events in Children and Young Adults," *New England Journal of Medicine*, 365, no. 20 (November 17, 2011): 1896–1904.

21   The American Heart Association's guidelines for assessing heart risk before ad-ministering ADHD drugs is reported on in Lisa Graham, "AHA Releases Recom-mendations on Cardiovascular Monitoring and the Use of ADHD Medications in Children with Heart Disease," *American Family Physician* 79, no. 10 (May 15, 2009): 905–10.

22   Evidence of the influence of ADHD drugs on psychotic symptoms is provided in Lynn E. MacKenzie, Sabina Abidi, Helen L. Fisher, et al., "Stimulant Medication and Psychotic Symptoms in Offspring of Parents with Mental Illness," *Pediatrics* 137, no. 1 (January 2016): e20152486.

23   The association between ADHD drugs and bone problems is reported on in Megan Brooks, "ADHD Drugs May Harm Bone Health: Study," *Psych Congress Network*, 2016. Retrieved from psychcongress.com/article/adhd-drugs-may-harm-bone-health-study-26693.

24   Reports of sudden death from psychostimulants is given in M. S. Gould, B. T. Walsh, J. L. Munfakh, et al., "Sudden Death and Use of Stimulant Medications in Youths," *American Journal of Psychiatry* 166, no. 9 (September 2009): 992–1001.

25   Research linking ADHD medication use with increased victimization by bullies is in Quyen M. Epstein-Ngo, Sean Esteban McCabe, Philip T. Veliz, et al., "Diversion of ADHD Stimulants and Victimization among Adolescents," *Journal of Pediatric Psychology* (November 19, 2015). Retrived from http://jpepsy.oxfordjournals.org/content/early/2015/11/19/jpepsy.jsv105.full.pdf+html.

26   Reports of teenage abuse of ADHD drugs is given on the National Council on Alco-holism and Drug Dependence Web site: "Almost 90 Percent of Teens Who Abuse ADHD Drugs Use Someone Else's Medication," March 10, 2016. Retrieved from ncadd.org/blogs/in-the-news/almost-90-percent-of-teens-who-abuse-adhd-drugs-use-someone-else-s-medication.

Notes

27 Increases in emergency hospital visits due to Adderall drug abuse by young adults are reported in Amy Kraft, "Adderall Misuse Rising Among Young Adults," CBS News, February 16, 2016. Retrieved from cbsnews.com/news/adderall-misuse -rising-among-young-adults.

28 For studies on children's positive attitudes toward ADHD medications see D. Efron, F. C. Jarman, and M. J. Barker, "Child and Parent Perceptions of Stimulant Medication Treatment in Attention Deficit Hyperactivity Disorder," *Journal of Paediatrics and Child Health* 34, no. 3 (June 1998): 288–92; and Lisa B. Thorell and Kerstin Dahlström, "Children's Self-Reports on Perceived Effects on Taking Stimulant Medication for ADHD," *Journal of Attention Disorders* 12, no. 5 (March 2009): 460–68.

29 Comments on young adolescents' negative experiences with ADHD drugs are from Alice Charach, Emanuela Yeung, Tiziana Volpe, et al., "Exploring Stimulant Treatment in ADHD: Narratives of Young Adolescents and Their Parents," *BMC Psychiatry* 14 (2014): 110.

30 The adolescent comment that the ADHD tablets were "in control of me" was from Chris Travella and John Visser, "'ADHD Does Bad Stuff to You': Young People's and Parents' Experiences and Perceptions of Attention Deficit Hyperactivity Disorder (ADHD)," *Emotional and Behavioural Difficulties* 11, no. 3 (September 2006): 205–16.

31 The drop-off in the use of ADHD medications during adolescence is reported in Suzanne McCarthy, Philip Asherson, David Coghill, et al., "Attention-Deficit Hyperactivity Disorder: Treatment Discontinuation in Adolescents and Young Adults," *British Journal of Psychiatry* 194, no. 3 (February 2009): 273–77.

32 The study which concluded that there was a better result from a lower dose of stimulant medication paired with a placebo than with a higher dose of stimulant medication by itself was Adrian D. Sandler, Corrine E. Glesne, and James W. Bodfish, "Conditioned Placebo Dose Reduction: A New Treatment in ADHD?" *Journal of Developmental and Behavioral Pediatrics* 31, no. 5 (June 2010): 369–375.

33 Two books that provide a pro-ADHD perspective for parents are Russell A. Barkley's *Taking Charge of ADHD: The Complete Authoritative Guide for Parents*, 3rd ed. (New York: Guilford, 2013); and Edward M. Hallowell and John J. Ratey's *Delivered from Distraction: Getting the Most Out of Life with Attention Deficit Disorder* (New York: Ballantine, 2005).

CHAPTER FOUR

1 Studies on cortical delay in children diagnosed with ADHD include P. Shaw, K. Eckstrand, W. Sharp, et al., "Attention-deficit/Hyperactivity Disorder Is Characterized by a Delay in Cortical Maturation," *Proceedings of the National Academy of Science U.S.A.* 104, no. 49 (December 4, 2007): 19649–54; Katya Rubia, "Neuro-Anatomic Evidence for the Maturational Delay Hypothesis of ADHD," *Proceedings of the National Academy of Sciences U.S.A.* 104, no. 50 (December 11, 2007): 19663–64; and Chandra S. Sripada, Daniel Kessler, and Mike Angstadt, "Lag in Maturation of the Brain's Intrinsic Functional Architecture in Attention-Deficit /Hyperactivity Disorder," *Proceedings of the National Academy of Sciences U. S. A.* 111, no. 39 (September 30, 2014): 14259–64.

2 The study showing a 50 percent drop in ADHD rates every five years is J. C. Hill and E. P. Schoener, "Age-Dependent Decline of Attention Deficit Hyperactivity Disorder," *American Journal of Psychiatry* 153, no. 9 (September 1996): 1143–46.

3   The study citing a 15 percent prevalence of ADHD-diagnosed twenty-five-year-olds
     is S. V. Faraone, J. Biederman, and E. Mick, "The Age-Dependent Decline of Atten-
     tion Deficit Hyperactivity Disorder: A Meta-Analysis of Follow-Up Studies," *Psy-
     chological Medicine* 36, no. 2 (February 2006): 159–65. By fudging their data to
     include young adults with ADHD in partial remission, the authors boosted the rate
     to 2.6 percent of all twenty-five-year-olds. However, the designation of "partial
     remission" can itself include a large measure of developmental delay.

4   The Icelandic study showing that the youngest children in class were most likely to be
     prescribed psychostimulants is Helga Zoëga, Unnur A. Valdimarsdóttir, and Sonia
     Hernández-Díaz, "Age, Academic Performance, and Stimulant Prescribing for ADHD:
     A Nationwide Cohort Study," *Pediatrics* 130, no. 6 (December 2012): 10112–18.

5   The British Columbia study showing a 30 percent greater likelihood being diagnosed
     with ADHD if the child's birthday is in December comes from Richard L. Morrow,
     E. Jane Garland, James M. Wright, et al., "Influence of Relative Age on Diagnosis
     and Treatment of Attention-Deficit/Hyperactivity Disorder in Children," *Canadian
     Medical Association Journal* 184, no. 7 (April 17, 2012): 755–62.

6   The quotation about age as a risk factor in ADHD diagnoses is from M. H. Chen,
     W. H. Lan, Y. M. Bai, et al., "Influence of Relative Age on Diagnosis and Treatment
     of Attention-Deficit Hyperactivity Disorder in Taiwanese Children," *Journal of Pe-
     diatrics* 172 (May 2016): 162–67.

7   The educator survey on changing attitudes and practices among kindergarten teach-
     ers from 1998 to 2010 is reported on in Daphna Bassok, Scott Latham, and Anna
     Rorem, "Is Kindergarten the New First Grade?" *AERA Open*, January 2016. Re-
     trieved from ero.sagepub.com/content/2/1/2332858415616358.

8   For an opinion piece on the rise of preschool suspensions see Denisha Jones and
     Diane Levin, "Here's Why Preschool Suspensions Are Harmful," *Education Week*,
     February 23, 2016. Retrieved from edweek.org/ew/articles/2016/02/24/heres-why
     -preschool-suspensions-are-harmful.html. Preschool tutoring is reported on in
     Samantha Kurtzman-Counter, "Cracking under Preschool Pressure," Huffington
     Post, June 2, 2011. Retrieved from huffingtonpost.com/samantha-kurtzmancounter/
     cracking-under-preschool-pressure_b_869926.html. The rise of academic preschools
     is criticized in Alison Gopnik, "Why Preschool Shouldn't Be Like School," *Slate*,
     March 16, 2011. Retrieved from slate.com/articles/double_x/doublex/2011/03/why_
     preschool_shouldnt_be_like_school.html.

9   Panksepp is quoted on the changing nature of play in "Science of the Brain as a
     Gateway to Understanding Play: An Interview with Jaak Panksepp," *American
     Journal of Play* 2, no. 3 (winter 2010): 247.

10   Rats' tendency to play less while dosed with psychostimulants is cited in Jaak Pank-
     sepp and Eric L. Scott, "Reflections on Rough and Tumble Play, Social Development,
     and Attention-Deficit Hyperactivity Disorders," in Aleta L. Meyer and Thomas P.
     Gullotta, eds., *Physical Activity Across the Lifespan*, Vol. 12 of *Issues in Children's
     and Families' Lives* (New York: Springer, 2012), 23–40.

11   One study on the positive impact of nature on ADHD symptoms is A. F. Taylor and
     F. E. Kuo, "Children with Attention Deficits Concentrate Better After Walk in the
     Park," *Journal of Attention Disorders* 12, no. 5 (March 2009): 402–09.

12   For a recent article on the significance of neoteny in evolution, see Mehmet Somela,
     Henriette Franz, Zheng Yana, et al., "Transcriptional Neoteny in the Human Brain,"
     Proceedings of the National Academy of Sciences U. S. A. 106, no. 14 (April 7,
     2009): 5743–48.

13   Stephen Jay Gould's observations about the importance of neoteny in human evolution are given in his book *Ontogeny and Phylogeny* (Cambridge, MA: Harvard University Press, 1977) and in a chapter, "A Biological Homage to Mickey Mouse," in *The Panda's Thumb: More Reflections in Natural History* (New York: Norton, 1992), 95-107.

14   Gould's characterization of humans as "permanent children" is quoted from his book *The Mismeasure of Man* (New York: Norton, 1981), 33.

15   Ashley Montagu's work on the physical and psychological dimensions of neoteny are in his book *Growing Young*, 2nd ed. (Westport, CT: Praeger, 1988).

16   Statistics on the prevalence of ADHD diagnoses among boys aged twelve to sixteen years are given in the National Center for Health Statistics, "Association between Diagnosed ADHD and Selected Characteristics among Children Aged 4–17 Years: United States, 2011–2013," CDC, May 2015. Retrieved from cdc.gov/nchs/data/data briefs/db201.htm.

17   Information on adolescent brain development and executive functioning is provided in Sarah-Jayne Blakemore and Suparna Choudhury, "Development of the Adolescent Brain: Implications for Executive Function and Social Cognition," *Journal of Child Psychology and Psychiatry* 47, nos. 3–4 (March–April 2006): 296–312.

18   For an article explaining the distinction between hot and cold cognition, see P. D. Zelazo and S. M. Carlson, "Hot and Cool Executive Function in Childhood and Adolescence: Development and Plasticity," *Child Development Perspectives* 6, no. 4 (June 7, 2012): 354–60.

19   Two recent books that look at the practical implications stemming from adolescent brain research are Thomas Armstrong, *The Power of the Adolescent Brain: Strategies for Teaching Middle and High School Students* (Alexandria, VA: ASCD, 2016); and Daniel J. Siegel, *Brainstorm: The Power and Purpose of the Adolescent Brain* (New York: Tarcher/Perigee, 2014).

20   The claim that ADHD symptoms at age three predict ADHD at age six is in Sara J. Bufferd, Lea R. Dougherty, Gabrielle A. Carlson, et al., "Psychiatric Disorders in Preschoolers: Continuity from Ages 3 to 6," *American Journal of Psychiatry* 169, no. 11 (November 2012), 1157–64.

21   An excellent book on the practical application of neuroplasticity research is Norman Doidge, *The Brain That Changes Itself: Stories of Personal Triumph from the Frontiers of Brain Science* (New York: Penguin, 2007).

CHAPTER FIVE

1   Statistics on the difference in prevalence rates of ADHD between boys and girls is provided in P. N. Pastor, C. A. Reuben, C. R. Duran, and L. D. Hawkins, "Association between Diagnosed ADHD and Selected Characteristics among Children Aged 4–17 Years: United States, 2011–2013," *NCHS Data Brief*, No 201 (Hyattsville, MD: National Center for Health Statistics, 2015).

2   Information on the under identification of girls with the Inattentive Type of ADD is given in Julia J. Rucklidge, "Gender Differences in Attention-Deficit/Hyperactivity Disorder," *Psychiatric Clinics of North America* 33, no. 2 (June 2010): 357–73.

3   Observations on a possible gender bias in the diagnosis of ADHD is found in Susan Hawthorne, "Facts, Values and ADHD: Gender Differences, Concepts and Practice," paper given at the International Association of Women Philosophers Symposium, June 25, 2010. Retrieved from http://ir.lib.uwo.ca/iaph/June25/Presentations/10/.

4   Natalie Angier's insightful comments on the risks of diagnosing typical boy behav-

ior as pathological are in her article "The Nation: The Debilitating Malady Called Boyhood," *New York Times*, July 24, 1994.

5   Information about the maturational differences between girls and boys is provided in Sol Lim, Cheol E. Han, Peter J. Uhlhaas, and Marcus Kaiser, "Preferential Detachment during Human Brain Development: Age- and Sex-Specific Structural Connectivity in Diffusion Tensor Imaging (DTI) Data," *Cerebral Cortex*, May 12, 2015. Retrieved from cercor.oxfordjournals.org/content/early/2013/12/13/cercor. bht333.full.

6   For evidence of continued frontal lobe maturation into young adulthood, see Elizabeth R. Sowell, Paul M. Thompson, Colin J. Holmes, et al., "In Vivo Evidence for Post-Adolescent Brain Maturation in Frontal and Striatal Regions," *Nature Neuroscience* 2, no. 10 (October 1999): 859–61. Note that postadolescent maturation continues as well in the striatum, which is another area considered to be key in the diagnosis of ADHD.

7   The information about gender differences in brain structures is given in J. E. Bramen, J. A. Hranilovich, R. E. Dahl, et al., "Puberty Influences Medial Temporal Lobe and Cortical Gray Matter Maturation Differently in Boys Than Girls Matched for Sexual Maturity," *Cerebral Cortex* 21, no. 3 (March 2011): 636–46.

8   The observation of greater physical activity among boys compared with girls is in Russell R. Pate, Karin A. Pfeiffer, Stewart G. Trost, et al., "Physical Activity among Children Attending Preschools," *Pediatrics* 114, no. 5 (November 2004): 1258–63.

9   Research on language processing differences between boys and girls is in Douglas D. Burman, Tali Bitan, and James R. Booth, "Sex Differences in Neural Processing of Language Among Children," *Neuropsychologia* 46, no. 5 (April 2008): 1349–62.

10   Evidence for girls' superiority in emotional self-regulation is provided in J. S. Matthews, Claire Cameron Ponitz, and Frederick J. Morrison, "Early Gender Differences in Self-Regulation and Academic Achievement," *Journal of Educational Psychology* 101, no. 3 (July 2009): 689–704.

11   Girls' superiority over boys in inhibition and self-control comes from Nicole M. Else-Quest, Janet Shibley Hyde, H. Hill Goldsmith, and Carol A. Van Hulle, "Gender Differences in Temperament: A Meta-Analysis," *Psychological Bulletin* 132, no. 1 (January 2006): 33–72.

12   Information about girls' superiority over boys in planning and attention is given in Jack A. Naglieri and Johannes Rojahn, "Gender Differences in Planning, Attention, Simultaneous, and Successive (PASS) Cognitive Processes and Achievement," *Journal of Educational Psychology* 93, no. 2 (May 2001): 430–37.

13   Figures on the predominance of women teachers in public education are from Household Data Annual Average, "11. Employed Persons by Detailed Occupation, Sex, Race, and Hispanic or Latino Ethnicity," Bureau of Labor Statistics, United States Department of Labor, 2015. Retrieved from bls.gov/cps/cpsaat11.htm.

14   The survey on male and female attitudes toward children's play was presented in Anette Sandberg and Ingrid Pramling-Samuelsson, "An Interview Study of Gender Differences in Preschool Teachers' Attitudes Toward Children's Play," *Early Childhood Education Journal* 32, no. 5 (April 2005): 297–305.

15   The bias toward diagnosing boys with ADHD even in the absence of full criteria is in Katrin Bruchmüller, Jürgen Margraf, and Silvia Schneider, "Is ADHD Diagnosed in Accord with Diagnostic Criteria? Overdiagnosis and Influence of Client Gender on Diagnosis," *Journal of Consulting and Clinical Psychology* 80, no. 1 (February 2012): 128–38.

Notes

16   The dominance of mothers in ADHD research is reported on in Ilina Singh, "Boys Will Be Boys: Fathers' Perspectives on ADHD Symptoms, Diagnosis, and Drug Treatment," *Harvard Review of Psychiatry* 11, no. 6 (October 2003): 308–16.

CHAPTER SIX

1   Some of the key books written by seminal progressive education leaders who've influenced me include Maria Montessori, *The Secret of Childhood* (New York: Ballantine, 1982); John Dewey, *Experience and Education* (New York: Free Press, 1997); Jean Piaget and Bärbel Inhelder, *The Psychology of the Child* (New York: Basic Books, 1969); Jerome Bruner, *The Process of Education* (Cambridge: Harvard University Press, 1977); John Holt, *How Children Fail* (Cambridge, MA: Da Capo, 1995); Jonathan Kozol, *Death at an Early Age* (New York: Plume, 1985); Howard Gardner, *Frames of Mind: The Theory of Multiple Intelligences* (New York: Basic Books, 2011); Deborah Meier, *The Power of Their Ideas* (Boston: Beacon Press, 2002); Susan Ohanian, *One Size Fits Few: The Folly of Educational Standards* (Portsmouth, NH: Heinemann, 1999) and Alfie Kohn, *The Schools Our Children Deserve* (Boston: Mariner Books, 2000).

2   The dialogue from *Ferris Bueller's Day Off* (1986), directed by John Hughes, can be retrieved from filmsite.org/bestspeeches38.html.

3   Sydney Zentall's foundational paper in what she refers to as the "theory of optimal stimulation" was "Optimal Stimulation as Rheoretical Basis of Hyperactivity," *American Journal of Orthopsychiatry* 45, no. 4 (July 1975): 549–63.

4   Sydney Zentall's research on the significance of spontaneous self-talk in hyperactive-identified kids is in her "Production Deficiencies in Elicited Language but Not in the Spontaneous Verbalizations of Hyperactive Children," *Journal of Abnormal Child Psychology* 16, no. 6 (December 1988): 657–73. Her research on the impact of color in the education of kids identified as hyperactive is summarized in Sydney S. Zentall and Ann M. Dwyer, "Color Effects on the Impulsivity and Activity of Hyperactive Children," *Journal of School Psychology* 27, no. 2 (summer 1989): 165–73.

5   The positive effect of choice and feedback on ADHD-diagnosed kids engaged in a computer task is presented in Deborah E. Bennett, Sydney S. Zentall, Brian F. French, and Karen Giorgetti-Borucki, "The Effects of Computer-Administered Choice on Students with and without Characteristics of Attention-Deficit/Hyperactivity Disorder," *Behavioral Disorders* 31, no. 2 (February 2006): 189–203.

6   The quotation on the importance of active learning for ADHD-diagnosed kids is in Rosemary E. Vile Junod, George J. DuPaul, Asha K. Jitendra, et al., "Classroom Observations of Students with and without ADHD: Differences across Types of Engagement," *Journal of School Psychology* 44, no. 2 (April 2006): 87–104.

7   The seminal article initiating a push for greater accountability in American education was U.S. Department of Education, "A Nation at Risk," April 1983. Retrieved from ed.gov/pubs/NatAtRisk/risk.html.

8   Diane Ravitch was quoted in Elizabeth Weil, "American Schools Are Failing Nonconformist Kids. Here's How," *New Republic*, September 2, 2013. Retrieved from newrepublic.com/article/114527/self-regulation-american-schools-are-failing -nonconformist-kids.

9   The quotation on the link between academic pressure and ADHD diagnoses is in Jeffrey P. Brosco and Anna Bona, "Changes in Academic Demands and Attention-Deficit/Hyperactivity Disorder in Young Children," *JAMA Pediatrics* 170, 4 (April 2016): 396–97.

10 The research on ADHD diagnoses of children from low socioeconomic backgrounds in states passing accountability laws after the No Child Left Behind law was discussed in Brent D. Fulton, Richard M. Scheffler, and Stephen P. Hinshaw, "State Variation in Increased ADHD Prevalence: Links to NCLB School Accountability and State Medication Laws," *Psychiatric Services* 66, no. 10 (October 1, 2015): 1074–82.
11 The quotation on the link between accountability laws and a rise in ADHD diagnoses and drug prescriptions is from Farasat A. S. Bokhari and Helen Schneider, "School Accountability Laws and the Consumption of Psychostimulants," *Journal of Health Economics* 30, no. 2 (March 2011): 355–72.
12 The survey that summarized ADHD-diagnosed children's attitudes toward school is in Maria Rogers and Rosemary Tannock, "Are Classrooms Meeting the Basic Psychological Needs of Children with ADHD Symptoms? A Self-Determination Theory Perspective," *Journal of Attention Disorders* 20 (December 10, 2013): 1–7.

CHAPTER SEVEN

1 One study that views parental stress as caused by ADHD-diagnosed children's behaviors is Jennifer Theule, Judith Wiener, Rosemary Tannock, and Jennifer M. Jenkins, "Parenting Stress in Families of Children with ADHD: A Meta-Analysis," *Journal of Emotional and Behavioral Disorders* 21, no. 1 (March 2013): 3–17.
2 The quotation on the scapegoating of children in dysfunctional families is from Soly Erlandsson and Elisabeth Punzi, "Challenging the ADHD Consensus," *International Journal of Qualitative Studies on Health and Well-Being* 11, no. 10 (2016): 3402.
3 Books by key thinkers who emphasized the influence of parent and caregivers on child development include Sigmund Freud, *Three Contributions to the Theory of Sex* (New York: Dutton, 1962); Carl Jung, *The Development of Personality*, Vol. 17: *Collected Works of C. G. Jung* (Princeton, NJ: Princeton University Press, 1981); Alfred Adler, *The Education of Children* (New York: Gutenberg, 2011); Erik Erikson, *Childhood and Society* (New York: Palgrave/Macmillan, 2011); John Bowlby, *A Secure Base: Parent-Child Attachment and Healthy Human Development* (New York: Basic Books, 1988); Carl Rogers, *Freedom to Learn: A View of What Education May Become* (Indianapolis, IN: Bobbs-Merrill, 1986); and Albert Bandura, *Social Learning Theory* (Englewood Cliffs, NJ: Prentice-Hall, 1976).
4 Key themes related to parent education of kids diagnosed with ADHD are given in, for example, Jennifer Theule et al., "Parenting Stress in Families of Children with ADHD."
5 Figures on the greater likelihood of ADHD diagnoses among children from low socioeconomic background compared with kids from wealthier backgrounds are from A. E. Russell, T. Ford, R. Williams, and G. Russell, "The Association between Socioeconomic Disadvantage and Attention Deficit/Hyperactivity Disorder (ADHD): A Systematic Review," *Child Psychiatry & Human Development* 47, no. 3 (June 2016): 440–458.
6 The unidirectional link from poverty to ADHD diagnoses is mentioned in, for example, Ginny Russell, Tamsin Ford, Rachel Rosenberg, and Susan Kelly, "The Association of Attention Deficit Hyperactivity Disorder with Socioeconomic Disadvantage: Alternative Explanations and Evidence," *Journal of Child Psychology and Psychiatry* 55, no. 5 (May 2014): 436–45.
7 Factors regarding growing up in poverty that are important in contributing to ADHD diagnoses are covered in Abigail Emma Russell, Tamsin Ford, and Ginny

Russell, "Socioeconomic Associations with ADHD: Findings from a Mediation Analysis," *PLoS One* 10, no. 6 (June 1, 2015): e0128248.

8   The Swedish study of one million children linking ADHD to single-parent families is A. Hjern, G. R. Weitoft, and F. Lindblad, "Social Adversity Predicts ADHD-Medication in School Children—A National Cohort Study," *Acta Paediatrica* 99, no. 6 (June 2010): 920–24.

9   Higher rates of ADHD in foster care are discussed in American Academy of Pediatrics, "Children in Foster Care Three Times More Likely to Have ADHD Diagnosis," October 23, 2015. Retrieved from https://www.aap.org/en-us/about-the-aap/aap-press-room/pages/Children-in-Foster-Care-Three-Times-More-Likely-to-Have-ADHD-Diagnosis.aspx.

10   The link between parental criticism and a failure in remission of ADHD symptoms in adolescence is discussed in E. D. Musser, S. L. Karalunas, N. Dieckmann, et al., "Attention-Deficit/Hyperactivity Disorder Developmental Trajectories Related to Parental Expressed Emotion," *Journal of Abnormal Psychology* 125, no. 2 (February 2016): 182–95.

11   Research on the causal connection between ADHD Inattentive Type and parental neglect and abuse is from Lijing Ouyang, Xiangming Fang, James Mercy, et al., "Attention-Deficit/Hyperactivity Disorder Symptoms and Child Maltreatment: A Population-Based Study," *Journal of Pediatrics* 153, no. 6 (December 2008): 851–56.

12   The Canadian study showing a sevenfold greater likelihood of an ADHD diagnosis if a child is abused comes from Esme Fuller-Thomson, Rukshan Mehta, and Angela Valeo, "Establishing a Link between Attention Deficit Disorder/Attention Deficit Hyperactivity Disorder and Childhood Physical Abuse," *Journal of Aggression, Maltreatment & Trauma* 23, no. 2 (2014): 188–98.

13   Elspeth Webb's comments on the impact of early exposure to violence to a potential ADHD diagnosis are in "Poverty, Maltreatment, and Attention Deficit Hyperactivity Disorder," *Archives of Disease in Childhood* 98, no. 6 (2013): 397–400.

14   The study linking high stress exposure to norepinephrine release and attention problems is Seung hye Lee, Dong-won Shin, and Mark A. Stein, "Increased Cortisol after Stress Is Associated with Variability in Response Time in ADHD Children," *Yonsei Medical Journal* 51, no. 2 (March 2010): 206–11.

15   For a discussion of the link between trauma and dopamine see Bruce D. Perry, "Traumatized Children: How Childhood Trauma Influences Brain Development," *Journal of the California Alliance for the Mentally Ill* 11, no. 1 (2000): 48–51.

16   Evidence for the negative impact of early trauma on executive functioning is presented in Victor G. Carrion and Shane S. Wong, "Can Traumatic Stress Alter the Brain? Understanding the Implications of Early Trauma on Brain Development and Learning," *Journal of Adolescent Health* 51, no. 2 suppl. (August 2012): S23–28.

17   L. Alan Sroufe is quoted in "Ritalin Gone Wrong," *New York Times*, January 29, 2012, SR1.

18   The study showing a link between a serotonin transporter gene variation, caregiver intrusiveness, and ADHD symptoms is Joana Baptista, Jay Belsky, Ana Mesquita, and Isabel Soares, "Serotonin Transporter Polymorphism Moderates the Effects of Caregiver Intrusiveness on ADHD Symptoms among Institutionalized Preschoolers," *European Child & Adolescent Psychiatry* (July 2016): 1–11. Retrieved from https://www.ncbi.nlm.nih.gov/pubmed/27430630.

19   Evidence for a gene-environment link between a *DRD4* seven-repeat allele, a child's sensation seeking, and low-quality parenting is presented in B. E. Sheese, P. M.

Notes

Voelker, M. K. Rothbart, and M. I. Posner, "Parenting Quality Interacts with Genetic Variation in Dopamine Receptor D4 to Influence Temperament in Early Childhood," *Developmental Psychopathology* 19, no. 4 (fall 2007): 1039–46.

CHAPTER EIGHT

1   Statistics on an average eight-second attention span in humans are reported on in Leon Watson, "Humans Have Shorter Attention Span Than Goldfish, Thanks to Smartphones," *Telegraph*, May 15, 2015. Retrieved from telegraph.co.uk/science/2016/03/12/humans-have-shorter-attention-span-than-goldfish-thanks-to-smart.

2   *The Honeymooners* episode "A Dog's Life" can be retrieved from youtube.com/watch?v=7Iv_zHJY2dM&list=PL-QYPAh7r9fw82cjk8JV4lBRPo5xH2fEw.

3   The trailer for the movie *Nerve* can be retrieved from youtube.com/watch?v=2PR-9MOPTI7g.

4   The definition of *jolts per minute* is from "Measuring Jolts Per Minute," *Media and Values* 62 (Spring 1993). Retrieved from medialit.org/reading-room/measuring-jolts-minute.

5   The quote denying the influence of TV and video games on ADHD is from Russell Barkley, Edwin H. Cook, Jr., Adele Diamond, et al., "International Consensus Statement on ADHD," *Clinical Child and Family Psychology Review* 5, no. 2 (June 2002): 90.

6   The experiment involving the introduction of television into three Canadian communities is the subject of Tannis MacBeth Williams and Alberta E. Siegel, eds., *The Impact of Television: A Natural Experiment in Three Communities* (Cambridge, MA: Academic Press, 1986).

7   The orienting response is discussed in Boguslaw Zernicki, "Pavlovian Orienting Reflex," *Acta Neurobiologiae Experimentalis* 47 (1987): 239–47.

8   The evolution of the concept of habituation in psychology is discussed in Richard F. Thompson, "Habituation: A History," *Neurobiology of Learning and Memory* 92, no. 2 (September 2009): 127–34.

9   Susan Weinschenk is quoted in her article "Why We're All Addicted to Texts, Twitter and Google," *Psychology Today*, September 11, 2012. Retrieved from psychologytoday.com/blog/brain-wise/201209/why-were-all-addicted-texts-twitter-and-google.

10 The link between striatal dopamine release and video games is given in M. J. Koepp, R. N. Gunn, A. D. Lawrence, et al., "Evidence for Striatal Dopamine Release during a Video Game," *Nature* 393, no. 6682 (May 1998): 266–68. The reduction of dopamine receptors in people with Internet addiction is reported in Sang Heea Kim, Sang-Hyuna Baik, Chang Soob Park, et al., "Reduced Striatal Dopamine D2 Receptors in People with Internet Addiction," *Neuroreport* 22, no. 8 (June 11, 2011): 407–11; and Haifeng Hou, Shaowe Jia, Shu Hu, and Rong Fan, "Reduced Striatal Dopamine Transporters in People with Internet Addiction Disorder," *Journal of Biomedicine and Biotechnology* 3 (March 13, 2012): e854524.

11 Research on the links between ADHD, reduced striatal dopamine activity, and abnormal dopamine transporters comes from P. Fusar-Poli, K. Rubia, G. Rossi, G. Sartori, and U. Balottin, "Striatal Dopamine Transporter Alterations in ADHD: Pathophysiology or Adaptation to Psychostimulants? A Meta-Analysis," *American Journal of Psychiatry* 169, no. 3 (March 2012): 264–72; Jing Wu, Haifan Xiao, Hongjuan Sun, et al., "Role of Dopamine Receptors in ADHD: A Systematic Meta-Analysis," *Molecular Neurobiology* 45, no. 3 (June 2012): 605–20; and Natalia del Campo, Tim D. Fryer, Young T. Hong, et al., "A Positron Emission Tomography

Notes

Study of Nigro-Striatal Dopaminergic Mechanisms Underlying Attention: Implications for ADHD and Its Treatment," *Brain* 136, part 11 (November 2013): 3252–70.

12 The study of 1,323 children that linked TV and video games to attention problems is Edward L. Swing, Douglas A. Gentile, Craig A. Anderson, and David A. Walsh, "Television and Video Game Exposure and the Development of Attention Problems," *Pediatrics* 126, no. 2 (August 2010): 214–21.

13 The study linking ADHD to Internet addiction is Ju-Yu Yen, Chih-Hung Ko, Cheng-Fang Yen, et al., "The Comorbid Psychiatric Symptoms of Internet Addiction: Attention Deficit and Hyperactivity Disorder (ADHD), Depression, Social Phobia, and Hostility," *Journal of Adolescent Health* 41, no. 1 (July 2007): 93–98.

14 The meta-analysis of studies that revealed a small but significant link between ADHD and media use is in Sanne W. C. Nikkelen, Patti M. Valkenburg, Mariette Huizinga, and Brad J. Bushman, "Media Use and ADHD-Related Behaviors in Children and Adolescents: A Meta-Analysis," *Developmental Psychology* 50, no. 9 (September 2014): 2228–41.

15 Dimitri A. Christakis is quoted in his editorial: "Rethinking Attention-Deficit/Hyperactivity Disorder," *JAMA Pediatrics* 170, no. 2 (February 2016), 110.

16 Statistics on media-viewing habits of kids ages eight to eighteen are from Victoria J. Rideout, Ulla G. Foehr, and Donald F. Roberts, "Generation M²: Media in the Lives of 8–18 Year Olds," Henry J. Kaiser Family Foundation, January 2010. Retrieved from kaiserfamilyfoundation.files.wordpress.com/2013/01/8010.pdf.

17 The statistic indicating that 30 percent of children's waking time is in front of a screen is from Christakis, "Rethinking Attention-Deficit/Hyperactivity Disorder."

18 Revised media guidelines given by the American Academy of Pediatrics are in Council on Communications and Media, "Media and Young Minds," *Pediatrics* 138, no. 5 (November 2016). Retrieved from pediatrics.aappublications.org/content/138/5/e20162591.

19 Jordan Shapiro is quoted from his article "The American Academy of Pediatrics Just Changed Their Guidelines on Kids and Screen Time," *Forbes*, September 30, 2015. Retrieved from forbes.com/sites/jordanshapiro/2015/09/30/the-american-academy-of-pediatrics-just-changed-their-guidelines-on-kids-and-screen-time/#368f8b8d137c.

20 The impact of chronic exposure to violent media on the prefrontal cortex is reported on in Tom A. Hummer, "Media Violence Effects on Brain Development: What Neuroimaging Has Revealed and What Lies Ahead," *American Behavioral Science* 59, no. 14 (December 2015): 1790–1806.

21 The differences in the impact of entertainment media and educational media on inhibition and emotion are in Frederick J. Zimmerman and Dimitri A. Christakis, "Associations between Content Types of Early Media Exposure and Subsequent Attentional Problems," *Pediatrics* 120, no. 5 (November 2007): 986–92.

22 The positive influence of nontechnological family activities on reducing hyperactivity are reported on in John Mark Froiland and Mark L. Davison, "Home Literacy, Television Viewing, Fidgeting and ADHD in Young Children," *Educational Psychology* 36, no. 8 (September 2016): 1–17.

23 McLuhan's prescient ideas about old and new media are most pithily expressed in Marshall McLuhan and Quentin Fiore, *The Medium Is the Massage: An Inventory of Effects* (Berkeley, CA: Gingko Press, 2001).

CHAPTER NINE

1   I discuss the mental health implications of there being no normal brain in my article "The Myth of the Normal Brain: Embracing Neurodiversity," *AMA Journal of Ethics* 17, no. 4 (April 1, 2015): 348–52.

2   The list of negative outcomes of ADHD in adulthood comes from Russell A. Barkley, "Fact Sheet: Attention Deficit Hyperactivity Disorder (ADHD) Topics." Retrieved from russellbarkley.org/factsheets/adhd-facts.pdf.

3   For a look at Goddard and the eugenics basis of early-twentieth-century special education see Stephen Jay Gould's award-winning book *The Mismeasure of Man* (New York: Norton, 1996); and James W. Trent, *Inventing the Feeble Mind: A History of Mental Retardation in the United States* (Berkeley: University of California Press, 1995). For information about Samuel Orton and Alfred Strauss, see Daniel P. Hallahan and Cecil D. Mercer, "Learning Disabilities: Historical Perspectives," paper presented at the Learning Disabilities Summit: Building a Foundation for the Future, Washington, D.C., August 27–28, 2001. Retrieved from ldaofky.org/LD/LD %20Historical%20Perspectives.pdf. For Samuel Kirk's account of "learning disabilities" see his "Learning Disabilities: A Historical Note," *Academic Therapy* 17, no. 1 (September 1981): 7. Kirk and Cruikshank's "invention" of learning disabilities in a Chicago hotel room in 1962 comes from a lecture I heard William Cruikshank give in 1976 in Montreal, Canada, at a meeting of the Canadian Association for Emotionally Disturbed Children.

4   The child's quotation of ADHD as a "disease eating on you," is from Chris Travella and John Visser, " 'ADHD Does Bad Stuff to You': Young People's and Parents' Experiences and Perceptions of Attention Deficit Hyperactivity Disorder (ADHD)," *Emotional and Behavioural Difficulties* 11, no. 3 (September 2006): 207.

5   The Italian psychologists are quoted in Antonio Iudici, Elena Faccio, Eleonora Belloni, and Norberto Costa, "The Use of the ADHD Diagnostic Label: What Implications Exist for Children and their Families?" *Procedia—Social and Behavioral Sciences* 122 (March 19, 2014): 508.

6   For a critical view of special education practices, see Beth Feri, "Doing a (Dis)service: Reimagining Special Education from a Disability Studies Perspective," in W. Ayers, T. Quinn, and D. Stovall, eds., *The Handbook of Social Justice in Education* (Mahwah, NJ: Lawrence Erlbaum, 2008). See also my book *In Their Own Way: Discovering and Encouraging Your Child's Multiple Intelligences* (New York: Tarcher/Penguin, 2000).

7   My dissertation was titled "Describing Strengths in Children Identified as 'Learning Disabled' Using Howard Gardner's Theory of Multiple Intelligences as an Organizing Framework," (San Francisco: California Institute of Integral Studies, 1987). Available from University Microfilms International, Ann Arbor, MI, number 48(08A).

8   The seminal text in the neurodiversity movement is autism rights activist Jim Sinclair's speech "Don't Mourn for Us," at the 1993 International Conference on Autism in Toronto, which appeared in the Autism Network International newsletter, *Our Voice* 1, no. 3 (1993). Retrieved from autreat.com/dont_mourn.html.

9   Harvey Blume is quoted in his article "Neurodiversity," *Atlantic*, September 1998. Retrieved from theatlantic.com/magazine/archive/1998/09/neurodiversity/305909. Origination of the term *neurodiversity* is also credited to autism activist Judy Singer in her undergraduate thesis, "Odd People In: The Birth of Community Amongst Peo-

Notes

ple on the Autistic Spectrum" (Sydney, Australia: University of Technology, Sydney, 1998).

10 See my two books on neurodiversity, Thomas Armstrong, *The Power of Neurodiversity: Unleashing the Advantages of Your Differently Wired Brain* (Cambridge, MA: Da Capo/Perseus, 2011); and Thomas Armstrong, *Neurodiversity in the Classroom: Strength-Based Strategies to Help Students with Special Needs Succeed in School and Life* (Alexandria, VA: ASCD, 2012).

11 Bonnie Cramond's discussion of the similarities between ADHD symptoms and creative behaviors are presented in her article "Attention-Deficit Hyperactivity Disorder and Creativity—What Is the Connection?" *Journal of Creative Behavior* 28, no. 3 (September 1994): 193–210.

12 The finding that ADHD-diagnosed adults did better on the Unusual Uses Task than non-ADHD-diagnosed adults is from Holly White and Priti Shah, "Uninhibited Imaginations: Creativity in Adults with Attention-Deficit/Hyperactivity Disorder," *Personality and Individual Differences* 40, no. 6 (April 2006): 1121–31.

13 The superior performance of ADHD-diagnosed adults on the Abbreviated Torrance Test for Adults is reported on in Holly White and Priti Shah, "Creative Style and Achievement in Adults with Attention-Deficit/Hyperactivity Disorder," *Personality and Individual Differences* 50, no. 5 (March 2011): 673–77.

14 The study on creative thinking in ADHD-diagnosed adolescents is A. Abraham, S. Windmann, R. Siefen, et al., "Creative Thinking in Adolescents with Attention Deficit Hyperactivity Disorder (ADHD)," *Child Neuropsychology* 12, no. 2 (April 2006): 111–23.

15 The study documenting the creativity of twelve- to thirteen-year-old children diagnosed with ADHD is Sapna Verma and Seema Kushwaha, "Creative Thinking and Attention Deficit Hyperactivity Disorder," *Journal of Psychosocial Research* 8, no. 2 (July–December 2013): 67–176.

16 The negative impact of ADHD drugs on the creative performance of ADHD-diagnosed children is reported on in Gracia González-Carpio Hernández and Juan Pedro Serrano Selva, "Medication and Creativity in Attention Deficit Hyperactivity Disorder (ADHD)," *Psicothema* 28, no. 1 (2016): 20–25.

17 An excellent article on ADHD in the lives of several successful and well-known entrepreneurs is Lois Gilman, "Career Advice from the Corner Office: Famous People with ADHD," *ADDitude*, December–January 2005. Retrieved from additudemag.com/adhd/article/754.html.

18 The study linking small firm entrepreneurs in France with ADHD symptoms is in Roy Thurik, Anis Khedhaouria, Olivier Torrès, and Ingrid Verheul, "ADHD Symptoms and Entrepreneurial Orientation of Small Firm Owners," *Applied Psychology* 65, no. 3 (July 2016): 568–86.

19 Paul Orfalea is quoted in Lois Gilman, "Career Advice from Powerful ADHD Executives," *ADDitude*, December–January 2005. Retrieved from additudemag.com/adhd/article/754.html#.

20 Martha Denckla's notation of ADHD-diagnosed kids' abilities in incidental attention are from her article "Biological Correlates of Learning and Attention: What Is Relevant to Learning Disability and Attention-Deficit Hyperactivity Disorder?" *Journal of Developmental and Behavioral Pediatrics* 2, ser. 17 (1996): 114–19.

21 Matthew Kutz is quoted in Thom Hartmann and Janie Bowman, *Think Fast! The ADD Experience* (Nevada City, CA: Underwood Books, 1996), 88.

22 For the value of off-task behaviors in the classroom, see Anne Hass Dyson, "The Value of 'Time Off Task': Young Children's Spontaneous Talk and Deliberate Text," *Harvard Educational Review* 57, no. 4 (1987): 396–420.

23 For research on the influence of irrelevant but novel stimuli on task performance in children diagnosed with ADHD, see Rosa van Mourik, Jaap Oosterlaan, Dirk J. Heslenfeld, et al., "When Distraction Is Not Distracting: A Behavioral and ERP Study on Distraction in ADHD," *Clinical Neurophysiology* 118, no. 8 (August 2007): 1855–65.

24 One of the first thinkers to promote the idea that people diagnosed with ADHD were hunters in a farmers world was political commentator and ADHD-diagnosed activist Thom Hartmann, in his book *ADD: A Different Perception* (Grass Valley, CA: Underwood-Miller, 1993). The idea gained currency within the professional community with the publication of P. S. Jensen, D. Mrazek, P. K. Knapp, et al., "Evolution and Revolution in Child Psychiatry: ADHD as a Disorder of Adaptation," *Journal of the American Academy of Child and Adolescent Psychiatry* 36, no. 12 (1997): 1672–79.

25 The study linking the *DRD4* gene to hunter-gatherer populations in Brazil is Luciana Tovo-Rodrigues, Sidia M. Callegari-Jacques, M. Luiza Petzl-Erler, et al., "Dopamine Receptor D4 Allele Distribution in Amerindians: A Reflection of Past Behavior Differences?" *American Journal of Physical Anthropology* 143, no. 3 (November 2010): 458–64.

26 There has been an uptick in the recognition of ADHD-related strengths in the adult population of ADHD-diagnosed individuals. See for example, Dale Archer, *The ADHD Advantage: What You Thought Was a Diagnosis May Be Your Greatest Strength* (New York: Avery, 2016). However, most of the popular literature related to children and adolescents diagnosed with ADHD is for the most part deficit oriented, an exception being two books by Laura Honos-Webb, *The Gift of ADHD: How to Transform Your Child's Problems into Strengths* (Oakland, CA: New Harbinger, 2010) and *The Gift of ADHD Activity Book: 101 Ways to Turn Your Child's Problems into Strengths* (Oakland, CA: New Harbinger, 2008).

CHAPTER TEN

1 The predicted rise in sales of ADHD drugs is reported in GBI [Global Business Intelligence] Research, "ADHD Therapeutics to 2020—Broadened Diagnostic Criteria and Growing Adult Prevalence to Drive Market Growth Despite Patent Expirations," July 2014. Retrieved from gbiresearch.com/report-store/market-reports/therapy-analysis/adhd-therapeutics-to-2020-broadened-diagnostic-criteria-and-growing-adult-prevalence-to-drive-market-growth-despite-patent-ex/tables.

2 Figures on the cost of ADHD drugs are taken from Evelyn Pringle and Martha Rosenberg, "Big Pharma's Newest Money-Making Scheme: Adult ADHD," *Alternet*, September 27, 2012. Retrieved from alternet.org/personal-health/big-pharmas-newest-money-making-scheme-adult-adhd.

3 A copy of the Alliant brochure can be retrieved from fda.gov/downloads/Drugs/GuidanceComplianceRegulatoryInformation/EnforcementActivitiesbyFDA/WarningLettersandNoticeofViolationLetterstoPharmaceuticalCompanies/ucm054004.pdf.

4 The recent approval of the flavored chewable ADHD drug Adzenys is reported on in Meghana Keshavan, "Tasty and Easy to Take, a New ADHD Drug Alarms Some Psychiatrists," Stat, May 23, 2016. Retrieved from statnews.com/2016/05/23/adhd-drug-concerns.

5 The document from the FDA that lifted the ban on direct-to-consumer advertising

Notes

was "Guidance for Industry: Consumer-Directed Broadcast Advertisements," U.S. Department of Health and Human Services, Food and Drug Administration, Center for Drug Evaluation and Research (CDER), August 1999. Retrieved from fda.gov/ohrms/dockets/ac/00/backgrd/3627b2bl.pdf.

6   Joe Dumit is quoted in his book *Drugs for Life: How Pharmaceutical Companies Define Our Health* (Durham, NC: Duke University Press, 2012), 14.

7   The link between direct-to-consumer advertising and increased drug sales is given in Julie M. Donohue, Marisa Cevasco, and Meredith B. Rosenthal, "A Decade of Direct-to-Consumer Advertising of Prescription Drugs," *New England Journal of Medicine* 357 (August 16, 2007): 673–81.

8   The Concerta and Adderall ads are displayed in Richard Feloni, "These Are the Ridiculous Ads Big Pharma Used to Convince Everyone They Have ADHD," Yahoo! Finance, December 16, 2013. Retrieved from finance.yahoo.com/news/ridiculous-ads-big-pharma-used-202922195.html.

9   The Adderall ad showing a mother hugging her son is displayed in Amanda Marcotte, "Who Wouldn't Want an Adderall Prescription?" *Slate*, December 16, 2013. Retrieved from slate.com/blogs/xx_factor/2013/12/16/selling_adhd_new_york_times_reports_on_the_big_business_of_attention_deficit.html.

10   The comic book for ADHD-diagnosed children titled "Medikidz Explain Living with ADHD" is available for a fee from medikidz.com/gb-en/shop/general-health/medikidz-explain-living-with-adhd.

11   Jonathan Leo and Jeffrey Lacasse are quoted from their book chapter "The Manipulation of Data and Attitudes about ADHD: A Study of Consumer Advertisement," in S. Tamimi and J. Leo, eds., *Rethinking ADD: From Brain to Culture* (New York: Palgrave Macmillan, 2009), 287–312. Retrieved from diginole.lib.fsu.edu/islandora/object/fsu:252721/datastream/PDF/view.

12   Shire's fraudulent claims about Adderall XL are reported on in U.S. Department of Justice, "Shire Pharmaceuticals LLC to Pay $56.5 Million to Resolve False Claims Act Allegations Relating to Drug Marketing and Promotion Practices," Justice News, September 24, 2014. Retrieved from justice.gov/opa/pr/shire-pharmaceuticals-llc-pay-565-million-resolve-false-claims-act-allegations-relating-drug.

13   Alan Schwarz is quoted from his article "The Selling of Attention Deficit Disorder," *New York Times*, December 14, 2013. Retrieved from nytimes.com/2013/12/15/health/the-selling-of-attention-deficit-disorder.html?pagewanted=all. See also his book *ADHD Nation: Children, Doctors, Big Pharma, and the Making of an American Epidemic* (New York: Scribner, 2016).

14   The report on the poor quality of content on drug company-sponsored Web sites devoted to ADHD is from J. Mitchell and J. Read, "Attention-Deficit Hyperactivity Disorder, Drug Companies and the Internet," *Clinical Child Psychology and Psychiatry* 17, no. 1 (January 2012): 121–39.

15   The PBS broadcast covering the links between CHADD and drug companies originally aired on October 13, 1995, and was part of John Merrow's regularly featured segment "Learning Matters" on *PBS NewsHour*. It was titled "A.D.D.—A Dubious Diagnosis?" and produced by John Tulenko. The video can be accessed at learningmatters.tv/blog/documentaries/watch-add-a-dubious-diagnosis/640. A written transcript can be retrieved from add-adhd.org/ritalin_CHADD_A.D.D.html.

16   Figures on CHADD money from drug companies and expenditures on conference, gala, and CEO salary are taken from Pringle and Rosenberg, "Big Pharma's Newest Money-Making Scheme: Adult ADHD."

Notes

17 The $3 million from Shire pharmaceutical to fund CHADD's monthly magazine is taken from Schwarz, "The Selling of Attention Deficit Disorder."

18 The story on the professional development seminar for psychiatrists paid for Shire pharmaceuticals is told in Schwarz, "The Selling of Attention Deficit Disorder."

19 The account of ADHD drug representative Brian Lutz's relations with Oakland-area psychiatrists is from Schwarz, "The Selling of Attention Deficit Disorder."

20 The account of Biederman, Wilens, and Spencer's failure to disclose support from ADHD drug companies is given in Gardiner Harris and Benedict Carey," Researchers Fail to Reveal Full Drug Pay," *New York Times*, June 8, 2008. Retrieved from nytimes.com/2008/06/08/us/08conflict.html.

21 Schwarz is quoted from his article, "The Selling of Attention Deficit Disorder."

22 A report of disciplinary measures taken against ADHD researchers Biederman, Wilens, and Spencer is given in Xi Yu, "Three Professors Face Sanctions following Harvard Medical School Inquiry," *Harvard Crimson*, July 2, 2011. Retrieved from thecrimson.com/article/2011/7/2/school-medical-harvard-investigation.

23 Drug company support disclosures are provided in a PowerPoint presentation by Russell A. Barkley titled "Deficient Emotional Self-Regulation Is a Core Component of ADHD: Evidence and Treatment Implications," 2009. Retrieved from ccf.buffalo .edu/pdf/BarkleySlides_CCFSpeakerSeries0910.pdf.

24 The American Psychiatric Association's links to drug companies are reported in Schwarz, "The Selling of Attention Deficit Disorder."

25 A copy of the Education for All Handicapped Children Act can be retrieved from govtrack.us/congress/bills/94/s6/text.

26 Congress's refusal to make attention deficit disorder a handicapping condition in the federal law is reported in Susan Moses, "Unusual Coalition Nixes Inclusion of A.D.D. in Bill," *APA Monitor* 21, no. 11 (November 1990): 37.

27 The letter from the U.S. Department of Education to state superintendents providing backdoor ways in which services for attention deficit disorder could be authorized under existing federal laws is reported in Susan Moses, "Letter on A.D.D. Kids Gets Mixed Reactions," *APA Monitor* 22, no. 12 (December 1991): 36–37.

28 Melina Sherman is quoted from her article, "The Cultural Production of a Pharmaceutical Market: The Making of ADHD," *International Journal of Communication* 9 (2015): 2190.

29 The figure on the median salary for special education teachers was taken from the "Occupational Outlook Handbook," U.S. Department of Labor, Bureau of Labor Statistics, December 17, 2015. Retrieved from bls.gov/ooh/education-training-and -library/special-education-teachers.htm.

30 One article on a new computerized brain training system designed to treat ADHD symptoms is Katherine Ellison, "Video Game Is Built to Be Prescribed to Children with A.D.H.D," *New York Times*, November 23, 2015. Available from well.blogs. nytimes.com/2015/11/23/video-game-is-built-to-be-prescribed-to-children-with-a -d-h-d.

31 FDA's letter warning Pearson against making false statements in advertising its ADHD Quotient System is reported on in Fink Densford, "FDA Warns Pearson on ADHD Device Claims," *Mass Device*, September 23, 2015. Retrieved from massdevice .com/fda-warns-pearson-on-adhd-device-claims.

CHAPTER ELEVEN

1   The reference to "nonexpert doctors," is from Russell A. Barkley, Edwin H. Cook, Adele Diamond, Alan Zemetkin, et al., "International Consensus Statement on ADHD," *Clinical Child and Family Psychology Review* 5, no. 2 (June 2002): 89.

2   The article linking early television exposure to attention problems is Dimitri A. Christakis, Frederick J. Zimmerman, David L. DiGiuseppe, and Carolyn A. McCarty, "Early Television Exposure and Subsequent Attentional Problems in Children," *Pediatrics* 113, no. 4 (April 2004): 708–13.

3   CHADD's article linking ADHD to a propensity to watch more television is Elizabeth P. Lorch and Richard Milich, "TV and Attention Problems in Children," *Attention*, June 2004. Retrieved from chadd.org/LinkClick.aspx?fileticket=eGmsqG9G6EI=.

4   WebMD's refutation of the "argument" that "ADHD is caused by bad parenting," is in "ADHD Myths and Facts—Topic Overview," Healthwise, November 14, 2014. Retrieved from webmd.com/add-adhd/childhood-adhd/tc/adhd-myths-and-facts-topic-overview.

5   For a history of homosexuality and the American Psychiatric Association's position on it, see Ronald Bayer, *Homosexuality and American Psychiatry: The Politics of Diagnosis* (Princeton, NJ: Princeton University Press, 1987). For the involvement of an American Psychological Association task force in advising the CIA on justifications for torture, see James Risen, "American Psychological Association Bolstered C.I.A. Torture Program, Report Says," *New York Times*, April 30, 2015. Retrieved from nytimes.com/2015/05/01/us/report-says-american-psychological-association-collaborated-on-torture-justification.html?_r=0.

6   Ruth Hughes is quoted in Tracey Harrington McCoy, "Richard Saul Says ADHD Does Not Exist. Not Everyone Agrees," *Newsweek*, February 25, 2014. Retrieved from http://bit.ly/2fk0htr.

7   Zeigler Dendy is quoted in Debra Viadero, "ADHD Experts Fear Brain-Growth Study Being Misconstrued," *Education Week*, December 3, 2007. Retrieved from edweek.org/ew/articles/2007/12/05/14adhd.h27.html?qs=attention+deficit+hyperactivity+disorder.

8   Ned Hallowell is quoted in his article, "ADHD in the Media: The Good, the Bad, and the Ridiculous," *ADDitude*. Retrieved from additudemag.com/adhdblogs/19/10626.html?no_redirect=true.

9   For a look at other reasoning fallacies used to support the ADHD position, see Gordon Tait, "The Logic of ADHD: A Brief Review of Fallacious Reasoning," *Studies in Philosophy and Education* 28, no. 3 (May 2009): 239–54.

CHAPTER TWELVE

1   Abraham Maslow is quoted from his book *The Psychology of Science: A Reconnaissance* (Chapel Hill, NC: Maurice Bassett, 1966), 15.

2   Richard Saul's book is *ADHD Does Not Exist: The Truth about Attention Deficit and Hyperactivity Disorder* (New York: Harper Wave, 2014).

3   The suggestion that ADHD should be considered as a spectrum rather than a discrete entity appears in Dimitri A. Christakis, "Rethinking Attention-Deficit/Hyperactivity Disorder," *JAMA Pediatrics* 170, no. 2 (2016): 109–10.

Notes

STRATEGY #1

1 The study linking fidgeting to better cognitive control is T. A. Hartanto, C. E. Krafft, A. M. Iosif, and J. B. Schweitzer, "A Trial-by-Trial Analysis Reveals More Intense Physical Activity Is Associated with Better Cognitive Control Performance in Attention-Deficit/Hyperactivity Disorder," *Child Neuropsychology* 22, no. 5 (2016): 618–26.

2 Julie B. Schweitzer's suggestion that fidgeting provides stimulation in the way that psychostimulants do is in Gretchen Reynolds, "Fidgeting May Benefit Children with A.D.H.D.," *New York Times*, June 24, 2015. Retrieved from well.blogs.nytimes.com/2015/06/24/fidgeting-may-benefit-children-with-a-d-h-d.

3 The use of fidgeting tools at Quaker School is reported on in Sumathi Reddy, "The Benefits of Fidgeting for Students with ADHD," *Wall Street Journal*, June 22, 2015. Retrieved from wsj.com/articles/the-benefits-of-fidgeting-for-students-with-adhd-1434994365.

4 The positive effects of doodling on thinking and behavior are reported in Steven Heller, "The Cognitive Benefits of Doodling," *Atlantic*, July 9, 2015. Retrieved from theatlantic.com/entertainment/archive/2015/07/doodling-for-cognitive-benefits/398027.

STRATEGY #3

1 The Pygmalion experiments are described and reported on in Robert Rosenthal and Lenore Jacobson, *Pygmalion in the Classroom: Teacher Expectation and Pupils' Intellectual Development* (New York: Crown, 2003).

2 The dialogue from "Leonardo da Vinci's IEP meeting" is an extract from a more complete conversation that appears on my Web site at institute4learning.com/blog/2013/02/19/leonardo-da-vincis-iep-meeting.

3 Patricia Cahill Paugh and Curt Dudley-Marling are quoted from their article " 'Speaking' Deficit into (or out of) Existence: How Language Constrains Classroom Teachers' Knowledge about Instructing Diverse Learners," *International Journal of Inclusive Education* 15, no. 8 (August 2011): 819.

STRATEGY #4

1 A good article on the positive impact of martial arts on self-regulation is Kimberly D. Lakes and William T. Hoyt, "Promoting Self-Regulation through School-Based Martial Arts Training," *Applied Developmental Psychology* 25, no. 3 (May–June 2004): 283–302.

STRATEGY #5

1 The poll reporting children's low daily activity in nature and high daily activity with technology is "Connecting America's Youth to Nature," Nature Conservancy. Retrieved from nature.org/newsfeatures/kids-in-nature/youth-and-nature-poll-results.pdf.

2 Research on the connection between sedentary behavior and obesity in children is provided in J. A. Mitchell, R. R. Pate, M. W. Beets, and P. R. Nader, "Time Spent in Sedentary Behavior and Changes in Childhood BMI: A Longitudinal Study from Ages 9 to 15 Years," *International Journal of Obesity* 37, no. 1 (January 2013): 54–60.

3 One article linking lower ADHD symptoms with time spent in nature is Andrea Faber Taylor and Frances E. (Ming) Kuo, "Could Exposure to Everyday Green Spaces Help Treat ADHD? Evidence from Children's Play Settings," *Applied Psychology Health and Wellbeing* 3, no. 3 (August 2011): 281–303.

Notes

4   The report that twenty minutes spent in a park could improve attention in ADHD-diagnosed children is from in A. F. Taylor and F. E. Kuo," Children with Attention Deficits Concentrate Better after Walk in the Park," *Journal of Attention Disorders* 12, no. 5 (March 2009): 402–09.

5   Richard Louv is quoted in "Beyond Meds: 3 Alternative ADHD Treatments That Ease Symptoms," *ADDitude.* Retrieved from additudemag.com/adhd/article/4924 -3.html.

STRATEGY #7

1   For a study on the use of transcendental meditation to improve ADHD symptoms, see Sarina J. Grosswald, William R. Stixrud, Fred Travis, and Mark A. Bateh, "Use of the Transcendental Meditation Technique to Reduce Symptoms of Attention Deficit Hyperactivity Disorder (ADHD) by Reducing Stress and Anxiety," *Current Issues in Education* 10, no. 2 (December 2008): 1–11.

STRATEGY #10

1   Comments of students at Mary Lee Burbank School from Holly Korbey, "How Standing Desks Can Help Students Focus in the Classroom," KQED News, October 21, 2014. Retrieved from kqed.org/mindshift/2014/10/21/how-standing-desks-can -help-students-focus-in-the-classroom.

2   The positive impact of stability balls on lessening ADHD symptoms is reported on in Alicia L. Fedewa and Heather E. Erwin, "Stability Balls and Students with Attention and Hyperactivity Concerns: Implications for On-Task and In-Seat Behavior," *American Journal of Occupational Therapy* 65 (July/August 2011): 393–99.

3   Research showing better cognitive performance for ADHD-diagnosed children when sitting in swivel chairs is provided in Dustin E. Sarver, Mark D. Rapport, Michael J. Kofler, et al., "Hyperactivity in Attention-Deficit/Hyperactivity Disorder (ADHD): Impairing Deficit or Compensatory Behavior?" *Journal of Abnormal Child Psychology* 43, no. 7 (October 2015): 1219–32.

STRATEGY #11

1   Statistics on the percentage of ADHD-diagnosed children being treated with complementary and alternative therapies (and the failure of most parents to report this to their physicians) is given in E. Chan, L. A. Rappaport, and K. J. Kemper, "Complementary and Alternative Therapies in Childhood Attention and Hyperactivity Problems," *Journal of Developmental & Behavioral Pediatrics* 24, no. 1 (February 2003): 4–8.

2   The statistic that fewer than 50 percent of doctors were interested in learning more about complementary and alternative therapies to treat ADHD is from Angela Huang, Kapila Seshadri, Tara Anne Matthews, and Barbara M. Ostfeld, "Parental Perspectives on Use, Benefits, and Physician Knowledge of Complementary and Alternative Medicine in Children with Autistic Disorder and Attention-Deficit/Hyperactivity Disorder," *Journal of Alternative and Complementary Medicine* 19, no. 9 (September 2013): 746–50.

3   Studies on the use of Traditional Chinese Medicine to treat ADHD include Xinqiang Ni, Yanli Zhang-James, Xinmin Han, and Shuang Lei, "Traditional Chinese Medicine in the Treatment of ADHD: A Review," *Child and Adolescent Psychiatric Clinics of North America* 23, no. 4 (October 2014): 853–81; and Tianping Zhong, Kai Wang, Meizhen Feng, et al., "Acupuncture and Psychological Treatment vs Drug Therapy in Treatment of Children with Attention Deficit Hyperactivity Disorder (ADHD)," *In-*

ternational Journal of Clinical Acupuncture 24, no. 4 (October–December 2015): 245–47.

4   One research article on the use of Ayurvedic medicine to improve processing speed in ADHD-diagnosed children is Harish Kumar Singhal, Neetu, Abhimanyu Kumar, and Moti Rai, "Ayurvedic Approach for Improving Reaction Time of Attention Deficit Hyperactivity Disorder Affected Children," *Ayu* 31, no. 3 (July–September 2010): 338–42.

5   For an article on the use of chiropractic methods to treat ADHD, see J. Alcantara and J. Davis, "The Chiropractic Care of Children with Attention-Deficit/Hyperactivity Disorder: A Retrospective Case Series," *Explore (NY)* 6, no. 3 (May–June 2010); 173–82.

6   One well-designed research study concluding that there was a positive impact on cognition and behavior from a homeopathic intervention with ADHD-diagnosed children is H. Frei, R. Everts, K. von Ammon, et al., "Homeopathic Treatment of Children with Attention Deficit Hyperactivity Disorder: A Randomized, Double Blind, Placebo Controlled Crossover Trial," *European Journal Pediatrics* 164, no. 12 (December 2005): 758–67.

7   A good article on the new pediatric integrative medicine subspecialty in medicine is Sunita Vohra, Soleil Surette, Deepika Mittra, et al., "Pediatric Integrative Medicine: Pediatrics' Newest Subspecialty?" *BMC Pediatrics* 12 (August 15, 2012): 123.

STRATEGY #12

1   Two studies, for example, on the influence of children and adolescent's ADHD behaviors in causing parental stress are Jennifer Theule, Judith Wiener, Rosemary Tannock, and Jennifer M. Jenkins, "Parenting Stress in Families of Children With ADHD: A Meta-Analysis," *Journal of Emotional and Behavioral Disorders* 21, No. 1 (March 2013): 3–17; and Judith Wiener, Daniella Biondic, Teresa Grimbos, and Monique Herbert, "Parenting Stress of Parents of Adolescents with Attention-Deficit Hyperactivity Disorder," *Journal of Abnormal Child Psychology* 44, No. 3 (April 2016): 561–74.

2   The research reporting a link between greater social support and better behavioral outcomes in children diagnosed with ADHD is from Richard E. A. Loren, Aaron J. Vaughn, Joshua M. Langberg, and Jessica E. M. Cyran, "Effects of an 8-Session Behavioral Parent Training Group for Parents of Children with ADHD on Child Impairment and Parenting Confidence," *Journal of Attention Disorders* 19, No. 2 (February 2015): 158–66.

STRATEGY #13

1   For a study which supports the idea of a protein breakfast being better than one containing only carbohydrates, see C. Keith Conners, *Feeding the Brain: How Foods Affect Children* (New York: Springer, 2001), 69.

STRATEGY #15

1   For two reviews on the positive impact of restriction and elimination diets in alleviating ADHD symptoms in children, see Joel T. Nigg and Kathleen Holton, "Restriction and Elimination Diets in ADHD Treatment," *Child & Adolescent Psychiatric Clinics of North America* 23, no. 4 (October 2014): 937–53; and University of Copenhagen, "Dietary Changes Help Some Children with ADHD," ScienceDaily, April 24, 2012. Retrieved from sciencedaily.com/releases/2012/04/120424121904.htm.

Notes

STRATEGY #16

1   Evidence for a link between musical training and improved executive functioning is provided in J. Zuk, C. Benjamin, A. Kenyon, and N. Gaab, "Behavioral and Neural Correlates of Executive Functioning in Musicians and Non-Musicians," *PLoS ONE* 9, no. 6 (2014): e99868.

2   The lead research of the Gamelan Project is quoted in Jane O'Brien, "Power of Art: Can Music Help Treat Children with Attention Disorders?" BBC News, March 5, 2013. Retrieved from bbc.com/news/magazine-21661689.

3   The positive link between music and dopamine transmission is reported in Den'etsu Sutoo and Kayo Akiyama, "Music Improves Dopaminergic Neurotransmission: Demonstration Based on the Effect of Music on Blood Pressure Regulation," *Brain Research* 1016, no. 2 (August 6, 2004): 255–62.

4   The differential impact of music on either helping or distracting boys diagnosed with ADHD is reported on in W. E. Pelham, Jr., D. A. Waschbusch, B. Hoza, et al., "Music and Video as Distractors for Boys with ADHD in the Classroom: Comparison with Controls, Individual Differences, and Medication Effects," *Journal of Abnormal Child Psychology* 39, no. 8 (November 2011): 1085–98.

STRATEGY #17

1   The link between self-monitoring and improved on-task performance on spelling tests is report in Karen R. Harris, Barbara Danoff Friedlander, Bruce Saddler, et al., "Self-Monitoring of Attention Versus Self-Monitoring of Academic Performance: Effects among Students with ADHD in the General Education Classroom," *Journal of Special Education* 39, no. 3 (2005): 145–56.

2   A review of the benefits of self-monitoring with students in special education is provided in L. A. Rafferty, "Step-by-Step: Teaching Students to Self-Monitor," *Teaching Exceptional Children* 43, no. 2 (2010): 50–58; and J. Webber, B. Scheuermann, C. McCall, and M. Coleman, "Research on Self-Monitoring As a Behavior Management Technique in Special Education Classrooms: A Descriptive Review," *Remedial & Special Education* 14, no. 2 (1993): 38–56.

STRATEGY #18

1   The use of more commanding and negative comments from parents of ADHD-diagnosed children compared with parents of typically developing children is reported in C. Johnson, "Parent Characteristics and Parent-Child Interactions in Families of Nonproblem Children and ADHD Children with Higher and Lower Levels of Oppositional-Defiant Behavior," *Journal of Abnormal Child Psychology* 24, no. 1 (February 1996): 85–104.

STRATEGY #19

1   The coercive cycle and the negative strategies used by parents in an ADHD household are described in Linda J. Pfiffner and Lauren M. Haack, "Behavior Management for School Aged Children with ADHD," *Child and Adolescent Psychiatric Clinic of North America* 23, no. 4 (October 2014): 731–46.

2   Parents of ADHD-diagnosed children report feeling less efficacy, less welcomed by school personnel, and less able to spend time with them is reported in Maria A. Rogers, Judith Wiener, Imola Marton, and Rosemary Tannock, "Parental Involvement in Children's Learning: Comparing Parents of Children with and without At-

tention-Deficit/Hyperactivity Disorder (ADHD)," *Journal of School Psychology* 47 (2009): 167–85.

3   The components of good parenting training courses are given in Centers for Disease Control and Prevention, "Parent Training Programs: Insight for Practitioners," CDC, 2009. Retrieved from cdc.gov/violenceprevention/pdf/parent_training_brief -a.pdf.

STRATEGY #20

1   The archetypal example of an overly compliant populace is, of course, the people of Nazi Germany between 1933 and 1945. What most people don't realize is that millions of the German people during this time were taking a psychostimulant called Pervitin, a methamphetamine-based drug that kept them energetic and productive. The drug was also used by Panzer divisions and the Luffwaffe during the invasion of France to keep them awake as they rolled or flew across the countryside to Paris. This only recently revealed story is detailed in Norman Ohler, *Blitzed: Drugs in Nazi Germany* (London: Allen Lane/Penguin Random House, 2016).

2   Studies failing to show a link between creative abilities and ADHD-diagnosed children and adolescents include J. B. Funk, J. B. Chessare, M. T. Weaver, and A. R. Exley, "Attention Deficit Hyperactivity Disorder, Creativity, and the Effects of Methylphenidate," *Pediatrics* 91, no. 4 (April 1993): 816–19; and Dione Healey and Julia J. Rucklidge, "An Exploration into the Creative Abilities of Children with ADHD," *Journal of Attention Disorders* 8, no. 3 (February 2005): 88–95.

STRATEGY #22

1   Experiments on the negative impact of crowding on children are described in Claudia D. Solari and Robert D. Mare, "Housing Crowding Effects on Children's Wellbeing," *Social Science Research* 41, no. 2 (March 2012): 464–76.

2   Carol S. Weinstein is quoted from her article "The Physical Environment of the School: A Review of the Research," *Review of Educational Research* 49, no. 4 (fall 1979): 585.

3   Anita R. Olds is quoted from her article "Designing Developmentally Optimal Classrooms for Children with Special Needs," in Samuel J. Meisels, ed., *Special Education and Development* (Baltimore, MD: University Park Press, 1979), 95.

STRATEGY #23

1   One article linking ADHD to a motivation deficit is N. D. Volkow, G-J Wang, J. H. Newcorn, et al., "Motivation Deficit in ADHD Is Associated with Dysfunction of the Dopamine Reward Pathway," *Molecular Psychiatry* 16, no. 11 (November 2011): 1147–54.

STRATEGY #24

1   Diana Baumrind's research on parenting styles is reported on in "Authoritative Parenting Revisited: History and Current Status," in Robert E. Larzelere, Amanda Sheffield Morris, and Amanda W. Harrist, eds., *Authoritative Parenting: Synthesizing Nurturance and Discipline for Optimal Child Development* (Washington, D.C.: American Psychological Association, 2013), 11–34.

STRATEGY #26

1   Jaak Panksepp's views on the importance of play in frontal lobe maturation are given in J. Panksepp, S. Siviy, and L. Normansell, "The Psychobiology of Play: Theoretical

and Methodological Perspectives." *Neuroscience and Behavioral Reviews* 8 (1984): 465–92. Panksepp's views on the connection between the disappearance of rough-and-tumble-play and ADHD diagnoses are shared in his article "Attention Deficit Hyperactivity Disorders, Psychostimulants, and Intolerance of Childhood Playfulness: A Tragedy in the Making?" *Current Directions in Psychological Science* 7, no. 3 (1998): 91–98.

2 Jaak Panksepp's conclusion that play supports the development of inhibition in children and that ADHD drugs reduce playfulness in both rats and children is reported on in his article, "Can Play Diminish ADHD and Facilitate the Construction of the Social Brain?" *Journal of the Canadian Academy of Child and Adolescent Psychiatry* 16, no. 2 (May 2007): 57–66.

3 For a fuller discussion of my thoughts on the links between technology, play, and ADHD symptoms, see my chapter "Attention Deficit Hyperactivity Disorder in Children: One Consequence of the Rise of Technologies and the Demise of Play," in Sharna Olfman, ed., *Work and No Play . . . How Educational Reforms Are Harming Our Preschoolers* (Westport, CT.: Praeger, 2003), 161–76.

STRATEGY #28

1 Edison is quoted in J. L. Elkhorne, "Edison—The Fabulous Drone," 73 *Magazine* 46, no. 3 (March 1967): 52.

2 The study linking ADHD-diagnosed adolescents with lower levels of resilience is Maria Angélica Regalla, Priscilla Guilherme, Pablo Aguilera, et al., "Attention Deficit Hyperactivity Disorder Is an Independent Risk Factor for Lower Resilience in Adolescents: A Pilot Study," *Trends in Psychiatry and Psychotherapy* 37, no. 3 (2015): 157–60.

3 The idea that the most important factor in building resilience in children is at least one strong, competent, and caring person in a child's life is given in Bari Walsh, "The Science of Resilience: Why Some Children Can Thrive Despite Adversity," Usable Knowledge, Harvard Graduate School of Education, March 23, 2015. Retrieved from gse.harvard.edu/news/uk/15/03/science-resilience.

STRATEGY #30

1 The research linking fast-food consumption with ADHD symptoms among Iranian children is reported in L. Azadbakht and A. Esmaillzadeh, "Dietary Patterns and Attention Deficit Hyperactivity Disorder among Iranian Children," *Nutrition* 28, no. 3 (March 2012): 242–49.

2 The Korean research showing a connection between a snack food diet and increased odds of having an ADHD diagnosis is reported in H. D. Woo, D. W. Kim, Y. S. Hong, et al., "Dietary Patterns in Children with Attention Deficit/Hyperactivity Disorder (ADHD)," *Nutrients* 6, no. 4 (April 2014): 1539–53.

3 The Australian research linking ADHD with a Western diet in adolescents is reported in A. L. Howard, M. Robinson, G. J. Smith, et al., "ADHD Is Associated with a 'Western' Dietary Pattern in Adolescents," *Journal of Attention Disorders* 15, no. 5 (July 2011): 403–11.

4 For a look at the influence of fast-food lobbies on government dietary guidelines, see Markham Heid, "Experts Say Lobbying Skewed the U.S. Dietary Guidelines," *Time Magazine*, January 8, 2016. Retrieved from time.com/4130043/lobbying-politics-dietary-guidelines.

Notes

STRATEGY #31

1   Shelley and Andy Raffino are quoted in Kirk Martin, "ADHD Children—What If There Really Isn't Anything Wrong?" Internet Special Education Resources. Retrieved from iser.com/adhd-normal.html.

STRATEGY #33

1   See Matthew R. Galvin, *Otto Learns About His Medicine: A Story about Medication for Children with ADHD* (Washington, D.C.: Magination, 2001).

2   Other examples of machine metaphors used to explain ADHD to kids can be found in Melvin D. Levine, *The Concentration Cockpit: Poster, Examiner's Guide, Explanatory Text and Record Form, Marker* (Portland, OR: Educators Publishing Service, 1997). "How Do You Explain ADHD to Your Child?" *ADDitude.* Retrieved from additudemag.com/adhd/article/9898.html; and in Carmine Gallo, "How a Popular TV Doc Has Learned to Explain ADHD Simply," *Forbes*, August 5, 2014.

3   Gerald Edelman is quoted in John Cornwell, "Master of Creation?" *London Times Online*, July 1, 2007.

4   Oliver Sacks is quoted in Edward Rothstein, "The Brain? It's a Jungle in There" *New York Times*, March 27, 2004. Retrieved from nytimes.com/2004/03/27/books/the-brain-it-s-a-jungle-in-there.html?_r=0.

5   The middle school student who learned about the neuroplasticity of the brain is quoted in Judy Willis, "How to Teach Students About the Brain," *Educational Leadership* 67, no. 4 (December 2009–January 2010). Retrieved from http://bit.ly/1SxJkYr.

STRATEGY #34

1   For a study showing how multitasking impairs performance in children diagnosed with ADHD, see Joshua B. Ewen, Jeffrey S. Moher, Balaji M. Lakshmanan, et al., "Multiple Task Interference Is Greater in Children with ADHD," *Developmental Neuropsychology* 37, no. 2 (February 2012): 119–133.

STRATEGY #35

1   Research showing reduction of ADHD symptoms in children diagnosed with ADHD who engaged in aerobic activity compared with a sedentary control group is reported in B. Hoza, A. L. Smith, E. K. Shoulberg, et al., "A Randomized Trial Examining the Effects of Aerobic Physical Activity on Attention-Deficit/Hyperactivity Disorder Symptoms in Young Children," *Journal of Abnormal Child Psychology* 43, no. 4 (May 2015): 655–67.

2   Improvement in ADHD symptoms among kindergarten through third grade children who engaged in a moderate-to-vigorous exercise program is reported in A. L. Smith, B. Hoza, K. Linnea, et al., "Pilot Physical Activity Intervention Reduces Severity of ADHD Symptoms in Young Children," *Journal of Attention Disorders* 17, no. 1 (January 2013): 70–82.

3   Jordan D. Metzl is quoted in "Increases in Physical Activity Linked to Decreases in ADHD," Phit America, June 24, 2014. Retrieved from phitamerica.org/PageFactory.aspx?PageID=2802.

STRATEGY #36

1   Parents of ADHD-diagnosed children who report teachers as less welcoming and more demanding are reported in Maria Rogers, Julia Boggia, Julia Ogg, and Robert

Volpe, "The Ecology of ADHD in the Schools," *Current Developmental Disorders Reports* 2, no. 1 (March 2015): 23–29.

2   For articles that report on the connection between parental involvement and better academic, behavior, and emotional outcomes for kids see S. Wilder," Effects of Parental Involvement on Academic Achievement: A Meta-Synthesis," *Educational Review* 66, no. 3 (2014): 377–97; Ming-Te Wang and Salam Sheikh-Khalil, "Does Parental Involvement Matter for Student Achievement and Mental Health in High School?" *Child Development* 85, no. 2 (March–April 2014): 10–62; and, Jacquelyn N. Raftery, Wendy S. Grolnick, and Elizabeth S. Flamm, "Families As Facilitators of Student Engagement: Toward a Home-School Partnership Model," in Sandra L. Christenson, Amy L. Reschly, and Cathy Wylie, eds., *Handbook of Research on Student Engagement* (New York: Springs, 2013), 343–64.

3   For a study that links teacher–parent communication with better behavioral outcomes for kids see George J. DuPaul, "School-Based Interventions for Students with Attention Deficit Hyperactivity Disorder: Current Status and Future Directions," *School Psychology Review* 36, no. 2 (2007): 183–94.

STRATEGY #37

1   For an article that reviews studies on the association between working memory and ADHD-diagnosed children, see Rhonda Martinussen, Jill Hayden, Sheilah Hogg-Johnson, and Rosemary Tannock, "A Meta-Analysis of Working Memory Impairments in Children with Attention-Deficit/Hyperactivity Disorder," *Journal of the American Academy of Child and Adolescent Psychiatry* 44, no. 4 (April 2005): 377–84.

2   The importance of pushing against limits to develop working memory among children diagnosed with ADHD is reported on in Torkel Klingberg, Elisabeth Fernell, Pernille J. Olesen, et al., "Computerized Training of Working Memory in Children with ADHD—A Randomized, Controlled Trial," *Journal of the American Academy of Child and Adolescent Psychiatry* 44, no. 2 (February 2005): 177–86.

STRATEGY #38

1   The figure that children spend seven hours each day on media is cited on the Web site. "Media and Children Communication Toolkit," American Association of Pediatrics. Retrieved from https://www.aap.org/en-us/advocacy-and-policy/aap-health-initiatives/pages/media-and-children.aspx.

2   The association between television exposure and negative school outcomes are enumerated in Jeffrey G. Johnson, Patricia Cohen, Stephanie Kasen, and Judith S. Brook, "Extensive Television Viewing and the Development of Attention and Learning Difficulties during Adolescence," *Archives of Pediatric and Adolescent Medicine* 161, no. 5 (2007): 480–86.

3   The connection between media use and shorter sleep is discussed in Christopher R. Engelhardt, Micah O. Mazurek, and Kristin Sohl, "Media Use and Sleep among Boys with Autism Spectrum Disorder, ADHD, or Typical Development," *Pediatrics* 132, no. 6 (December 2013): 1081–89. The association between a TV in the bedroom and increased weekday screen time is reported in Charmaine B. Loa, Molly E. Waring, Sherry L. Pagoto, and Stephenie C. Lemon, "A Television in the Bedroom Is Associated with Higher Weekday Screen Time among Youth with Attention Deficit Hyperactivity Disorder (ADD/ADHD)," *Preventive Medicine Reports* 2 (2015): 1–3.

4   The link between violent media and aggression in kids is discussed in Dimitri

Christakis, "Virtual Violence," *Pediatrics* 138, no. 2 (August 2016): e2 0161298. A possible gene–environment interaction with respect to ADHD-related behaviors and media violence is explored in Sanne W. C. Nikkelen, Helen G. M. Vossen, Patti M. Valkenburg, et al., "Media Violence and Children's ADHD-Related Behaviors: A Genetic Susceptibility Perspective," *Journal of Communication* 64 (2014): 42–60.

STRATEGY #39

1   The phenomenon of hyperfocus is discussed in Jenara Nerenberg, "Hyperfocus: The Other Side of Adult ADHD," CNN Online, July 15, 2016. Retrieved from cnn .com/2016/07/15/health/adult-adhd-hyperfocus.
2   To read more about the concept of flow, see Mihály Csíkszentmihályi's popular book on the topic: *Flow: The Psychology of Optimal Experience* (New York: Harper Perennial Modern Classics, 2008).

STRATEGY #42

1   Two articles that cover the prevalence of emotional dysregulation among ADHD-diagnosed children and the neuroanatomical basis of dysregulation are R. Vela, "Neuroanatomical Basis of Emotional Dysregulation in Children and Adults with ADHD," *European Psychiatry* 33, suppl. (March 2016): S447; and Philip Shaw, Argyris Stringaris, Joel Nigg, and Ellen Leibenluft, "Emotion Dysregulation in Attention Deficit Hyperactivity Disorder," *American Journal of Psychiatry* 171, no. 3 (March 2014): 276–93.

STRATEGY #43

1   For a good introduction to mindfulness meditation, see Jon Kabat-Zinn, *Wherever You Go, There You Are* (New York: Hachette Books, 2005).
2   Studies that cover the positive impact of mindfulness meditation on ADHD symptoms include E. van de Weijer-Bergsma, A. R. Formsma, E. I. de Bruin, and S. M. Bögels, "The Effectiveness of Mindfulness Training on Behavioral Problems and Attentional Functioning in Adolescents with ADHD," *Journal of Child and Family Studies* 21, no. 5 (October 2012): 775–87; S. van der Oord, S. M. Bögels, and D. Peijnenburg, "The Effectiveness of Mindfulness Training for Children with ADHD and Mindful Parenting for their Parents," *Journal of Child and Family Studies* 21, no. 1 (February 2012): 139–47; and V. Modesto-Lowe, P. Farahmand, M. Chaplin, and L. Sarro, "Does Mindfulness Meditation Improve Attention in Attention Deficit Hyperactivity Disorder?" *World Journal of Psychiatry* 5, no. 4 (December 2015): 397–403.

STRATEGY #44

1   Lev Vygotsky's views on the development of internalized language can be found in his seminal book, *Thought and Language*, rev. ed. (Cambridge, MA: MIT Press, 1986).
2   The positive impact of allowing children with ADHD-related behaviors to engage in spontaneous self-talk is explored in Adam Winsler, Louis Manfra, and Rafael M. Diaz, "Should I Let Them Talk?: Private Speech and Task Performance among Preschool Children with and without Behavior Problems," *Early Childhood Research Quarterly* 22 (2007): 215–31.
3   Zentall's observation that children identified as hyperactive will not talk when asked to but talk a lot if they are not supposed to are in her article "Production Deficiencies

in Elicited Language but Not in the Spontaneous Verbalizations of Hyperactive Children," *Journal of Abnormal Child Psychology* 16, no. 6 (December 1988): 657–73.

STRATEGY #47

1   Statistics on the number of available apps are taken from "Number of Apps Available in Leading App Stores As of June 2016," *Statistika—The Statistics Portal.* Retrieved from statista.com/statistics/276623/number-of-apps-available-in-leading-app-stores.

STRATEGY #48

1   Survey data on the positive impact of the mentoring program Eye to Eye are taken from their Web site at "Student Outcomes." Retrieved from eyetoeyenational.org/programs/our_outcomes.html.

2   The link between student mentoring and positive academic and school attendance outcomes for kids identified as having ADHD or LD is reported in Nancy K. Glomb, Leigh D. Buckley, Esther D. Minskoff, and Sherrita Rogers, "The Learning Leaders Mentoring Program for Children with ADHD and Learning Disabilities," *Preventing School Failure: Alternative Education for Children and Youth* 50, no. 4 (2006): 31–35.

3   Marcus Soutra is quoted in his article "Building a Powerful Mentoring Relationship: Tips from My Experience As a Child with ADHD and Dyslexia," Understood—For Learning and Attention Issues, January 25, 2016. Retrieved at http://u.org/29fRZVH.

4   Quoted in Soutra, "Building a Powerful Mentoring Relationship."

STRATEGY #49

1   Olympic champion Michael Phelps's story about succeeding with ADHD is provided in Patrick Barkham, "What Can Athletes with ADHD Teach Us About the Condition?" *The Guardian*, August 1, 2012.

2   The positive cognitive, social, and behavioral outcomes of ADHD kids engaged in sports are reported in K. D. Kang, J. W. Choi, S. G. Kang, and D. H. Han, "Sports Therapy for Attention, Cognitions and Sociality," *International Journal of Sports Medicine* 32, no. 12 (2011): 953–59.

3   The association between swimming and improved inhibition of impulsive behaviors in children diagnosed with ADHD is in Yu-Kai Chang, Chiao-Ling Hung, Chung-Ju Huang, et al., "Effects of an Aquatic Exercise Program on Inhibitory Control in Children with ADHD: A Preliminary Study," *Archives of Clinical Neuropsychology* 29, no. 3 (May 2014): 217–23.

STRATEGY #50

1   For a rundown on the positive impact of implementing high stimulation interventions such as light, color, and animals in the classroom, see Sydney S. Zentall, "Theory- and Evidence-Based Strategies for Children with Attentional Problems," *Psychology in the Schools* 42, no. 8 (2005): 821–36.

STRATEGY #51

1   For an article that discusses late prefrontal brain maturation in adolescents, see E. A. Crone and R. E. Dahl, "Understanding Adolescence as a Period of Social-Affective Engagement and Goal Flexibility," *Nature Reviews Neuroscience* 13, no. 9 (2012): 636–50.

Notes

2   Zig Ziglar is quoted in Lilly Walters, *Secrets of Superstar Speakers: Wisdom from the Greatest Motivators of Our Time* (New York: McGraw-Hill, 2000), 96.

STRATEGY #53

1   Henry Adams is quoted from his autobiography, *The Education of Henry Adams* (Radford, VA: Wilder, 2009), 194.
2   The association between a preschooler's negative or stressful relationship with his preschool teacher and referral for special education in elementary school is covered in Jordan Buckrop, Amy Roberts, and Jennifer LoCasale-Crouch, "Children's Preschool Classroom Experiences and Associations with Early Elementary Special Education Referral," *Early Childhood Research Quarterly* 36 (2016): 452–61.
3   The Pygmalion experiments are covered in Robert Rosenthal and Lenore Jacobson, *Pygmalion in the Classroom: Teacher Expectation and Pupils' Intellectual Development* (New York: Crown, 2003).
4   The impact of high school teachers' high expectations for students on college graduation rates is covered in Ulrich Boser, Megan Wilhelm, and Robert Hanna, "The Power of the Pygmalion Effect: Teachers Expectations Strongly Predict College Completion," Center for American Progress, October 6, 2014. Retrieved from americanprogress.org/issues/education/report/2014/10/06/96806/the-power-of-the-pygmalion-effect.

STRATEGY #54

1   For an example of a skeptical perspective on the value of neurofeedback to treat ADHD symptoms, see Russell Barkley's editorial commentary on "EEG and Neurofeedback Findings in ADHD," *ADHD Report* 11, no. 3 (2003): 7–9.
2   For a report on the history of studies assessing the value of neurofeedback in treating ADHD see Martijn Arnsa, Hartmut Heinrich, and Ute Strehle, "Evaluation of Neurofeedback in ADHD: The Long and Winding Road," *Biological Psychology* 95 (January 2014): 108–15.
3   The study showing improved symptoms in ADHD-diagnosed students who engaged in neurofeedback compared with those who did cognitive training or nothing (control group) is Naomi J. Steiner, Elizabeth C. Frenette, Kirsten M. Rene, et al., "In-School Neurofeedback Training for ADHD: Sustained Improvements from a Randomized Control Trial," *Pediatrics* 133, no. 3 (March 2014): 483–92.

STRATEGY #55

1   Ashley Montagu's ideas about the significance of human touch are related in his book *Touching: The Human Significance of the Skin* (New York: William Morrow, 1986).
2   For studies that link touch and massage with positive behavioral and emotional outcomes for children and adolescents diagnosed with ADHD, see T. F. Field, O. Quintino, M. Hernandez-Reif, and G. Koslovsky, "Adolescents with Attention Deficit Hyperactivity Disorder Benefit from Massage Therapy," *Adolescence* 33 (1998): 103–08; and Barbara Maddigan, Pamela Hodgson, Sylvia Heath, et al., "The Effects of Massage Therapy & Exercise Therapy on Children/Adolescents with Attention Deficit Hyperactivity Disorder," *Canadian Child and Adolescent Psychiatry Review* 12, no. 2 (March 2003): 40–43.

STRATEGY #57

1   The association between laughter and lower cortisol levels is documented in Lee S. Berk, Stanley A. Tan, and Dottie Berk, "Cortisol and Catecholamine Stress Hormone

Decrease Is Associated with the Behavior of Perceptual Anticipation of Mirthful Laughter," *FASEB Journal* 22, no. 1 (March 2008): 946.

2   The link between laughter and endorphins is explored in R. I. M. Dunbar, Rebecca Baron, Anna Frangou, et al., "Social Laughter Is Correlated with an Elevated Pain Threshold," *Proceedings of the Royal Society B* (2011). Retrieved from rspb.royal societypublishing.org/content/royprsb/early/2011/09/12/rspb.2011.1373.full.pdf.

3   Jaak Panksepp's views on playful laughter as a positive evolutionary development are shared in Jaak Panksepp, "Neuroevolutionary Sources of Laughter and Social Joy: Modeling Primal Human Laughter in Laboratory Rats," *Behavioural Brain Research* 182 (2007): 231–44.

4   The idea that most laughter occurs as a response to other people's laughter is from Robert Provine, *Laughter: A Scientific Investigation* (New York: Penguin, 2001).

5   Peter Jaksa's anecdote about the value of humor and getting attention is given in his article "Laughing Matters," *ADDitude*. Retrieved from additudemag.com/adhd/article /797.html.

STRATEGY #58

1   Zig Ziglar is quoted from his book *Raising Positive Kids in a Negative World* (New York: Ballantine, 1989), 130.

2   For the study on the preference of ADHD-diagnosed children for time with parents as a reward, see R. D. Hill, D. Olympia, and K.C. Angelbuer, "A Comparison of Preference for Familial, Social, and Material Rewards between Hyperactive and Non-Hyperactive Boys," *School Psychology International* 12, no. 3 (August 1991): 225–29.

STRATEGY #59

1   The foundational work that explores the theory of multiple intelligences is Howard Gardner's book *Frames of Mind: The Theory of Multiple Intelligences* (New York: Basic Books, 2011). His book *Multiple Intelligences: New Horizons in Theory and Practice* (New York: Basic Books, 2006) looks at the impact of his theory on educational practices.

STRATEGY #60

1   The link between learned helplessness and ADHD-diagnosed boys is explored in Richard Milich and Mimi Okazaki, "An Examination of Learned Helplessness among Attention-Deficit Hyperactivity Disordered Boys," *Journal of Abnormal Child Psychology* 19, no. 5 (October 1991): 607–23.

2   For an article reviewing the academic and self-regulatory benefits of a growth mindset, see Veronika Job, Gregory M. Walton, Katharina Bernecker, and Carol S. Dweck, "Implicit Theories About Willpower Predict Self-Regulation and Grades in Everyday Life," *Journal of Personality and Social Psychology* 108, no. 4 (2015): 637–47. See also Carol Dweck's best-selling book on the subject, *Mindset: The New Psychology of Success* (New York: Ballantine, 2007).

STRATEGY #62

1   The article that explores the association between sunlight and lower rates of ADHD diagnoses in the United States is M. Arns, K. B. van der Heijden, L. E. Arnold, and J. L. Kenemans, "Geographic Variation in the Prevalence of Attention-Deficit/Hyperactivity Disorder: The Sunny Perspective," *Biological Psychiatry* 74, no. 8 (October 2013): 585–90.

2   For information about the negative human impact of screen illumination from com-
     puters, tablets, smartphones, and other devices, see "Blue Light Has a Dark Side,"
     Harvard Health Letter, September 2, 2015. Retrieved from health.harvard.edu/
     staying-healthy/blue-light-has-a-dark-side.

STRATEGY #63

1   A meta-analysis of studies on the positive effect of omega-3 supplements in reduc-
     ing ADHD symptoms is Elizabeth Hawkey and Joel T. Nigg, "Omega-3 Fatty Acid
     and ADHD: Blood Level Analysis and Meta-Analytic Extension of Supplementation
     Trials," *Clinical Psychology Review* 34, no. 6 (August 2014): 496–505.

2   The Dutch study that demonstrated improved attention from eating margarine
     supplemented with omega-3 fatty acids is reported on in D. J. Bos, B. Oranje, E. S.
     Veerhoek, et al., "Reduced Symptoms of Inattention after Dietary Omega-3 Fatty
     Acid Supplementation in Boys with and without Attention Deficit/Hyperactivity
     Disorder," *Neuropsychopharmacology* 40, no. 10 (September 2015): 2298–306.

STRATEGY #64

1   Murray Bowen is quoted from his book *Family Therapy in Clinical Practice* (Lan-
     ham, MD: Jason Aronson, 1993), 129.

2   For an article that discusses the prevalence of adversity, parental psychopathology,
     and life stress in families of children diagnosed with ADHD, see Carla A. Counts,
     Joel T. Nigg, Julie Ann Stawicki, et al., "Family Adversity in DSM-IV ADHD Com-
     bined and Inattentive Subtypes and Associated Disruptive Behavior Problems,"
     Journal of the American Academy of Child and Adolescent Psychiatry 44, no. 7
     (July 2005): 690–98.

STRATEGY #65

1   For evidence from brain scan studies that the brains of ADHD-diagnosed kids show
     greater responses to novel stimuli, see Jana Tegelbeckers, Nico Bunzeck, Emrah Duzel,
     et al., "Altered Salience Processing in Attention Deficit Hyperactivity Disorder,"
     Human Brain Mapping 36, no. 6 (June 2015): 2049–60.

2   The association between ADHD and dopamine genes is explored in V. Kustanovich,
     J. Ishii, L. Crawford, et al., "Transmission Disequilibrium Testing of Dopamine-
     Related Candidate Gene Polymorphisms in ADHD: Confirmation of Association of
     ADHD with DRD4 and DRD5," *Molecular Psychiatry* 9 (2004): 711–17.

3   For the study that revealed better performance among ADHD-diagnosed children
     when presented with nonrelevant distractions, see R. van Mourik, J. Oosterlaan,
     D. J. Heslenfeld, et al., "When Distraction Is Not Distracting: A Behavioral and ERP
     Study on Distraction in ADHD," *Clinical Neurophysiology* 118, no. 8 (August
     2007): 1855–65.

STRATEGY #66

1   James Evans is quoted in Thomas G. West, *In the Mind's Eye: Visual Thinkers,
     Gifted People with Learning Difficulties, Computer Images, and the Ironies of
     Creativity*, 2nd ed. (Buffalo, NY: Prometheus, 2009), 84.

STRATEGY #69

1   For a history of the use of aromatherapy in ancient times, see Farid Alakbarov,
     "Aromatic Herbal Baths of the Ancients," *HerbalGram* 57 (2003): 40–49.

Notes

2   For a critical review of research in the use of aromatherapy, see, Myeong Soo Lee, Jiae Choia, Paul Posadzki, and Edzard Ernst, "Aromatherapy for Health Care: An Overview of Systematic Reviews," *Maturitas* 71, no. 3 (March 2012): 257–60.

3   For a study that found greater odor sensitivity in children diagnosed with ADHD, see M. Romanos, T. J. Renner, M. Schecklmann, et al., "Improved Odor Sensitivity in Attention-Deficit/Hyperactivity Disorder," *Biological Psychiatry* 64, no. 11 (December 1, 2008): 938–40.

4   For a study that links ylang-ylang with a calmer mood, see Mark Moss, Steven Hewitt, Lucy Moss, and Keith Wesnes, "Modulation of Cognitive Performance and Mood by Aromas of Peppermint and Ylang-Ylang," *International Journal of Neuroscience* 118, no. 1 (2008): 59–77.

STRATEGY #71

1   Sanford Newmark is quoted in "Are ADHD Medications Overprescribed?" *Wall Street Journal*, February 14, 2013. Retrieved from wsj.com/articles/SB10000872396 390444301704577631591596516110.

2   For a complete discussion of these and other candidates that mimic the symptoms of ADHD, see Richard Saul, *ADHD Does Not Exist: The Truth About Attention Deficit and Hyperactivity Disorder* (New York: Harper Wave, 2014).

STRATEGY #72

1   The anecdote about Mary Ann Moon and her two kids was taken from Anne Scheck, "Find Your Focus with Natural ADHD Treatments," *ADDitude*, June–July 2005. Retrieved from additudemag.com/adhd/article/883.html.

STRATEGY #74

1   Thomas and Sydney Zentall are quoted on the aversive nature of punitive time out for hyperactive children in Sydney S. Zentall and Thomas R. Zentall, "Optimal Stimulation: A Model of Disordered Activity and Performance in Normal and Deviant Children," *Psychological Bulletin* 94, no. 3 (1983): 461.

2   Jane Nelsen is quoted from her book *Positive Discipline* (New York: Ballantine, 2006), 163.

STRATEGY #75

1   The ADHD-diagnosed adolescent boy's words about how it feels to go to school are in Robert Brooks, "Loneliness, Self-Efficacy, and Hope: Often Neglected Dimensions of the Learning Process." Retrieved from drrobertbrooks.com/pdf/0703.pdf.

2   The study in which ADHD-diagnosed children reported that they believed a core dimension of their real selves was persistently bad despite medication is reported on in Ilina Singh, "Clinical Implications of Ethical Concepts: Moral Self-Understandings in Children Taking Methylphenidate for ADHD," *Clinical Child Psychology and Psychiatry* 12, no. 2 (2007): 167–82.

3   The youth who said "ADHD does bad stuff to you," was quoted in Chris Travella and John Visser, " 'ADHD Does Bad Stuff to You': Young People's and Parents' Experiences and Perceptions of Attention Deficit Hyperactivity Disorder (ADHD)," *Emotional and Behavioural Difficulties* 11, no. 3 (September 2006): 205–16.

4   The negative impact of praise on children with low self-esteem is explored in Eddie Brummelman, Jennifer Crocker, and Brad J. Bushman, "The Praise Paradox: When

and Why Praise Backfires in Children with Low Self-Esteem," *Child Development Perspectives* 10, no. 2 (June 2016): 111–15.

5   Pablo Casals is quoted in Pablo Casals and Albert Eugene Kahn, *Joys and Sorrows: Reflections* (New York: Simon & Schuster, 1970), 295.

STRATEGY #76

1   Figures on the number of U.S. chemicals that affect the nervous system are from Anna Esparham, Randall G. Evans, Leigh E. Wagner, and Jeanne A. Drisko, "Pediatric Integrative Medicine Approaches to Attention Deficit Hyperactivity Disorder (ADHD)," *Children* 1, no. 2 (2014): 186–207.

2   Larry Silver's list of toxic chemicals in everyday household items is given in his article, "Cause of ADHD: Toxic Risk Factors," *ADDitude*. Retrieved from additude mag.com/adhd/article/8388.html.

3   The authors are quoted on the link between lead and ADHD in their article, Joel T. Nigg, Molly Nikolas, G. Mark Knottnerus, et al., "Confirmation and Extension of Association of Blood Lead with Attention-Deficit/Hyperactivity Disorder (ADHD) and ADHD Symptom Domains at Population-Typical Exposure Levels," *Journal of Child Psychology and Psychiatry* 51, no. 1 (January 2010): 58–65.

4   The link between secondhand smoke and ADHD is reported on in Wendy Max, Hai-Yen Sung, and Yanling Shi, "Attention Deficit Hyperactivity Disorder among Children Exposed to Secondhand Smoke: A Logistic Regression Analysis of Secondary Data," *International Journal of Nursing Studies* 50, no. 6 (June 2013): 797.

STRATEGY #77

1   Sleep recommendations for children and adolescents come from National Sleep Foundation, "National Sleep Foundation Recommends New Sleep Times," February 2, 2015. Retrieved from: sleepfoundation.org/media-center/press-release/national-sleep-foundation-recommends-new-sleep-times.

2   The percentage of children and adolescents getting less than eight hours of sleep per night is from Julia F. Dewald, Anne M. Meijer, Frans J. Oort, et al., "The Influence of Sleep Quality, Sleep Duration and Sleepiness on School Performance in Children and Adolescents: A Meta-Analytic Review," *Sleep Medicine Reviews* 14, no. 3 (June 2010): 179–89.

3   The link between ADHD-diagnosed kids and shorter sleep duration is from E. Juulia Paavonen, Katri Räikkönen, Jari Lahti, Niina Komsi, et al., "Short Sleep Duration and Behavioral Symptoms of Attention-Deficit/Hyperactivity Disorder in Healthy 7- to 8-Year-Old Children," *Pediatrics* 123, no. 5 (May 2009): e857–64.

4   For a discussion of sleep problems associated with an ADHD diagnosis in children, see V. Sung, H. Hiscock, E. Sciberras, and D. Efron, "Sleep Problems in Children with Attention-Deficit/Hyperactivity Disorder: Prevalence and the Effect on the Child and Family," *Archives of Pediatric and Adolescent Medicine* 162, no. 4 (April 2008): 336–42.

5   Parent reports of problematic behaviors preceding sleep in children and adolescents diagnosed with ADHD are from Judith A. Owens, "A Clinical Overview of Sleep and Attention-Deficit/Hyperactivity Disorder in Children and Adolescents," *Journal of the Canadian Academy of Child and Adolescent Psychiatry* 18, no. 2 (May 2009): 92–102.

6   The report suggesting that good sleep hygiene plus melatonin can ameliorate sleep problems in children and adolescents diagnosed with ADHD is from M. S. Weiss,

Notes

M. B. Wasdell, M. M. Bomben, et al., "Sleep Hygiene and Melatonin Treatment for Children and Adolescents with ADHD and Initial Insomnia," *Journal of the American Academy of Child and Adolescent Psychiatry* 45, no. 5 (May 2006): 512–19.

STRATEGY #78

1 On negative adult outcomes of people with ADHD, see, for example: J. Biederman, C. R. Petty, K. Y. Woodworth, et al., "Adult Outcome of Attention-Deficit/Hyperactivity Disorder: A Controlled 16-Year Follow-Up Study," *Journal of Clinical Psychiatry* 73 (July 2012): 941–50.

STRATEGY #80

1 The Lebanese study linking chess playing to improved concentration and listening skills in ADHD-identified students is from Ladrie Mohammad, Nour ElDaoua, and Sara Ibrahim El-Shamieh, "The Effect of Playing Chess on the Concentration of ADHD Students in the 2nd Cycle," *Procedia—Social and Behavioral Sciences* 192 (May 2015): 638–43.

2 The Spanish study linking chess training to decreased severity of ADHD symptoms is discussed in Hilario Blasco-Fontecilla, Marisa Gonzalez-Perez, Raquel Garcia-Lopez, et al., "Efficacy of Chess Training for the Treatment of ADHD: A Prospective, Open Label Study," *Revista de Psiquiatría y Salud Mental* (English Edition) 9, no. 1 (January–March 2016): 13–21.

3 The connection between playing the Chinese game Go and improved executive functioning is explored in Se Hee Kim, Doug Hyun Han, Young Sik Lee, et al., "Baduk (the Game of Go) Improved Cognitive Function and Brain Activity in Children with Attention Deficit Hyperactivity Disorder," *Psychiatry Investigation* 11, no. 2 (2014): 143–51.

STRATEGY #81

1 For an article exploring the value of cross-age teaching and its positive impact on the tutor, see Peter Tymms and Christine Merrell, "Cross-Age Peer Learning," *Evidence-Based Education* 7, no. 1 (spring 2015): 18–19. The value of using cross-age teaching with kids showing ADHD-related symptoms is discussed in Brigid A. Vilardo, George J. DuPaul, Lee Kern, and Robin L. Hojnoski, "Cross-Age Peer Coaching: Enhancing the Peer Interactions of Children Exhibiting Symptoms of ADHD," *Child & Family Behavior Therapy* 35, no. 1 (2013): 63–81.

STRATEGY #82

1 Examples of articles that guide parents in telling their kids about their ADHD diagnosis include Madeline Vann, "Talking to Kids About ADHD," *Everyday Health*, September 28, 2011. Retrieved from everydayhealth.com/add-adhd/talking-to-kids-about-adhd.aspx; and Heather Hatfield, "8 Tips for Talking with Your Child About ADHD," *WebMD*. Retrieved from webmd.com/add-adhd/childhood-adhd/features/adhd-talking-to-child.

2 The association between positive illusory bias and children diagnosed with ADHD is discussed in Julie Sarno Owens, Matthew E. Goldfine, Nicole M. Evangelista, et al., "A Critical Review of Self-perceptions and the Positive Illusory Bias in Children with ADHD," *Clinical Child and Family Psychology Review* 10, no. 4 (December 2007): 335–51.

STRATEGY #83

1   For the study that concludes computerized instruction is superior to teacher-directed learning for students diagnosed with ADHD, see Julie Clarfield and Gary Stoner, "The Effects of Computerized Reading Instruction on the Academic Performance of Students Identified with ADHD," *School Psychology Review* 34, no. 2 (March 2005): 246–54.

2   The study that concluded computerized learning in mathematics was better than seatwork in the same subject is discussed in Jennifer A. Mautone, George J. DuPaul, and Asha K. Jitendra, "The Effects of Computer-Assisted Instruction on the Mathematics Performance and Classroom Behavior of Children with ADHD," *Journal of Attention Disorders* 9, no. 1 (August 2005): 301–12.

STRATEGY #84

1   Clark C. Abt is quoted from his book *Serious Games* (New York: Viking Press, 1970), 9.

2   Improvements for children diagnosed with ADHD in working memory, social skills, and time management due to playing the computer game Plan-It-Commander are reported in K. C. Bul, P. M. Kato, S. Van der Oord, et. al., "Behavioral Outcome Effects of Serious Gaming As an Adjunct to Treatment for Children with Attention-Deficit/Hyperactivity Disorder: A Randomized Controlled Trial," *Journal of Medical Internet Research* 18, no. 2 (February 2016): e26.

3   Improvements in ADHD-diagnosed children associated with playing the computer game Project EVO are reported on in Katherine Ellison, "Video Game Is Built to Be Prescribed to Children with A.D.H.D.," Well blog, *New York Times*, November 23, 2015.

4   ADHD-diagnosed students' positive statements about their experiences with the computer game Minecraft are in Randy Kulman, "Why Is Minecraft So Appealing to Children with ADHD?" *Learning Works for Kids*, March 4, 2015. Retrieved from learningworksforkids.com/2015/03/minecraft-appealing-children-adhd.

5   The positive impact of Minecraft on executive functioning skills is reported on in Cathy Risberg, "More Than Just a Video Game: Tips for Using Minecraft to Personalize the Curriculum and Promote Creativity, Collaboration, and Problem Solving," *IAGC Journal* (2015): 44–48. Retrieved from imsa.edu/sites/default/files/2015-iagc-journal_1.pdf#page=44.

STRATEGY #85

1   Students' virtual tours using Nearpod VR goggles are reported on in John Gaudiosi, "These Two School Districts Are Teaching through Virtual Reality," *Forbes*, February 25, 2016.

2   The use of The Virtual Classroom to help children diagnosed with ADHD learn to deal with distractions is suggested in Leanna M. Withrow, Phillip A. K. Hash, and Keith B. Holten, "Managing ADHD in Children: Are You Doing Enough?" *Journal of Family Practice* 60, no. 4 (April 2011): E1–3.

3   The use of virtual reality applications to teach road-crossing safety and driving skills to adolescents diagnosed with ADHD are described in T. A. Clancy, J. J. Rucklidge, and D. Owen, "Road-Crossing Safety in Virtual Reality: A Comparison of Adolescents with and without ADHD," *Journal of Clinical Child and Adolescent Psychology* 35, no. 2 (June 2006): 203–15; and Daniel J. Cox, Mohan Punja, Katie

Powers, et al., "Manual Transmission Enhances Attention and Driving Performance of ADHD Adolescent Males Pilot Study," *Journal of Attention Disorders* 10, no. 2 (November 2006): 212–16.

4   Reflections on the positive potential of using virtual reality with children diagnosed with ADHD are given in Shimon Shiri, Ariel Tenenbaum, Orly Sapir-Budnero, and Isaiah D. Wexler, "Elevating Hope Among Children with Attention Deficit and Hyperactivity Disorder through Virtual Reality," *Frontiers of Human Neuroscience* 8 (May 2014): 198.

5   Reports of accidents suffered by users of Pokémon Go are covered in Sharon Gaudin, "Pokémon Go Craze Shows Apple an Augmented Reality Future," *Computerworld,* July 27, 2016. Retrieved from bit.ly/2arJS3s.

STRATEGY #87

1   The figure on the number of children practicing yoga in the United States is from Marlynn Wei, "More Than Just a Game: Yoga for School-Age Children," Harvard Health Blog, Harvard Medical School, January 29, 2016. Retrieved from health.harvard.edu/blog/more-than-just-a-game-yoga-for-school-age-children-201601299055.

2   The study showing the positive influence of yoga instruction on ADHD-diagnosed children's improvements with task behaviors related to classroom assignments is discussed in Heather L. Peck, Thomas Kehle, Melissa A. Bray, and Lea A. Theodore, "Yoga As an Intervention for Children with Attention Problems," *School Psychology Review* 34, no. 3 (2005): 415–24.

3   For the study reporting on improvements in ADHD symptoms after eight sessions of yoga instruction, see V. R. Hariprasad, R. Arasappa, S. Varambally, et al., "Feasibility and Efficacy of Yoga As an Add-On Intervention in Attention Deficit-Hyperactivity Disorder: An Exploratory Study," *Indian Journal of Psychiatry* 55, Suppl. 3 (July 2013): S379–84.

4   The German study reporting decreases in ADHD symptoms after yoga instruction is discussed in J. Haffner, J. Roos, N. Goldstein, et al., "The Effectiveness of Body-Oriented Methods of Therapy in the Treatment of Attention-Deficit Hyperactivity Disorder (ADHD): Results of a Controlled Pilot Study," *Zeitschrift für Kinder-und Jugendpsychiatrie und Psychotherapie* 34, no. 1 (January 2006): 37–47.

5   The yoga activities described here, plus many others that can be successfully used with kids diagnosed with ADHD, can be found in Stacey Turis, "Say Yes to Yoga for Kids with Attention Deficit," *ADDitude*. Retrieved from additudemag.com/adhd blogs/27/10006.html; and Dennis Thompson, Jr., "Bending Energy: ADHD Kids Benefit from Yoga," Everyday Health. Retrieved from everydayhealth.com/adhd/bending-energy-adhd-kids-benefit-from-yoga.aspx.

STRATEGY #88

1   The child who identified with a therapy horse is quoted in Madeline Vann, "Equine Therapy for ADHD Treatment," Everyday Health, August 8, 2013. Retrieved from everydayhealth.com/add-adhd/equine-therapy-for-adhd-treatment.aspx.

2   The study reporting on reduction in ADHD symptoms after a canine-assisted intervention is described in Sabrina E. B. Schuck, Natasha A. Emmerson, Aubrey H. Fine, and Kimberley D. Lakes, "Canine-Assisted Therapy for Children with ADHD: Preliminary Findings from the Positive Assertive Cooperative Kids Study," *Journal of Attention Disorders* 19, no. 2 (February 2015): 125–37.

3   The many benefits of animal therapies for ADHD symptoms are discussed in

Caroline Busch, Lara Tucha, Alzbeta Talarovicova, et al., "Animal-Assisted Interventions for Children with Attention Deficit/Hyperactivity Disorder: A Theoretical Review and Consideration of Future Research Directions," *Psychological Reports* 118, no. 1 (February 2016): 292–331.

STRATEGY #89
1 For an example of an early-interventionist perspective, see Joan L. Luby, "Dispelling the 'They'll Grow Out of It' Myth: Implications for Intervention," *American Journal of Psychiatry* 169, no. 11 (November 2012): 1127–29.

STRATEGY #90
1 Statistics on co-morbidities of ADHD with anxiety and mood disorders are provided in Beth Krone and Jeffrey H. Newcorn, "Comorbidity of ADHD and Anxiety Disorders: Diagnosis and Treatment Across the Lifespan," in Lenard A. Adler, Thomas J. Spencer, and Timothy E. Wilens, eds., *Attention-Deficit Hyperactivity Disorder in Adults and Children* (Cambridge, UK: Cambridge University Press, 2015), 98; and Gavin L. Brunsvold, Godehard Oepen, Edward J. Federman, and Richard Akins, "Comorbid Depression and ADHD in Children and Adolescents," *Psychiatric Times*, September 1, 2008.
2 For reports on the positive impact of different psychotherapeutic approaches in ameliorating ADHD-related symptoms in children and adolescents, see K. M. Antshel, S. V. Faraone, and M. Gordon, "Cognitive Behavioral Treatment Outcomes in Adolescent ADHD," *Journal of Attention Disorders* 18, no. 6 (August 2014): 483–95; Benedict Carey, "Early Behavior Therapy Found to Aid Children with A.D.H.D.," *New York Times*, February 17, 2016; and Francine Conway, "The Use of Empathy and Transference As Interventions in Psychotherapy with Attention Deficit Hyperactive Disorder Latency-Aged Boys," *Psychotherapy* 51, no. 1 (March 2014), 104–09.

STRATEGY #93
1 Peer rejection figures for children diagnosed with ADHD are from B. Hoza, S. Mrug, A. C. Gerdes, et al., "What Aspects of Peer Relationships Are Impaired in Children with Attention-Deficit/Hyperactivity Disorder?," *Journal of Consulting and Clinical Psychology* 73, no. 3 (June 2005): 411–23.

STRATEGY #94
1 The American Academy of Pediatrics quote on the importance of physical education programs before medication is used is taken from "Medication for Children with an Attention Deficit Disorder," *Pediatrics* 80, no. 5 (November 1987): 758. It's a measure of the acceptance which stimulant medication has attained in our society today that this phrase was not included in this association's 2011 revised policy statement on medication. See Subcommittee on Attention-Deficit/Hyperactivity Disorder, Steering Committee on Quality Improvement and Management, "ADHD: Clinical Practice Guideline for the Diagnosis, Evaluation, and Treatment of Attention-Deficit/Hyperactivity Disorder in Children and Adolescents," 2011. Available at http://pediatrics.aappublications.org/content/pediatrics/early/2011/10/14/peds.2011-2654.full.pdf.
2 The percentage of schools requiring 150–225 minutes per week of physical education was taken from School Health Policies and Programs Study (SHPPS): Physical Education, Centers for Disease Control and Prevention, 2006. Retrieved from cdc.gov/healthyyouth/shpps/2006/factsheets/pdf/fs_physicaleducation_shpps2006.pdf.

3   The figure for the percentage of school administrators reporting cutbacks on physical education programs and recess due to academic accountability pressures is from H. W. Kohl and H. D. Cook, eds., *Educating the Student Body: Taking Physical Activity and Physical Education to School* (Washington, D.C.: National Academies Press, 2013).

4   The Madison Junior High School PE program is described in "New PE Trend Stresses Fitness and Fun," *Education World*. Retrieved from educationworld.com/a_curr/curr346.shtml.

5   The Woodford County Schools PE program is described in Caralee Adams, "The P.E. Shift," *Scholastic* (Spring 2013). Retrieved from scholastic.com/browse/article.jsp?id=3757966.

6   Jeffrey Alexander is quoted from his article "Hyperactive Children: Which Sports Have the Right Stuff," *Physician and Sports Medicine* 18, no. 4 (April 1990): 106.

STRATEGY #95

1   David Neeleman is quoted in Lois Gilman, "Career Advice from the Corner Office: Famous People with ADHD," *ADDitude*, December–January 2005. Retrieved from additudemag.com/adhd/article/754.html.

2   The link between higher education students with ADHD-like behavior and entrepreneurial interests is reported in Ingrid Verheul, Joern Block, Katrin Burmeister-Lamp, et al., "ADHD-Like Behavior and Entrepreneurial Intentions," *Small Business Economics* 45, no. 2 (June 2015): 85–101.

3   The association of poorer executive functioning and risk-taking with positive entrepreneurial traits is made in Mario Hayek and Michael Harvey, "Attention Deficit/Hyperactive Disorder As an Entrepreneurial 'Marker' among Family Business Members: A Social Learning Perspective," *Journal of Family Business Management* 2, no. 1 (2012): 6–22.

STRATEGY #96

1   The study demonstrating improved handwriting of ADHD-diagnosed children when writing on colored as opposed to black or white paper is discussed in Margarete Imhof, "Effects of Color Stimulation on Handwriting Performance of Children with ADHD without and with Additional Learning Disabilities," *European Child & Adolescent Psychiatry* 13, no. 3 (2004): 191–98.

2   The use of a yellow highlighter pen to improve on-task behaviors and problem solving in girls at risk for ADHD is reported on in Suneeta Kercood, Sydney S. Zentall, Megan Vinh, and Kinsey Tom-Wright, "Attentional Cuing in Math Word Problems for Girls At-Risk for ADHD and Their Peers in General Education Settings," *Contemporary Educational Psychology* 37, no. 1 (January 2012): 106–112.

STRATEGY #97

1   Claire's story is featured in Jeff Rasmussen, "A Girl with A Blog—ADHD Role Model," *ADHD Kids Rock*, February 18, 2016. Retrieved from adhdkidsrock.com/a-girl-with-a-blog-adhd-role-model.

2   The Facebook survey was reported in Amy Gajaria, Emanuela Yeung, Tara Goodale, and Alice Charach, "Beliefs About Attention-Deficit/Hyperactivity Disorder and Response to Stereotypes: Youth Postings in Facebook Groups," *Journal of Adolescent Health* 49, no. 1 (July 2011): 15–20.

Notes

STRATEGY #98

1   For the study linking lower neighborhood support with greater odds of developing ADHD and higher levels of ADHD severity, see Nooshin Razani, Joan F. Hilton, Bonnie L. Halpern-Felsher, et al., "Neighborhood Characteristics and ADHD: Results of a National Study," *Journal of Attention Disorders* 19, no. 9 (September 2015): 731–40.

STRATEGY #99

1   For a discussion of the importance of project-based experiential learning from these two educational luminaries, see John Dewey, *Experience and Education* (New York: Free Press, 1997); and Howard Gardner, *The Disciplined Mind: Beyond Facts and Standardized Tests, the K–12 Education That Every Child Deserves* (New York: Basic Books, 2000).

2   The butterfly project was described in Wayne D'Orio, "The Power of Project Learning," *Scholastic*. Retrieved from scholastic.com/browse/article.jsp?id=3751748.

3   The clean-water project was described in Michael Golden, "Active Learning through Project-Based Learning," *SEEN—Southeast Education Network*, June 12, 2014. Retrieved from seenmagazine.us/Articles/Article-Detail/articleid/3977/active-learning-through-project-based-learning.

4   Jonathan Mooney and David Cole are quoted from their book, *Learning Outside the Lines: Two Ivy League Students with Learning Disabilities and ADHD Give You the Tools for Academic Success and Educational Revolution* (New York: Touchstone, 2000).

5   The Buck Institute's book on project-based learning is by John Larmer, John Mergendoller, and Suzie Boss, *Setting the Standard for Project Based Learning: A Proven Approach to Rigorous Classroom Instruction* (Alexandria, VA: ASCD, 2015).

INDEX

Index

Index

misleading or false advertising, 65–66
profiting from products and services, 69–71
Edelman, Gerald, 155–56
education
industry benefitting, 69–70
standards, 41–43
See also classrooms; homeschooling; schools; special education services; teachers
Education, U.S. Department of, 69–70
educational resources
computer learning programs, 258–59
mobile apps, 182–83
online learning, 168–70
educational strategies, xiv, 90
Education for All Handicapped Children Act (1975), 69
Einstein, Albert, 250
Eli Lilly, 18, 67
elimination diets, 121–22
Elkind, David, 35
emotional self-regulation skills, 172–75, 183
emotional strategies, xv, 91
entertainment media, limiting, 165–66
entrepreneurship
linking ADHD with, 61
supporting in kids, 281–82
environment. *See* family environment; home environment
environmental contaminants, 242–44
environmental influences
brain neuroplasticity and, 32–33
gene-environment interactions, 14, 49
See also family environment
equipment and furniture, 111–12
Erikson, Erik, 235
Erlandsson, Soly, 45–46
evaluation. *See* diagnosing ADHD
Evans, James, 220–21
Every Student Succeeds Act (ESSA), 42, 279
executive function skills
adversity diminishing, 46–47
chess improving, 253
goal-setting related to, 189–90
lack of, enabling entrepreneurship, 281
maturation and, 13, 28, 32, 35–36
metacognition related to, 170–72

mindfulness meditation improving, 175
music improving, 123
video games improving, 259–60
exercise
family exercise and recreation, 178–79
promoting daily, 159–61
See also martial arts; sports involvement; yoga
expectations, cultural, 29–30
expectations, teacher and parent, 98–99, 194
Eye to Eye coalition, 184, 185

Faccio, Elena, 59
families
chore organization, 295
diet cooperation, 122
exercise and recreation, 178–79
family meetings, 103–5
family therapy, 216–17
family time suggestions, 54–55, 204–6
humor and laughter in, 202
negative family patterns, 129
novel experiences for, 218–19
positive strategies for, xiv, 91
family environment, 45–49
adversity and trauma, 46–48
gene-environment interactions, 49
influencing diagnosis and treatment, 48–49
parental stress contributing to, 45–46
family meetings, 103–5
family systems theory, 216, 217
family therapy, 216–17
fast food *vs.* healthier options, 150–51
FDA (Federal Drug Administration), 65
Feingold diet, 122
fidgeting behavior, 95–96
financial interests. *See* economic interests
flow experiences, promoting, 166–68
focus and concentration
chess improving, 252
computerized learning programs benefitting, 258
eliminating distractions, 157–59
flow experiences, 166–68
focusing techniques, 105–7, 251
hyperfocus, 167
mindfulness meditation for, 175–76

Index

food additives, 121–22
food allergens, 121–22
Food and Drug Administration (FDA), 18, 64–65, 66
free play
  importance of, 29–31, 142–44
  learning through, 44
  making time for, 142–44
  See also hands-on learning
full inclusion, supporting, 153–55
furniture and equipment, 111–12

games. *See* chess games; computer games and programs; video games
Gardner, Howard, 206–7, 256, 289
gender bias in school, 36–37
  See also boys and ADHD
genes
  adaptive selection hypothesis, 62–63
  gene-environment interactions, 14, 49
Glenn, H. Stephen, 126–27
goal-setting skills, 183, 189–92
Goleman, Daniel, 256
Gould, Stephen Jay, 31
Growing Young (Montagu), 31
growth mind-set, 208–10

habituation, 51–52
Hallowell, Edward (Ned), 24, 75–76
hands-on learning, 109–10
  See also free play
hearing and vision problems, ruling out, 231
Hickey, Philip, 12
Hinshaw, Stephen, 19
history of ADHD, 8–11
home environment
  behavior contracts, 273–74
  choices and decisions, 120–21
  consistent rules, routines, and transitions in, 139–40
  cross-age tutoring in, 255
  flow experiences, 167–68
  free play guidelines, 143–44
  growth mind-set, developing, 209
  incidental learning strategy in, 229–30
  learning through movement, 200–201
  organizational strategies, 294–96
  project-based learning, 290–91

real-life tasks in, 236–37
stimulating activities, 188–89
study areas, 135, 213
study strategies for, 233–34
toxins in, 242–44
See also families; family environment
homeopathy, 114
home-school communication, 161–63, 194–95
homeschooling, 264
  See also project-based learning
homework
  coaching child with, 145
  color tip, 283–84
  computer use, 258–59
  mobile app for, 182
  organizing, 182, 294
  sessions, physical movement and, 200–201
  sessions, tools and furniture for, 112
  strength-based learning strategies, 152
  study areas, 135, 213
  study strategies, 233–34
Hughes, Ruth, 75
humor and laughter, 201–3
hyperactivity
  drugs controlling, 16–17, 18
  equipment benefitting, 111–12
  learning spaces and, 134–35
hyperfocus process, 167
hyperkinesis, 3
hyperkinetic disorder (HKD), 10
hyperkinetic reaction of childhood term, 9

identities, constructing, 255–57
imagination and visualization, 250–52
"I" messages, 127–28
immature behavior. *See* developmental factors
impulsivity
  as ADHD symptom, 5–6
  characteristics of, 5–6
  genetic adaptation and, 62
  psychosocial factors and, 49
inadequacy, behavior motivated by, 223
inattention
  as ADHD symptom, 5–6
  carbohydrate-rich foods related to, 117

Index

characteristics of, 6
equipment aiding, 111–12
genetic adaptation and, 62
incidental learning strategy, 228–30
music benefitting, 123–24
related to working memory, 164
self-monitoring apps for, 293
See also focus and concentration
Inattentive Type, 5, 34
incidental learning, 61–62, 228–30
Individualized Education Program (IEP), 70, 163
Individuals with Disabilities Education Act (IDEA), 69–70
information processing, self-talk and, 177
Institute of Human Development, 138–39
instructions
step-by-step videos aids, 293
strategies for delivering, 148–49
working memory related to following, 163–65
intelligence. *See* multiple intelligences
interdisciplinary approach to ADHD, 78–81
child-centered model, 80
comprehensive solutions, 81
conventional treatment, 78
diagnostic factors to consider, 80–81
neurobiological model, 78, 79–80
See also strategies, 101 nondrug
interests and activities, 136–38
internally empowering behavior modification, 224–27
International Classification of Diseases (ICD), 10
International Consensus Statement on ADHD (2002), 7, 50–51, 72, 74, 76
the Internet. *See* media use; web sites
Intuniv, 66
Iudici, Antonio, 59

Jaksa, Peter, 202
Johns Hopkins University, 18, 22
journaling, 171, 256
junk food, limiting, 150–51
junk media. *See* media use

Kabat-Zinn, Jon, 175
Khan Academy, 168

kindergartens and preschools, 29–30
Krager, John, 18

labeling children
as ADHD, xv, 133, 255–56
economic interests behind, 64
as lacking in motivation, 136
negative labels applied, 58–59
Last Child in the Woods (Louv), 101
late-blooming children, 268–70
lead exposure, 243–44
learned helplessness, 208–9
learning activities, stimulating, 187–89
learning approaches
active learning, 39–41
free play, 29–31
hands-on learning, 109–10
incidental learning, 228–30
learning through movement, 200–201
multiple intelligences theory, 206–8
project-based, 289–91
strength-based learning, 151–53
See also cross-age tutoring
learning disabilities
as co-morbidity, 14–15
creation of term, 59
ruling out, 232
learning spaces, 134–35
Leo, Jonathan, 66
light, natural and full-spectrum, 212–14
listening to child. *See* active listening
logical consequences, 211–12
Louv, Richard, 103

manipulative materials, 110
martial arts, 100–101
maturation of the brain, 13, 27–29, 268–70
McKay, Gary D., 128
McLuhan, Marshall, 55
media use, 50–55
brain impacted by, 51–53
entertainment media, limiting, 165–66
guidelines for, 54–55
linked to rise of ADHD diagnoses, 50–51
shortened attention spans, 50
social media, 284–86
studies linking ADHD with, 53, 54–55

Index

rejection by peers, 277–78
relationships. *See* parent-child relationship; parent-teacher relationship; social networks; social skills
relative age, related to diagnosis and treatment, 29
relaxation exercises, 180–81
resilience, building in child, 146–48
rewards and consequences
  behavior contracts, 273–74
  behavior modification programs, 224–27
  natural and logical consequences, 210–12
  See also discipline
Richwood Pharmaceuticals, 18
Ritalin (methylphenidate hydrochloride), 16–17, 18, 20
Rivera, Jessica, 22
role models, 220–21
role-playing (social situations), 278
rules and routines, establishing, 139–40
Running on Ritalin (Diller), 18

Safer, Daniel, 18
Saul, Richard, 11, 75, 80, 231–32
schooling options (alternative), 263–64
schools, 38–44
  academic standards, 41–43
  "canaries in the coal mine" analogy, 44
  increased accountability in, 43–44
  learning practices in, 39–41
  medication use in, 38–39
  optimal stimulation theory, 40
  See also classrooms; learning approaches; teachers
Schwarz, Alan, 66, 67–68
Schweitzer, Julie B., 95
scientists, and drug company subsidies, 68
screen time, limiting, 54–55, 165
self-assessment inventories, 256
self-awareness, promoting, 255–57
  See also self-monitoring skills
self-care, parental, 115–16
self-control. *See* emotional self-regulation skills
self-esteem
  enhanced by cross-age tutoring, 254

positive role models and, 220–21
  raising, 240–42
self-monitoring skills, 124–26, 183, 293
self-regulating emotions, 172–75, 183
self smart intelligence, 207
self-talk, spontaneous, 177–78
serotonin, 49, 117
Setting the Standard for Project Based Learning (Buck Institute for Education), 290
Shapiro, Jordan, 54
Shire Pharmaceuticals, 65–66, 67–68
Silver, Larry, 242–43
sleep
  disorders, ruling out, 231
  issues, 245–47
  light exposure affecting, 213
smoke exposure, secondhand, 243
social adversity, role of, 46–47
social media, 284–86
social networks, 276, 286–88
social skills, 277–78
social strategies, xiv, 92
Soutra, Marcus, 184–85
special education services
  legislation, 69–70
  vs. full inclusion classrooms, 153–54
speech, spontaneous, 177–78
speech software, 292
Spencer, Thomas, J., 68
spontaneous self-talk, 177–78
sports involvement, 185–87
  See also exercise; martial arts; physical education programs
Sroufe, L. Alan, 13–14, 48–49, 73
Still, George, 8–9
stimulants. *See* medication; specific psychostimulant drugs
stimulation
  bodily stimulation, need for, 198–99
  hands-on learning providing, 109–10
  in the learning environment, 187–89, 269
  overstimulation hypothesis, 53
strategies, 101 nondrug
  by approach, xiv–xv, 87–92
  questionnaire for choosing, xv, 82–87
  suggestions for using, 81–82

Index

Index

Waldorf schools, 263
walks and hikes, 161
web sites
   creating a blog, 284–86
   drug company ties to, 66
   online safety, 285
Weinschenk, Susan, 52–53
Wilens, Timothy E., 68
word smart intelligence, 207
work-around strategies, 291–93

working memory, strengthening, 163–65, 183
worst practices learning, 39–40

yoga, 265

Zentall, Sydney S., 40, 177, 188, 238–39
Zentall, Thomas, 238–39
Ziglar, Zig, 204

ABOUT THE AUTHOR

Thomas Armstrong, PhD, is a psychologist, learning specialist, and consultant to educational groups around the world. He has written for *Family Circle, Ladies' Home Journal,* and *Parenting* magazine, and is the author of sixteen books, including *Awakening Your Child's Natural Genius.*